Pete McCarthy was born in Warrington to an Irish mother and an English father. He is the writer and performer of many series for radio and television, including 'Desperately Seeking Something', 'X Marks the Spot' and 'Travelog'. His critically-acclaimed debut, McCARTHY'S BAR, was a world-wide best-seller and took the award for Newcomer of the Year at the British Book Awards. THE ROAD TO McCARTHY is his second book.

PRAISE FOR McCARTHY'S BAR

'An acutely observed and often hilarious series of snapshots of a country that can induce an onrush of sentimental cliché. A funny and believable travelogue'
The Sunday Times

'McCARTHY'S BAR is so unrelentingly funny it needs to be taken in small doses . . . When it comes to playing stooge in ridiculous travel situations, he makes Michael Palin look shy and Bill Bryson look positively sombre'
The Australian

'A wonderfully funny journey'
Express on Sunday

'Wonderful . . . It's a surprise to discover that this is McCarthy's first book because he is an excellent writer, enthralling his readers with vivid descriptions of the Irish countryside, wonderful comic timing and a knack for the telling phrase. This is a hugely enjoyable book, heartfelt, self-aware and very funny . . . full of funny anecdotes, keen observation, and an intelligent exploration of what it means to be Irish, to belong here'
Kilkenny People

Also by Pete McCarthy

McCarthy's Bar

THE ROAD TO McCARTHY

PETE McCARTHY

Hodder & Stoughton

Copyright © 2002 by Pete McCarthy

First published in Great Britain in 2002 by Hodder and Stoughton
First published in paperback in 2003 by Hodder and Stoughton
A Lir paperpack
A division of Hodder Headline

The right of Pete McCarthy to be identified as the Author
of the Work has been asserted by him in accordance with the
Copyright, Designs and Patents Act 1988.

Photograph of author as a child in toy car © Ken Robinson
Photograph of mining 'nugget': Anchorage Museum of History and Art
Maps by Neil Gower
Extract from *The Fields of Athenry* by kind permission of
Peter St John © Pete St John (Saint Music)

3 5 7 9 10 8 6 4

A CIP catalogue record for this title
is available from the British Library

ISBN 0 340 76607 7

Typeset in Monotype Sabon by
Rowland Phototypesetting Ltd,
Bury St Edmunds, Suffolk
Printed and bound in Great Britain by
Mackays of Chatham Ltd, Chatham, Kent

Hodder and Stoughton
A division of Hodder Headline
338 Euston Road
London NW1 3BH

To the West Cork McCarthys, wherever they may be

CONTENTS

THE ROAD TO McCARTHY

The author sets out on his journey

1

ATTACK OF THE KILLER MACAQUES

It had seemed a romantic idea to arrive in the port of Tangier, and the continent of Africa, by sea; but the painfully early hour of my flight to Gibraltar, where I will catch the ferry to Morocco, has already turned romance sour. An alarm clock ringing at four in the morning in the middle of an English winter is a cruel and unnatural thing. Manufacturers should build in an override mechanism to stop it from happening, like they do with trucks and coaches to prevent them going over sixty and killing even more people. The fear of getting up so early pollutes my sleep, filling it with nervous, guilty, premature awakenings, as well as nightmares of having overslept and missed the taxi, the flight and the rest of my life.

It's frosty and still dark as we board the plane at a shopping mall with an overcrowded airport attached somewhere in Sussex. The young man in the seat next to me is Estonian, like his friend across the aisle. When breakfast is served he orders two quarter-bottles of red wine from a surprised stewardess and knocks them back at high speed with his sausage, bacon, mushrooms and powdered egg. Then he eats the muesli and yoghurt. It's so early my brain isn't working properly, and I'm struggling to decipher the meaning of such extreme behaviour.

The Estonians are accompanied by a hearty English business type in a Winnie-the-Pooh-on-a-balloon tie who is keen to show that he's in charge. He keeps telling the Estonians very boring things in a loud, slow voice with all definite and indefinite articles removed, like whisky trader talking to injuns about heap powerful thundersticks. When the stewardess comes to collect the breakfast debris my Estonian orders a gin and tonic to wash the wine down, while his friend opts for another cup of tea and some port. I have been to Estonia twice, and can report that it is an enigmatic country, with a glorious tradition of choral singing.

We're crossing southern Spain when the pilot comes on the intercom to tell us that the weather isn't very nice in Gibraltar. Very windy, apparently. More than fifty miles an hour.

'Under the circumstances it would be hazardous to attempt a landing. We'll get back to you in a few minutes to let you know what's happening.'

'WINDY!' shouts Winnie the Pooh at the Estonians. 'NOT LANDING! DANGEROUS! GO! SOMEWHERE! ELSE!'

He's using his right hand to mime what he thinks is a change of direction, but the Estonians think is a plane crash. They have taken on the haunted look of men who are about to plummet from 36,000 feet and don't know whether to use their last seconds to proposition the hostess or order more gin and port.

Before they can decide we enter a cloud and the plane starts pitching and bumping in the most terrifying manner. It feels as if the controls have been seized by two teenage boys who are pulling and pressing everything in sight to see who can make a wing fall off first. Clouds look such gentle, fluffy things, so what the hell's inside them that can cause aircraft so much grief? Monsters? A giant anvil? Gods who are displeased with us? Not for the first time I find myself wondering whether you pass out as soon as the fuselage cracks and you hit the cold air, or whether you remain conscious and have a brilliant but eye-watering view all the way to the ground, or sharks.

We ricochet down through the clouds and suddenly we're clear of them, descending rapidly but seemingly still in control. The PA system bing-bongs and the pilot is back on the airwaves.

'We've decided we'll try and give it a go anyway.'

His voice is alarmingly casual. I suppose he's hoping to re-assure us, but his words couldn't be more worrying if they'd been spoken with a slur and preceded by the phrase 'Ah, sod it'. Though we've spent the last two hours flying over land, we're now very close to something that looks like the sea. I can see white tops on the waves. I can see individual drops of water, but no sign of land anywhere, as we go into an abrupt gung-ho bank to the right that suggests our man may be a frustrated fighter pilot who failed the psychological profiling. All around me pas-sengers are exchanging panic-stricken glances with complete strangers with whom they've so far been scrupulously avoiding any kind of eye contact.

And now there it is in front of us, the Rock itself, massive, grey, broody, windswept; but, above all, very solid-looking. The PA pings back on.

'I'm afraid this may be a little bumpy.' And that's it. He's gone quiet. Perhaps one of the stewards has managed to force a towel into his mouth before he could add, 'but I really couldn't give a toss.' We're hurtling flat and low across the water, straight towards the Rock. Why are we so low? To get below the radar? Are we going to bomb it? They're on our side, aren't they? We're so low over the spray that I can feel it on my face; or is that just the Estonians crying? And now there's the airstrip straight ahead of us, immediately beneath the enormous bulk of the Rock. At close range it really does look dauntingly dense. If we do hit it, it seems unlikely we'll have the option of surviving for ten days by eating each other.

A brutal gust of wind strikes the plane, tipping the wing on my side up towards the Rock, then down towards the seabed. We take another belt, then another, and now it's rolling crazily, feeling as if we're about to flip over like one of those eejits who fly upside down over Biggin Hill for charity on Bank Holiday Monday. We're dropping ever lower, rolling from side to side in newer and scarier ways, when without warning the G Force sucks back our stomachs and flattens out our internal organs like offal on a dinner plate as we surge into a steep, last-minute climb. I can see people in Gibraltar going to work in their cars and thinking, 'What in God's name was that?' But they're receding rapidly into the distance as we climb back to a safe, or possibly unsafe, height. Confident now that he's given the Red Baron the slip, our man is back on the PA, but sounding strangely low-key and matter-of-fact.

'Well, as you can see . . .'

Pause.

'We were unable to land at Gibraltar. We'll keep you posted.'

He sounds curiously post-orgasmic, and we have to suppress dreadful images of what's been going on in the cockpit.

Ten minutes later, we're dropping down over calm sea and miles and miles of pristine deserted sandy beach to land in Tangier, which is where I want to be tomorrow, but not today. As I'm wondering whether to accept the fact that I'm already in Morocco and save myself the bother of going back to Europe by plane just so that I can come back to Morocco by boat, the pilot comes back on the speaker and says that we are just refuelling. We can't get off until we arrive at our new destination, which may, or may not be, Málaga. Terrific. I'm going to spend the rest of the day retracing my steps so that I can pay extra money to come back here a slower way first thing tomorrow. Good plan.

'And can I ask you please not to use mobile phones while we're refuelling?' he adds.

4

The Winnie the Pooh businessman immediately gets out his mobile and phones Kirsty at head office to tell her she can't call him with any messages for the foreseeable as we're on the runway at Tan-bloody-gier and aren't allowed to use mobiles for safety reasons. The call continues for about seven minutes while he explains to Kirsty exactly why it is that he isn't currently able to use the mobile and would she be a poppet and call Jonathan direct and tell him it looks like he's going to have to cancel the two thirty with Telecom and the fucking Spaniards? Thanks, love. As he snaps the phone shut, he throws a defiant look in my direction for listening to his conversation. He's glowing with the it's-a-free-country-so-why-shouldn't-I stroppiness you get when you try and reason with someone whose dog has just fouled the pavement outside a nursery school.

There is an unspoken agreement that requires us all to collaborate in the pretence that we are unable to hear the conversations and monologues that other people are having into their mobile phones. In one of the more unpredictable shifts in British social behaviour of the last decade, a hitherto reticent nation has taken to shouting intimate details of its social, emotional and sexual life into the faces of complete strangers, who are required to pretend that they aren't there and haven't heard. Under no circumstances must you acknowledge your existence by joining in and saying, 'She sounds a right bitch', or 'What a coincidence, I'm on a train too.' I recently spent the journey from London Euston to Warrington sitting shoulder-to-shoulder with a man of about my own age. Not once did we speak, or even let on that the other one was there. Yet during a half-hour delay in Crewe – because Virgin were unable to find a train driver, in Crewe – he took out his mobile and, holding it just inches from my head, launched into a fraught conversation with his daughter. She lives with his ex-wife in Southampton, and he'd just paid her a visit that he knew – and now so did I, and so did the Alan Bennett and Thora Hird couple on the other side of the table eating home-made tongue and cucumber sandwiches on their way back to Lytham St Anne's – hadn't gone well. Not well at all. I believed his protestations when he said he'd behaved badly and was sorry, that he loved his daughters and missed them terribly, but that he and Mummy just couldn't be together any more, look you know why, angel; and by the time the sun was setting in a haze of tropical colours behind Fiddlers Ferry Power Station to announce our arrival in Warrington, the debris of his personal life was laid out before us like forensic evidence at a rail crash enquiry. So I said the only thing one really can say in these circumstances – 'excuse me' – and got off.

On the return trip south I found myself crammed into one end of the Victoria–Brighton service with a shy-looking Sikh couple, their three young daughters and Grandma. At East Croydon a bare-midriffed multiply-pierced teenager came striding along the platform arguing with her phone. She climbed in through the nearest door, which she left open for a customer liaison operative to slam violently shut behind her, and sat down opposite Grandma.

'Bollocks!' she shouted as the girls gazed on, mesmerised by her fashion sense. 'Bollocks! I never? I bloody never!' Grandma caught Mum's eye for a second but no one said anything. 'Twat!' she continued. 'Twat! Lying twat!' before bursting into tears, gurgling and snottering into the phone. 'You don't know why? You don't know why? I'll tell you why then shall I? Shall I? Right. Because I fakkin lav you, you cant, that's why. Now fakk off and leave me alone.' Then she sat there and pretended that we hadn't heard, and so did we. She got off at Redhill, in case you're ever in the area.

When we finally land at Málaga we're told to collect our luggage from carousel twelve. After a walk so long and arduous it could have been sponsored to raise funds for mental health, we reach the carousels only to find they begin at number twenty. The people who've just arrived from Luton on a flight that was actually supposed to land here are looking incredibly smug, the bastards, as chaos and confusion reign in our camp. A woman in a viscose blouse covered in corporate logos turns up holding a clipboard over her head, bringing to mind that holy man in India who's been holding his arm up in the air for five years. It seems we're in the wrong terminal. No, there's been a mistranslation. Right terminal, but they've changed the carousel numbers since last time. She won't rest until she's found out which one used to be twelve.

The people from Luton have had tapas, drinks and a couple of hours on the beach by the time our luggage appears. We're herded onto three waiting coaches and given mineral water and egg sandwiches from a big cardboard box. The Estonians have managed to get a six-pack of San Miguel from somewhere, while Winnie is tapping away at his laptop, because a top executive can never rest. The driver waits until almost, but not quite, everyone has got on, then takes us on an extended coach tour of the Costa del Sol. This isn't something I'd have booked for, but it turns out to be quite diverting. I thought they'd finished the Costa del Sol years ago and started on somewhere else by now, but apparently not. The scale of unfinished construction is astonishing. Motionless cranes and half-built apartment blocks litter the coast to Marbella, yet there's not a builder to be seen. Like the migration of lemmings and the homing instinct of salmon, the disappearance of builders from unfinished jobs remains one of the unfathomable mysteries of our time.

Traffic is heavy, and we're held up at roadworks outside an Irish pub called Rory's Taverna Irlandesa, so one way and another it's five o'clock in the evening when we get to Gibraltar, rather than ten in the morning as planned. So much for my day exploring the Rock. I'm going to have as much time to get an intimate feel for the place as a coachload of camcordered Korean pensioners who are having a cream tea in Anne Hathaway's cottage and are due at Beatrix Potter's house for dinner.

'Bland Travel', says the big sign across the street as our coach pulls in at the airport, and it has been. Our bags are taken from the bus and put on the airport luggage carousel in a desperate attempt to hoodwink us into thinking we've just arrived by plane. A bit of Zen helps at times like this. It's important to remind yourself that life, death, money, happiness are all an illusion, as is the feeling that you left England much, much earlier in your life – sometime in childhood, probably – and all your adult years have been spent driving through building sites in glaring sunshine on a coach full of angry people who smell of egg sandwiches.

I get my bag and walk out into arrivals. Three enormous British soldiers in camouflage fatigues are standing by the door, their body language suggesting that they have been sent to kill everyone on the coach. The sight of them triggers memories of Gibraltar's most famous news story of recent decades, when the SAS shot an IRA bomb team dead on the streets. As I approach them I find myself speculating that MI5 have probably kept a list of everyone in the country who thought it might have been a better plan to arrest and prosecute the suspects rather than shoot them in the head, so I'm relieved when I manage to slip past them without incident. I get into a taxi with the subject of shoot to kill and trying the British military for murder racing through my mind. At least I'll have something to talk about if I find myself in a pub full of squaddies this evening and need a bit of light-hearted banter at closing time.

At the hotel I accelerate past Winnie and the Estonians, who have arrived first but are struggling to get their luggage out of a minibus. Winnie clocks me as I flash past, and even though I haven't used my elbows or cut him up in the revolving door he's obviously gutted when I get the last sea-view room. Perhaps next time he'll think on to ask Kirsty to phone ahead and put a hold on a Superior Sea-view Executive Mini Suite with Complimentary Membership of the Business Centre and Health Club plus a basket of hard fruit in cellophane.

I'm delighted to discover I'm able to stand in the shower

covered in luxury hair-or-body shampoo and admire an enormous battleship anchored in the Med, or whatever that water outside is called. I haven't quite got my bearings yet. As I dry myself vigorously in possible view of the sailors, I remember that experience has taught me that you can sometimes meet interesting and colourful people in hotel bars in old colonial outposts. I head downstairs for an aperitif, only to find a Welsh businessman asking an engineer from Birmingham, 'So are there still bauxite deposits to be exploited out there?' I turn on my heel and flee so fast that my Blundstones burn skidmarks in the *Bienvenudo* mat.

Out in reception the Estonians – aftershaved-up, hair gleaming, feet and fingers tapping nervously in anticipation – are sitting on a wicker sofa waiting for Winnie. The lads look hot to trot. They have polished their shoes till the laces shine and are both wearing long-sleeved white shirts with the cuffs folded back. Winnie, I fancy, will choose something more appropriate to his status: a lightweight linen-effect jacket and slacks combination perhaps, one of those that you can either buy separately or as a suit, which is a great idea when you think about it.

It's light until well after seven, so I take a stroll down the hill for a look at Gibraltar town. By a traffic island opposite Queen's Cinema I happen upon Trafalgar Cemetery. Cemeteries cheer me up no end when I'm abroad, so I head through the gate and down some steps into a tranquil oasis of palm trees and gravestones. The whine of mopeds and rumble of diesel engines seem distant. A discreet sign says that many who died at Trafalgar and Algeciras are lying here. Next to the gate a stone is set in the wall.

IN A DIRECT LINE
TWENTY-ONE FEET FROM THIS STONE
LIES THE BODY OF
CHARLOTTE BOLTON,
2 MAY 1800.
BORN IN MINORCA, THIRTY-SIX YEARS.

The stone is strangely decorated with primitive carvings. There is a row of classical urns along the top, then below the inscription are three ghoullish black-winged angels, one of them grinning, or possibly gurning, in menacing fashion. The composition is completed by a skull and crossbones and an empty coffin. A date on the bottom says '67. What can it all mean? Did hippies do it in 1967? One of them carving, while the other sat on a gravestone blowing bubbles through a little plastic hoop on a stick? Or was the picture of the coffin a joke left by Victorian grave robbers in 1867, who might have taken a break from their ghoulish work to sit on these very steps and share some cheese and beer?

There's another stone set in the wall nearby.

SACRED TO THE MEMORY OF
WILLIAM GRAVE AGED 38 YEARS
MASTER OF HMS CAESAR
WHO FELL
WHILE CONSPICUOUSLY EXERTING HIMSELF
IN THE BATTLE OF ALGECIRAS
ON JULY 6TH
AD 1801
BY NATURE HE WAS PENETRATING AND RESOLUTE
HE WAS COURTEOUS IN HIS DEPORTMENT
IRREPROACHABLE IN HIS MORALS

It says it was put here 'by his fellow officers'. The question is, are the words heartfelt, or were they just taking the piss? After all, the armed forces have a long tradition of savage humour, and there is a distinctly ironic tone to 'while conspicuously exerting himself'. It might be implying that this was the first time he'd got off his fat arse since about 1775, and he only went and got himself killed. If you take it like that, the last three lines could be read as a tongue-in-cheek dig at a spineless slob who liked to put it about a bit when he'd had a few drinks. It's a distinct possibility, though I feel bad for even thinking it. I walk away reflecting how sad it is that poor Mr Grave doesn't even have a grave.

Gibraltar town is a curious hybrid, one part contemporary Spain to three parts the England of thirty years ago, with more cannons per square inch than any other duty-free zone in the world. As I pass through a gate into the old town there's a chap sitting behind a glass panel in the wall. The sign says he's a sentry of the 25th Regiment of the King's Own Scottish Borderers, who came here as reinforcements during the Great Siege of 1782. He's draped in a checked blanket and looks fed up, which is perfectly understandable. The sign also says that there's a guy from Gloucestershire in another glassed-up oubliette on the opposite side of the street, but the traffic lights are against me, so I decide to take their word for it and press on in search of the soul of Gibraltar, or perhaps a nice little bar.

Walking through the main pedestrian street as the shops pull down their shutters for the night, the sense of being in Britain rather than the Mediterranean is heightened by the impressive numbers of UK winos setting up alfresco cocktail bars in doorways. Perhaps a well-meaning vicar scooped them all up in an old school bus one night and dropped them off here. They seem happy enough. The warm climate, laughably cheap booze and comforting familiarity of brand-named doorways such as Mothercare, M&S and Thresher must make this a top winter destination. After all, long cheap winter breaks featuring excessive drinking at budget prices have been attracting British retirees to hotels just across the border in Spain for decades, so it's heart-warming to see the underclass finally getting their share. The cosmopolitan experience of sleeping rough on the Continent seems likely to produce a more discerning and sophisticated generation of street drinkers. These guys will return to Britain in the spring ready to spread the word that although turps is fine as an aperitif, especially in the open air, it's a white spirit and really is best with fish.

The smaller shops have some interesting artefacts in their windows. There's an unusual lace-effect toilet-roll holder that can hide two rolls at once, which must save on embarrassment. A green twinset is labelled 'green twinset', but the sun-faded box of liquorice allsorts in the newsagent's next door is enigmatically captioned 'English Allsorts'. Perhaps it's a Spanish shop owner, and he wants to make it clear where the blame lies.

Outside Roy's II Chip Shop & Restaurant an illuminated perspex noticeboard is displaying colour photographs of the food. Egg and chips have been emphatically in the public domain for many years now and really don't need their portrait taking, but there they are. Look. An egg. And some chips. On a plate. And Roy hasn't stopped there. Photo No. 7 is billed 'Bread & Butter' and is as good as its word, featuring a round of sliced bread, cut in two, with butter. Now no one will be able to say, 'What the bloody hell's this?' when the waiter plonks it on the table. No. 13 is a double-header, 'Mushy Peas/Baked Beans', and it exerts a hypnotic effect, featuring two round bowlfuls, one green, the other brown, peering out like strange eyes. If there's a Roy's II, there must be a Roy's I, and possibly several more. The omens for indigenous cuisine aren't good.

To tell the truth, I'd been secretly hoping for tapas or paella, or anything Spanish really, but everywhere I look there are blackboards advertising pies and full English breakfasts. For the time being I decide to settle for a couple of drinks and a bag of nuts, but in a bar rather than the doorway of that shoe shop with those three high-spirited lads with cuts on their faces who are calling me over. I delve off into the back lanes in search of a likely looking place and find that the street names are top class: Bishop Rapello's Ramp, Pitman's Alley, Serfaty's Passage, Nelson's Dirt Box, Boschett's Steps, Ragged Staff Wharf, Tuckey's Lane, The Plump, Benzimra's Alley.

I made one of them up.

At the top of a narrow ramp, passage, or alley a sign outside a pub catches my attention. 'Flower of Scotland', it says, then, 'All food home-made', above a blackboard that's completely blank. It looks promising. The Irish have dominated the overseas nostalgia-for-home pub for long enough, and it's about time someone else had a go. As I prepare to enter the bar though, my confidence is momentarily undermined by the FEB factor.

Some years ago at the Edinburgh Festival I realised that many of the locals kept referring to those of us who were members of visiting theatrical troupes from England as FEBs. Delivered with a smile, it was a witty and I have to say endearing way of calling us Fucking English Bastards to our faces. One Christmas I received a tartan calendar in the post. You lifted up the two Scottie dogs on the front cover to reveal the legend, 'Happy Hogmanay ya FEB,' scrawled in Biro.

I stride in through the door, trying to suppress all memories of that English kid in Peebles who had seven shades kicked out of him by his painty-faced schoolmates the week *Braveheart* came out. Inside, I have to say, it's a shock, but once you've walked in you can't just walk out again, can you? The carpet is blue and green tartan, while the upholstery – all of it – is red and yellow tartan. It's like walking into a deranged psychedelic movie: *Fear and Loathing in Dumfries – a savage journey to the heart of the Scottish dream.*

The place is small – like a living-room with a bar in, and don't be snobbish, we've all been in a few of those – but unlike most small living-rooms they've gone for two tellies, one on each side, so that if you sit in the middle of the room you get stereo, except it's two different channels, Sky News and Sky Not News, which can affect your concentration. The bar itself is built of brick, and brings to mind the two other little piggies in the children's story who built their bars out of straw and sticks. I'm greeted by a charming barmaid with a big smile and a Paisley accent.

'What can I get ya, doll?'

She pours me a half-pint of witheringly strong gin and tonic, which costs about the same as a box of matches would back home. I'm just looking round for a free table when, standing at the end of the bar with his wife, I notice a shaven-headed bulked-up guy in his fifties. He looks as if he owns a large vicious dog that he's left locked up in a tiny bedsit with nothing to eat and the telly turned up loud. Suddenly he bursts out laughing, and in an act of good-natured yet terrifying horseplay punches his wife on the shoulder and knocks her backwards off her bar stool. She hits the tartan with a thump, screams, laughs, then kicks him on the shin, but makes no attempt to get up.

Meanwhile behind me a man is holding an eight-year-old boy upside down by the ankles and shaking him, also good-naturedly, in the confident style that comes from many years' exposure to massive quantities of duty-free blue-label vodka. The other customers are similarly boisterous – let's face it, they're scaring me – but they're not all, I'm at pains to stress, Scottish. The jolly wife-beater, for example, is from the West Midlands. The child-suspender sounds as if he has only recently been hounded out of Leeds by vigilantes. The bar may claim to be Scottish, but its clientèle has selected itself by temperament rather than nationality.

I realise I'm in a difficult situation. This is clearly not the sort of place where you should risk eye contact with the regulars; yet taking out a book and reading it might be seen as a dangerous act of provocation. I pick a table and decide to keep a low profile by watching the televisions instead. I'm beginning to go wall-eyed when a couple in their sixties come and sit opposite me and start whacking back the bevy at a tremendous rate. He's on family-size rum and Coke, while she's gone for extra-strength cider. They must have been over here pickling themselves on cheap booze for years. I can't tell where they're from, because they're not speaking to each other. Ciderwoman looks up and spots me staring at them. She leans forward and beckons me closer, with an expert arch of the eyebrows and a practised flick of the head.

What am I going to get? I wonder. A public warning, or a row of stitches in my nose?

'Do you speak English?'

I nod, and say that I do.

'What time do the pubs shut in Gibraltar, love?'

She's got a Yorkshire accent. They've just got off the evening plane. No problem landing, apparently. Bang on time. We chat for a few minutes, swapping happy memories of spectacular brawls outside Kiko's Polynesian NiteSpot in Pontefract, before I pick my way through the vivid soft furnishings and potential concussion cases to the relative safety of the dark, semi-deserted streets.

I've just turned the corner when a thickset woman appears from behind a parked car and takes up a position in the middle of the narrow street, facing me. She's holding a two-piece pool cue which she very purposefully starts screwing together, as if about to begin a match, or a punishment beating. 'I'll give you two more minutes. All right?'

What have I done? What does she want me to do? Please, not the face! And then I hear another voice behind me. 'Aye, all right, all right, keep yer hair on.'

I turn and see her husband, or manager or opponent or commanding officer, coming out of a doorway behind me. Snarling and bickering at each other, and completely oblivious of my existence, they head off up the street and disappear into the shadows. Centuries of military occupation have coloured the mood of this town. I turn onto Winston Churchill Avenue, where I flag down a taxi and head back to the sanctuary of the hotel.

There are no photos of bread and butter outside the hotel restaurant, but I take a chance and go in anyway. The maître d' scowls at his watch and seems to greet my request for a table for one with a glare of sublimated anger, though I suppose it's possible that there was so much gin in that G and T that it's poisoned my view of mankind. It's a big yellow room, with a guitarist who looks like Demis Roussos on steroids strumming away at the far end next to the sweet trolley. Only five of the forty-odd tables are occupied, the diners cooped together in one corner of the cavernous room like away supporters who've been kept behind in the stadium until the home fans have been safely dispersed by riot police with dogs.

I order calamari and scallops in ginger and tomato something, followed by roast hake with pickled things and braised fennel. The food is exemplary, but the waiter thinks I am a time-wasting wanker. This is one of the prices you pay for asking for a table for one, but it's worth it. I know some people can't bear the thought of dining alone in public, sitting there advertising your Johnny-No-Mates status, isolated among the gleeful groups of friends and couples of ever-so-slightly inebriated lovers. I have to say, though, that I love it. To pretend to be laughing at something in the book you appear to be reading, while in reality tuning in to the conversation at the next table, is one of the great gastronomic pleasures, with the added advantage of being entirely unreliant on whatever's turned up on your plate. Restaurant critics frequently warn that it's impossible to get a good table if you're eating alone; but once you understand that 'good' actually means 'close to that couple over there who look a bit angry and drunk', dinner for one becomes a very entertaining option.

So I'm pretending to read the book about Tangier that I didn't dare get out in the Scottish pub when a couple in their forties finish their coffee and get up to leave. They look urban and modern. She's quite svelte, while he's noticeably overweight. At the table between me and them sit an ancient English couple who look as if they've been coming here ever since William Graves's funeral. She's in elegant black, with a single string of pearls, and he's got a cream linen suit, a military tie and a twitch. They must be pushing ninety, and good luck to them for being this far from home, even if home is only a suite on the third floor. They're making no attempt to disguise the fact that they have temporarily abandoned their sherry trifle to stare at the couple who are leaving. Suddenly he speaks in a booming, John Gielgud voice.

'Good God! Look at the size of him! He's absolutely enormous!'

'Extraordinary!' exclaims his wife. 'How on earth could she bear to let him make love to her? He'd crush her like an egg!'

'Well, she'd have to, and that's an end to it.'

As each table empties, the departing diners get the same treatment: 'Do you think they were Belgian?' 'What bizarre hair!' 'I can't abide that sort of thing.' I decide to hang on until they've gone so that they can't say anything horrid about me. As they leave, they give me a dignified but restrained 'Goodnight' and totter towards the door, where he says something vicious-sounding that I can't quite hear. She scrutinises me, then mutters in agreement. The moment they disappear the guitarist stops playing, the big lights come on and I'm left to eat my crème caramel while contemptuous waiters re-set the tables for breakfast all round me.

To tell the truth, I made two of those street names up.

At breakfast I'm served by the same guys who were setting the tables when I went to bed. They still hate me. By eight o'clock I'm down at the port for the ferry to Tangier, where there is no ferry. The wind that dropped last night just long enough for Ciderwoman to land has started up again, and there will be no boats today. Winnie and the Estonians are checking out as I check back in to the hotel I've just checked out of. A phone call confirms that there's nothing sailing from Algeciras, just along the Spanish coast. I have to face the fact that I am not going to get to Tangier today. Still, I was there for a few minutes yesterday. Mustn't grumble. I've been presented with the opportunity to spend a windy February day in Gibraltar and I should make the most of it. It's just that I've absolutely no idea what to do.

A leaflet in the hotel lobby claims that no visit to Gibraltar is complete without a trip up the Rock to see St Michael's Cave and the Other Attractions, and I decide to believe the propaganda. Of course I can walk if I do not want to call a taxi, says the man at the concierge desk when I ask. 'Just keep going up and up,' he says. 'You are fit? Well, it is very easy.'

The road does indeed go up and up, and up, following the coast with spectacular views over the harbour and ocean. The lush vegetation concealing hillside government buildings reminds me of Hong Kong. After half an hour there's a sign that says 'Upper Peak Nature Reserve'. It warns that you enter at your own risk. What risk is that then? 'Apes,' it says. What – the Barbary Apes? There's a picture of one of them on the leaflet. Are they in a zoo up here, then? Or are they free-range? I have vague memories of learning something about them at primary school, but I can't remember what it was. Are they vicious predators, or gentle companions? Carnivorous, or herbivorous? An endangered species, or farmed commercially for supermarket salami? I realise I know nothing at all about them except that they live here, rather than Marbella, or Màlaga. I half thought they were mythological. Are they big or small? Must be small, eh? So why are they called apes, then? Apes are big, aren't they? As big as us, at least. If I'd had any sense I'd have bought a guidebook and swotted up on them, but I didn't. I'm completely unprepared, and have no idea what to expect.

I'm also the only person walking.

There have been occasional taxis and tour minibuses passing me on the way up, but I seem to be the only person on foot.

Just the one for the apes to concentrate on, then?

So what am I supposed to do if they attack? I seem to remember something on a BBC Bristol wildlife programme about showing apes your bottom when cornered. Or is it that they show you their bottoms? You'd want to make sure you got it right. You'd probably only get the one chance.

After another quarter-hour of much harder foot slog than that swine of a concierge had even hinted at, I come to a ticket booth where I have to pay a fiver to get in, even though I'm not sure what I'm getting in to. It's not like Longleat, is it, some wretched safari park full of wild animals, with me the only pedestrian? There's a monument ahead, looking south towards Africa over the best view so far. There's also a group of about ten people, English by the look of it, who've just got out of a minibus together.

'If you wish, you may take a picture of the Pillars of Hercules,' says their dapper little guide, with the grim resignation of a man who knows he is wasting his life.

'Try and bloody pretend, Lisa! Just try and look as if you're having a good time,' says a woman to her companion, her daughter perhaps, or maybe a recently released prisoner placed under her supervision by the courts. 'It's the Pillars of Bloody Hercules, you know.'

Lisa rolls her eyes and moans, 'I am, I am having a good time. What's the problem?'

Lisa is a thirty-something bleached blonde with terrifying hips. After giving it a lot of thought this morning she has decided to come up the Rock wearing painted-on jeans with no pockets and stitched seams up the front, a T-shirt decorated with a painting of a leopard highlighted in sequins, and a short denim jacket with silver studs on the back. She's doing her best to see the point of the wonders of the Mediterranean, but you sense that deep down she'd rather be spending the weekend in Center Parcs sloshing around in a jacuzzi with Peter Stringfellow.

A sign on the monument says that in ancient times this point was known as Mons Calpe, one of the Pillars of Hercules, entrance to Hades and the end of the known world. Lisa, however, doesn't give a shit about mythology, and has just tottered back to the minibus on her improbable shoes to have a fag while she waits for the others.

A little further on up the road I come to another sign. DO NOT FEED THE MACAQUES.

What? What the hell are macaques then? They're parrots, aren't they? Or are the bloody macaques in fact the bleeding apes? They've always got another name for things, haven't they, to make you feel ignorant and inadequate for calling them Barbary apes, or sausage dogs, or Eskimos or whatever? The sign continues: THERE HAS BEEN AN EXCESS OF MONKEY – oh, I see, they're monkeys now, are they? – OF MONKEY/HUMAN INTERACTIONS. THIS RESULTS IN THE MONKEYS BECOMING STRESSED AND THEY WILL BITE.

Blimey. Not might. WILL.

DO NOT CARRY VISIBLE ITEMS OF FOOD. THE MONKEYS WILL – there's that sense of certainty again, just when I don't want it – TRY AND STEAL THESE ITEMS AND BECOME AGGRESSIVE.

It doesn't specify how aggressive, but it doesn't have to. I already understand why no one else is walking to the flaming caves. I don't even like caves that much. I've only come because there didn't seem to be anything else to do. I've already seen the Scottish soldier in the glass case, and he was smashing, but you wouldn't want to go twice. Come to think of it, when I paid my £5 the man at the ticket booth asked me what vehicle I was in. When I said I was walking he looked baffled, as if I had said I was walking to Tangier, which at this rate I might have to.

Suddenly they're standing there in the road in front of me. Two of the bastards. I was hoping they'd turn out to be tiny and ornamental, but they're actually rather big, like a couple of stooped, overweight hairy jockeys. They've got me on my own now, just like they've been planning, one to keep lookout while the other frisks me for food. Luckily I'm not carrying any – but what if they think I am? *What if they mistake my fingers for bags of sausages they think I'm trying to sneak past them?* They won't be happy. They probably hate that kind of thing. No doubt about it, I'm in a difficult situation. There's a sign saying that this is where the Queen and Prince Philip stood on 10 May 1954. I bet they didn't get harassed by bloody monkeys. The prince probably thought they were just inbred locals and made a joke about them to somebody from the High Commission.

And then, thank God, a tourist minibus, rejoicing in the splendid title of ParodyTur, comes round the corner and stops for the inmates to admire the view. And wouldn't you know it, my two would-be muggers have started acting all cuddly and cute, as if they hadn't really been planning to do me over for the sausages in the first place. One of the devious little buggers jumps on the roof of the minibus and starts showing off. Its friend doesn't seem interested, probably seen it all before, and just sits on the wall picking insects off its well-fed tummy. The one on the roof's having a whale of a time, cavorting round like a very drunk uncle at a wedding reception, when without warning the minibus drives off. The monkey seems delighted. Perhaps this is their equivalent of riding on the roofs of underground trains. Feeling a new surge of confidence, I take a long hard look at the one that's been left behind, but the sneaky little bully isn't looking quite so cocky now he's on his own. He's adopted a self-effacing 'you must have imagined it' air that suggests he isn't keen to take me on for the sausages single-handed.

As ParodyTur disappears round the next bend, the monkey on the roof appears to be breakdancing. It's clear he hasn't considered the possibility that he might be on his way to Seville, or Stuttgart.

There's a café and shop when you reach the cave, with a handful of coach and taxi drivers hanging around outside, talking about football, and what scum their passengers are. I've been fantasising about a cold beer and a nice snack – some olives and Serrano ham and Manchego cheese, that kind of thing – but the sign says: BURGER EGG BACON SAUSAGE & CHIPS. Or PIE CHIPS & PEAS. There are two kinds of pie: STEAK & KIDNEY, or MACAQ— I mean BEEF & ONION.

The shop is also advertising 'Souveniers', but it's never a good idea to buy something from a place that can't spell it. Lots of cafés these days are advertising 'Expresso', and there's a takeaway in Brighton that sells 'Chickin'. Not to me it doesn't.

All things considered, the cave is very nice. It's top notch, as caves go. It's got stalagmites and stalactites in the appropriate places, wherever they are. I'm not sure I'd build a day round it though. Here's Lisa and her friends again. I hadn't wanted to mention it earlier, but she's really rather shrill.

'There's a 'orrible smell, ain't there?' she shrieks.

'Nah there ain't. It's brilliant,' says the bloke with her. 'Look at that cave. It's like the inside of a giant rotten tooth.'

There's spooky muzak, and moody low-level light that would be atmospheric if it weren't for Lisa, and the muzak. The information cards say that the Romans and Phoenicians were familiar with the cave. They believed it to be bottomless, a gateway to the Underworld and an undersea link to Africa, which is how all the apes, monkeys and macaques got here. The Victorians used to have picnics, marriages, concerts and even duels down here, illuminated by soldiers 'perched' on the stala . . . er, the ones that go upwards.

In a niche in the rocks is a tableau of waxwork figures. A Stone Age man is holding up a leg of some kind of meat to his weather-beaten family around a campfire, or perhaps it's the Glastonbury Festival and he's barbecuing tofu. I'm about to move on when two American women and a man sidle up next to me.

'Hey, this is nothing,' says the first lady, turning on her heel to go.

'Sure it is, there's some little guys,' says the man.

'Okay,' she says and gets her camera out.

'Hey, stand back so you get them all in.'

'Okay.'

Click.

Gone.

As they disappear up the damp steps in the direction of Lisa's voice, I realise that at no time did they remark, or even speculate, on what the figures might be. What will they say to the folks back home when they show them their vacation pictures?

'Here are some little guys in a cave.'

'That's neat.'

'They're kinda cute. Who are they?'

'I dunno. And this is us outside the cave with a gorilla.'

Back outside I discover that the road is a circular one, so I just continue straight ahead to go back down into town. For the first couple of hundred yards there are lots of people, their numbers almost matched by the freeloading, panhandling apes. One of them is sitting on a railing with a big view behind him, having his picture taken with the people from Parody and Bland. There's a parked van with six of them sitting on top. A little girl is crying inconsolably. Her father is telling her mother that it's nothing, it's just that one of them leaped out in front of her, but it didn't mean any harm. Yeah, right. Some father. He hasn't even considered the possibility that the beast was after her sausages.

I head off down the hill and soon it's deserted again, with no sign of people or monkeys. I take the opportunity to stop for a pee in the lush vegetation, and suddenly one of them is standing there, watching me. It seems interested. Bloody hell. How am I meant to behave? Brash? Embarrassed? Mysterious? Under the circumstances I don't think I can do mysterious. What if . . . ? What if . . . ? Fingernails like razors, apparently. They fancy a snack, they get a snack.

It lets me finish though, and when I do, I swear it winks.

There are more dubious mannequins in a ruin on the way down, where I discover that during the Great Siege a sheep's head and feet would sell for three weeks' wages. It also says that a man from the Lancashire Fusiliers received 30,000 lashes in the course of his fourteen-year posting, which suggests either that corporal punishment doesn't work, or that Lancashire lads are right hard nuts.

I'm hot and hungry when I get back to town in mid-afternoon.

It's time to give up on the search for anything Spanish, so I sit outside a café in John McIntosh Square and order a beer and a toasted ham and cheese sandwich. The toastie, when it comes, turns out to be two rounds of recently defrosted sliced brown bread, toasted, then filled with cold cheese and ham. Let's make this clear. The cheese hasn't been melted, or hotted up in any way. They've just made toast, and put cold stuff in it. This really isn't on, especially if you travel the world on a diet consisting largely of toasted ham and cheese sandwiches. But it's impossible to legislate against this kind of thing. Every time you order a toasted sandwich you can't tap the waitress on the shoulder and try to assuage the nagging undertow of worry by saying, 'The cheese will be melted, won't it?' They look at you as if you're mental, because everyone knows the cheese has to be hot and hazardous to the mouth. So why would anyone serve Cheddar like this, sweaty but still strangely cold, as if it's suffering from a tropical fever? Now the ham has started sweating too; and as the principal ingredient of square plastic packet ham is water, this is oozing out to make the fevered cheese even clammier.

I'm so whacked from the walk though, and so relieved that the ape didn't rip off any crucial body parts and eat them, that I haven't the energy to complain. I just down the beer and ask for the bill. But the waitress notices I've dismantled the sandwich and abandoned it in horror and deducts the cost, which is a result I suppose, apart from the fact that I'm still starving, and have now got alcohol coursing through my system with nothing to absorb it.

I'm back at the hotel eating an apple from the ornamental display at reception and planning what to do tonight – according to the paper, Scrabble Club meets in the hall in the square at seven thirty – when the concierge tells me he's just heard that the Algeciras to Tangier ferry is running again. There'll be nothing from Gibraltar for at least thirty-six hours, but Algeciras is only forty minutes across the border by taxi. Once again I check out of the hotel I checked out of and into earlier in the day.

In less than ten minutes I'm in the back of a taxi heading for the Spanish border.

'Sodom was a church picnic and Gomorrah a convention of girl scouts compared to Tangier, which contained more thieves, black marketeers, spies, thugs, phonies, beachcombers, expatriates, degenerates, characters, operators, bandits, bums, tramps, politicians and charlatans than any place I've ever visited.' So wrote Robert Ruark in 1950. Samuel Pepys made Tangier sound pretty sexy too: 'A nest of papacy where Irish troops and Roman bastards could disport themselves unchecked.' 'Spectacular view,' raved Tennessee Williams, 'every possible discomfort.'

I'm just thinking that someone at the tourist board should collect all these quotes and stick them on the front of a nice glossy brochure when the Spanish taxi driver catches my eye in the rear-view mirror. I look up from the book I'm reading.

'You been in Tangier before?'

I tell him I haven't.

'Take care, my friend. My cousin is in prison there for smuggling tobacco. Eight years. All food and clothes must be taken in to him, or there is just bread and water. Naked. If you want even to wash your friends must bring the water. This place makes *Midnight Express* look like a top hotel with pool.' Perhaps noticing that I'm about to burst into tears he turns his head, looks me in the eye and grins.

'But don't worry. Morocco treats tourists very well. You want to change some currency?'

It's early evening as the ferry leaves Algeciras under a cover of grey cloud, with a late winter chill in the air. I seem to be the only English speaker on board apart from a backpacker across the bar who's reading a novel called *Backpack*. This is depressing. Surely he can think of other ways to enrich his gap year. At any rate, he shouldn't be reading books about the activity he's currently engaged in. It is an existentialist nightmare that will end in chaos. If there were a book called *Three Fat Lorry Drivers Drinking, Smoking and Playing Cards*, then the three guys at the next table would be reading it, rather than doing it. Nothing would get done, society would grind to a halt, and it would all be literature's fault.

The idea of arriving in Africa by ferry was to help me feel a spiritual connection with the traders and smugglers, pirates and soldiers who have been navigating these legendary straits for countless millennia. The exotic atmosphere of this floating bazaar would give me time to prepare myself for the ancient mysteries of the casbah. I'm reminding myself of this as I sit in a harshly lit plastic and vinyl bar, listening to Phil Collins, surrounded by screaming children, and drinking a small gin and tonic that's just cost me more than a litre of duty-free. We're heading for a Muslim country, so I'm the only one drinking alcohol.

The bar closes as we approach Tangier, and I go for a walk on deck. Even though it's dark I can see the white buildings of the old town, the medina, framing the port like an amphitheatre. I'm trying my best to luxuriate in this special moment of arrival by ship in the most notorious port in North Africa, when the purser replaces Phil Collins with some superannuated bat from Nashville warbling, 'C'est la vie say the old folks, It goes to show you never can tell.' You certainly can't. Travel can be full of surprises. Sometimes they're not even the surprises you expect.

I go back into the lounge to collect my bag, and everything starts vibrating as the engines go into reverse for docking. Bottles and glasses start tap-dancing eerily across tables as if at some nautical séance. All around me people are shouting into mobile phones, saying, 'I am on a boat,' or, 'I'm just outside Haywards Heath, I'll be home in twenty minutes,' in Arabic.

At the port there's no sign of the MacCarthy brothers from Belfast, who are the reason I'm making the trip. They'd arranged to meet me off the morning ferry, so I suppose there's no reason to expect them to be here tonight. Instead I'm confronted by a scrum of taxi drivers hungry for business. Backpacker Boy shows a moment's fatal indecision, hesitates, and is immediately mobbed, disappearing from view like an English scrum-half on the wrong end of a good shoeing from the All Blacks' pack. I've decided to scan the drivers' faces and make a decisive move towards the first one that appeals. It works a treat and in moments I'm heading off in a white Merc, just as Backpacker is about to be penalised for not releasing the ball.

As we set off I ask the driver '*Combien?*' to give the impression I know what I'm doing, which of course I don't. The drive feels like a scene from an exotic film noir. The streets of the port are lined with decaying hotels and cafés, their pavement tables full even on a winter's night. The air hangs heavy with the promise of adventure, intrigue and the thrill of the unknown. I suspect that, whatever your purpose, arriving in Tangier by night will make you feel like you've come to the right place.

The driver seems delighted at the childlike pleasure I'm taking from the street scenes and boasts that Tangier is '*une ville internationale*'. The King is in residence, he says, which is why the streets are decorated with fairy lights, bought, if I understand his French correctly, from a bankrupt seaside resort in Lincolnshire.

My hotel room has been booked for a week, but this doesn't stop reception denying all knowledge of me and saying that they are full. This always happens when I try and book anywhere half-decent. The more elaborate the preparations and the more upmarket the hotel, the less likely they are to have heard of me. Perhaps if I had matching luggage, fewer carrier bags and a jacket draped around my shoulders with the sleeves hanging loose, it wouldn't happen so often; but I suspect that even if I arrived by Ferrari with Nicole Kidman, a butler and a masseur, I'd still come across as an impostor.

After a quarter of an hour of arguing they suddenly remember me and ask me to fill in a registration form headed 'Please write very legibly. This is applicable to married women even when accompanied by husband.' This is my fourth check in or out of the day. It's after ten when I drop the bag in the room and hit the streets.

The boulevards of the fin-de-siècle new town are thronged with men promenading and packed into cafés watching football on TV. The astonishing thing for a visitor from Britain, apart from the absence of women, is the fact that it's Saturday night and *all these men are sober*. I've walked several hundred yards, and no one has urinated in a shop doorway or thrown a litterbin across the street while singing 'No Surrender to the IRA'. It's hard not to feel a faint pang of nostalgia for the colourful traditions of small-town England.

In a snack bar that's trying to be a restaurant I order a seafood pizza, then ask for the carte des vins. '*Oh, pardon,*' says the waitress, '*pas d'alcool.*' I'm faced with the distressing prospect of eating pizza without the wine that's the only way of making it seem like food. Surely the only point of pizza's existence is to encourage the consumption of cheap red wine? Unspeakable rotgut that would otherwise end up in Andalusian pickle jars and Romanian cigarette lighters tastes like premier cru when accompanied by a pepperoni and chilli thin crust with extra garlic. Looks like it'll have to be water, then. Mind you, the young Moroccan at the next table has got a Quattro Staggioni that he's just covered in ketchup and is now washing down with a litre of Coke. I've always been disturbed by people who drink Coke or Pepsi with a meal, but perhaps he's got the right idea. Pizza is children's birthday party food, and deserves no respect.

Back in my room, the dough still expanding inside me, I combat the pizza afterburn, heart palpitations and flashbacks of genital mutilation by macaque with a glass or two of the wittily named Spanish brandy, Soberano. Mysterious chanting and the cries of cockerels float across the night sky to my palm-fronded balcony as I sit propped up in bed, glass of brandy in hand, and consider the strange series of events that have conspired to bring me here tonight.

2

PITY THE POOR EMIGRANT

When I was a kid I couldn't understand how Irish aristocrats with Irish names who lived in big houses in Ireland came to be sitting in the British House of Lords. Still don't, to be honest. Nor did I have any real notion of an ancient Gaelic aristocracy. But I do remember my uncle telling me, when I was over in West Cork on holiday, that McCarthy was a royal name and we were descended from ancient high kings of Ireland. Nothing special about that, mind. Everybody else called McCarthy was royal too, which from what I knew about Ireland in those days – West Cork, basically – meant about 80 per cent of the population. There were a few Crowleys and O'Donovans about the place, but apparently they were just McCarthys who'd changed their names. And either all of us were kings, or none of us.

So it came as a surprise when some years later a BBC Radio producer told me that I had a clan chief to whom I owed my allegiance; but the head of the McCarthy family, he said, was not Irish. He was a Moroccan, who lived in Tangier, and was known as the McCarthy Moor. Fantastic, I thought. A Moor!

Like Othello! We discussed it over a few pints, and decided that the original McCarthys must have been a nomadic tribe from North Africa who sometime in pre-history had, like the Celts, emigrated north to Ireland. Over Singapore noodles and a couple of bottles of wine we further deduced that the unaccustomed moistness of the Irish climate must have broken down their skin pigment, a kind of genetic rusting process that led inevitably over the centuries to red hair and freckles. And so it was that I began to tell anybody who'd listen that the ancient kings from whom I was descended were Moroccans, and that one day I would travel to Morocco and share a water pipe and a bowl of couscous with the Moor himself.

It was, of course, utter, utter bollocks, as my uncle pointed out to me when I told him of my discovery, although he used to be a headmaster and phrased it much more eloquently than that. There were, he told me, a few fantasists and nut jobs going about the place claiming direct descent from ancient Gaelic princes, kings, gods, saints and little people, but it was a small country and royal blood was no truer of them than it was of all the rest of us. Morocco, though, had never been involved. Even the Romans had never been to Ireland. St Patrick was about as exotic as things got, and he was Welsh.

I gave the matter no further thought until I was in Galway a couple of years ago browsing in one of those shops that sell bogwood-in-poteen keyrings and Irish family coats-of-arms for people from Chicago to sew on to their golf bags, when an article in a cheaply photocopied Celtic fanzine called *Caledonian Fringe* or *Gael Force* or *Diasporic Paddy* or some such caught my attention.

The North American MacCarthy Clan Gathering in August will be presided over by the MacCarthy Mór, Dr Terence MacCarthy, Prince of Desmond.

Not Moor then.

Mór.

Probably a Gaelic word meaning 'Moroccan'! Now I'd be able to prove to my uncle that I'd been right all along, and that everyone in West Cork was, if you looked at things from the right angle, African. The gist of the article was that hundreds, possibly thousands of Americans and Canadians called McCarthy, MacCarthy and McCartney would be gathering for a weekend of clan-related activities by a river somewhere in deepest Nova Scotia. It sounded too good to miss. There would be esoteric ceremonies, and indiscriminate bonding, and business cards embossed with shamrocks would be exchanged. We would dress up in strange togs, learn the magic words, and discover where we came from. With luck there'd be re-creations of ancient Celtic rituals featuring half-naked Yanks covered in green paint, and I would be able to drink heavily with policemen from Boston and mental health professionals from Toronto who had never been near Ireland in their lives. We would sing the old songs together, to which none of us knew all the words. In Nova Scotia!

But how to contact them? There was a website address, but that was no good to me as I haven't got a computer – not because I'm some sort of technophobe, but because I know them to be the spawn of Beelzebub – so I phoned a friend in Cork who logged, as I believe it's called, on, and he came right back with the news.

Sorry, clan gathering cancelled.

Some sort of problem with the main man.

Seems he's staying at home.

In Morocco.

A whole arcane world of medieval Gaelic princely shenanigans – quite probably involving the wearing of emerald-coloured tights – of whose existence I had been completely and sadly unaware had revealed itself to me, only to snatch itself away at the last moment. I felt cheated. I decided to go to Morocco, meet the Moor, and lay claim to my roots.

It turned out to be impossible. Phone calls and letters to likely sounding contacts went unanswered. Nobody in the mysterious world of Gaelic heraldry wanted to talk about it, while Irish people living in the real world told me it was a load of unbelievable old shite, and I'd be better off steering well clear of these mad feckers unless I wanted to end up minus large amounts of cash Riverdancing in plaid trousers in a Holiday Inn at two o'clock in the morning.

Then a friend who'd been making some enquiries for me got a call from someone claiming to represent some manner of ceremonial Celtic Guard, an order of armed Gaelic gentlemen who accompany and defend the Mór on all his overseas trips. And the word was that the man himself was indeed in Morocco, but would speak to no one.

No one. Understand?

Then two things happened.

First of all I managed to get hold of a book on Gaelic history with a foreword written by the MacCarthy Mór himself. There was also a photograph. He wasn't a Moroccan fella at all. Rather pale and Irish-looking, in fact; and decked out in a dinner jacket covered in fancy badges and decorations.

The second was an article in the Irish edition of the *Sunday Times* saying that the Irish government had withdrawn 'courtesy recognition' of the MacCarthy Mór, who it described as 'a Belfast historian of humble origins'. Suggesting that his genealogy had been declared suspect, the paper said that MacCarthy was indeed in Morocco, adding ominously: 'He may yet face legal challenges from dozens of disgruntled Irish Americans to whom he sold and rented titles.'

The ceremonial Guard also got a mention: 'A uniform of rust kilts, grey military shirts and black berets. One member carried an axe.'

What in God's name could it all mean?

I was hooked, but my attempts to make contact with the Mór

were, if anything, making reverse progress. The Tangier hotel in which he had been a long-term resident denied ever having heard of him. I did succeed in making contact with a count who had for years been one of MacCarthy's supporters. 'When you phone him, make sure you've got a donkey handy,' advised the intermediary who gave me the number, 'so that he can talk the hind leg off it.' In a series of extended telephone conversations – during which I took on the role of donkey, none being available locally – the loquacious count denounced his former mentor as a charlatan, and urged me to avoid any contact with him. He saw no contradiction, however, in continuing to use his title, despite the fact that it had been bestowed on him by MacCarthy himself. On the other end of the phone I ee-awed in disbelief, but I don't think he noticed. I had entered a peculiar realm in which, as I was to learn to my cost on more than one occasion, interested combatants armed with vast quantities of minute, unverifiable and unlikely-sounding historical detail talk and talk and talk at you until you have a very bad headache indeed.

After several weeks I was no closer to the elusive Mór, but I had managed to piece together the essential facts of the story. Since 1948 the Irish state has been conferring 'courtesy recognition' on the proven heirs of the traditional Gaelic chiefships which were swept away under Anglo-Norman, later British, rule. In 1991, after a decade of petitioning, the Chief Herald of Ireland authorised Terence MacCarthy, a historian and the son of a Belfast ballroom dancing instructor, to use the title MacCarthy Mór, Prince of Desmond. In some eyes this made him potential heir to the high kingship of Ireland, even though the job no longer exists, on account of the inconvenient existence of a republic. Throughout the nineties MacCarthy adopted a high profile, publishing historical books, proselytising for Gaelic culture, being photographed with dignitaries, and making public appearances at clan gatherings in North America. And then, as reported in the *Sunday Times*, the Irish government withdrew its recognition, and the Chief Herald issued a statement: 'It appears that reliance was placed to an excessive degree on uncorroborated statements and uncertified copies, transcriptions, or summaries of documents, the originals of which were not produced or were said to have been destroyed by fire, flood or explosion.'

As a consequence of the alleged fires, floods and explosions, MacCarthy was duly stripped of his title – in effect, they said, because he wasn't who he claimed to be. In reply the ex-Mór wrote that the Chief Herald, 'a mere civil servant of a republic', had no 'right to alter the successional laws of Gaelic Ireland'. Each side accused the other of selling titles to gullible Americans – which, like many people, I'd always assumed to be a cornerstone of the Irish economy and therefore to be encouraged – and, in a welter of claim and counterclaim, MacCarthy announced he was abdicating, withdrawing from public life, and going to ground in Tangier, where he had been living on and off for twelve years with his associate, Andrew, the Count of Clandermond.

'I shall not comment again on this affair. I shall not answer any correspondence, nor stoop to defend myself, or any member of my family, from any further defamatory attacks by self-interested trouble-makers, self-acclaimed experts, scandal-mongers or title hunters.'

By now I had realised that it needed an experienced investigative journalist with a precise and analytical mind to crack this peculiar case and establish the facts once and for all. That ruled me out, then. In any case I felt no urge to prove anything. Most Irish people I've spoken to regard these titles, and the anachronistic world of Gaelic chivalry, genealogical purity and vicious back-biting that surrounds them, as a bit of a game. They may be of some importance to the tourist industry, they tell you, though not so important as genuine aristocracy like U2, Daniel O'Donnell, and Fungi the Dolphin. Rather than caring who was right and who was wrong, I found myself intrigued by what it all said about contemporary Ireland. A Dublin academic offered me his take on the affair: 'In England you have a class system, and everyone knows how it works. In America they have no class system, and everyone knows how it works. And in Ireland, we have a class system, and no one knows how it works.'

There was also a surreal and peculiarly Irish dimension to the whole business, placing it firmly in the grand tradition of Flann O'Brien, Sam Beckett and Spike Milligan. In 1923 the Public Records Office in Dublin was blown up by the IRA and all records destroyed, so that, when push comes to shove, hardly anybody in the country can prove they are who they say they are.

Yet I remained eager to meet the man at the centre of the controversy. I didn't want to cross-examine him, but I was intrigued to know what kind of guy might be claiming, rightly or wrongly, to be my chief. Who are my clan anyway? Senator Joe, the witch-hunter? Mary, the novelist? Mick, the football manager? John, the ex-Beirut hostage? Perhaps. Someone cornered me in Cork airport this year, and said 'Tell me, Mr McCarthy – do you still see a lot of that Brian Keenan?'

I read learned tomes on clan history and discovered all manner of obscure information, most of which is far too boring to pass on; though I was pleased to discover that a McCarthy is reputed to have invented whiskey, and that in remotest Alaska there is a town called McCarthy, population seventeen. One day, I thought, I'll go there. Maybe I'll drink some whiskey when I arrive. And that was about it. I had reluctantly decided to leave the MacCarthy affair to more accomplished investigators when I got a phone call from a friend of a friend. Terence MacCarthy had passed his title – the one that the Irish government had withdrawn – to his younger brother Conor, who lives in Belfast.

And would I like to go over to meet him?

Though it's not the most direct route, I decided to travel to Northern Ireland via Cork, where I had a dole office to visit.

*

Another thing I found difficult to understand as a kid, I thought, as the plane crossed the Welsh coast and headed out over the Irish Sea, was that lots of people were still living in Ireland, even though so many had gone away. It was always the place we went to, but it was better known as a place that people went from. Growing up midway between Liverpool and Manchester there seemed to be more Irish about the place than there were in Cork itself. Everyone I knew seemed to have a parent, or a funny auld pissed-up granddad, or an auntie with a moustache who was always saying the rosary, someone at any rate to tie them into an awareness of an Irish past and a consequent shared cultural identity. Even though you had a flat Lancashire accent – unless you came from Liverpool itself, in which case your accent was a poetically heightened dialect of Dublin – and were immersed in English pop music and politics and sport and literature, part of you was always aware of coming from, if no longer belonging to, another tribe. When England played Ireland at football or rugby it was impossible to know who to support, because either way you'd feel like a traitor. Should you cheer for the land of your birth, your accent and your dad, against the poor downtrodden colonised persecuted underdogs, while your mammy fought back the tears on the other side of the room? Or did you go for the romance of oppression, the pride of a displaced nation in exile, and your cousin singing 'Kevin Barry' at a family wedding, and turn your back on the country that had made you what you were, given you education and prosperity and friendships, Shakespeare, the Small Faces and The Who? These were impossible choices. I'm sure most of us were relieved when the Ireland v. England match and the existential uncertainties that accompanied it had passed for another year, and we could return to the simple eternal truths that nobody in Lancashire ever need question – you know – all southerners are bastards. So are Yorkshiremen. That kind of thing.

Religion was part of the identity. Every priest and nun you

came across – and in our neck of the woods there were hundreds of them – talked just like your uncles and aunties. I was aware on an intellectual level that the Catholic Church was Roman, and therefore in some way inherently Italian, but as far as I could make out in practice it had been comprehensively hijacked by the Irish.

There were other connections reinforcing our links with the homeland where we'd never lived: the John McCormack records, the Irish dancing lessons from the nuns at primary school, and the two parcels that arrived without fail every year. The first was a small box containing the St Patrick's Day shamrock. The second, arriving days before Christmas, was a plucked turkey in a hessian sack. No box, no letter, no fancy wrapping. Just a sack, with stamps on, and a huge turkey inside. It's probably illegal now to send nude poultry through the post, though I believe there's a shop in Amsterdam that will send you photographs. Even as a kid, I can remember thinking there was a wonderful deadpan humour about living in the UK, with our central heating and supermarkets and motorways, and receiving food parcels from people who had no running water in the house. And it seems the practice was worldwide. A man in Toronto told me of a similar sack arriving from the family in Sligo for his emigrant parents. The turkey went straight from sack to oven with a minimum of fuss. An hour and a half later there was a tremendous explosion and the door blew off the oven. His mother had failed to spot the bottle of poteen with which the bird had been stuffed.

There's an ornamental fishpond in the arrivals hall, which also doubles as the departures hall, at Cork airport. As I was sitting waiting for my taxi a thickset man with high blood pressure walked by with his son, a chubby, red-faced ten-year-old wearing chunky platform-soled Cuban-heeled boots with big gold buckles. Maybe he was ahead of the fashion, or perhaps he had a club foot. The boy became very animated and pointed at the oversized goldfish in the pond.

'Look at them big ones, Da.'

Then he had another idea.

'Look at the big fat juicy ones, Da!'

In the space of a single thought the fish had been transformed from ornamental exhibit to nice tasty meal with spuds, apple pie and custard, demonstrating that the transcendent abilities of the human imagination should never be underestimated.

The taxi arrived and twenty minutes later, after a journey enlivened by the radio phone-in – 'Gerry, my mother taught us to share a biscuit! I wouldn't have a dishwasher in the house. Sure, it's exercise, you wouldn't want to seize up now' – I was getting out on the waterfront in Cobh.

Cork has the second-largest natural harbour in the world, a land-enclosed deepwater haven entered from the Atlantic by a single mile-wide channel. Cobh sits on the Great Island, facing the harbour entrance, row upon row of rather grand nineteenth-century houses terraced dramatically up the hillside. Many are newly painted in vivid colours, but otherwise the twentieth century didn't make much impact on the look of the place, and the twenty-first hasn't yet had time to.

At the centre of the town towards the top of the hill looms the grey granite bulk of St Colman's Cathedral with its 300-foot spire and forty-nine bells, which makes you wonder why they didn't go for the full half-century. Its scale is massively at odds with the proportions of the rest of the town, as if a life-size building has been constructed next to one of those miniature model villages they build in places where there's nothing else for tourists to do, so they go and have their photo taken standing next to houses that only come up to their knees. I once went to a park in China where they have miniature versions of everywhere else in China, to save you the bother of going. You can cross the Great Wall and the Terracotta Warriors off your list on the same afternoon. You can see the logic. It frees up all that travelling time for other things, which makes your life seem longer and more action-packed than it really is.

The cathedral is so huge that on a clear day they can probably see it from Ellis Island in New York, but the heavy-handed symbolism of its dominant position is showing signs of wearing thin; as I arrived the town was bristling with placards proclaiming 'No Change To Cobh Cathedral'. Perhaps they were planning to add a plastic conservatory or double garage, or paint it red, yellow and purple, like the houses along the main street. Discreet enquiries in a waterfront pub, however, revealed that the slogans of protest represented an unprecedented show of opposition to the Church's plans to relocate the Italian marble altar rails and create a more appropriately modern open-plan worship space. The word on the streets, or at least in the bar, or at least from the only other guy in there, was that although the protestors have public opinion on their side, they face a tough fight. The devout afternoon drinker told me of the awe in which he held the dioccsan authorities.

'Ya don't feck with those bastards,' he said, backlit for a moment by a vivid beam of sunshine through the pub's stained-glass window – the Almighty's searchlight perhaps, marking him out for the wrath of the bishop and the red card of eternal damnation.

Back out in the crisp fresh air, and ever mindful of the fact that the humble potato is the only vegetable to contain all the nutrients needed for survival, provided you can force enough of them down, I bought a bag of chips to play yang to the drink's yin. I found a seat in the sun near the renovated bandstand from which I could gaze out towards the prison on Spike Island and beyond it, through the break in the headlands, to the open waters of the Atlantic. For many people the view back through this harbour entrance would have been their last glimpse of home. For more than a century Cobh was the great port of Irish emigration. In the decades following the Great Famine of the 1840s 3.7 million people left Ireland, the vast majority of them from here.

My uncle sailed from Cobh to Boston. Nothing special about that. Every family in the country must have had someone leave from here. The town was famous for its American wakes, all-night vigils of celebration and mourning for those about to leave, and who in all probability would never be seen again. Perhaps I'm being fanciful, but I've always felt that the weight of numbers who passed through here, and the volume of tears of goodbye that were shed, have left an indelible mark on the soul of the place. And that's before you even think of the *Titanic*. I was starting to get gloomy. Even the chips were beginning to depress me. I dumped them in an ornate British Empire rubbish bin, where they attracted the immediate attention of one of those fearless ostrich-sized seagulls that have become alarmingly commonplace in recent years, and will one day inherit the earth.

The town was known as the Cove of Cork until 1849, when Queen Victoria, no doubt in a magnanimous gesture of famine solidarity, paid a visit. She painted some watercolours, and also made an entry in her diary: 'the day was grey and excessively muggy, which is the nature of the Irish climate.' In the wake of this definitive meteorological assessment, the name of the town was changed to Queenstown in her honour. It reverted to Cove, this time with the Irish spelling of Cobh, after home rule in 1921.

I'd made the detour to Cobh to catch up on one of my favourite stories. I first heard it from an alcoholically-enhanced fiddle player at a late-night session in a West Cork bar. Even by the infinitely flexible standards of truthfulness that apply on such occasions, it was clearly a preposterous yarn.

'So this fella's out of work and signing on, the roof leaks and he's bringing up three kids on his own. Anyway, doesn't he go and win a million on the Lotto? So how do you think he spends it?'

I don't know, I thought. I can't imagine. I don't even believe the first part of the story.

'He only goes out and buys the feckin' *dole* office, that's all. Then triples its rent. What a man, eh? What a star!'

Ireland has few urban myths, due to a shortage of urbs, but plenty of tall stories. This, it turned out, wasn't one of them. I visited Cobh a few years ago and was able to confirm that, on 22 October 1995, unemployed single parent Vince Keaney did indeed win a million and buy the local dole office. It's a deeply satisfying story, with a powerful sense of poetic justice that gives it the quality of a contemporary myth or fable. But Mr Keaney didn't just buy the place for the craic or the revenge, though I'm sure those elements both played a part. A more pragmatic force was also at work. He was aware that in a previous life the dole office in question – situated on a decaying wharf in the centre of town – had housed the White Star Shipping Line, and that it was through these offices, and from this wharf, on 11 April 1912, that the final 123 passengers embarked on the *Titanic*.

Vince had a plan, which he explained to me when I tracked him down shortly after his win. He was going to evict the dole bastards, buy off the handful of fishermen who still operated from the near-derelict sheds, and invest his fortune in a Titanic bar and restaurant. The man's a loon, I thought, as he showed me the original designs for the ship's tiles, railings and staircases, a charming and engaging loon who's going to lose the lot for believing his own legend. In 1999 I wrote that 'disaster is widely predicted once again.'

I heard no more of Vince and his plan to tip a boatload of money into the sea until a little while ago, when a letter arrived telling me I was no threat to Nostradamus, because the Titanic Bar was up and running. Best of all, didn't they have a survivor of the original disaster – an elderly lady who was a tiny baby when the ship struck the iceberg – coming to open the place? This sounded in such appalling taste that I felt I really had to go and see for myself. I also owed Mr Keaney an apology for doubting his ability to pull off the kind of hare-brained scheme that most of us would dream up at two o'clock in the morning, write down on a scrap of paper, and then be unable to read the following day. Drunken notes to yourself explore the outer limits of the human psyche, and can only be understood when read in the same state of inebriation as when they were written. I can only presume that Vince woke up a couple of days after his win, found a stained beer mat on which he'd written BUY DOLE FECK FISHERMEN OFF BOOK LIFEBOAT BABY, and could actually understand what it meant.

So I'd come to Cobh on my way to Belfast, having invested £9.99 in one of those absurd England–Ireland airfares that crop up with increasing frequency these days, the ones where we all wonder if someone's going to come and chuck us off just before take-off and tell us they were only joking. In the good old days, it used to cost a fortune to fly to Ireland. You knew where you stood then. Today, though, the whole thing is enough to subvert your faith in the entire global economy. How can it possibly cost £9.99 to fly to Ireland, when it's £160 to go to Manchester on the train, and there are hardly any buses any more because buses don't make economic sense? It sounds to me as if someone woke with a hangover one morning, found a piece of paper on which they'd written TEN QUID PLANE A HUNDRED AND SIXTY QUID TRAIN NO BLOODY BUSES, and somehow it got implemented. Crazed nocturnal inspiration can play an important role in our imaginative lives, but it's no basis for an integrated transport system.

Along the shore ahead of me next to the post office I could see a handsome newly painted yellow and white building where the scabby old dole office used to be. Titanic Queenstown, said the sign, over a flag of the White Star Shipping Line. Directly across the street was a shop called 'English'. Perhaps it used to be called 'Irish' but was renamed when Victoria visited.

Vince is one of those men who can wear cravats, brocade waistcoats and Panama hats and come out of it looking like a colourful roué, rather than a twat. Like many Irishmen before him he served in the Royal Navy, then embarked on the successful career in unemployment that led eventually to his celebrated win and purchase. Despite the fact that his new toy must have absorbed the million and a fair bit more besides, he has such an unconcealed glee in the project that you're almost convinced it might be a sound idea.

'This used to be the most miserable room in town. Well, take a look at it now.'

The signing-on hall has been transformed into an upmarket restaurant, modelled on the design of the Palm Court Café on A deck of the *Titanic*. The sea views are extensive, though not as extensive as the *Titanic*'s. The restaurant appeared to be open – people were sitting at tables eating at any rate – but there was an inaugural dinner scheduled for the next night in the presence of the *Titanic* survivor. What if she hated it? If she screamed, 'This is a travesty and a desecration!' and threw herself through one of the handsome sash windows into the harbour, or on to the yuppies eating satay on the jetty?

'Ah, she'll be fine,' said Vince, 'we've had two openings already. She knows the drill. She's a wonderful woman.'

As far as I could make out, about seventeen openings were planned. This made me feel marginally less special for receiving an invitation, especially as I'd phoned up and asked for one. As a general rule I find this usually works very well in Ireland, where social etiquette is less rigid than in England. If you really want to go to something, then you're probably the sort of person they're looking for anyway, so why not come along?

There's a big bar downstairs, which was full of local types who looked as though they'd either finished work for the day, or never started. The room isn't a replica of the ship's first-class lounge, so much as an improvisation around its designs. There's a wonderful back bar mirror with wooden surround.

'Indian rosewood, from her sister ship, the *Mauretania*,' said

Vince. There are lots of other memorabilia, including the harbour logbook displayed in a glass case, and open at the *Titanic*'s fateful handwritten entry. The overall effect is either deeply impressive or wildly kitsch, depending on your point of view.

Vince gave me a guided tour of the Gents, followed by the Ladies, where our arrival did nothing to interrupt the vigorous application of mascara. Both facilities have been kitted out with period marblework and authentic-looking sinks with original taps, though my favourite detail was the bucketful of ice cubes that had been dumped in the urinals. Vince said they'd had some tourists in who'd been fascinated by the toilet fittings.

'Did these things really come from the *Titanic*? How did you get them up from the bottom of the ocean?'

After buying me a couple of drinks, then forcing me to write a handwritten correction next to my previously published comments, Vince suggested we take a jaunt along the front. In the street just along from the restaurant there's a wooden hut that operates as the taxi control centre.

'It was built in 1886 as a beverage stall for departing emigrants. Once a year twenty-five or thirty men used to push it up the street, then back again, which meant they didn't have to pay rates. Look, you can still see the wheels.'

And so you can.

Walking east along the harbour we came to a bench, known locally as the Bench, where conversation has been held and wisdom dispensed for many generations. The stretch of shore beyond it is known as the Holy Ground.

'Not like in the song "The Holy Ground"?'

'The very same.'

'I thought the song was about, you know, the whole of Ireland. The Holy Ground.'

'Ah, no, this is it here.'

It's a traditional drinking song, sung when I was a kid in any social club you cared to go into, and made popular by the likes of the Clancy Brothers and, in Liverpool, the Spinners. Remember them? Remember their jumpers?

> *Adieu my fair young maiden*
> *A thousand times adieu*
> *We must bid farewell to the Holy Ground*
> *And the girls that we love true.*
> *We will sail the salt sea over*
> *And return again for sure*
> *To seek the girls who wait for us*
> *In the Holy Ground once more.*
> *(Fine girl you are!)*
> *You're the girl that I adore*
> *And still I live in hopes to see*
> *The Holy Ground once more.*
> *(Fine girl you are!)*

Sacred ground, then, where virtuous young wives waved their menfolk off to sea and remained chaste until their return?

'Ah, no.'

The guy who had been in the pub dissing the bishop had sidled up and taken his place on the Bench, where, as tradition demanded, he was engaging in conversation and dispensing wisdom.

'They were a bunch of feckin' hoors! 'Twas all brothels along here, a bit of a party for the randy auld sailors. Of course they don't like you saying it, but feck 'em, for it's the truth.'

'It's a very close-knit community round here.' Vince smiled. 'The original tenements were knocked down in Dev's time, and new houses built. The boxer Jack Doyle grew up and lived here. Remember him?'

No. So was it true – about the brothels?

'Well . . .' As a pillar of the local community Vince was potentially compromised.

'Course it's true,' chimed in the Bishop Basher.

45

'Well, there are those who think that the song was written in an ironic voice,' volunteered Vince.

'Wasn't it funny now, when the Pope came over. He gets off the plane and kisses the runway and the band start playing "The Holy Ground", a song about a bunch of feckin' hoors. Ah, Jaysus, we were pissing ourselves laughing down here.'

'It was an incongruous moment,' conceded Vince.

'On that headland over there' – the Basher was pointing to the west of the harbour mouth – 'they found a grave dating from 300 BC. Imagine that now.' He had clearly decided I needed a tour guide, and to be fair he did have an impassioned, unpredictable quality not normally found in official guides, but then usually they haven't been drinking all day, more's the pity. The thought of lairy, unkempt dipsos shouting and slurring and weeping their way round Westminster Abbey and Stratford-upon-Avon before hugging their visitors and asking for the bus fare home is most appealing.

'Seeorther?'

He was pointing to a distant industrial building across the water.

'Viagra factory! True! Export-quality Viagra, made in Ireland! And over there?'

He was pointing to Spike Island, so I said, 'Spike Island?'

He ignored me and said, 'Spike Island!' Then he said, 'That's where the Brits put their political prisoners. John Mitchel. You know about him?'

I said I didn't.

'No, me neither. But they kept him out there. Can't blame 'em like.'

I agreed that indeed you couldn't. You couldn't blame 'em at all. And so, having improved my knowledge of John Mitchel, though only marginally, the tour was concluded, and the Bishop Basher meandered home to sleep it off or have a few more, whichever seemed the better idea at the time.

We wandered up through the town and while Vince nipped home to sort out a room for me I decided to have a look round the cathedral, check out the altar rails, and see what all the fuss was about. What I wasn't expecting was to find the bishop himself, addressing a party of devout-looking coach passengers. As I backed out of the door as inconspicuously as I could, he fixed me with a withering look that made me sure he knew I'd been talking about him in the pub.

So one thing led to another, as tends to happen, and we ended up in a cosy bar full of people talking and drinking and smoking, while a singer with big sideburns played all the old songs on several instruments at once. Then the room went quiet and everyone stood as he played the national anthem, indicating that it was now an hour and a half past closing time. Then we all carried on drinking. A man from Manchester told me he once approached a barman in a small village in the west of Ireland at one o'clock in the morning and asked when they closed. 'October,' came the reply.

The singer came over to join the table and we fell into conversation. He'd been on the road playing music all his adult life, in show bands and rock bands and traditional Irish bands, solos and duos, in pubs and clubs and big concrete dance-halls on the edges of tiny villages. It turned out that he grew up in one of those villages, where a favourite old aunt of mine was a teacher. Excited at this unlikely connection – even though by now I should know that in this part of the world there are no degrees of separation, rather than the usual seven – I asked did he know her?

'Sure, I did. She taught me for five years.'

He took a drink.

'So, what was she like?'

'She was a vicious auld bitch.'

The Chinese takeaway that should have been closed was open,

possibly because it knew that the closed pub was open too, so we headed back to Vince's imposing Regency terrace with a leaking carrier bag full of noodles and duck. We washed them down with neat malt whiskey, an imaginative combination which I can't recommend highly enough, especially if you feel your life's stuck in a rut. Then we sat up talking for hours about things I can't remember. Perhaps I should have written them down on a piece of paper. Perhaps I did. I know that at one point we went on a tour of the house, a gloriously unmodernised wonderland of ancient wood and plaster, bohemian clutter and horror movie landings, the sort of place you expect someone to say, 'You'll be sleeping in Igor's room tonight.' So naturally I was thrilled when Vince refilled my glass and said, 'You'll be sleeping in Igor's room tonight.' There really was a lodger called Igor, a young Croatian who was maître d' at the Titanic and was away for the night.

I was about to head for Igor's room when Vince said he had something to show me. While converting the dole office he found several trunks and boxes in the attic dating back to the nineteenth century and the building's heyday as headquarters of the White Star Line. He showed me tickets, luggage labels, timetables, rules and regulations, all waiting to be catalogued and eventually put on display. He'd also found letters tucked under the eaves of the building, some of them in the original envelopes. He gave me one to read before I went to sleep. I propped myself up in Igor's bed and began. It bore the writer's address in Liverpool and the date, 13 August 1884.

'My own darling husband.'

Next thing I knew the sun was streaming through cracks in the shutters. The letter was lying on the bed next to me. I got up and opened the shutters to look at the harbour and was hit by blinding sunlight of such vicious and painful intensity that it seemed likely I had been turned into a pillar of salt. My mouth tasted as if Michael Barrymore had died in it during the night.

There was no sign of Vince anywhere, so I went downstairs, cleared up the duck, the noodles, the empty glasses and forty or fifty of Vince's dog-ends, drank six or seven pints of water, and settled down at the table to read the letter.

It was six pages long, but written on two sheets of paper. Page six was written in fainter script at right angles across the words on page one, and page five across page four in the same way, presumably to save paper. The hand was so urgent that the emotion leaped off the page.

August 13th 1884

My own darling husband,

This is my second letter to Queenstown, and I do sincerely hope and trust it will find you in the very best of health. I am very well with the exception of the toothache which has driven me mad this week. Your dear Bertie is very poorly with a bilious attack it is the first he has had and I blame myself a good deal for it. I have not given the child any opiate Medicine for four months and he has been drinking a great deal of milk this hot weather and he has bread and milk and rice pudding every day and sometimes an egg. So what with the hot weather and what he eats, he has required medicine which I have neglected to give him for I do dread the Struggle I have to get him to take anything he tells me to take it myself.

Mother and Bert and I were to have gone up to Lizzie's yesterday but Bert took ill just as we were ready to start. And the poor little darling was in a dreadful way about it he thought he was doing something wrong by vomiting and he says 'mama I will be a good boy I wont spit all my bread and milk out again' he was sick ten times in less than a hour and every time he would say I'll tell my Papa when he comes home, then he will make me better he is always talking about his Papa especially when anything goes wrong with him and he is not a bit better at going to bed . . . he sits up on the pillows and puts the clothes over his head like a bus driver he says, and after he had been in bed a short time he called out Mama is Papa downstairs I think I can hear him, it was just a little scheme of his to be brought downstairs again.

Oh Jack my darling when I do look at him a long time I can see such a likeness of you in him and his head is the very same shape as yours and so are his eyes and mouth but his nose is not like yours at present but I think it will grow like yours but all the rest of him his legs and body and everything are the exact model of yours. Oh Jack my love what an awful long passage you are making the time seems longer this last month than all the others. I do hope you will arrive soon I am so longing to see you I feel so anxious to know the condition of your health and I do hope the ship will come to Liverpool for a great many reasons and now my precious Darling Husband I don't think I can say anymore and I am not going to write anymore till you arrive this is the fourth letter I have written two to Queenstown and two to Falmouth I hope you will get them all. And now my love I will finish with my fondest love and heaps of kisses from your ever Loving deserted and faithful wife Louie.

I headed out for some early morning fresh air to clear my head. It was half past one in the afternoon.

A big night was planned at the Titanic and Igor would be back in town, so I was booked into a guest-house up the road, the only place I've ever stayed whose former owner once had a job as Napoleon's doctor on St Helena. My room had a perfect view of the harbour, the cathedral and the bishop's bedroom. After checking my pockets for illegible notes that might give some clue to what we were talking about last night, I waved to the bishop, who didn't wave back, then stepped out towards the waterfront.

As I walked down the hill in unseasonable early evening sunshine I found myself thinking of Louie and Bert. Whatever became of the poor kid? Did they ever find his feckless pa? Did anyone warn the poor little bugger off all that milk and rice pudding? He'd have been better off staying on the opium. I wanted to go to Liverpool, knock on the door and find out what the hell happened. It's been a long time, but social services move very slowly sometimes. Someone must know something.

In the 1760s John Wesley, founder of Methodism, visited Cobh and won himself lots of friends by declaring it a 'godless place' and 'a sink full of sinners'. Part of his legacy is a magnificent pillared and colonnaded Wesleyan chapel, built in 1873 as a monument to the virtues of abstinence, and these days doing grand business as Pillars Bar. It probably isn't fair to say that this represents Ireland's revenge on Wesley, but I'd like to say it anyway. At the very least, someone's having a good-natured little joke with him. Inside are more pillars, giving the bar a wonderfully ornate ambience that reminds me not so much of a typical Irish pub as of a magnificently baroque gay bar I once happened upon in a deconsecrated chapel in Majorca.

As I drank my pint, the passing of each mouthful was marked by a creamy line on the surface of the glass. I found myself thinking of tree rings for carbon dating, or the descending generations on a family tree – a warning sign that my all-day hangover was in imminent danger of interacting with Cobh's melancholy history to produce a cocktail of lethal sentimentality.

There's no denying, though, the huge and burgeoning modern need to know where we come from. When I was a kid it seemed most children would grow up, leave home, then live in the next street to their parents. That doesn't happen so much now. As we become more socially and geographically mobile, so the need to belong to some collective past has rocketed; not an invented need, a plastic heritage, as some cynics suggest, but a genuine yearning that's always been there, but is no longer satisfied. And for many people, it struck me as I left Pillars and headed down the hill past a woman in Celtic jewellery and avant-garde knitwear who was either in a famous band or else thought she was, God's gone missing too. He may be back one day, but until then people will seek the reassurance of a wider human context, a bigger picture in which their own walk-on role gives life meaning and significance. Everybody wants to be in a good story. It's a natural impulse to shape the random events we live through into coherent narrative, otherwise our lives would feel like experimental theatre or abstract painting, which would be a complete bloody nightmare. We need a good plot, and if God isn't available to provide it then an epic human story stretching back in time across far-flung continents fits the bill nicely. And so history and archaeology are all over our televisions, and genealogical websites implode under the volume of 'hits', I believe they're called. Americans come to European archives, and Europeans go to Australian prison records, and people tramp round the west of Ireland going into every pub that bears their name and wondering at their place in it all. In a world that lives increasingly in the moment, it's important to remember where we've come from, or we may wake up one morning unable to remember who we are. As I reached the Titanic a journey was beginning to take shape inside my head. I should probably write it down on a piece of paper, I thought, or I may have forgotten it by morning.

The inaugural dinner was to be held in the Dean Room – named after the guest of honour, disaster survivor Mulvena Dean – but the warm-up was in the bar downstairs. Sleek and poised in black jacket, black polo neck and black bags under the eyes, Vince was working the room with energy and poise, giving an almost-convincing impersonation of a man who'd had a quiet night in, a cup of Horlicks and nine hours' sleep last night. 'In a town of talkers, Vince is a doer,' said Eamon, a definite talker in a lost-at-sea beard and stained nautical jumper, who looked so completely at home on the bar stool next to me it seemed possible he was part of the memorabilia. Perhaps he'd been cloned from

DNA on a fragment of *Titanic* timber and next year, when re-
furbishments are complete, he'll end up on display in a glass case
under the telly.

The Dean Room has huge wood-framed windows, salvaged
from a local house when they were discarded in favour of that
maintenance-free UPVC that turns grey and falls out after fifteen
years. We were able to look out on the tugboats passing on the
water outside, and beyond them the harbour mouth through
which so many – convicts and famine victims, unmarried women
and unemployed men, and maybe even Louie's Jack himself –
once passed on their way to uncertain and mostly unrecorded
futures. I had a seat next to Mulvena, a trim and sparky woman
who was an eight-month-old baby when the ship went down. I
felt awkward and didn't know what to talk about. Should I ask
her if she enjoyed the movie? Would she be amused by the ice
cubes in the urinals? She turned out to be good company, and
well used to being trotted out for *Titanic*-related events.

'I think they think I am the *Titanic* in America. Some of them
are obsessed. One man wrote asking for a lock of my hair.'

So what did she think of that?

'I thought he was a nutcase.'

Her father was a Hampshire publican who decided in 1912 to
make a new life as a tobacconist in Kansas. A house and business
were arranged, but her father went down with the ship. Her
mother survived, and together they went back with nothing to
her grandparents' farm in Hampshire.

'When I was eight a vet came to see one of my grandmother's
cows. He saw my mother as well and married her.'

The food and wine were good, Igor floated effortlessly around
the room, and a man at the far end of the table asked me was I
aware my family were ancient kings in Munster, and did I know
about this fella in Morocco, the one they say is the McCarthy
king? I said that I did, but it was hard to hear what he said next,
because people kept coming through to peer at Mulvena, which

didn't seem to bother her, and Vince told her she'd be better off in Ireland, where pensioners travel free on buses and trains and have their mortgages and fuel and phone paid. Yeah, but other than that, said the guy down the table, it's everyone for themselves. 'There was much more social acceptance of struggling and being poor twenty years ago than there is now. Communities looked after their own. That's all but disappeared now thanks to the Celtic feckin' Tiger.'

We were draining the bottles for a final toast when two big, heavily perspiring men who looked as if they'd made illicit fortunes from bent dairy farming came through to pay their respects, as if we were in some downmarket Irish remake of *The God-father*. The one in charge had a thick moustache, large glasses, stripy shirt, red face and an iffy syrup. Suddenly he closed his eyes, threw back his head and launched into an impassioned rendering of 'The Fields of Athenry', the tale of deportation and loss that has already achieved traditional classic status, despite having been written in the 1980s. It's one of those stirring melodies that make people feel proud and sad and nostalgic and indignant and free, even if they've not the faintest idea what it's about. Tonight's version was delivered like a masterclass in pub singing technique, with peculiar vibratos and strange warbles in unexpected places.

> *By-ee the lonely prison wall-uh!*
> *I-ee heard a young girl call-ee-ee-ing, uh*
> *Michael! They are a-taking you ah-way-ee,*
> *For you stole Trevelyn's corn, ugh!*
> *So the young might see the mor, mor, mor, or-or-or-ning, eh*
> *Now a preeson ship lahs awaitin' – awaitin', inabay, ee.*

And we all joined in on the chorus, really, really quietly, like a murmur of conversation from a distant room.

> *Lo lie-ee, the fields of Athenry . . .*

'Altogether now!' he shouted, and we sang even quieter. Some of us were just humming. My God, it was embarrassing. The Dairy Gangster was turning redder as he built to what I can only describe as a climax. It seemed possible he might explode all over Mulvena. She's a nice lady, though. I don't expect she'd have complained.

Back at Napoleon's doctor's house a few of us sat up for a quick nightcap that lasted till almost daybreak. What happens to all the late-night conversation that goes on in Ireland? There's far too much of it for anyone to remember. But I do recall someone telling me about the sinking of the *Lusitania*, when one of the bodies laid out on the quayside at Cobh got up and walked away; and about the cabaret turns on the nineteenth-century transatlantic liners, which he swore included performing polar bears; and the waterfront flophouses, where musicians were hired to wake the sleepers and make them dance while another shift slept in their beds. And I learned that the John Mitchel imprisoned on Spike Island was a famous political activist, who was transported from Cobh to Van Diemen's Land, which we agreed sounded much scarier than Tasmania; and that Cromwell, in an early pilot scheme for ethnic cleansing, transported the Irish to work as slaves in the West Indies; and that the *Titanic* was only moored in Cobh for an hour and a half.

'Mind you,' said someone, 'we tend to play that down a bit.'

Before I went to bed I wrote myself a note: VDL, NY?17/3?/ or WINDIES?? MORROCCO????

With any luck it would still make sense in the morning. As I was falling asleep I remembered something.

There's only one R in Morocco.

Next day on the way to Belfast I found a marvellous story in the newspaper.

A Dublin supermarket had been closed down the previous

week because of infestation by mice. Vermin Relations Representatives, or whatever they call rat-catchers these days, were called in and the problem was quickly eradicated. But now the shop had been closed down again because the mice had been replaced, in a pleasing piece of synchronicity, by an elusive and incontinent stray cat. 'The cat has been urinating on the food,' said a supermarket spokesman, 'but we don't know which food.' You can see their problem. I've always had my suspicions about prawn cocktail crisps, and supermarket coleslaw, but it's very difficult to prove anything. Staff, continued the report, had engaged in a sit-in to try and capture the creature and conclusively identify the pee-soaked food. 'The cat may be the straw that broke the camel's back,' said the supermarket spin-doctor, in the first suggestion so far that infestation by dromedary was also a problem.

I haven't spent much time in Northern Ireland apart from once seeing Daniel O'Donnell stripped to the waist and covered in shaving foam in a toilet in Coleraine. Other than that, the place is a bit of a mystery to me.

'It's a mystery to most people here too,' said Mark the Pagan. I once made a television series, three in fact, in which I encountered pagans, wiccans, dowsers, Odinists, witches, shamans and druids. The Kaos Magicians were rather alarming, stomping round in moonlit woods brandishing human skulls and bones; and so was the woman who ran the bed and breakfast in Glastonbury and claimed to be growing a second spine, which she said proved she was from Atlantis. Other than that the British pagans seemed bright and sincere, and I liked them. I also enjoyed Iceland, where a majority of the population believes in elves, the elf stones in which they live, and the existence of parallel dimensions in which the elf population operate, and into which we occasionally experience slippage. After the series I got letters from anti-pagans congratulating me for showing them up as the dangerous loons they really are; letters from pagans thanking me for giving them a fair crack of the whip; and a letter in six different colours of felt-tip from a bloke in Doncaster who said I was going to lose my immortal soul. I was invited to speak at pagan gatherings, and to open a new coven in Birmingham, just round the corner from the Bull Ring.

And now my occult credentials were having an unexpected pay-off. Ireland is a small country, and people soon knew that I was asking questions about the MacCarthy Mór. It seems Conor MacCarthy, the brother and heir of my clan chief in exile, had heard of my interest and was determined to avoid me, until his friends in Belfast's tiny pagan community – of which there is no mention in the Good Friday Agreement – gave me a glowing reference. Without my sun-worshipping, sweat-lodging, spirit-channelling shamanistic past I would never have got to meet him. Perhaps the Earth Spirit was guiding my progress.

I arrived in the afternoon and made my way as instructed to a pagan café in a shopping arcade. As he poured my coffee the guy behind the counter said, 'The druid who used to wear the fox on his head says hi.' I was sorry to hear he'd stopped wearing the fox. It suited him, and was a big hit when we went for a pub lunch in Oxfordshire. I might not recognise him without it.

After half an hour Conor arrived, a scholarly looking thirty-something with a nose and hairline that made him look alarmingly like my own younger brother. He was accompanied by his brother Tommy, an entirely different physical type, stockier, sandier, with less of the academic and more of the street lad about him. One of the first things he told me was that he was planning to move away from Belfast because so many friends had been killed in the course of the Troubles. After bombarding me for an hour with the kind of incomprehensibly complex historical and genealogical detail that I now know is par for the course in the bitterly contested world of Gaelic heraldry, I felt another headache coming on, and suggested we adjourn to the pub. As well as being able to get a drink, there was the bonus of loud music, so that if they started going into too much detail I could just keep saying, 'What?' without appearing rude.

Over a few pints, a Thai meal, a few more pints, and dozens of cigarettes, Conor explained his family's position, with Tommy on back-up vocals. In 1905, they claimed, at a clan gathering in Nantes in Brittany, the title of MacCarthy Mór was passed to their grandfather under the ancient Gaelic principle of tanistry, by which authority is passed on by consensus to the most able, rather than to the male first-born. He in turn passed the title to their father who, despite his humble circumstances as a dancing teacher and proprietor of the Cordoba nightclub in Belfast, exercised the office of clan chief until 1980, when he abdicated in favour of Terence. Aware of their family's chiefly status, they grew up in a Catholic Gaelic monarchist household, apart from Tommy who was fostered and raised – 'in keeping with an old Irish tradition', they told me, somewhat mysteriously – by 'one of the few Republican Presbyterian families in Belfast'. Are you with me so far? Good. Because since then all three brothers have converted to the Eastern Orthodox Tridentine Church of the Western Patriarchy, of which they are passionate devotees.

After several hours of this it all started to sound quite matter-of-fact, and I was able to give a half-decent impression of a man who has conversations like this all the time. I'd no idea how much of it I understood, but I couldn't help liking their company. They were impassioned and funny and unpredictable, and, as pub talk goes, it was a lot more fun than football or the lottery or the fact that the same Ikea bed costs much more in the UK than it does in France or Spain.

They walked me to a minicab office and, ever the perfect hosts, insisted I took the first car. The driver said my bed and breakfast was in a mainly student area. As he dropped me off, the students were mainly off their faces and trying to find their way home from one of those 20p alcopop and vodka mixer promotional nights at which the first fifteen drinks are free. Two English girls were shrieking and dodging the traffic and trying to walk the white line in the middle of the road, while their friend performed cartwheels and handsprings along it. She sounded as though she came from Huddersfield, though she could have been a Surrey girl with a bad chest.

My room had three single divans with Readers' Wives headboards, and enough melamine wardrobes and dressing-tables to stock a medium-sized second-hand shop in Widnes. As I lay in bed listening to a high-spirited young academic vomiting in someone's garden, I realised that Terence MacCarthy had hardly been mentioned. There'd certainly been no suggestion that I might be able to make contact with him.

Ten days later I got a phone call from Conor asking if I'd like to come and meet them in Morocco. VDL, NY and WINDIES would have to wait.

3

McCARTHY'S
CASBAH

Tangier is the oldest city in Morocco, by tradition the place where Hercules wrenched apart Africa and Spain to create for his son a city protected by the sea. It was a Roman capital, before being disputed for centuries by Arabs and Berbers, and subsequently a possession of Spain, then Portugal, who gave it to Charles II of England as a wedding present in 1661. Samuel Pepys was appointed treasurer of the city, and hated it with a passion. 'A hell of brimstone and fire and Egypt's plagues . . . a place of the world I would last send a young man to, but to hell.' Britain abandoned it in 1684, having first blown up the quays and burned down the casbah, presumably as part of some philanthropic job-creation initiative designed to help the locals.

The city is blessed with both Atlantic and Mediterranean coastlines, big beaches, an ancient medina and a French-style *ville nouvelle*. A large European population was established in the nineteenth century, but it was from the 1920s to the 1960s, during its years as an international tax-free port, that it gained

a reputation as an anything-goes playground for the decadent, the artistic and the generally whacked-out. The city echoes still to tales of Matisse and Saint-Saëns, Marlene Dietrich and Errol Flynn, Joe Orton and Oscar Wilde, Barbara Hutton and Truman Capote, Paul Bowles, Gertrude Stein, Allen Ginsberg, William Burroughs and Jack Kerouac. 'In Tangier,' wrote Kerouac, 'everything is possible – and everything that isn't possible is possible too.' And he only went there on his holidays.

I've been catching up on my Tangier reading during a languid breakfast of fruit and pastries and fresh-squeezed orange juice in the hotel dining-room, looking out on the Med through dazzling winter sunshine. At the far end of the almost-deserted room a loud bohemian-posh English woman is eating, smoking and talking at the same time. She is also sketching the waiter, who has been required to pose, tray on upturned hand.

'Big mouths are always a problem, dahling,' she bellows, and there's no one in the room who'd disagree.

I've been reading Joe Orton's diaries and his extraordinarily frank, shocking and hilarious account of his hashish-enhanced sexual adventures in Tangier. I've just reached the bit where a Moroccan boy boasts to Joe that he 'takes it up to the last hair', when the smiling young waiter appears at my elbow with more coffee. He looks at my book, then deep into my eyes. 'Is this an interesting book, sir?' I don't know what to say. What if he thinks I'm reading it so that people will know I'm up for this sort of caper myself? I tell him it's by a famous English writer who is dead now, and is about his stay in Tangier in 1967. He looks thoughtful. 'Nineteen sixty-seven,' he says, 'that is a very long time ago.'

After breakfast I try and plan my day, but it isn't proving as straightforward as I'd hoped. My missed rendezvous with the MacCarthy brothers at yesterday morning's ferry could prove costly. They don't know where I'm staying, and I have only two ways of contacting them in Tangier: a mobile phone number which I have been trying all morning and which doesn't work; and an address written in biro on a scrap of paper which I have either left behind in England, or lost. Luckily I can remember the name of the street: Rue des Postes. They're staying at a pension, possibly number twelve, that's run by an Irish woman. The two men at hotel reception, however, have just assured me that there is no such pension in Tangier, and that the street does not exist. Under the circumstances, it's hard to see how I'm going to find them, short of walking around until I bump into them. I eventually settle on a plan that is more coherent than that, but only marginally so. I will go out and search for the street that doesn't exist, pausing occasionally to phone the mobile that doesn't work. Relentless pursuit of the non-existent by the clueless armed with the unworkable is bound to turn up something sooner or later.

I walk out of the hotel into a sunlit confusion of the medieval and the modern, business suits and veils, djellabahs and Levis, T-shirts and fezes, wondering which way to head. I plunge into the crowd trying to look as if I'm in control but feeling like a character in a period movie whose plot I don't understand, half expecting Peter Lorre to pop out of a doorway at any moment. By walking as if I know where I'm going and it's important to get there quickly, even though I'm lost already, I'm hoping to avoid all hassle. I know that in many Moroccan cities unofficial guides and street touts can be the bane of your life and that it is important to see them off politely but firmly, unless you want them to shadow every waking moment of your trip. No problem. I will discourage their attentions by being aloof, preoccupied and terribly British. 'Leave me alone,' my sophisticated body language will say, 'I am not some naïve tourist. I've been about a bit, so don't mess with me.'

'You want to rent a house?'

The cheery voice comes from somewhere to my right and I spin round instinctively, even though I already have a lovely hotel room. Why the hell would I need a house?

'I know German man. He has perfect house for bar restaurant but he needs business partner. Or maybe he will rent house to you if I ask him.'

This is so absurd, so outlandish, such a parody of what I knew was bound to happen that I give a big smile. He smiles back, and that's it. It's all over. Five minutes, day one, and he has me. He is my guide, and I am his creature. He knows it. I know it. There's no escaping now.

'I see you leave hotel.'

He's been watching me! He's seen me coming out! Targeted me, followed me. I should be outraged, but I'm not. What nerve, I'm thinking, what bottle.

'You must be very careful, my friend. In Tangier are many bad people will try to be your guide. You must not go with them. If you like I will show you.'

He's very good at this.

'What is your name, my friend?'

It's important I don't tell him anything about myself, especially my name.

'Peter.'

Damn. Why did I do that?

'My name is Mohammed.'

He's about thirty, with liquid doe-brown eyes, and looks like he's been sleeping rough since a year last Ramadan. I, on the other hand, have been munching croissants in a fancy hotel. The moral high ground is definitely his.

'Come with me. I show you casbah.'

I tell him I don't want to go to the casbah, I must find somewhere else first. Suddenly, he's all ears. Where? Where do I have to find? Which street? What people? Why? When? Who? How? Let me help! He's moving round and round on the spot in an agitated manner, anxious for any snippet of information so he can pick up the scent and head off in pursuit. I'll have to be careful here. I don't want to play all my cards at once. Information is power. It might be better to keep him at arm's length. Don't get too familiar. Don't tell him the name of the street.

'I'm looking for Rue des Postes.'

I can't believe I said that. I really didn't mean to. There'll be no getting rid of him now. He'll know all my business if I'm not careful. I'll just have to make sure he clears off once he's helped me find the street. There's absolutely no need for him to know which house I'm going to, or who I'm meeting.

'I am looking for two Irish men.'

'Irish? What is Irish?'

'Irish. You know, from Ireland. They are staying in a guest-house. Pension? Small hotel? In Rue des Postes. Do you know it?'

I'm feeling foolish for giving so much away, but I don't seem to be able to help it. It's as if some kind of truth drug has been administered. I've only known him about a minute and a half, yet already Mohammed seems to have some kind of psychological hold over me, as if he knows what I'm thinking. Perhaps I'm not even saying these things out loud. Maybe he's just reading my mind. It's possible. He could be part Vulcan. Morocco's exactly the sort of place aliens would make for. I haven't been here long, but already it seems to have far more that would be of interest to intergalactic life forms than Roswell, say, or Wiltshire. It certainly seems to encourage extravagant thought processes.

'Rue des Postes,' he says. 'Yes. I know this place.'

But he's pausing. He looks unsure. He doesn't know, does he? He's just trying to humour me. He doesn't bloody know!

'Where is it, Peter?'

See, told you. *He's* asking *me* where it is. But I don't know. That's the whole point! That's why I'm asking him. So why am I saying, 'I think it must be quite near the port.'

His face lights up and he starts walking on the spot again.

'The port? This is good. Come. Come. This way.'

We plunge off down a side street, Mohammed leading the way. It's too late to try and explain that this is just guesswork and that the person who may or may not be the head of the Mac-Carthy clan, and therefore a potential contender for the throne of Ireland if it should ever come up for grabs, though at the moment it has to be said that doesn't seem likely – that this person had only mentioned in passing that it was no problem to meet me at the port, 'because it's not far at all'. He was probably just being polite, and anyway now that I'm here I can see that nowhere in Tangier is actually that far from the port. This non-existent street could be virtually anywhere. No matter though. We're off, and if not exactly running, walking very briskly. We pass the gloriously dilapidated Spanish-looking Théâtre Cervantes. Below us the bay gleams in the sunshine and I'm thinking it must be wonderful to live in a city where the water is always visible from the centre like this. And then two men walk past, one in a fez, one in a little gold embroidered hat, and I stop thinking about the water and start thinking how lucky these guys are to come from a place where you can wear headgear like this without any sense of irony or fear of looking ridiculous. I don't seem to be able to stick with any thought for very long at the moment. Perhaps my powers of concentration aren't what they used to be.

'Maybe it is near here.'

He asks a man selling grilled fish, but he looks hostile and shakes his head, so we thread through the traffic to cross the narrow street and end up at one of the archways leading into the medina.

'You like to see casbah?'

No, I don't want to see the bloody casbah, I want to see the MacCarthy Bleedin' Mór, Prince of Feckin' Desmond, and to be perfectly frank it's looking less likely by the minute. On an impulse I pause in the middle of the street and ask a policeman or soldier or traffic warden or bus conductor, a man in a uniform anyway, but he shakes his head too, then takes a couple of assertive strides, blows a whistle and points at a lad on a moped. I'm hot and bothered now with all this charging about, and also conscious that I'm the only Western face on the street. We've wandered into a part of town with no carpet shops or MasterCard stickers. They clearly don't cater for tourists round here, unless they're tourists looking for hardware or electrical fittings or coffins who are prepared to pay cash.

After a few minutes I've had enough and decide to hail a taxi. Mohammed pushes past me and gets in first and the driver nods at the mention of the street name. Back up the hill we go, away from the port, obviously, past my hotel, naturally, past the spot where I met Mohammed a little while ago, inevitably, and then we pull over at a crossroads. We're 100 yards from where we started, in the opposite direction to the way we walked. I pay the driver, who smiles and waves as he drives off. The street signs are all in Arabic.

'So which street is it?'

'It is one of these.'

'But there are four streets here, Mohammed. Which one?'

'Yes. One of these. Or very close to here. We find it now, Peter. Come.'

And the whole thing happens again. This way. That way. Past orange stalls and fish stalls and a cybercafé, misdirected by two people who clearly haven't heard of it but don't want to disappoint us, until a man in a fabric shop sends us back to where we first got out of the taxi, and I notice a sign on the wall that I hadn't seen before. And it's in French. Perhaps someone stuck it up as we walked away from the taxi. RUE DES POSTES, it says. I point it out to Mohammed, who's looking the other way.

'Yes,' he says. 'Ah, yes. Des Postes. I am good guide, yes?'

In the cybercafé we ask if they know of a pension run by an Irish lady, which they don't, or if they've seen two Irish men in here, which they haven't. A man washing a car on the street also knows nothing. I feel like a secret policeman trying to find the Resistance among a patriotic and tight-lipped population. On the off-chance that I've remembered the number on the scrap of paper correctly we approach number twelve, a detached Spanish-style villa with colourful tile work, and ring the bell. After a couple of minutes a Moroccan woman in a veil comes to the door, denies all knowledge of pensions, Irishmen, and anything else we want to know, and sends us packing. Mohammed shrugs and smiles.

'You like to drink mint tea? In Morocco, everyone drink mint tea.'

We go to a café, where I order mint tea and he orders Coke. Not to worry, he says, soon I will find my friends. In the meantime would I like to see the casbah? Would I like to visit the beach? Perhaps we go out of town, see the caves of Hercules? And all the time I'm feeling like a fool for letting him insinuate himself so easily, yet guilty for coming from an affluent country so that to him I'm impossibly wealthy, even though to me I'm not. And now he's asking can I help him? After all, he found the street for me, he knew it was near here but he is poor, hasn't showered for many days, needs fingernails cutting, needs scissors. Well, what can you say? Of course I'll help. I give him twenty dirhams. He laughs disdainfully and asks for more. I give him another five. He winces, shrugs, smiles. As we're haggling I realise it reminds me of something: Joe Orton's account of post-coital bartering with the boys he picked up on the beach. Mind you, he'd had sex with them. I've only had a cup of tea with Mohammed.

'I meet you tomorrow at ten, Peter, same place, by the cannons on Boulevard Pasteur?'

I disappear into the cushioned lounges and exquisite tiled court-yards of the hotel, knowing that the becloaked pantalooned flunky will bar Mohammed's way if he should try to follow. Part of me feels bad for letting him attach himself and fleece me in this way, while the other part feels guilty for not giving the poor guy much more money.

One thing is certain though.

At ten tomorrow morning I'll be as far from Boulevard Pasteur as I can get.

Later in the afternoon, after a short hallucinatory nap, I try and get to the bottom of the mystery of the Rue des Postes. I've decided to confront the concierge with the fact that it does exist, because I've just been there. He is charming and personable, while sticking firmly to the alternative reality that there is no such place. It stands to reason therefore that the alleged pension I am seeking cannot exist either. The clear implication is that I am either mistaken or mad. I can take my pick.

While we've been talking a man with an air of elegantly crumpled Frenchness has been sitting in a chair in the lobby. He's got a small mobile phone in his hand and is gazing at it fixedly as people do all over the world these days, as if in an act of worship. As I turn from the desk he catches my eye and smiles.

'Monsieur, there is something you should know.'

He explains that most streets have now been renamed in Arabic, though a few still have their old French names; and to complicate matters further some have two entirely different names, one in each language, that do not translate as each other. What a fantastic system. It's as if, say, Oxford Street were also called the Meadow Where a Thousand Petals Bloom, only in another language with an entirely different alphabet. Many locals are oblivious to the French names, which is why nobody had heard of Rue des Postes. Shameful ignorance of such crucial local information is one of the joys of travelling alone. Like near-castration by Barbary ape, it's the kind of meaningful inter-action with local culture that makes it worth getting out of bed in the morning.

I do what I can to find the elusive Irishmen. I try and look for T. MacCarthy in the telephone book, but the hotel switchboard and the international phone-fax bureau at the top of the street both tell me that Tangier doesn't have a telephone book. I've been here less than a day, but already this seems plausible. I walk to the tourist office to make enquiries, but it has a broken window and is closed, or possibly abandoned. I'm not sure what else to do. Perhaps I should try and start acting like a private detective. I put on a jacket and sit at the hotel bar looking as mysterious as I can manage. In the film I would slip the barman a bank note and he would give me the information. In real life, however, he ignores me. When I ask him if an Irish prince ever comes in here he shakes his head in scornful disbelief. He's probably been talk-ing to the concierge and the breakfast waiter. They've all got my number by now. The English Pervert. They'll have spotted me reading Joe Orton, and will do whatever it takes to stop me having my filthy way with their brothers and sons.

Early in the evening I head down towards the medina in the most purposeful and preoccupied manner I can manage, and this time nobody bothers me. I stride briskly through the street traders in Grand Socco, their alarm clocks and belts and handbags laid out on the ground, and take a seat outside a café. All around me there is shouting and laughter, hustlers selling crêpes and Islamic CDs and underwear, women carrying carpets and boxes of oranges. Half the people in the city are frantically busy doing things, while the other half are sitting at cafés watching them. Men keep coming into the café to greet and hug other men, join them for a quick mint tea, then move on. I feel as if I'm at the theatre, separate from the action that's unfolding before me. The actors all know precisely how the play fits together and understand the significance of everything, while I can only sit and observe the spectacle.

As I get up to leave, marvelling at the exotic and impenetrable foreignness of it all, I notice that the café has filled up with rows of men staring impassively at a TV in the corner. Curious as to what is exerting such a powerful spell over them – the King perhaps, or a spiritual or military leader – I poke my head round the door. They are all watching an old episode of *Cheers*. The mood is serious, almost sombre. Perhaps they've just heard that Coach is dead and have been overwhelmed by the hollow emptiness of life.

On the way back to the hotel I stop at a bakery and buy some kind of custardy-creamy-filled croissanty-type affair which I smuggle past the room service police and eat in my room for dinner. It's rather strange. I can't work out whether its savoury lemony-cheesy flavour is intentional, or whether it's just a sweet one that's gone rancid in the heat. Never mind. The role of tension and uncertainty in gastronomy is frequently underrated, particularly late at night. I pour a decent-sized tumbler of Soberano to chase the ambiguous pastry, and turn on the TV.

Hotels all over the world now have CNN the way they used to have trouser presses and Gideon's Bibles. I'm hoping for a global political update, but instead I get the result of the

University of Wisconsin football match, proving once again that CNN has no equal when it comes to providing world news from all over the USA. Over on BBC Bland International there's some pleasure to be had from wondering whether the presenter or the viewer will lose the will to live first. This is a pale shadow of the BBC as we have known it, like turning up to see Manchester United and getting the Wythenshawe Youth Team instead. I'm halfway through the brandy now and getting angry, unable to understand why they're spending licence payers' money on hotel guests who have twenty other channels to watch, when they could be spending it on proper terrestrial TV programmes about decking and water features instead. This is terrible. I'd rather watch a still photograph of the hotel lobby. Luckily they're showing one on Channel 3. After a while it gets a bit predictable, like watching a repeat of a programme you already saw repeated not long ago, so I drain my glass and settle for an early night. Wisconsin beat Notre Dame, by the way. Massacre, by the sound of it.

Next morning at ten I slip out of a side entrance through the hotel garden and car park and go and hide in the medina a long way from Boulevard Pasteur. It's a wasted effort, because Mohammed finds me anyway. I'm outside a café watching a woman carrying a goat under her arm and leading a sheep on a rope, and wondering how she settled on these particular priorities, when I realise he's standing in a doorway across the road watching me, like Harry Lime in *The Third Man*, only scruffier. Slowly, painfully slowly – this guy's a master of suspense – he comes across to join me. He exudes a colossal sense of wounded pride and hurt and disappointment.

'So, Peter. You do not come this morning like you promise.'

So I tell him a lie, a pointless lie which gains me nothing. A small amount of money changes hands, and we go our separate ways. In one masterful stroke he has established the basic ground rules: wherever I go in this city he will find me, I will let him guide me and then I will give him some money. Even if he doesn't guide me, I'll have to give him money for finding me. That's just the way it's going to be.

It's lunchtime, and I'm about to enter a promising-looking restaurant on the edge of the casbah when I notice an old man sitting daydreaming in the street. I turn into the doorway and he totters to his feet and goes into what is either a large cupboard or a small office, where he presses an antique bellpush. As I reach the restaurant at the top of a flight of stairs an ancient retainer in green fez and maroon pantaloons has responded to his call and is there to meet me. He shows me into a dazzlingly ornate room with tiled floors and walls, green and yellow glass skylights, embroidered wall hangings and cushions, marble fireplaces, Islamic arches and hand-made rugs. It's empty apart from five Berber tribesmen in traditional dress sitting at a table in the centre. They've probably been bringing animals to market and have popped in for lunch before heading back to the mountains.

I'm congratulating myself on my unerring ability to sniff out the most authentic places when the doors open and a party of about forty tourists in terrifying leisurewear pile in, tooled up to the eyeballs with video and photographic equipment. The authentic tribespeople burst into action, producing an extraordinary selection of nose flutes, radical ukuleles and camel-skin timpani from underneath their seats and robes. The tour party, an uneasy alliance of French and American – though under interrogation I couldn't rule out the possibility that some of them might be Swiss – burst into action, shooting the shit out of everything that moves with state-of-the-art idiot-proof camcorders. Some of them have those digital stills cameras that display instant pictures, so that now people can take their holiday snaps and bore their friends with them at the same time.

The authentic tribespeople from the mountains, who I now realise are a coach party cabaret turn from a block of flats up the road, are playing wonderful music, wailing and pounding and drawing haunting, searing melodies from their strange instruments. It's a thrill to be in the same room as them, a fact that hasn't been lost on the visitors, who are lining up to use the band as props. They are poking their heads in between the musicians, grinning and gurning as the flashbulbs pop, treating them for all the world as if they're one of those stick-your-head-through-the-hole-in-the-plywood jobs you see on the pier. As I get up to leave after a grey and greasy chicken tagine the band are passing the hat round, bowing and smiling at the tourists and repeating over and over again the same Berber word: 'Thank you,' perhaps, or possibly 'Wanker.'

I spend the afternoon reading and dozing in the hotel garden, where the orange trees are jiggling in a gentle breeze. It's like a perfect English summer's day, warm enough to have any self-respecting Brit stripped to the waist drinking a can of Stella in the lottery queue; but officially it is still winter. Mediterranean etiquette demands that the pool remains closed, and that the Moroccans, Spanish and French who are my fellow guests remain fully kitted out in winter woollies and cashmere coats.

In the hotel bookcase I found a copy of *Tangier: City of the Dream* by Iain Finlayson. It documents the recent history of the city, and bristles with scandalous tales of Burroughs, Paul Bowles and the artistic demi-monde. I'm fascinated by his account of Mohammed Mrabet, a storyteller who dictated his tales onto Bowles's tape recorder and won a reputation as a major figure in modern Arab literature. He was also a wild and crazy guy, a Moroccan Marlon Brando lookalike who became sexually involved with a variety of Western women, men and couples. I'm intrigued by the sound of his book, *Love With a Few Hairs*, published in London in 1967, a tale, according to Finlayson, of 'a European being taken for a ride by a young Moroccan man who skilfully plays him for personal advantage'. It sounds like it might shed some light on my situation with my own Mohammed, and I decide to find a copy, even though I haven't seen a bookshop yet.

By evening I need a walk but I'm worried that Mohammed will nab me again as soon as I leave the hotel. I edge out into the street and scan the likely doorways and alcoves, but there's no sign of him. He's brilliant. As soon as you think you know how he operates, he changes the pattern to keep you guessing. Wait a minute – is that him over there?

No.

It's just after dark when I find myself a seat on the outside terrace of a run-down café just outside the medina, where three tiny pedestrian streets packed with shops and market stalls converge. There's a cassette stall with loud Islamic music distorting from speakers that aren't big enough to cope. Closest to me is an increasingly desperate-looking man who keeps arranging and rearranging stonewashed jeans and denim handbags on a blanket on the ground. He hasn't made a sale in the hour I've been here. I've been watching life come and go and reflecting on the beautiful energetic confusion of it all, thinking how redistribution of the West's wealth is probably a jolly good thing, when a guy comes and sits too close to me. It's clear that he's going to try and strike up a conversation and scam me in some way, so I'm ready for him.

'Hello, my friend.'

'Hello.'

'You know me?'

'I don't think so.'

'I see you earlier, in hotel? Remember? I change my clothes now.'

It seems unlikely. I can't think of a hotel in the world that would let him through the door, let alone offer him a job. He looks like a particularly unscrupulous pirate, or the kind of assassin you'd be forced to hire if you were on a very limited budget, yet even as I'm thinking this I'm chiding myself for making such a glib and superficial judgement. Why think the worst of the guy? All right, so he's another poor Moroccan, but

that doesn't give me the right to condemn him. Yes, it's unlikely
he works at my hotel, but what's so special about a fancy hotel?
Who the hell do I think I am anyway?

'My name is Mustafa.'

He offers me his hand and I shake it.

'What is your name?'

In an instant I consider a plethora of misleading pseudonyms,
noms de plume and aliases to throw him off the scent. I know I
mustn't give anything away. After all, I've already told Mohammed
my name and it would be foolish to repeat the mistake.

'Peter.'

It doesn't matter, though, because he's so stoned he forgets it
immediately. Do I have a guide? Did he take me to the casbah?
He's not a very good guide then, says Mustafa, because tomorrow
is Friday, Muslim holy day. Casbah will be closed. I tell him I
know. Ah, yes, he says, but also closed Saturday, Sunday and
Monday. For festival.

'What festival?'

'We kill sheep. So maybe you visit casbah now, see snake-
charmers, acrobats, fire.'

He pauses, then goes for it.

'And camels.'

'Camels?'

'Yes, William. Camels. Come. I show you.'

I know he isn't government approved, and probably doesn't
subscribe to any professional code of conduct in the way that
estate agents and contract killers do; but I think I'd feel a bit of
a Charlie if the casbah stayed closed for the duration of whatever
this festival is and I had to go home and tell people I hadn't even
seen the wretched place, but I'd managed a pizza and a few beers
in the hotel bar instead. It's not very adventurous, is it? I know
he's probably a bit dodgy, but the dope seems to have made him
quite mellow, and I'm actually starting to feel like I know my
way around. After all, what can happen really?

Actually, on second thoughts, a lot might happen. Don't bother. It isn't worth the risk. Just say no.

'Okay.'

This is crazy. I've already got Mohammed. At this rate I'm going to end up with more guides than Lonely Planet. Whatever happens now I have to give this guy some money as well. I'm beginning to realise that I'm not very good at this.

We stand to leave, and Mustafa insists on several clenched-fist handshakes.

'What is your name?'

'Still Peter.'

'Peter. You. Me. We are like brother.'

We head off into the medina, heading up the hill to the casbah, the fortress within a fortress, maze within a maze, where once no outsider was permitted to tread. Soon we're climbing steps and the buzz of the night-time market is falling away behind us. I'm aware of our footsteps, and the sound of my heart racing.

'Here are Jewish houses. Later I show you film-star house. What is your name? Ah, where you from? I know English people. Not rich like American film star. Jean-Claude Van Damme, he make movie in this house. You are afraid? Do not be afraid. No one hurt you here, William. You are with me. Like brother. See there? They sell knives. To kill sheep. For festival.'

We're inside the casbah walls now – 'bottom half Phoenician, top Portuguese' – and in a maze of medieval alleyways, all sense of direction long since lost. He's pointing out a selection of interesting doors.

'Here German. Swiss here. This lady has art gallery. Where you from? Ah, here English film star. Tony Williams. You know him? Here other Englishman. We call him Eric. Skinhead.'

We seem to be getting nearer the centre, where the acrobats and camels and snake-charmers must be. Here's the women's mosque, full of children singing and chanting verses from the

Koran. Round the corner and – no, it's dark again, and I'm very uneasy now. If I reach out I can touch the walls on either side. But now there are some small children in a doorway playing, and a woman in traditional dress with a baby, a biblical image that's immediately superseded by a businessman with an expensive blouson and briefcase making his way home. The alley opens out and we stop briefly to admire the great mosque, or at least as much of it as you can see in the dark, before moving on and stopping outside a house with gates. Mustafa looks proud. This is clearly a highlight of the tour.

'Here Barbara Hutton house. Come.'

He shakes and rattles the gate till it opens. I take a couple of paces back.

'Come. Now!'

He makes me walk ahead of him up the path, a sensible precaution on his part in case there's a Doberman that's been trained to leap from a first-floor window and rip out a man's throat before he hits the ground.

'Swiss man live here now. When he here carpet' – he gestures – 'all way to gate. Come. You like to see port?'

He climbs over a wall onto the cliff edge and points to the lights of the ferry port far below us. He wants me to follow him to the brink of the abyss, but years of living near one of the world's top suicide spots have sullied the charms of sea-pounded cliffs, and I decline with as much manly nonchalance as I can muster. A few feet away I see the orange glow of a cigarette, and realise a man is sitting on the wall watching me. An undercover member of the tourist police looking after my interests, perhaps; or maybe an international trafficker in human organs who is running low on stock.

We emerge into what seems to be a central square, though there's no sign of any festival. An elderly couple in traditional dress are sitting outside their house, which I find strangely comforting, but then we plunge into the dark maze again and Mustafa starts reassuring me about money. He says he knows I am not an American film star and it won't cost too much. There are some heavy-looking guys kicking a football around in a courtyard. We walk through. Someone says something and everyone laughs. If anything goes wrong now I wouldn't have a clue how to get out of here. I knew this was stupid. Why did I do it? And *where are the bloody camels and snake-charmers then*? Now he's saying we must go into a quiet place – how much quieter can it get? – somewhere private where I can pay him for the tour, not here in public where the chancers and low-lifes and bad guys might see us. He slinks into the most sinister and threatening alleyway I've ever seen in my life and I realise I have to make a stand. No, I say, let's go back so that I know where I am.

He pauses. This could go either way.

'Okay. We go back now, William.'

'Not William. Peter.'

'Yes, Peter. How many sons you have?'

He's got three, all under the age of two, he says, and all very hungry. We're returning to the comfort of crowded streets.

'This coffee bar. Rolling Stones make film here one time. You afraid?'

Well, I can't deny I'm sweating, though whether from fear or walking too fast up too many hills or wearing too many clothes, I really couldn't say. We approach two women standing chatting at a pump. They go silent as we pass.

'Free water. Good drink. You like to wash maybe?'

There's water cascading down the steps as we descend. I'm reminded of something I read today about how in heavy rain the casbah steps get very slippy. Apparently a woman fell on her arse and got washed away down the hill in a storm. Popped out dead in Tangier Bay a day or two later. *There aren't going to be any camels, are there*? How would you get the bloody things up here anyway? It'd be a nightmare. He's still giving a running spiel – this door knob, these doors, that roof, those tiles – as we enter one more dark place and I'm sure he's going to confront me, or his accomplice will be there with gleaming teeth and a sheep-killing knife. And then we pop out into the street with steps we'd been up earlier, and probably for the only time in my life I'm relieved to find myself outside Jean-Claude Van Damme's house. We're only a couple of hundred yards from Grand Socco, so I don't feel uneasy about stepping into a doorway with him. From what I've seen so far, twenty dirhams seems to be the going rate. I'll give him thirty.

'You insult me.'

We've been less than an hour and this is more than an official guide would earn. But Mustafa is sneering now.

'I am better than official guide. Official guides all from south. I am from Tangier Bay.'

A local guide for local people. The evening is beginning to take on an unpleasantly Royston Vaseyesque quality. It could get nasty. Hang on, I've got some change. Another eight. Thirty-eight altogether.

This only makes it worse.

'Four hundred Americans pay me.'

Silly sods, spoiling it for everybody else.

'But I do not expect that. Two hundred only.'

I haven't even got that much on me. I've got a hundred note and the thirty-eight I've already offered him. So I produce the hundred and take back the thirty-eight. Naturally he refuses, and he's angry now because he knows I've got the other thirty-eight and he wants the lot. There's a guy in a hood by a stall on the street and he's heard us arguing. He turns round and says something to Mustafa in Arabic. Could be, 'Leave him alone.' Could be, 'Make the bastard pay.' I've no idea. I'm sweating hard now, wondering what he'll do next, clutching at the straw that if he really does work in the hotel then I'll be able to find him and have him taken away to that horrible prison for bread and water in the nude. Look, I tell him, take the hundred, but thirty-eight is all I've got left and I need that for tea and a sandwich. And a massive brandy, though I don't mention that.

'Sandwich is only seven. You think you need thirty-eight for sandwich? I must feed three babies!'

And all the years of liberal guilt about African famine, and images of child labour and civil war and refugees and Lenny Henry and Griff Rhys-Jones on *Comic Relief* digging wells and ploughing fields with oxen come flooding in, even though he's turned mean and this is not a pleasant situation, and I give him the lot.

He refuses.

'No. You must give with love in your heart.'

He's just rubbing it in now.

'I am. I am. With love. With love! Look!'

He smiles. And we do the clenched fist handshake thing again.

'With love. Like brother. Goodbye, William.'

He disappears with the cash and I notice the brass plate. We've been conducting our negotiations in the doorway of a firm of lawyers.

Back at the hotel I change out of my fear-soaked clothes, shower, then reach for the caramel-flavoured comfort of the Soberano. I turn on CNN and discover that the skiing championships in Salt Lake City have been abandoned because of heavy snow. Over on BBC Bland International there are pictures, but for some reason no sound. I'm tempted to say that this is an improvement, but in fact it's worse. Only marginally, though.

I go to bed, but lie there in the dark unable to sleep. I'd been hoping the brandy might calm me down but I'm still feeling alert, albeit a little rattled and frayed around the edges. Why aren't I sleepy then? Maybe it's low-alcohol brandy. That'd be a dirty trick. I must check the label in the morning.

As I drift into restless half-sleep I keep thinking how stupid I've been this evening and asking myself the same question.

Where was bloody Mohammed when I needed him?

*

Next morning I'm feeling a bit lonely and blue so I go down to the front desk and ask if there have been any messages for me, which there haven't. This isn't surprising, as I haven't told anybody I'm staying here. I feel even worse now.

I decide to make a final concerted attempt to find the Mac-Carthys. If it fails I will give up and go home. The mobile is still unobtainable and the pension doesn't exist, so I phone the only other contact number I have, the café in Belfast. Mark the Pagan says that Terence is a friend of the King of Morocco, so perhaps I should contact the palace and ask him. This doesn't strike me as a promising line of enquiry, so I head to a travel agent's to check the availability of flights home.

As I'm waiting to speak to someone it strikes me that this office – the fan, the blinds, and the two heavy men with moustaches sitting behind the desk in perspiration-marked shirts – is another scene from the North African B-feature film noir in which I've fetched up. I ought to strike a match on my thumbnail and light an untipped cigarette to show them I mean business, but I'm not even wearing a hat. Mind you, I have just had an idea.

'I'm trying to contact a friend of mine who flies from Tangier to Ireland quite often. His name is MacCarthy.'

'Macarthur?'

'MacCarthy. His passport says he is an Irish prince.'

'Prince? Prince Macarthur?'

'No. MacCarthy. Prince of Desmond.'

'Desmond? Ah, Desmond!'

There's a burst of animated conversation, a flick through an address book, a spool through a computer screen passenger list and then he dials a number.

'Desmond? One moment please.'

As I take the phone I notice the blind is playing horizontal lines of sunlight and shadow across my face and body. Very *Maltese Falcon*. This is perfect.

'Hello? Is this Terence MacCarthy?'

'*Bitte?*'

'Terence. Prince of Desmond. The MacCarthy Mór?'

'Desmond? I am sorry? Desmond has returned in Germany. He is in Köln. Who is speaking please?'

They've given me the number of a German antique dealer called Desmond and I'm speaking to his boyfriend. I make my apologies and decide to leave this film before the end. As I thank the men and turn to leave one of them is looking at his computer screen. It's a confidential passenger list, which he is not allowed to disclose to me.

'Look here. Two MacCarthys. C and T. In twelve days they return to Belfast. And here, a phone number in Tangier.'

Conor and Tommy are already in the hotel lobby when I arrive, smoking at least one cigarette each. When I met them that night in Belfast it seemed I was the only person in the city not chain-smoking, apart from the drunken Huddersfield lass cartwheeling along the white line, and I expect her friends had one on the go for her when she'd finished. At half past seven the following morning at Belfast airport a poorly-looking man who smelled of closing time asked the girl at the till for 'twenty of your cheapest please, love'. Entering the fug of smoke that engulfed the danger-ously crowded Beer & Fried Breakfast Zone was like walking back into a long-vanished decade when signs said 'Spitting Pro-hibited', and cigarettes were widely believed to be good for the throat. Unseen coughers hacked and gruffed somewhere deep in the fetid smog, reinforcing the impression that Belfast might be a bit of a smokers' town. I didn't have time to check, but it's possible that little knots of non-smokers were huddled pariah-like in doorways outside the terminal building, indulging their shameful habit.

'Aye, well, maybe that's what thirty years of killing does to a town,' says Tommy as we leave the hotel, crushing my glib observations like a tab end on a grease-encrusted breakfast plate, before lighting up a couple more.

It's Tommy's first time in Morocco and he can't have enough of it.

'I love the chaos. It's like Ireland, only with more colours.'

Lots of people in Belfast had warned him not to come to Tangier, mind. 'They said it's meant to be a very dangerous place.' He laughs, effortlessly blowing smoke out of his nose as he speaks. ' "You don't want to be going out on the streets there at night, Tom," they said, "not with some of those fellas around. Can't get a drink so they're all on the whacky backy. Cut your throat soon as look at you." ' He laughs again, and smoke comes out of his ears and through the top of his head.

We're on our way to the pension that doesn't exist. Even against the riotous backdrop of Tangier's streets they're a stand-out couple of guys, and it's a miracle I haven't bumped into them sooner. Squat and mischievous in one of the few Donegal tweed jackets in Morocco, Tommy has the air of a rough and ready Belfast lad who hasn't wasted his money on health clubs and grooming products. Conor, angular and serious-looking in his de Valera specs, is dressed in the defiant long black raincoat of a Nick Cave fan on holiday in a sunny place. They're good company, and completely unfazed by the several days of non-communication which has almost sent me home early.

'Ah, we knew we'd bump into each other one way or another,' says Conor disarmingly. 'If you hadn't found us we'd probably have come to the hotel at the weekend. We thought you'd probably be staying there.'

As we turn into Rue des Postes, the same man is cleaning the same car as last time I was here. He smiles and waves and generally greets the MacCarthy brothers like long-lost relatives as we turn into the gateway of number twelve, the house where the Moroccan lady gave me the bum's rush on my previous visit. I tell them what happened, expecting them to be outraged.

'Ah, yes, that would be the Fatima,' explains Conor.

'She's been trained to deny everything,' adds Tommy helpfully.

'It's a very delicate situation,' concludes Conor.

I've no idea what they're on about.

After symbolically acknowledging that it's still technically the morning by drinking a foul cup of instant coffee – imported direct from Northern Ireland to improve the quality of Moroccan life – there's unanimous agreement that it's now morally acceptable to move on to the duty-free Bushmills, particularly if we drink it out of the same mugs. And, after all, haven't we just managed to meet up with each other? And there does seem to be a bit of a chill in the air today. And anyway, isn't a lunchtime aperitif a very civilised way to carry on? Well, not really, not if you don't actually have any lunch, but it seems churlish to point out the lack of solids to underpin the alcohol as we stride confidently out into the afternoon sunshine, where the man is still washing his car. He must be some kind of secret policeman or government spy. Before he comes to do the car each day he probably sits in a café reading an upside-down newspaper – *though of course you wouldn't know it was upside down if you didn't read Arabic!* The crafty bastard. If I'd had just one more mug of whiskey I'd probably be feeling reckless enough to denounce him publicly and blow his cover. Luckily I'm simultaneously both sober and intoxicated enough to realise that nonsense masquerading as piercing insight is one of the side effects of drinking whiskey in daylight on an empty stomach. It's only a short step from here to the two-hour memory lapses, grazed knuckles and inexplicable cuts on the forehead, and that isn't a road we want to go down, which is why we've stopped drinking and come out to do a bit of sightseeing instead. We manage a quick and uneventful mooch around a market that sells flowers and meat, then adjourn to a bar for a drink.

Unlike my mint tea binges of the past week, which have been in warm, colourful, public, Islamic places, the bar is dark, chilled and completely empty except for the three of us. There's as much indication that this is Morocco as there is in the bar of the Sheffield Travelodge. The waiter brings enough complimentary bowls of nuts, cheese, olives and pizza to stock a Harvester All-You-Can-Eat-Buffet and the world starts to feel a more grounded place. Conversation, though, is completely away with the fairies. Tommy and Conor are gifted improvisers with an instinctive ability to finish each other's sentences. One of them takes an idea from the other, runs and riffs with it in oblique and unexpected directions until it is unrecognisable, only for the originator to seize the concept anew and carry it into deep and hitherto un-explored areas. It's ensemble playing, like jazz, but I'm not in the band yet. I've always been considered a bit of a lippy bastard in England, so it's enjoyable to spend time in the company of the kind of people who make me look like the strong silent type.

But through all the conversational loops, we keep returning to the concept of Irish monarchy and of the MacCarthy Mór, the title claimed by Conor since his brother's abdication. He says he'll debate his family's claim to the title with anybody, while at the same time protesting that he is a reluctant claimant to the post. All the time there is the unspoken and increasingly mys-terious fact of his elder brother Terence's exile in Tangier. I've come here specifically to meet him, yet so far the possibility of our getting together hasn't been mentioned. Luckily I have a plan that has always worked before, which is: do nothing, and see what happens.

What happens is we go to a Chinese restaurant on top of a newly built concrete block of shops. The brothers don't want to eat – just the drinking and the smoking will be fine – but they're aware of my obsession with Singapore noodles and feel it's impor-tant some should be made available. And sure enough, there they are on the menu: *Nouilles mélange fruits de mer façon Singapore*. When they arrive they turn out to be fat spaghetti tossed with mixed marinated pickled seafood. Number seventeen, the shredded roast duck is, if anything, even more peculiar. It comes in a thick gravy of what tastes like Marmite, lard and chocolate, topped with a green glacé cherry. I know that Chinese restaurateurs like to adapt their cuisine to local tastes and ingredients, but occasionally I get the feeling that something far more disturbing is going on.

We leave, taking the second bottle of Moroccan red with us, and return to the roof of the pension that doesn't exist, where the boys entertain me with unprintable Belfast gossip about which local politician beats his wife, which is seriously ill, who is really the head of the IRA and which assassinations were carried out by the SAS. The view over the old town and the sea must be virtually the same as the one enjoyed by Matisse when he painted *View of Tangier Bay* from a hotel room not far from here. Unfortunately it's dark, so you can't see anything except the arches of the illuminated golden M. I'm wondering whether there's any chance that it might not be what I think it is and might stand for, say, mosque, when Tommy catches my eye and leans across, grinning emphatically as he lights a cigarette with the end of another.

'You know, Peter, people in Northern Ireland really don't like the English.'

I'm immediately on edge. It's not clear whether for the purpose of this conversation I'm English or Irish. I've had so much to drink I'm not really sure myself. As we're four floors up I decide to proceed with caution. I take advantage of the rare pause to ask a question.

'But what about the Loyalists? All the people in the North who regard themselves as British?'

'Are you kidding? They hate the feckin' English most of all. Particularly the posh ones from the south. Can't stand the smug bastards.'

Have I told him I live in the South? I can't remember. It's been a long day. Back on the mint tea tomorrow, that's for sure.

'You don't seem English but.'

There's another pause. I don't know whether it's a good one or a bad one.

'I don't usually feel at ease with English people. There is one thing that worries me, mind.'

I think he's smiling in the dark, but I can't be sure.

'What's that?'

'This tremendous interest you have in food. It's very un-Irish, you know.'

I walk back to the hotel past countless stray cats and find myself thinking of life's imperfections. In an ideal world, it would have been the beer first, then the red wine, and then the whiskey. I suppose we can only try our best.

Café Portes is a split-level confection of swirling ceilings, marble floors and wrought-iron banisters and balustrades, an elegant Moorish art deco extravagance straight out of *Casablanca*. Since its heyday it's gone teetotal and the cocktail bar, though not re-moved, has been emphatically bricked up. The original Madame Porte was a fascist sympathiser and the place was once a hotbed of Italian and German spies, though you can't help thinking they mustn't have been very good spies if everyone knew where to find them. 'The Pimpernel? He is eating cake in Café Portes with the Silver Eagle.'

Petit déjeuner complet is very good and costs next to nothing. I'm halfway through a wafer-thin grilled cheese sandwich filled with deliciously un-Gibraltarian melted cheese, when a cloak-and-dagger voice hisses in my ear in a peculiar mockney accent.

'*Tellygraph*, sir? *Dily Tellygraph*? Aww this moanin's Inglish pipers!'

I turn and find a wizened Moroccan newspaper vendor bran-dishing the full range of English titles. RAILTRACK, say the head-lines, reminding me what I'm missing at home. PARKER BOWLES. BIG BROTHER. FOOT AND MOUTH.

'Piper, sir? 'Ow are you t'day, sir? Lavely moanin'.'

I can only imagine that he must be a survivor of the post-war anything-goes years, when the street traders of Tangier were renowned for their ability to mimic the many different accents they heard. I haven't said a word though, so how did he know which accent to pick?

'Go on, sir. *Tellygraph*. 'Ave a quick shufty if you like.'

Cor luv-a-duck, 'ees gawn over the top now. At the moment, life is strange enough without the added complication of a *Daily Telegraph* leader. I decline with all the dignity I can muster: 'No fanks, me old cock sparrar,' pay my bill and leave.

I'm walking back towards the hotel along Boulevard Pasteur when another ageing spiv marks me out from the mid-morning crowds and falls in step alongside me. 'No money, no honey,' he incants, in a strange monotone that sounds not unlike Blur. 'No money, no honey.' Why is he doing this? Is he trying to tell me he has neither money nor honey, but would like some of each? 'No money, no honey.' Or is he letting me know that I won't be getting any honey unless I can guarantee cash up-front? 'No money, no honey.' Perhaps it's Moroccan rhyming slang. 'No money, no honey, no money no honey – Gawd bless you, sah!' And with that he turns away and crosses the road, for all I know on his way to the British Consulate to audition for the new Guy Ritchie movie.

At the top of the street I bump into Tommy and Conor, who have selected the outside tables of the Café de France as their early morning smoking venue.

I join the brothers for coffee, and we are immediately besieged by the entire black economy of Tangier. Three times in as many minutes Conor is propositioned by shoeshine boys who don't give Tommy and me a second glance, and three times he declines. A boy with withered arms asks for money and we give him some, then a woman tries to sell us a tray of things, but we don't know what they are. She says they're very good, mind. And then there's a loud noise in my right ear. 'Miaoowh!'

I turn and see a lady in traditional dress, smiling sweetly at me. She leans forward.

'Miaoowh! Meee-owwh!'

'Ah,' says Conor, assessing the situation in an instant. 'It's the lady who miaows.'

'How are you today?' enquires Tommy. She seems fine. She's washing her paws now.

The queue of street people waiting to perform for us is taking on the proportions of a medium-sized carnival, so we leave and walk down into the medina. We've passed through the crowds and are heading down a deserted alley when someone hisses from a doorway.

'Hash!'

This time there's no reassuringly comic Britpop accent. A tough-looking young man has stepped out in front of us, brandishing a huge lump of cannabis on the palm of his hand.

'Hash? You like? You like? Speak English? American?'

Or perhaps he's selling henna. Or Oxo.

'Tá faitíos orm nach geaitheann muid tobac,' says Conor.

'Tá sé go dona don tsláinte,' adds Tommy.

The man narrows his eyes, then disappears back into the shadows.

'Whenever things get heavy, we just speak Irish,' says Conor.

'Confuses the fuck out of them,' explains Tommy.

At the top of the alleyway, on a hill looking out across the harbour to Spain, is the Hotel Continentale. It's a masterpiece of decaying fin-de-siècle opulence that was probably never that opulent in the first place. The lobby is a riot of stained glass, ancient tiles, and cushions to lie down on while you wait for something to happen. The check-in desk is straight out of all those movies where someone's trying to find a cheap room to hide from the bad guys, but you know they'll find him because as soon as he's gone upstairs the clerk will phone a sinister man in a cheap suit and dob him in. A numbered board behind the desk hangs heavy with the kind of big metal key-shaped keys you used to get before they invented those useless plastic cards you stick in the lock but the red light keeps coming on, so you have to go back downstairs and ask some grumpy youth for help.

I've always been a sucker for clapped-out colonial hotels. The Bella Vista in Macau, Raffles in Singapore and the Eastern & Oriental in Penang were all impossibly seductive in the days when it cost next to nothing to stay and everything was either broken, peeling, or scuttling across your bedroom floor. They've all been refurbished now. One day it will probably happen here, and a mini-bar corporation and CNN provider will move into the Continentale and lay on conference facilities, complimentary sewing kits and those paper seals across the toilet that have finally taken the bottom-related paranoia out of international travel.

Just off the lobby is a large bazaar selling carpets and lamps and antiques.

'Come and meet Jimmy,' says Conor. We're immediately and vigorously embraced by a thickset Moroccan in his fifties. 'Ah, my boys!' He beams. 'My Irish boys!' He turns towards a young couple who are browsing on the other side of the shop and shouts. 'Where you from?'

'Canada,' says the man.

'Pogue Mahone!' shouts Moroccan Jimmy.

'I'm sorry?' says the Canadian.

'It means "Kiss my arse" in Irish,' says Jimmy.

'Interesting,' says the Canadian.

Jimmy listens to me speak for a few seconds, then says, 'Where you from? Yorkshire?'

'No,' I say, 'but good try. Lancashire.'

'Eccleston?' asks Jimmy.

This is unnervingly accurate. Eccleston is the small suburb of St Helens where the Brothers beat me relentlessly for seven years, with occasional pauses for lessons and exams. To this day, if I see a man in a long black gown with a white collar, I instinctively bend over and lift my blazer up. Luckily there's no one who fits that description in the shop.

I tell Jimmy he's very good at accents.

'I have very good man in Eccleston. East Lancs Road. Export-import. Tom Digby. You know him?'

Strangely enough there was a Tom Digby a couple of years above me at school. Top mod. Fourteen-inch centre vent and a silver Lambretta with aerials and fur. He used to go and see Georgie Fame at the all-nighters at the Twisted Wheel in Manchester, and I used to go to the youth club on a pushbike and have to be home by half-past nine. I'd like to think he's a dealer in Moroccan antiques now. It must have been an ideal career option for someone with a taste for expensive mohair suits.

Jimmy embraces us several more times and promises me big discount when I return, and we head down through the medina towards the beach. The breeze has dropped and it's sunny and warm. At five minutes to one we hear the call to prayer, not broadcast on loudspeakers as in some Islamic countries, but unamplified and strangely atmospheric. Conor says that the King has banned the use of speakers. 'When the fundamentalists objected he pointed out that they were a Western invention unknown to the Prophet. That foxed them.'

As we turn a corner our way is blocked by a small crowd gathered in a tiny square. They are watching two guys in suits pushing and slapping a frightened and impoverished-looking youth in a cheap leather blouson. No one is attempting to intervene and I'm wondering what to do when a film camera bursts through the doors of a café, gliding along a gleaming set of tracks I'd somehow failed to notice. Clustered around it are a dozen or so extremely good-looking people of all ages and sexes, olive-skinned and wearing exquisite clothes that are casual, stylish and expensive. The cameraman has the luxuriantly flowing black curly hair, the charisma and the trousers of a classical god who has landed among mortals. It is an Italian film crew, I realise, as my almost threadbare, not recently ironed Australian pub T-shirt clings to my clammy back in shame.

Why do Italians pursue us around the globe like this with their impeccable dress sense? Until now, Tommy, Conor and I have been coping quite well, doing our best to blend into the surroundings, and not looking too shabby considering where we're from. But now the bloody Italians are here, making us look like three ageing potatoes in need of a good scrub and peel; a fact that hasn't been lost on one of the local shoeshine boys, who once again singles out Conor and offers to buff his boots until he can see the Italians' ear studs reflected in them. For the fourth time this morning Conor says no, but he's clearly rattled by the overwhelming Moroccan consensus on the state of his footwear.

We're about to remove ourselves from the Italians' sphere of influence when I look up and see Mohammed standing in a doorway, smiling knowingly in my direction. I realise that for the first time since I've been here I haven't been worried about bumping into him, and now I've bumped into him. His timing is impeccable. It seems possible that he is shadowing me twenty-four hours a day, waiting for the moment of maximum impact. As I pour the Soberano and switch on CNN at one o'clock in the morning, he may be lying face down on top of the wardrobe, taking notes and waiting till the time is right.

'So, Peter. You find your friends?'

He gives Tommy and Conor a lingering look as if to say, 'I know your game.'

'You stay in Rue des Postes? Is there one small hotel there?'

'Tá muid ag obair do Rúnseirbhís na hÉireann,' says Tommy.

'Tá plean ag Éirinn Maracó a thógáil,' agrees Conor.

'Where you go now?' asks Mohammed.

'An bhfuil a fhios ag do mháthair go bhfuil tú amuigh?' says Tommy.

I'm feeling guilty about trying to avoid him, even though any escape can only be temporary.

And then he says, 'Peter. I watch you. You like writing. So maybe you like to meet famous Moroccan writer. Friend of Paul Bowles. Makes translations with him. Storyteller. He is my friend also. Many years.'

While the MacCarthy brothers smoke heavily in Irish by my side, Mohammed tells me he has been watching me sitting at cafés, writing in books or sometimes reading them. He probably also knows my PIN number, my postcode and my mother's birthday, but he's holding them back for another occasion.

'So, you like to meet famous Moroccan writer? Good man. Old man now, with nice house not far from here. His wife make pilgrimage to Mecca. His name is Mohammed Mrabet.'

I'm shocked rigid. This is impossible! I've never taken the book I've been reading about Bowles and Mrabet out of the hotel. So how does he know? Why is he making up such an outlandish story? What is he setting me up for? Where does he really want to take me?

'We can go tomorrow? I tell him you come. Make a time. What time you like?'

Mrabet was a big name here in the 1950s. Surely he must be dead by now? And even if he's not, he wouldn't be hanging out with low-life like Mohammed. This is madness. I mustn't go off anywhere with this man. I could end up chained to a radiator, or worse.

'Two o'clock tomorrow? Outside your hotel?'

I feel tired and powerless to resist.

'Okay. Two o'clock.'

He smiles and is gone.

'You should be careful there,' wheezes Tommy, finishing the packet. 'They could be after your kidneys.'

The beachfront has a dilapidated feel, run-down but not without charm. It hasn't had the global brand makeover yet, but I suppose that's only a matter of time. Games of football are in progress on the wide, sandy spaces. New apartments, built with hashish-generated dirhams that can't be exported, stand half-finished among the builders' rubble. Near the far end of the beach is the Windmill, a drinking den and pick-up joint once frequented by Joe Orton, Kenneth Williams, and other assorted expats who, by Orton's own account, could have perved for England in the Perving Olympics, and won gold. It looks desolate and closed up, whether for winter or for ever it's hard to tell. There's nothing to mark it out as a literary shrine, no memorial of any kind. A blue plaque would be nice, with Orton's name and dates, and perhaps a silhouetted depiction of men engaged in acts of gross indecency. If I can find the British Embassy I'll pop a note through and suggest it.

We pass an Indian restaurant where the first item on the menu is chicken lollipop, which I'm sure would have amused Joe, and then install ourselves in one of the few beach cafés that seems to open all the year round. We're the only customers on a covered blue veranda looking out on some kids playing beach volleyball. Our three beers are served with a plate of grilled sardines, some boquerones, a dish of paella and some octopus and rice salad. The next round comes with meat and potato stew, and a tomato, green bean and coriander salad. The third beer is accompanied by stewed fish and vegetables and spiced chicken wings. We finish with just the one for the road, plus two whole grilled plaice and a platter of shell-on prawns fried in garlic. Pogged, tipsy and ready for a siesta, we ask for the bill. The twelve beers come to £12. Lunch, on the other hand, is free. The owner explains that the banquet was just a complimentary bar snack; like a free whelk in a Southend pub on a Sunday lunchtime, I suppose, only better. He says he does this every day. So there you are. Provided you're prepared to drink yourself to a standstill twice a day, you could dine extremely well in Tangier for absolutely nothing. It must be the best value in the Mediterranean.

Tommy has called their regular taxi driver on the mobile. After quarter of an hour he still hasn't come, and I think I know what's happened. For seven years I travelled the world making programmes with a charming and hilarious Ulsterman blessed with a strong County Down accent that made no concession to people who had learned standard English from Linguaphone or the BBC World Service. From Moscow to Vanuatu, from China to Marrakech, I watched as he told anecdotes, explained camera shots and paid compliments to people who couldn't understand anything he was saying. Then, when he'd finished, one of us would translate. Clearly the same thing is going on here.

Another five minutes pass, and I try and imply as tactfully as possible that the combination of crackly mobile phone and difficult accent may mean that the driver has not fully understood. Tommy phones him again, which compounds the confusion. Conor takes over and establishes that the guy must have understood at least a few words, because he is waiting for us at our intended destination.

Ten minutes later he turns up and we get in. Taking care to speak slowly and distinctly, Tommy tells him to take us back to the place he has just driven from. The driver takes us somewhere else. It seems easiest just to get out. We're saying our goodbyes and trying to work out where we are when the phone that doesn't work starts ringing. It is Terence, the ex-MacCarthy Mór. The three of us are invited for cocktails tomorrow at five. Conor smiles.

'He says he saw you today, Peter.'

'Where?'

'Having breakfast in Café Portes.'

Bloody hell.

'Why didn't he come and say hello?'

'He didn't feel it was socially correct to come and introduce himself there. He says it's a pity you didn't buy a paper. That guy's prices are the cheapest in town.'

This city is starting to spook me. I feel like I'm under constant

surveillance. Mind you, Mohammed was probably hiding somewhere in Portes, watching Terence watching me.

I wonder who's watching Mohammed?

Don't you hate those siestas where you wake up at half past nine
in the evening and there's nothing really much to do, except have
a little drink and then go back to sleep again? With such deranged
sleep patterns, it's amazing the Mediterranean nations are as sane
as they are. I get up and turn on the TV. BBC Bland International
still has pictures but no sound. It's been like this for days now.
There must be so few people watching that nobody's phoned up
to tell them about the fault. Or perhaps they've decided to cut
the budget and invest the money in a gardening makeover website
instead. Over on Eurosport there's a football match with ambient
crowd sound – cheering, whistling, catcalling, firecrackers –
but no commentary. I try and watch, but it's an odd experience.
The game loses all context, and you have to draw on your own
inner resources to give it significance. I discover that I haven't
got any.

It gets even stranger when the football is over. I'm still trying
to come to terms with the fact that someone I don't know has
beaten someone else I don't know, or possibly there's been a
draw, in a country I can't identify, when the tennis comes on.
This, too, is commentary-free. All you can hear is the whack of
the ball and the grunts of the players, whoever the hell they are.
I really haven't a clue. It's just two blokes on a red court on a
green background in a gym. Is it any good? I don't know. There's
no one to tell me. Click. CNN is looking at the stories behind the
US stock market. Click. A Spanish channel is showing Andalusian
agitprop theatre performed by men with funny stick-on noses.
Click.

Ah! They've got the sound back on BBC Bland. There must
have been another management reshuffle and a subsequent change
in policy while I've been channel-hopping. There's an excellent

story about a man from Georgia in the former USSR who is swimming two kilometres in freezing seawater with his hands and legs fastened tight with leather straps. 'It is a way of bringing pride to Georgia by demonstrating our ancient ways,' says the subtitles beneath a shot of a pervily-bound, hypothermic man. One day he hopes to swim the Dardanelles like this.

The next item is also from Georgia. They've obviously decided to get their money's worth out of the poor bastard they've sent there. This one's about a teenage boy who's just walked the thirty ks from his village to Tbilisi football stadium, bouncing a ball on his head.

'I wanted to make a statement of national self-belief,' says the youth, bouncing a ball on his head. It just goes to show what young people can achieve if they have the right motivation.

Over on Eurosport quiet tennis has been replaced by commentary-free cycling. I'm beginning to understand the appeal of being an international businessman. As well as all the free shower gel, you'd be able to watch stuff like this all the time.

I drift off to sleep and become embroiled in confused dreams of Mohammed Mrabet, the MacCarthy Mór. He is an eerie composite of two people I have never met, and speaks with an impenetrable accent. I try and dream a commentary by way of explanation, but none is available.

When I leave the hotel at two the next day, Mohammed is lurking in the street waiting for me. He looks particularly shifty today. Perhaps this is to be the big sting.

'So, Peter, we go to meet Mohammed Mrabet?'

I've been expecting a last-minute change of plan but it looks like he's going to persist with this literary fantasy until I call his bluff. As we're getting into a taxi, a Moroccan businessman in suit and tie clocks the situation – naïve half-wit tourist heading off to the boonies with ruthless cut-throat vagrant – and gestures to me. '*No!*' he mouths, shaking his head. '*Don't!*' As we drive off, he repeats the signal. He'll be a key witness when they do the reconstruction on *Crimewatch Morocco*.

Mohammed says something I don't understand to the driver, while I try and think happy thoughts and suppress the visions of kidnap and mutilation that are springing up uninvited from the depths. We head out of the centre of town, down streets I've never seen, where the traditional buildings give way to nondescript modern flats. Mohammed is grinning and reassuring me that everything is okay, but it isn't easy to relax. No one knows where I am, and Tommy reckons they're after my kidneys. It would be a pity to end up minus vital internal organs just hours before I'm meant to be meeting the MacCarthy ex-Mór.

I know I shouldn't be here, but the possibility of meeting the renegade storyteller is too unlikely to pass by. But does my Mohammed really know him? Is Mrabet even alive? Or is this the equivalent of me pouncing on some unsuspecting Japanese tourist in the Lake District and telling him I'm taking him to meet Beatrix Potter?

'Mohammed Mrabet has very nice house. Nice area,' says Mohammed, as we get out at a noisy traffic roundabout in a dusty concrete suburb. On the pavement nearby three men are busily creating antiques out of coffee tables that were made earlier in the day. We turn off the main drag and trudge up a potholed hill. Ahead of us a young man stands leaning against a wall, where the street forks. Is he a lookout? An accomplice? A policeman who will hold me down and hide the drugs up my arse before dragging me off to that prison where your friends have to bring in water if you want to have a wash? We walk past, he ignores us, and we stop outside a nondescript block of low-rise housing. Mohammed knocks on the door. I'm half hoping there'll be no reply. A shutter upstairs moves, but I'm too late to see who it was. 'You see him?' No, I didn't. Is this all part of the plan?

The door is opened by a poorly looking man with a winning smile. He's in his sixties and is smaller than I'd expected after reading those raucous accounts of him beating people up. That's if it's really him, of course. He gives a painful-sounding cough, and I notice that his sallow skin has a distinctly yellow tinge. Yellow.

That's a sign of iffy kidneys, isn't it?

I call him by his name and ask in French if it's okay to meet, and he says it is. He takes us upstairs to a space with no windows or natural light, a kind of room within a room where we sit on low cushions in a large alcove. The TV and Calor gas heater are both on. There's a low table spread with pens and coloured inks and other art materials and lots of biscuits, and an overpowering smell of hashish, as if dozens of art students have spent many years in here watching *Countdown*. He makes tea as the other Mohammed looks on, grinning as if to say, 'See, I told you we were friends.' There's an easy feeling between the two of them that makes it clear he's been telling the truth. We sit down on the cushions to talk. I'm trying to reconcile the lurid account I read this morning of Mrabet breaking up a homosexual orgy with a broken vodka glass, with the frail and gentle old man who's sitting before me.

He carefully fills a long, dark, wooden pipe with hashish, fires it up and tells me how he was put in prison when he was fourteen after finding a stolen safe and filling his trousers with money from it. He'd served seven months of a twelve-year sentence when they found the real robbers and released him. At any rate, I think that's the story. He delivers it first in Arabic, then again in French, then refills the pipe and starts telling me about Paul Bowles and the society of the free port in the years before Moroccan independence. He gets very excited.

'*Oui, internationale*, whoaaah! Woooh! *C'était* ... *une salade niçoise. Tu comprends? Très* ... *mixte.*' He says that Elia Kazan offered him a part in a movie but wanted him naked, frolicking with a girl. He wouldn't do it.

'Everyone see Mohammed Mrabet – like that? *Non, non, non!*

Tennessee Williams, he tells me I should do it. Plenty money. But money does not matter. For naked? *Non.*'

He explains that his stories come from an oral tradition, and mix his life and his dreams with older legends and spontaneous improvisation. He says he can neither read nor write. He asks if I am a writer, then tells me he needs a new *collaborateur – 'pour traduire'* – as he has more stories to tell the world. He reels off a list of a dozen or more countries in which he's published, but says that the royalties don't bring in much money. In a moment of shame, I realise that I'm waiting for him to try and hit on me for cash, but it doesn't happen. He's very dignified and by now, surely, extremely stoned. He shows me the intricate pen and ink Islamo-psychedelic pictures he's been working on, and it's clear I can buy one if I want. They're not really to my taste though, and I can't bring myself to get one as a literary souvenir, a little piece of him to take back. But my mind's buzzing at the thought of a possible collaboration with this near-legendary figure, the man who was the link between the ancient tradition of North African storytelling and the cranked-up world of the beats. He's probably been stuck indoors smoking himself to a standstill for years. He must meet hardly any outsiders. This could be a real opportunity! I could rediscover the renegade genius of Moroccan letters. It's an international event! Look – he's even giving me his home telephone number. I am his solitary connection with the outside world. I'll phone the publishers from the hotel.

I thank him for his time and I'm just getting up to leave when there is a knock at the door. He looks at his watch and pulls a face. 'French journalists.' What? He shrugs. 'I have to live.' He comes to the door to let us out and let the next lot in, but there's been a mix-up and it's not French journalists – it's a Spanish TV producer and his assistant instead. The French journalists are due in an hour. I feel my collaboration with the reclusive genius hurtling away into the rapidly receding distance.

Outside we flag a taxi and head back into town before Melvyn

Bragg can show up with a crew from the *South Bank Show*. Mohammed is clearly elated, and who can blame him? He has delivered. He worked out that I wasn't interested in sightseeing or entering into a partnership with a German restaurant owner. He reckoned I needed a literary encounter, so he's laid one on. As we get out of the taxi and I'm paying the driver, Mohammed goes for the hard sell.

'Give me three hundred dirham please, Peter. For blanket. Very cold at night where I live. No furniture. No blanket. These clothes I wear, Australian boy gave them to me. You have clothes you can give? Please, Peter, give me one shirt, one trouser.'

I give him the 300 but decide to hang on to my clothes for the time being. But he's still not happy and I'm not feeling proud. He senses this and becomes increasingly blunt.

'Peter, you rich. I am poor. You give me more money now. For nothing. Just give me. Five hundred. Please.'

I say I'll see him again before I leave. Well, obviously I will. I'll have no choice.

4

THE LAST GOOSE

It's just before five as the taxi pulls up outside a pink-walled villa glowing warm in the evening sunshine on a hillside on the outskirts of the city. I have it on good authority – well, Conor and Tommy told me – that two neighbouring houses are owned by the King and the princess. Of Morocco, not Munster.

A gate in the wall opens and Terence MacCarthy comes out to greet us. He's a large, rotund man in his forties, smiling and jolly, wearing a well-pressed V-neck woollie over a collar and tie, fixed with what looks like a diamond tie pin. To my practised eye, it's clear at a glance that this man is either a brilliant and wrongly deposed Irish clan chief, who has spent his life labouring tirelessly on behalf of his people; or else a deluded and cynical impostor, who has exploited the office of chief for his own aggrandisement. The problem is, I've no idea which.

Nor do I have any intention of subjecting him to a ferocious interrogation regarding his bona fides. I realised early in life that I'd make a hopeless magistrate or immigration official because if someone seems likeable, and most people do, then I believe everything they tell me. I am, however, keen to have a few drinks with him and see what turns up. If the Spanish Inquisition or Jo Stalin or Senator Joe McCarthy had abandoned their rigidly methodical approaches in favour of cocktails and a few nibbles, they might have achieved a lot more than they did.

Ireland has been transformed in recent years by a mania for building very new houses in very old places, so it seems appropriate that this self-styled deposed Irish prince should be living in a newly built villa on an ancient hillside in this prehistoric port. Inside, the house feels formally European with few concessions to local style. It is spotless and pristine, with not so much as a newspaper or teacup casually discarded, as if an estate agent is expected to turn up at any moment with a prospective purchaser. The walls are hung with Greek and Russian Orthodox icons. Incense burns. Ethereal ecclesiastical chants issue forth from high-quality hidden speakers.

Conor and Tommy have gone rather stiff and formal on me, as if they feel we are privileged to be here. You don't get the impression they'd ever barge in uninvited, turn on the football and grab a couple of lagers from the fridge. Although Conor has claimed the title of Mór, Terence is the accomplished historian with many years' experience living the role, and it appears that the younger brother still instinctively defers to the elder, whatever the official pecking order.

Terence introduces me to his long-time companion, Andrew, and Andrew's mother, Betty. 'My cousins,' says Terence enigmatically, by way of non-explanation. Andrew also styles himself the Fifth Count of Clandermond, a title bestowed on him by Terence. They have known each other since childhood. Betty is over on a visit from Ireland. Though Tangier has always had a reputation as a hot spot for smuggling, I suspect Betty may be the only person ever to have crossed the border carrying Irish sausages, Cheddar cheese and black pudding. She should be aware, however, that transporting meat on international airlines can be a risky business.

I once knew an elderly lady, a former fashion editor for *Vogue*, who lived in a flat on Hove seafront. Each year she used to spend Christmas and New Year in Venice, always taking essential festive paraphernalia with her from home. One year the airline managed to lose the suitcase in which she'd packed a Christmas pudding and a small frozen turkey, so she had to have pasta instead. The luggage turned up the following March, by which time she'd forgotten about the turkey. She opened the bag to reveal unspeakable scenes of maggot apocalypse, into which she threw up. After that she always carried items of poultry in her hand luggage.

Betty and Andrew leave to keep a dinner appointment and Terence offers us drinks. He's not at all what I'd been expecting. I realise I've been hoping for some kind of medieval warlord with a big cloak and daft beard, all ceremonial daggers and hearty laughter. But he is sharp and playful – though clearly slightly wary of me – funny and camp, and talks so much he makes his two hyper-loquacious brothers look like members of a silent order that encourages smoking. I ask for a gin and tonic. He raises an amused eyebrow.

'Well, how terribly English.'

He pours me one with no ice or lemon and I try not to rise to the bait.

'Yes, well, I am English.'

'Really?'

'Well, sort of. Half and half. You know?'

'Then you'll understand the nature of the relationship between the two countries.'

'I'm not sure anyone could claim to understand that.'

'It's perfectly simple.'

There's a theatrical pause for maximum outrage as he checks that we're all listening. We are.

'Ireland,' says Terence, 'is an invention of the English. It is a construct, a fiction. As a political entity Ireland does not exist.'

He's enjoying this. It's not the opening gambit I'd been

expecting from a potential claimant to the Irish throne, but it was worth coming to Tangier just to encounter such an outrageous point of view. As I gulp the gin and the brothers weather down the paintwork with nicotine, Terence launches into a compelling monologue about how English kings and the Roman Catholic Church combined to steal or crush all that was indigenous and Gaelic – a wrong that has been compounded by the present, he believes illegitimate, Irish state which was founded on lies.

'There is a pretence that Ireland has always been green and republican, Catholic and Utopian, a place of equality where chiefs were voted into office and there was no aristocracy. This is rubbish of the highest order.'

Ireland, he repeats, was invented by the English. Historically it was four kingdoms – Ulster, Munster, Connaught and Leinster – and that is the way it should be now.

'More gin?'

Absolutely.

Anyway, he says, it was the Anglo-Norman way to lump disparate places together for ease of administration and domination. The island was Gaelic but not 'Ireland' until the English, and he says it again, 'made it up'. Then in the modern age de Valera – 'an American Spaniard, and how Gaelic is that?' – institutionalised a lie in which, says Terence, Sinn Fein and all the rest of them are equally complicit.

'That dancing-at-the-crossroads pigs-in-the-kitchen anti-pluralistic myth in which Protestants were unwelcome, anti-intellectual priests were given power and Roman Catholicism became a test of your Irishness, all based on a past that never existed. This is a made-up Ireland. It simply never was so.'

At one point, he reads aloud from one of his books. He has the manner of a potentate holding court but is also very funny, as if he believes in everything he is saying, but also has an underlying sense of the apparent absurdity of his position. The present Irish government, he says, is 'an occupying power'.

As the evening wears on, I decide that it's not for me to judge whether or not Terence is who he says he is; that's for him to know, and others to decide. Yet I'm much taken by his colourful arguments – the more unpalatable they are, the more he seems to relish them – and by the breadth of his historical knowledge. Informed at all times by a prodigious sense of humour and tempered with generous doses of pseudo-aristocratic pretentiousness and unreconstructed snobbery, he's a one-off in a world of production-line opinions. Here's a man who openly proclaims to hold Sinn Fein, the Ulster Unionists, the Irish Republic and the British government in equal contempt. You might question the logic, but you have to admit it's an original point of view. It's unlikely that the notion of solving the problems of partition and sectarianism by dividing 'Ireland' into four hereditary monarchies is one that's come under serious scrutiny in Stormont, Whitehall and Dublin in the last twenty years of negotiations. Maybe that's what's been holding them back.

The evening takes on a more sombre tone when he touches, without any prompting from me, on his abdication, overthrow, disgrace, call it what you will. He claims none of the other Gaelic chiefs currently recognised by the Occupying Power would be able to pass the tests of provenance that have been applied to him. He's been targeted, he says, because he upset people with his political ideas, his thoughts on de Valera, and for denouncing the hijack of the Gaelic chiefs by the heritage and tourist industries. He returns to the theme of anti-intellectualism, waspishly pointing out that the visionary authors of whom Ireland is now so proud – Wilde, Joyce, Beckett – were all forced into exile. The parallel I'm expected to draw is clear. I remind him of Joyce's line from *A Portrait of the Artist*: 'Ireland is the old sow that eats her own farrow.'

'They should put that on the bloody brochures,' says Terence. 'Instead of *ciad mil failte*.'

As we head for the taxi that's waiting outside the gate he

produces two thick leather-bound foolscap volumes and hands them to me.

'These are my Tangier diaries. You might be interested to read them. No one else has.'

I take them, though it's not clear why he's taken me into his confidence in this way. As I get into the car, he leans across.

'If it's wild geese they want, then I'll be the last goose.'

Back in my room at the hotel I take the diaries and sit on the balcony. The night-lit port is framed between two arches and there's a faint hum of traffic as the city goes about its never-ending business. '*Strait Talk – The Tangier Journals of Terence MacCarthy Mór, Prince of Desmond*', says the title page.

The diaries cover thirteen years, and run to nearly 600 pages. Warm rain is falling on the palms outside my balcony as I drain the last of the Soberano. A dog howls and an ethereal wailing emanates from the edge of the medina. I head for my bed and find the cover has been turned back and a room-service breakfast menu is sitting on my pillow.

Somewhere out there Mohammed is trying to get to sleep on a floor.

The next day is the last before I leave. When I wake the weather has broken. It's cool and raining hard, which softens the blow of going back to the English winter. I borrow an umbrella and walk up the street for coffee and croissants in the Café de Paris. No one is having a business meeting, or reading, or eating with that sense of purpose and urgency that suggests that time is short. The brown bench seats and curved leather armchairs are filled with men, only men, all gazing attentively at the activity in the street outside. They're either much calmer people than we are, genuinely at ease with the concept of relaxation, or all as stoned as Mohammed Mrabet.

When I get back to the hotel the guy on the front desk

announces that I have a message. I'm very excited, as this is my first one. Perhaps now the staff will see that I am someone to be reckoned with, and not just another English pervert on vacation. The MacCarthys have called to say they are going up to the Rif Mountains for the day, and I'm invited to join them. Ten minutes later Conor is in the lobby to collect me. His funereal raincoat is flecked with rain and looks pleased to be earning its living for the first time in weeks. The change in the weather seems to have given him a more expansive air. A man and his mackintosh who are used to the Northern Ireland climate must relish the feeble challenge of Moroccan drizzle.

Two taxis have been chartered for our journey. We give our passports to one of the drivers, who takes them off for scrutiny by some obscure government agency. We're heading into a notorious hashish-producing area, so they probably need to make a note of who we are for ease of administration when we're kidnapped by dealers or shot by the secret police later this afternoon.

The rain has stopped as we drive south out of the city, but the roads are flooded and children are splashing and paddling in the water as our driver carefully negotiates the waves. It's not long before we're out of town, driving on dry roads through sunlit green countryside with huge mountains on the horizon. Old men on mules outnumber the passing cars. Terence conducts a scurrilous and entertaining monologue for the duration of our two-hour journey. There is no mention of last night's Irish issues. Today's targets are the seedy carryings-on and hopeless pretensions of Tangier's self-appointed expat high society. It's been viciously lampooned in his diaries, and there's plenty more where that came from.

'They have bizarre priorities. If someone were to receive a letter on lined notepaper or be presented with the wrong kind of calling card, they would talk about nothing else for the rest of the week, even while the servants were being buggered in the garden.'

By the time we reach Tétouan, I'm fully briefed on the intricacies of the feud between the leather-clad diesel dyke with the monkey wrench and the would-be society hostess 'who wears long white gloves at all times and walks round as if she's looking for a flower show to open'. Tétouan is famous for being the place where – well, actually, it isn't famous at all, it's just the place where the daughter of Cleopatra and Mark Antony is reputed to have come to live. The town's most noteworthy feature is a singularly unimpressive little trickle of a stream. The story goes that when the princess expressed misgivings about leaving Egypt because she would miss the River Nile, they told her, 'Don't worry, they've got one just like it in Tétouan.' We pass a noxious rubbish dump on the edge of town and enter stunningly beautiful mountain and valley scenery that remains unbroken for the rest of the journey. Terence's commentary rises effortlessly to the occasion.

'He believed his house to be the most prestigious salon in Tangier, yet it was never cleaned. It was so filthy that you thought it was carpet when in fact it was fungus. Of course, he's in exile now for alleged pederast activity. Tangier is where you're meant to be exiled to. Exile from Tangier is getting rather low down the scale.'

On a sharp bend a car has gone through the feeble wall and over the edge and is being pulled back up on a dubious-looking rope by a battered old van. A dozen men are standing round, watching with an air of 'I told you so' expertise and discussing camshafts and brake discs just as they would anywhere else in the world. Terence, meanwhile, is telling us the saga of the consular official who was arrested at a border crossing and locked up for years when a dog that didn't know it wasn't supposed to sniff diplomatic cars found 190 pounds of hashish built into the doors. The word is that the smart smugglers have started concealing their gear up a pet dog's bottom, so that the sniffer hound's interest will be mistaken for flirting.

The free-range nature of the conversation is most exhilarating. Tour guides are traditionally expected to talk about the buildings and landscape around them, but I'm beginning to realise that this is a huge mistake. Scandal, libel and intrigue that have no immediate connection with the landscape through which you are passing, but are delivered in artful counterpoint to it, make for a far more entertaining day out. If those tourists you see going round London on open-topped buses were being regaled with squalid tales of alcoholism, shop-lifting and intravenous drug use among the cuckolded wives of army officers and bishops, they'd go back home with a much more positive impression of the country.

For the last few miles as the road has climbed ever higher we've been waved at enthusiastically from the roadside by happy, smiling locals. They are, I'm assured, hashish producers, who presume the only reason Europeans venture into these hills is to score. If you are naïve enough to buy, there's a good chance your dealer will phone the police and you'll be arrested a couple of hours later in the marketplace with the maximum of fuss just as you're buying hand-made wooden toys to take home for the kiddies. I'm told all this in a confidential monotone by our driver, as Terence and Conor yatter away in the back, and it's reassuring to know I'm in such reliable and law-abiding hands in so potentially dangerous an area. Then he says, 'If you want drugs, better I bring them to your hotel. Then there is no problem.'

The sunshine of the valleys has given way to dank mountain mist and drizzle as we approach the ancient town of Chaouèn. It's reputed to be one of the most beautiful spots in Morocco, but doesn't look its best on such a melancholy day. For centuries this was a secret Berber stronghold, and it remained hidden and undiscovered by Europeans until 1920. The first Spaniards to arrive reported that medieval dialects were still being spoken. Two antique steamrollers stand on the edge of town overlooking the gorge, abandoned when their work was completed in the

1920s. As we approach the old town it's clear that the edges of this once-secret place are expanding ever outwards in a ribbon of new, cheaply constructed development that will soon destroy much of its appeal. A boom in tourism is either planned or expected. We get out of the cars on the edge of the medina and the chill, moist air envelops us like February in Donegal. Terence suggests a livener in the empty and bitterly cold bar of a nearby hotel. As we drink, the owner stands on the bar performing strange contortions as he tries to fit an enormous and extremely kitsch mirror to the wall. Terence has selected the Roman Catholic clergy as his topic, a subject on which he has opinions as vigorous and extreme as his thoughts on everything else.

'These men were anti-intellectuals from the pig-owning classes who presided for decades over the mental and spiritual decline of the people.' It's a legitimate point of view, though not one that's likely to win him universal popularity in Ireland. Tommy joins in with a story about the priest who made his early years a misery. A naïve and lingering childhood belief that God must really be on his side and not the priest's was eventually borne out when the hated cleric caught fire one Sunday during Benediction.

'The hem of his cassock got caught in the thurible the altar boy was swinging, and whoosh! Up the bastard went.'

We have lunch in a serene high-ceilinged room hidden down a medieval alleyway. A sign on the wall says, '*Défence de fumer des drogues*'. It's a favourite haunt of Terence's and he's uncompromisingly enthusiastic about the food.

'You must try the carrot soup. It's wank-a-dead-dog's-dick good.'

In a world of clichéd restaurant reviews this stands out as a refreshingly original classification. Perhaps it will find its way into the guidebook and provide an alternative to those tired old stars, rosettes and chef's hats symbols that have ruled the roost for so long. Pudding is *tarte au citron*, 'made with crumbled digestive biscuits to an old *Blue Peter* recipe', according to

Terence, who then volunteers something so scandalous and filthy about one of the programme's most famous presenters that I've been trying to forget it ever since.

Over coffee all three brothers regale me with the story of a Mac-Carthy who was murdered while working as a missionary. Most of him was eaten, though his head somehow survived. Inspired by Australian Aborigines who have successfully claimed bones from British museums, the brothers are hoping to repossess the head and bring it back to Ireland. This seems unlikely, as it is currently revered as a sacred fetish object in a glass case somewhere in Africa. Conor suggests that I might like to undertake its recovery on behalf of the clan. I have a brief vision of myself wheezing through the jungle with a severed head tucked under my arm, pursued by irate and extremely fit fetish devotees, and decline.

'It wasn't so much the fact that they ate him that upset our family,' says Terence, 'but the fact that they ate him on a Friday, in Lent.'

In the street outside I buy a camel-skin lampshade that reminds me of the leathery skin on my ancestor's skull, even though I've never seen the wretched thing and hope I never will. The young man who sells it to me presumes I must be Canadian, because I try and barter in French as well as English. I've never been called Canadian before, and I'm unsure how to react. I shake my head.

'So where you from?'

'England. And Ireland.'

'England? England?'

He suddenly seems disappointed in me.

'England football hooligans! Very bad men! Very bad!'

It's a salutary experience to discover you've been negatively stereotyped by the hill tribes of northern Morocco.

The word 'hooligan' is derived from the name of a particularly wild Irish family, as anyone in England will tell you. In Ireland, mind you, it's said to have its origins in the antics of a tribe of English nutters from Liverpool, so who knows where the truth lies? One thing everyone seems agreed on is that 'riff-raff' and 'ruffians' refer to marauders from the Rif Mountains of Morocco; like the guys who are still at the roadside optimistically trying to sell us hashish as we roar past at fifty miles an hour on the way back to Tangier. By the broken wall there is no sign of the recovery van or spectators, but the crashed car is still visible, about seventy-five feet further down the mountainside than it had been earlier. When travelling on perilous roads in hashish-producing areas, it's probably best to allow a few extra hours for roadside recovery.

Back in Tangier the weather has cleared by late afternoon and Tommy, Conor and I take a walk in the casbah. Despite bright daylight we get emphatically lost. Luckily there's no sign of Mustafa. An old man notices our plight, gives us clear and explicit directions, and we still can't find our way out. We spend another half-hour imprisoned in a dream-like maze of arm's-width alleyways, blue sky just a narrow slit overhead, as the boys babble non-stop of MacCarthy clan history, of how Terence was stitched up by a corrupt establishment, and of the deeds of Finnian MacCarthy, the Great Wolf of the Irish, who slaughtered the Normans, before coming to an untimely end himself. So what happened to him?

'Killed by the feckin' Normans.'

I've no idea whether or not Conor is my clan chief, though I fear the probabilities are against it, but he and Tommy are like those previously undiscovered distant relatives you meet at a wedding and with whom you get on famously. I've always enjoyed the kind of comedy where you don't know whether or not you're meant to be laughing, and the two of them have this quality. They're like an off-the-wall Gaelic double act performing their work in translation into English.

Eventually we emerge in a familiar part of the medina. The street resounds to loud and strange taped music that's probably

Arab or Berber, but could easily be the kind of Afro-Irish-Anarcho fusion you hear hippies playing in Galway and Goa. The weather must have improved in Salt Lake City because inside a café men are watching the giant slalom.

Our conversation turns to the subject of hangovers. Conor tells me about a holiday a few years ago with a friend who went out to play golf while suffering a severe reaction to the night before. At the first tee he was struck by lightning, which lifted him off his feet and knocked him flat to the ground.

'When he came round, he didn't realise what had happened. He only knew he was lying on the floor, feeling terrible, and presumed it must just be a much worse hangover than usual. So he went back to the chalet for a lie down.'

Tommy's in stitches at the thought of it, and with good reason.

'A few weeks later, he was staying on a caravan site in Sligo,' says Conor, 'and didn't he get hit by lightning again?'

'Aye,' says Tommy, wiping his eyes, 'it was like he was on a personal mission to disprove the proverb.'

Conor says it's time for them to leave. Though we're all still full from carrot soup à la dead dog and cheesecake *Blue Peter*, the brothers are expected for dinner.

'Terence and Andrew are cooking Irish stew. We mustn't be late.'

Café Central was where Burroughs, Ginsberg and their boho entourage chugged absinthe and made whoopee in the 1950s. These days no alcohol is allowed in the medina, which is why I'm enjoying the novel experience of drinking orange juice after dark on a Saturday night. It's not as bad as you'd imagine. If you're desperate, you could always pretend there's a UK measure of vodka in it. There could be. It's so small you'd never notice.

There is no sign outside Café Central to let you know that this is Café Central. It's on Petit Socco, the tiny square that also doesn't display its name. This means that if you go out looking for Café Central on Petit Socco you're at a double disadvantage. The only way to find it is by a process of elimination. At first you'll walk straight through Petit Socco because it's so small it doesn't seem much like a square, but once you understand that nowhere else looks anything at all like a square you realise that must have been it.

The café is a large, crumbling oblong room that may have seen better days, though it seems unlikely. Pink and green pillars support a high ceiling, handsomely appointed with fluorescent strip lights hung with cobwebs like fishnet stockings. The only service point is a tiny tiled bar opposite the doorway which boasts the same espresso machine Burroughs might have enjoyed. It's hard to work out how they make a living here. The profit margins on coffee, tea and orange juice must be tiny, and that's all they appear to sell. An old man sits in the window, rolling little balls of hashish between his fingers, and smoking them in a long wooden pipe. Two other men are muttering conspiratorially in the corner. On a giant screen at the far end of the room people are skiing. No one is watching. Sky Sports Two is God's, and Rupert's, way of reminding us that wherever in the world we escape to, we live in a tawdry and imperfect universe. If it weren't for the screen, the crumbling exoticism of the café would be impossibly romantic. It occurs to me that in a strange way the screen is a reverse metaphor, a paradoxical reminder that this is not a movie, but real life. Perhaps I'm getting a bit of blowback from the old guy in the window.

That must be it. I'm getting high on passive dope-smoking. Orange juice wouldn't have this effect. Now I've started thinking that the big unglazed window that looks out on to the street is itself a kind of screen. It frames the action! I can just sit and watch the rich cast of characters enter and leave the movie as they walk by: a man on crutches, a boy in a Nike anorak with three live chickens, a blind man begging, a cleaning woman with a bucket, a kid on a scooter in an Obi Wan Kenobi costume, a prophet Isaiah look-alike. I've started feeling hungry now.

I take a stroll out through the medina to the *ville nouvelle*. The streets seem much busier at night than by day. At one corner a man has laid out his stock of wallets and alarm clocks on a blanket by the kerbside. An old Mercedes saloon reverses out of the side street and runs over them. The alarms on the clocks start going off indiscriminately and the argument is gathering momentum as I turn the corner.

As I walk I realise how fond I have become of Tangier. Like Mohammed, it has crept up on me without my really noticing. It's the closest African city to Europe, but it never features in those lists of fashionable places to go for the weekend. It has no famous attractions that must not be missed; which, in a strange way, is the biggest attraction of all. Freed from the tyranny of sights that must be seen in the company of lots of other mugs with cameras, the city itself becomes the star. I realise I've become familiar with it without making any conscious effort. Petit Socco and Grand Socco have come to feel like home from home. Landmarks are now taken for granted. There is Matisse's famous window; here is the Great Mosque; that is where Orton and Halliwell, and before them Tennessee Williams, rented an apartment. As I scout the street for a restaurant likely to serve wine, it feels as if I'm no longer walking with an affected sense of purpose and belonging, but have subliminally acquired a genuine one. It must have been good stuff the old man was smoking.

I climb a flight of stairs to a Spanish restaurant. The landing opens into a bare and noisy bar full of men who look like lorry drivers, captains of smuggling boats and mercenaries on leave for the weekend. Everyone is shouting and drinking brandy and eating tapas off paper napkins. I adjourn to a calmer though no less spartan dining-room, where I have salade niçoise and calamari. It's served with a half-litre jug of rancid white wine that you wouldn't use to dress a wound. I enjoy it enormously. There's a charming old waiter who looks and dresses like Bela Lugosi in

Plan 9 From Outer Space. When I've finished eating he pours a complimentary digestif of half a pint of Muscatel to take away the taste of the wine.

I'm flying in the morning, but it's Saturday night and I'm frightened I might miss something if I go to bed early. I head back to Café Central to find the place has been transformed in my absence. It's packed to the rafters with men watching Real Madrid on the giant screen. I sit outside as their cheers and roars echo through the alleyways. An old man in a hooded robe sits alone at the table next to me. He's either speaking into a concealed hands-free mobile phone, or talking to himself. After a little while an old woman in a veil appears from around the corner and starts giving him a tremendous bollocking. She shouts and shouts for two or three minutes and then, bollocking complete, leaves as quickly as she'd appeared. He decides, wisely it seems to me, to stay put for a while. A few minutes later she appears again. This time, though, she doesn't even give him the time of day, but just blanks him and walks right on past. I'm trying to work out what's been going on between them when I notice that this time she's also carrying a toilet seat looped over her left arm, like a handbag. Once again I'm completely out of my depth. The certainties of Europe seem far away, even though that continent is visible from the end of the street.

My thoughts turn to poor old Mohammed. I haven't seen him for a couple of days and I'm leaving in the morning. I wonder what's become of him? I hope he's all right. A few days ago I sat for a quarter of an hour at a second-floor window at the front of the hotel watching him trying to watch me. Though he always finds me eventually, I've become more accomplished at avoiding him, and more brazen about giving him the slip. I've been going in and out of the hotel through the garden or rear car park entrance. Sometimes I've tried getting up unnaturally early, or hiding till he's gone. Once I spotted him in the street and just turned and ran away through the crowds, hoping he hadn't seen me, but thinking how I've always enjoyed this scene in the cinema, the one where the sweaty bloke in the safari suit gets chased through the souks by the bad guys. I managed to escape without knocking over a single souvenir stall.

And then I remember that first taxi journey, and its sense of being in the opening scene of a movie, and I understand what Mohammed has brought to my trip. He has helped turn a documentary into a drama, by giving it character, conflict and a through line. And because I never see him come or go, it actually seems as if he's been edited in and out. He has plagued my life with his stalking and lurking; but he's also put me in my own film noir, constantly looking over my shoulder, never able to relax when walking the streets. It would have been a much poorer movie without him.

The match ends, the crowds disperse and I walk back to the hotel for the last time, realising that the shadows hold no surprises any more. As I walk, I find myself wondering about Mohammed. Where is he? I hope nothing's happened to him. I feel a slight pang of regret. Perhaps he's met someone else! That's it. I'm jealous. *He's seeing another tourist.* Someone richer than me. More generous, at any rate. I should have given him more than I did. Even my loose change is a fortune to him. I'm kicking myself now. And in a strange way, I'm missing him.

'So, Peter! You go tomorrow?'

The voice comes hissing out of the darkness, and scares me rigid. Just twenty yards from the hotel, and he's come out of a doorway I didn't even know existed.

'Please, you must help me now. Please. Give me five hundred, Peter, for blanket. Where I live, no furniture, no blanket. Five hundred! Some tourists give me money for nothing, but I have been helping you. Please. Your shoes! Take them off. Yes! Give me your shoes! You have trouser for me? Old trouser? Please, trouser, trouser . . .'

*

Next morning Conor and Tommy are in the lobby to see me off. They have a full complement of cigarettes, though Conor claims to be on the point of giving up.

'You wouldn't want to be catching cancer in a third world country.'

As my taxi drives off from the front of the hotel Mohammed is watching from a doorway. I don't see him, but I know he's there.

The road to the airport, as is traditional with roads to airports, takes us through the drabbest areas of town. Flocks of sheep are grazing on wasteland outside cheap concrete apartment blocks. Some have their own shepherds. The driver says they will all be slaughtered next week inside the apartments, and the bay will run red with their blood.

We land at Gatwick in the dark, in driving rain. Inside the terminal everything looks grey. On the journey home from the airport no one follows me, there's foot and mouth on the radio, and I don't see a single person wearing a fez.

Sometimes home movies can seem very dull.

5

UNREPENTANT FENIAN BASTARDS

I keep telling myself it could be worse, but it's hard to imagine how. The first bottle just hit the wall behind me, and the crowd have scented blood. They've started to move towards me now, tipping over tables and crunching glass into the floorboards with their steel-capped boots, as the bar staff pull down the shutters and run for cover. I'm trying to look on the bright side, but the omens aren't good, and there's no way off the stage without fighting my way through them. They hated me from the start.

'Good evening,' I said.

'Gedoffyafuckinenglishbasstar!' they screamed, and it's been downhill ever since.

I can hear sirens out on 29th Street, so maybe the cops will get to me before the crowd can wreak a terrible vengeance for Culloden, the Highland Clearances and the poll tax. In a final attempt to calm them down I step up to the mike. I'm searching for the right words to defuse the situation and save my skin, so naturally I'm devastated to hear myself saying, 'Think you're hard, don't you? Well, don't forget who won the World Cup in 1966!' They're going mental now, reaching out at me and trying to grab an arm or a leg, like the Zombies in *Dawn of the Dead* when they cornered that guy, ripped out his large intestine, then unravelled and ate it.

I'm starting to wish I'd never got involved in book readings. They seem like very dangerous events. Ah, good. The cops, pushing through the crowd to the front. No, it's the paramedics. They want to know where's the guy who's been maimed.

'We've nae maimed him yet,' says a big guy I recognise from the bar in Gibraltar. 'Could ye no' give us a few minutes?'

'Sure, no problem. Back in ten,' says the medic, and they turn and go.

For days now I've been rerunning this scenario in my head. What had started out as a happy-go-lucky trip to New York to experience the world's biggest St Patrick's Day celebrations has been transformed into a journey to the heart of darkness. It had seemed the most natural thing in the world to say yes when I was asked if I'd like to do some sort of performance or reading while I was in Manhattan. How glamorous it would sound to say I was doing a gig in New York City. It would conjure up images of Carnegie Hall or Madison Square Garden, with Woody Allen, Norman Mailer and Frank McCourt in the front row. But now I know the reality: I will be standing on some beer crates in a bar full of baying jet-lagged drunks, very few of whom are likely to be avid readers.

A few days after returning from Tangier I had a phone call from the woman who was organising the event. It was clear from her voice that something was wrong. She was trying hard to sound upbeat, but had the unmistakable tone of someone who was concealing the terrible truth from a patient, or a victim.

'Our literary events are very popular.'

'Good.'

'It's just . . . look, it's nothing, you'll probably be okay – but, y'know, it's the Wednesday before St Patrick's Day . . .'

I said I knew that. That's why I was coming.

'Oh, okay, so you know that all the Celtic boys will be in town.'

Which Celtic boys? Don't say it. Oh, God, no! Please don't say it.

'Oh, y'know, the football fans? From Glasgow? They come over every year for Paddy's Day for the whole week, and they go kind of crazy. It's wild. Thing is, they use this bar as their headquarters. By Wednesday there'll be a whole bunch of 'em in here. It might not be like a regular reading. They kind of, drink a lot? And that, like, frightens away the regular audience? So you might be faced with a lotta very drunk Scots guys. But hey! Some of them are pretty cool. Just wanted you to know. I'm sure everything will be okay.'

So I told her I was sure everything would be okay too, and then she said it again, which is when I knew I was really in trouble. And then she said, 'Hey, you've got an Irish name, but you sound like, English?'

I said she had a good ear for accents, and she said, 'I wonder if the Scots guys will notice your accent, only, y'know, they can get a little like – boisterous?'

Oh, I doubt it, I said, as my bowels turned to acid rain and my mouth dried up and shrivelled like a Christian Brother's heart. I doubt it.

I'm sure everything will be okay.

It's a bitterly cold morning as I wait for the train to the airport, so cold that a pool of last night's sick has frozen to the platform. I'm only guessing that it's last night's. Most stations aren't manned these days because it isn't cost-effective, so there's no one to collect the tickets, or the sick. Official policy is to rely on gradual dispersal by rook and magpie, unless they strike lucky and someone slips and mops it up with the back of their overcoat. Mind you, hardly anyone on the platform is wearing an overcoat.

It's below zero but a young man has just walked past me, hunched and wincing against the cold, wearing a thin polyester suit. A few feeble nylon anorak-affairs are in evidence, and a sprinkling of those piss-poor raincoats that aren't even waterproof. There are few hats or gloves. Everyone is displaying the distinctive body language and corned beef cheeks of terminal hypothermia. We really should know better. If it drops below sixty in the south of France the fur coats are out and the shitzus are togged up in designer thermals with sequinned piping and flared trousers. Is our national aversion to high quality winter clothing caused by poverty or machismo? Or could it be an act of defiance? Unlike cashmere and lambswool, nylon jackets and manmade-fibre suits are non-absorbent, which means that if we take a tumble on an icy, poorly maintained platform, they won't mop up the vomit. Good thing too. That's someone else's job.

As we pull out of the station the guard announces that refreshments will not be served today as one of the wheels has fallen off the trolley. This beautifully-chosen metaphor for the entire railway system provokes a burst of spontaneous laughter and gives everyone a lot more pleasure than they'd have got from one of the tea-flavoured drinks. Announcements on British trains remain the best reason for choosing rail travel over the car, or mule. 'Complimentary tea and coffee is now being served in the buffet,' announced the steward on my two-and-a-half-hour-late West Coast Express recently. 'Any passengers wishing to purchase complimentary tea and coffee please make your way to the buffet now.'

One night I was on a train packed with commuters that came to a stop in a dark field for no apparent reason. The world-weary guard announced that he was sorry for the delay, in one of those voices that lets you know he isn't really. Then he came back on, said there were two trains stopped on the line ahead of us and one backed up behind, and he had 'absolutely no idea' when we'd get moving. By the third time his patience had snapped and he had made an executive decision to disregard his terms of employment and tell us the truth. 'Well,' he said in a sardonic sing-song. 'I've still no idea how long we'll be stuck here, because apparently there's someone "threatening to commit suicide" on a bridge up ahead.' People lowered books and newspapers at this point, looking at each other as if to say, 'Did he really say that?' Then he continued. 'Suicide? Suicide? Looking for bloody attention if you ask me. I'll keep you posted if he jumps.'

It's not long before we're rattling past the long-term car park, which means we must only be about twenty miles from the airport. It's a smooth check-in, and in no time I'm walking through Business Class to my seat in Economy. The aisle is blocked by a stewardess who is trying to ply a business passenger with free champagne.

'No, thank you.'

He fixes her with the forced half-smile and morally superior glare of a Jet-lag Nazi.

'Just water for me.'

Well, give it to me then, you self-righteous sod. How dare you turn your nose up at something any normal person would be gagging for? Why are you paying extra for stuff you don't want? I'm still reeling at the injustice of it all when the woman across the aisle, who looks like the MD of a company that tests cosmetics on animals and is proud of it, makes her order in an unsmiling monotone.

'No. No alcohol. Just still water. And no meals.'

'None?'

'That's what I said.'

No chance for the crew to spit in them then. As the stewardess moves to let me pass through I catch her eye and say, 'I'll have their champagne if you like.'

I'm trying to sound like I'm joking, but we both know I mean it. So she fixes me with the pond-life glare she's just been on the receiving end of from the Cosmetics Bitch.

'Get down the back with the rest of the ballast, you desperate loser,' she says, taking care to phrase it, 'I'm sorry, sir.' My spirit broken, I trudge past the dividing curtain into the terrifying netherworld of psychotic children, Antipodean backpackers and competition winners from the *Daily Star* with whom I will spend the next eight hours jostling for elbow space with my knees touching my chin. It'll be the best part of an hour before the first sniff of a drink, and it won't be Veuve bloody Cliquot. They should make an example of those two ingrates. The captain should come out and point: 'Oi! You! And you! Off! Go on, off!' Economy would echo to the sound of proletarian laughter as we guzzled their booze and divvied up their bags of freebies like looters after the revolution.

The in-flight magazine compounds the damage with a preachy article warning not to drink alcohol for at least twenty-four hours before flying – let alone on the plane itself – because of the health risks. This puritanical guff makes me even more tense than I already am at the prospect of take-off, and therefore more in need of the drink or two that most of us require in order to relax and block out the mental reruns of every air disaster we've ever seen. A tipsy plane is a happy plane, it seems to me, merrily oblivious of the terrifying fact that we are seven miles above the unforgiving glaciers of Greenland with no visible means of support. What health risks, anyway? Flying is dangerous, sober or drunk. So why not run whiney articles telling people they'd be much safer if they got off and stayed at home instead? Mind you, that can be dangerous as well. A friend of mine was at home knitting when the ceiling fell in on her – plaster in her hair, rubble down the cleavage, the lot. The insurance bastards refused to pay, of course, because they said it was an old house, so it was fair wear and tear. She wasn't even drinking at the time, which goes to show you can't blame alcohol for everything.

The plane's only half full so, unlike Jet-lag Nazi and the

Cosmetics Bitch, I've got a row of three seats to myself. No champagne, but three seats, and a pile of newspapers. Time spent in the USA offers many delights, but I think it's fair to say that news from other countries isn't one of them. A booster dose of British journalism will help me cope when Europe hasn't been mentioned in any news media for more than two weeks and I'm beginning to question the reality of my existence.

As we take off I'm reading that someone has stolen forty-six bloodhounds from a kennel in Kent, and a fifteen-year-old girl has been given breast implants as a birthday present by her mum and dad, who sound like smashing people. And a police sergeant has been found guilty of indecently exposing himself to a ninety-three-year-old woman in the old people's home where he'd been visiting his father. Unfortunately for him he was recorded in the act by a security camera; yet he still pleaded not guilty, saying that his zip had broken and his undercarriage had spontaneously popped out of its own accord – wait, it gets better – but he hadn't noticed because he's twenty-one stone and hasn't been able to see past his stomach for some time. You can see his predicament. All manner of stuff could have been going on down there for years and he'd never have had a clue.

We've crossed the Scottish coast before the trolley appears at the far end of the aisle. I'm just deciding what to order for my two colleagues in the empty seats next to me who've gone to stretch their legs when there's a tremendous crash and a yelp of pain. The hostie, who was walking backwards down the aisle pulling the booze cart in her wake, has stumbled and fallen, banging against a Jewish gentleman in the aisle seat, and bringing the trolley and its contents tumbling down on top of her like an amorous drunk. Perhaps she got lumbered with the three-wheeled trolley off the train. Anyway, now she's lying on her back, her uniform covered in miniatures of gin and brandy, like Father Jack's wildest fantasy. The elderly American lady across from me catches my eye and explains what happened.

'The cart overturned, and then she went down on the man in the yarmulke.'

Well, why not? You can see her point. 'Heck, I'm down here already, and I've always wondered what it would be like. May as well give it a go.' Eventually she gets up, dusts herself down, and brings us drinks, and more drinks, which we all knock back with no apparent ill effects. I do develop a chest pain which in the course of the flight relocates itself to my shoulder blades, but in a way this is a plus, as it induces dark thoughts of the probability of cancer, which takes my mind off the likelihood of crashing.

A short sleep and we're heading down the New England coast towards New York. I take a final look at the papers before entering international news quarantine and find a gripping account of an English murder trial in which the evidence has been compromised by the police, who refused to attend the scene of the crime for an hour after the 999 call 'in case the murderer was still there'. Yes, you can see how awkward that could have been. Much safer to sit outside in the squad car eating Kentucky Fried Chicken for an hour. If anyone in New York tries to suggest that Britain is going down the gurgler, as they sometimes do, I will tell them this tale of heroic British bobbies and watch them squirm.

We come in to land under a steely grey sky, the last traces of snow still visible in the outer suburbs. Perhaps I should have gone to the West Indies after all. There'd have been no snow there. Montserrat almost got the vote. I was tempted by the prospect of spending St Patrick's Day, which I've always associated with the dim light and bare trees of England, Ireland and Budapest, on a sunny tropical island, especially one where the saint's day is said to be celebrated with particular fervour. Some linguists believe that the local patois, like that of Barbados, is descended from the Irish brogue, a theory that has been hotly disputed by rival linguists and academics, who have been prepared to travel long distances to debate their case at seminars and conferences on some of the most beautiful beaches in the world. The prospect of Paddy's Day festivities on a sun-drenched Caribbean island was most attractive. Fat spliffs would be rolled, made entirely of shamrock, and we would skank on the beach to the heavy dub sounds of 'Paddy McGinty's Goat'. Another time, perhaps.

For years I've been hearing stories of New York's St Patrick's Day Parade, still the biggest in the world. It's either a glorious celebration of Celtic pride and the achievements of Irish America, or a shame-making Disneyfication of stomach-turning paddywackery and drunken sentimentality, depending on whom you believe. I figured it was time to find out for myself. The trip to Cobh gave me the final nudge I needed. I decided to come and see the parade, and maybe even march in it, if that's possible without being a member of a religious order, Irish band or paramilitary fund-raising organisation. Perhaps if I packed a dog collar, dark glasses and a beret I could lurk in a side street and tag along when Gerry Adams or the Corrs walked past.

I was also keen to know how an English accent would go down. A friend of mine narrowly escaped a vicious beating for being English in a New York Irish bar on Paddy's Day a few years ago. He was able to see the funny side of it because he was Irish, while his American would-be assailants had never even set foot in the country, though they had seen *The Quiet Man* and *Michael Collins*. My mixed Anglo-Irish Catholic-Protestant parentage might not count for much if I find myself cornered by guys like this and try to persuade them that history perhaps isn't so black and white as it's sometimes painted. I have an ace up my sleeve, though, a fact of which few people seem aware.

The New York St Patrick's Day Parade was founded by the British army.

I've decided I'll only mention this as a last resort, as there's a good chance it will only make matters worse.

*

I don't know about you, but the first person I see when I arrive in America is always that big pear-shaped woman in blue polyester trousers and white uniform shirt with epaulettes, patrolling the no-man's-land before you get to Immigration. It's unclear what her function is, as she never speaks; she's just walkin' tough, walkin' strong, like a Wild West sheriff, or a steroid freak from the gym. You must have seen her. She's in San Francisco and Boston, Miami and LA. 'Welcome to America,' says her gun and her prodigious transatlantic bottom. 'This is how we do things over here. You got a problem with that?' No, ma'am, I surely don't. This time, though, she's walking up to me. Hundreds of people converging on the twenty-five immigration queues and she's picked me. What have I done?

'Purpose of your visit?'

I always feel guilty entering America, on account of having worked for two days as a chef without a permit, and without any of the skills normally associated with being a chef, in Flagstaff, Arizona, in the 1970s. I explained my accent by saying I was from Massachusetts, and it seemed to do the trick. The busboy had never been further than Tucson and wanted to know if the cowboys in Boston dressed the same as in Arizona. His world crumbled when I told him there were no cowboys in Boston. Years later I saw some people dressed as cowboys on their way to a Wild West club in Boston, Lincs., which just goes to show you should never generalise. Perhaps she's keeping me talking so they can drop a net on me and drag me off to a back room where FBI agents who look like Henry Kissinger and Jack Ruby will be waiting to shoot my buttocks full of truth serum.

'Vacation.'

Holiday! I should have said holiday. She'll know I'm only trying to talk like them to ingratiate myself, which is a sure sign of guilt. I'm going to get locked up and gang-raped for cooking burgers and spaghetti in Arizona twenty years ago, and for making the Chef's Salad. It was the restaurant's recipe, but it should have been an arrestable offence. Strips of Kraft processed cheese with shredded white cabbage and tinned sweetcorn in Thousand Island dressing? Do me a favour.

'Okay. Wait in line twenty-one.'

Two minutes, and I'm through. For the benefit of American government officials I'd just like to point out that the stuff about Flagstaff was a joke and didn't really happen, and anyway it'd be hard to find that dishwasher even if he existed, which he doesn't. If anyone tries to tell you I worked in a junk shop as well, it's a lie.

I take the airport bus to Grand Central Station, then a cab to the Upper East Side, where I'm staying in my friend's spare room. An awning covers the street outside the entrance, and a uniformed doorman in cap and greatcoat lets you in, which is very stylish, and also costs you $1,000 in tips at Christmas. There's nobody home and it'd be tempting to lie down and sleep for a couple of hours if I didn't know that the key to avoiding jet-lag – apart from not drinking for a year before getting the plane and consuming only double-distilled mineral water and Royal Jelly while you're in the air – is to stay up until the local bedtime. This can be a tough order when you arrive in Australia at five o'clock in the morning, but at four o'clock in the afternoon in Manhattan it's a breeze, provided you embrace that goobly, out-of-body sensation as a positive. Jet-lag frequently creates the feeling that you are observing rather than participating in life, an experience which is intensified by being in New York, where every square inch is familiar from countless films and TV shows. The only difference between the Manhattan you know from the movies and cop shows and the one that's there when you get off the plane, is the fact that you're in it, and you've never seen that in a film.

As I meander downtown from 72nd Street it strikes me that in a peculiar way Manhattan looks less modern and more traditional – less what we think of as 'Americanised' – than does Britain these days. There are small grocers, delis, bars, florists and cleaners, all bearing the name of a family or an individual instead of an international chain or brand, so that the city still retains much of its early twentieth-century charm. Though it reaches for the sky, at street level it's surprisingly intimate, and just how you want it to be, like going to a concert and being relieved when the band play all their hits rather than experimental new stuff that everybody hates. Taxis are yellow, steam rises from the subway vents and you feel like applauding as if Bob Dylan had just launched into 'Positively Fourth Street', only with a tune you can recognise.

After walking aimlessly for an hour and a half I've reached the corner of Second Avenue and 20th Street. Jet-lag is starting to assert itself, and I feel as if my veins are filled with lead. I need somewhere to sit down, and right across the street is McCarthy's Bar and Grill. It would be perverse not to go in.

A barmaid with a fierce Dublin accent, her face illuminated by eight TVs, is leaning on the counter and moaning about Christmas in New York to the only other person in the bar, a sales rep from a drinks company. He's from Dublin too.

'At home everything closes for two weeks,' she says. 'It's brilliant. Jesus, you can drink yourself to a standstill. Here, though, one bloody day and that's it.'

'Aye, I know.'

'Do you know what I had?'

'What's that?'

'Beans. Feckin' baked beans on Christmas Day.'

'Are you not happy here then?'

'Ah, no, not really. I'd as soon go home but I'm going to try and stick it out for the year like. Otherwise people will just say, "Oh, you've come home early."'

'Which you will have.'

'Aye, and I won't give 'em the satisfaction of taking the piss. I couldn't stand that. I'd rather stay here and be miserable.'

She instinctively understands that the purpose of travel is to be able to tell your friends about it and make them feel that staying at home was a poorer option, even if it wasn't.

There's a heap of magazines and papers and leaflets on the table in the corner. On top of the pile is a flyer for an Irish play called *Howie the Rookie* that is playing off-off Broadway. 'A mind-blowing slice of Dublin street life', claims the blurb. 'Cooler than NYC in Winter.' There's also a three-month-old copy of an Irish-American newspaper in which Gerry Adams has his own column. 'I love Christmas,' writes Gerry. 'Not the mad commercialism which threatens to replace the magic of that wonderful story of the birth of the baby Jesus in a stable at Bethlehem . . .' I double-check in case this is a satirical magazine and it's a spoof, but it doesn't appear to be. There's no sign of a balancing article by Ian Paisley entitled 'The Lord Gave Us Many Words and the Greatest of These is No', so I can only presume it's a republican publication.

The barmaid's moaning about American TV now, even though she's got eight of them on, so I drink up and decide to adjourn to the next bar I see, which is Paddy Maguire's Pub. In the men's room is a handwritten sign saying: ONE ARM URINAL PUSH UPS.

Step one	place free hand on wall
Step two	lean forward bending at elbow until forehead is three inches from wall
Step three	push yourself back to starting position
Step four	shout 'i am special'

I try it and discover that it immediately induces a sense of inner calm and well-being. I may have stumbled on a form of t'ai chi for the drinking classes. As I'm drying my hands two construction workers come in. 'Twenty-five?' asks one. 'Twenty-five!' confirms the other. They high-five, then start undoing their flies. In the mirror I can see them rocking back and forth at the urinal chanting, 'I am special,' in unison. If you hadn't read the sign this could be very alarming.

I ought to go back to the apartment and unpack and start winding down for bed, but then I'd have to admit that's what I did on my first day in New York. Like the barmaid from Dublin, I don't want to admit defeat. Instead I get a taxi and ask the Sikh driver to take me to a bar called Rocky Sullivan's, which is where I'm due to do the reading. I figure it might be reassuring to spend some time there and make it feel like home before the tartan army arrive next week.

It's tucked away among a line of Indian and Pakistani cafés near the police precinct on Lexington Avenue. From outside it's nothing special, but as soon as you go in it's clear that you may have stumbled upon a world-class bar. There are steps that go down from the street into the room, a symbol of moral descent that sets a promising tone. It's long and narrow, with an ageing wooden bar on the right and a tiny stage at the far end, which has no visible means of escape. There's grime on the floorboards and nicotine on the ceiling. I'd been expecting another Irish theme bar, but there's no sign of production-line Celtic bric-à-brac. Instead there's a set of Virgin Mary fairy lights around the top of the mirror, and a black T-shirt hanging in front of it proclaiming in bold letters: UNREPENTANT FENIAN BASTARD.

I take a seat on a stool at the bar and ease myself into the situation. There's a handful of customers and a murmur of conversation above the juke-box. Christy Moore has just finished, and now the Undertones are singing 'My Perfect Cousin'. There's a single window on to the street that's a perfect frame for the telegenic yellow cabs that cruise constantly by like an ambient video installation. A note written on a scrap of paper is taped to the mirror next to the till. STRAIGHT OUT THE FUCKIN WINDOW, it says. Perhaps it's intended as a conversation piece. I ask the dark-haired young American woman behind the bar about it.

'Well,' she says, 'that's from the last time Shane MacGowan was in here – you know? The singer from the Pogues, the Popes, whatever he calls the band now? It was three in the morning and the manager said we're closed and Shane said he wasn't going anywhere. Oh, no? says the manager. No, says Shane, and I'd like to see how you think you'll get me out. Well, says the manager, I was thinking you could go straight out the fuckin' window. Fair enough, says Shane, and drinks up and goes home.'

And the T-shirt?

'It's a quote from a song by a band call Seanchai. They gig here on Fridays.'

'What kind of music do they play?'

'Irish republican hip-hop. Will you have another?'

There's a sweetly optimistic note to her voice and it might seem callous to say no, so I say yes instead. While she's pouring it she points to a painting hanging over the bar. A man's face peers out at me through the gloom. 'James Cagney,' she says. 'A self-portrait, in oils. The genuine article.'

A wild-looking guy on the stool next to me suddenly bursts into action, reaching into a bag on the floor. He produces a painting and passes it to me. It's a watercolour portrait of the hunger-striker Bobby Sands. This is such a parody of the kind of thing you expect to happen in Irish-American bars that I'm not sure how to react. Maybe it's an initiation rite. 'Colour is my strength,' he mutters, in a half-distracted voice. 'I'm a great colourist, just something natural I seem to have.' My pint is served, and he puts the picture in his bag and goes back to his drink. On the screen at the end of the room the cabs are still streaming by.

I'm just thinking that, as well as framing the street action for a drinker looking out, the window also frames the drinker for, say, a drive-by assassin looking in – no one ever said travelling alone would be cheerful – when the guy drinking Jim Beam on the stool on the other side of me says it's getting cold outside.

He's a big fella in his late thirties with a moustache, an unkempt all-purpose rock-and-roll haircut and a T-shirt with a picture of some mental-looking frizzy-haired guitar player. He points to it.

'Ted Nugent,' he says. 'Remember Ted?'

I nod, meaning not really, but that's not going to stop the anecdote.

'Ted was the spirit of rock-and-roll, but he was never drunk, never stoned. All that drug paraphernalia on his album covers – Ted says he didn't know what it was even for. Never did drugs, never got drunk.'

He takes a mouthful of Beam.

'Guess he just had a vivid imagination.'

'Same again?' says the barmaid.

I nod.

'Ted's a serious hunter now. And a main man of the NRA. You English? You have the NRA over there? National Rifle Association? Hey! England! Arright!'

The Bobby Sands artist has looked up at the mention of the word England. He stares as the Moustache clinks his glass against mine.

'Rock-and-roll, man! Went to see Ozzy Osbourne at the Garden. Had a seat behind the stage. Could see Ozzy reading his lyrics, all that satanic stuff and weird shit off of the screen on the speaker box, with a little bouncing ball on the words to keep him on the pace. And Motorhead? Lemmie? Shit. Saw them at the Garden too. Summer. I was wearing shorts. This heavy-metal high-school kid in back of me puked on my leg and in my sneaker.

'He's like, "Oh, gee, dude! Sorry, dude!"'

'So I waited twenty minutes cos I didn't want to miss "Killed by Death" cos it's an awesome song, then I went to the bathroom to wash the puke off. Place was full of black magic heavy-metal kids in there like, twenty years younger than me?

'"Oh, dude, man, someone barfed on your leg."'

' "Yeah," I said, "thanks for that." Waited twenty minutes to get the puke out of my sneaker though. Love that song, man.'

He drains his glass and says goodbye. I'm flagging now, so just one for the road and that'll be it. As I offer the ten-dollar bill she knocks on the counter and turns away, leaving me confused. Have I been barred? The Bobby Sands man comes to my rescue. 'The knock means it's on the house,' he says. 'It means you are a valued customer who has bought several drinks and tipped appropriately though not over-generously. They like you here.' This lulls me into an exaggerated sense of belonging so I casually mention my forthcoming event, in the hope that the barmaid will reassure me and say how good it's going to be.

'Oh, yeah,' she says. 'We get a nice crowd for the readings. You know, people who like to listen. They'll even "shh" if someone's talking in back.' This is exactly what I need to hear. Then she says, 'Oh, no!'

She's raised her hands to her mouth.

'You're the guy who's here in Paddy's Week?'

Unless I run away to Montserrat.

'Has no one told you about . . .'

'The Celtic boys?'

She nods.

'Is it true?'

She nods again and winces in sympathy. She is looking for straws at which to clutch and bright sides on which to look. Hang on, it's worked. She's smiling. Everything really will be okay!

'Look at it this way. They'll probably be so drunk they won't even notice you.'

I'm doing my best to fan the dying embers of optimism, but the glow is fading to black.

'And if they do, just remember that the head of homicide will probably be here.'

The head of homicide? What in God's name is she saying?

That Glasgow's top killer is going to be here? Their main murder man? The head of homicide! One unguarded remark about Scottish goalkeepers or deep-fried Cadbury's Creme Eggs and I'll be sleeping with the herrings.

'Yeah, from the Precinct House up the block? The NYPD? He drinks in here.'

That's not so bad then. In a way it's quite reassuring. The head of the New York Police murder department will be on hand. I'll tell him the one about the British coppers not going into the house in case the murderer was still there. That'll cheer him up.

'Hey, don't worry. If things get real bad I guess he can just shoot them.'

I bet this doesn't happen at Hay-on-Wye.

'Hey, just joking. One more for the road?'

A wonderful thing happens next morning at dawn. There are no blinds or curtains on my eighth-floor window so the first light wakes me, a low and amber-glowing winter sun hitting the apartment blocks across the street and making them glow orange and pink. It's a luminous Arizona-canyon colour that is quite unexpected in the heart of the city. I get up to take a better look and see that despite the deceptively clear sky it's been snowing in the night. It looks like there's a couple of inches on the street far below, where some early risers are already shovelling the sidewalks clear.

Another wonderful thing is the plumbing. I get in the shower after everyone has left for school and work and I'm immediately flattened against the tiling by a violent torrent that would do credit to the South Korean riot police. Why do American showers knock you over, while ours have all the oomph of Barbie's watering can? Is it something to do with the Hoover Dam? In the apartment upstairs a man is doing early morning singing exercises in a powerful tenor. That's American service for you. Singing in the shower is actually provided, though city and state taxes won't be included, and terms and conditions may apply.

As I head out into the street the doorman holds the door open for me, but on balance I'd rather have the $1,000. All along the street people are clearing snow with plastic shovels. A woman in a puffa jacket and moon boots is pulling a little girl on a toboggan. As I search for somewhere to have breakfast I pass a woman wearing a full-length mink coat over blue jeans. She has an expensively hairy dog on a diamanté leash. The creature is squatting in the snow. When it's finished she bends down and fills a plastic bag with her pooper scooper, then tries to wipe the snow from the smug mutt's nether regions with what looks like a chamois-lined pine-scented Doggie-Do Disposer from the Pet Hygiene Emporium on Fifth Avenue. It's probably been made to measure to fit his nooks and crannies. After all, they have gymnasiums for dogs in this town. And cigar clubs, for all I know.

Once she's satisfied that the dog's bum is free of unpleasantness she folds up the cloth and the evil little parcel, pops them into a paper bag and puts the lot in the pocket of her coat. A visitor from another planet might presume that people picking up dog shit on the streets had been sentenced to it by the courts rather than freely choosing it as a 365-day-a-year activity. I'm just hoping there's a warm spell and she forgets about it until November.

I find an old-style diner but the counter seats are all taken, so I take a booth instead. A 110-year-old Rumanian waiter brings me the menu. All breakfasts, it says – and there are dozens of them – come with three eggs. Can you imagine asking for three eggs with your breakfast in Britain? They'd call the vice squad. I once asked for two in a B&B in Norfolk and there was an incident. I order and start to pick through a pile of newspapers and listings magazines. A thin, severe-looking woman, wearing the kind of coat you'd see at a bad-taste party in Brighton, comes and sits at the next table. The Aged Rumanian comes across, forces a smile from beneath the decades of oppression and says, 'Are you ready to order?'

'Hey!' snarls the Coat. 'Gimme a break! I didn't even look at the menu yet. Jesus Christ!'

This is her way of saying, 'No, thank you,' or 'I just need a few more minutes.' I heard a radio programme a little while ago about street rage and shopping rage in New York. They reckoned it happens because they all live in apartments that aren't quite big enough. Maybe this woman lives in a closet and sleeps standing up in the coat.

Time Out New York carries a five-star review of the play I saw advertised yesterday, *Howie the Rookie*. 'Writer Mark O'Rowe,' it says, 'does more with a few words than most playwrights accomplish in an entire scene. His profane unsentimental prose adds yet another distinctive voice to the latest Irish playwriting renaissance. This is a seventy-five-minute dramatic torpedo.' I make a note of the number, even though going to the theatre on your own is even sadder than sitting in a bar on your own. Only a bit, mind.

Breakfast arrives, and it is massive. There's so much other stuff that you hardly notice the three eggs, yet it costs about the same as a croissant would in London. Speaking of London, there's a photo of Ken Livingstone in the *New York Times*. He's been in town to pick up a few tips on how a big city works, so that he can try and make it happen in London. His visit is reported with an amused detachment. When someone asked him how he liked to spend his time when he wasn't doing politics, Ken replied, 'Drinking excessively.' The paper was impressed. No American politician, it said, would have dared make such a reply. That'll be because they're not sufficiently relaxed or at ease with themselves, because they don't drink excessively enough.

As I leave the diner I spot a payphone in the corner and decide to seize the moment to book for *Howie the Rookie*.

The show is sold out for the rest of the run.

Bloated and egg-bound, I head out on to the street. Most people are dressed stylishly and effectively against the cold, in marked contrast to the Oxfam Spring Collection on the railway station yesterday morning. I'm puzzled, though, when I see first one person, then another, and another all wearing thick knitted headbands round their foreheads and ears, leaving their heads, frequently bald, sticking out the top like an egg – I can't stop thinking of eggs just now – without a cosy. Is it a fashion statement? Or just an economy hat, a factory second bought cheap because the middle bit, the warm, important bit, is missing? I've always presumed that people who don't wear hats in cold weather just can't be bothered to lift their hands up and put something on their head. But if you're going to take the trouble to put something up there, it might as well have a middle.

I go to the subway and take the downtown 6 train to Grand Central Station, then walk to the New York Public Library where I will spend the day finding out about St Patrick's Day in America, and keeping warm.

It's dark when I leave the library, and the snow has thawed. The streets are wet and slushy as I splash through the rush-hour crowds along 34th Street towards Madison Square Garden. Towering Gotham-Gothic buildings on the north side of the street vividly evoke the old New York. I'm surprised how many parts of town have retained this classic early twentieth-century feel. I'm also surprised how few obese people I've seen today, though maybe I shouldn't be. New Yorkers like to congratulate themselves on not having fallen victim to the thick-shake-and-fries-with-that epidemic of lardy-arseness that plagues the rest of the nation. In the library today I discovered a lengthy correspondence in one of the New York papers about how far out of town you had to travel before you were in Buttville, where the colossal buttocks begin.

Opposite Madison Square Garden on Eighth Avenue is Tír na nÓg, an upmarket Irish theme pub and restaurant with grand mock-heroic-heraldic, ancient-Druidy, high-chieftain-of-Ireland décor. It's packed with ice hockey fans warming up for the New York Rangers seven o'clock puck-off across the street. This isn't a great place for two people who've never met to try and find each other, so I stand near the bar looking hot and anxious in the hope that's what the other guy will be expecting. It seems to do the trick.

John McCarthy is the New York representative of the Clan McCarthy Association, with which our man in Tangier was involved before his fall from grace, and has met Terence on several occasions. He's a banker, just back from a two-year posting to Surrey, which he loved. His brother, though, refused point-blank to visit him because of what England has done to Ireland. 'He says he'll never set foot there as long as he lives,' says John. I've never heard of anyone boycotting Surrey for ideological reasons – though it could catch on in Lancashire and Yorkshire – and I'm intrigued. As the hockey fans leave the bar and the noise subsides, I ask about his brother's refusal to sully his shoes with the morally tainted soil of Esher. Is this because they're Irish immigrants?

'Not really. Our McCarthys got here way before the American Revolution. They backed the wrong side and had to run away to Ontario. But my mother's grandmother was Irish. That's good enough in this town.'

John has an intriguing angle on the MacCarthy Mór controversy.

'You must remember that Hollywood movies have happy endings. Americans are very nostalgic people.'

He breaks off to order more drinks while I try to figure out where this is going.

'Here's the way I see it. I've read Terence's books and I thought they were great stories. I read 'em, I close 'em, and I put 'em back on the shelf. And d'you know what? I don't want to know whether they're true or not.'

He takes a drink and a pause for thought.

'It doesn't actually matter whether they're true, or whether his claim to be Prince of Desmond was true. The point was, it brought people together. It was a fraternal organisation. C'mon! We knew we weren't really related. So what? It was a starting point. It's shot to hell now with this scandal. Only the Irish government can sort this out. And there's some people put a lot of work into this clan thing. And a lot of money. Hell, we're Americans. Business is important to us. And there could have been a lot of tourist business generated by this clan thing.'

He says I should try and make contact with the head of the clan association, Larry McCarthy, who has had extensive dealings with the former MacCarthy Mór. Unfortunately he lives 2,000 miles away in Montana.

'We once went to Montana to buy a dog. Sure is beautiful country out there.'

A thickset young man comes and sits at the stool next to us and asks if we'd like tickets for the hockey. 'There's nearly half the game left. They're good seats, six rows from the ice.'

John says he has to take the train home after this drink, but I'm tempted. I'm about to ask the tout how much the tickets cost when he reads my mind and tells me.

'Excellent seats. Really. Hundred-and-eighty-dollar seats.'

How much? God in heaven! I'm still recovering from when schoolboy admission at Warrington Rugby League Club went up from six pence to nine pence. And you could go and see the Beatles on the way home, pay for your bus fare, a fish supper and two weeks' holiday in Southport and still have change from half a crown.

'So how much do you want for them?'

'Nothing, man. I'm a bartender here. I don't want anything. The tickets are comps. My buddy couldn't make it. Here, take it.'

John and I say our farewells and he disappears into the subway while I try and find my way into Madison Square Garden. I'm feeling a bit intimidated, not wanting the genuine fans and the stewards to mark me down as some lightweight tourist, turning up when the game's almost over without even knowing the rules. Even though I'm in possession of a bona fide multiply-logo'ed $180 ticket I find myself inventing stories to explain my lateness. Do you never reach a point in your life when you cease to be scared of authority figures, even when right is on your side? I blame the Brothers, who taught us through bitter experience that just because you're right it doesn't mean you're not going to get a bloody good hammering for being wrong. I got a letter the other week from an old schoolmate: 'A few of us still get together and talk about how it never did us any harm, as we twitch and spill beer on each other.'

The Garden is a deserted maze of brightly illuminated corridors with a strange rumbling coming from somewhere deep inside, as if the mother ship may have landed. The stewards seem astounded to be presented with an intact ticket so late in the day, but lose interest in me before I can tell them my cover story. They direct me into a huge bowl of noise where the fans are as well-lit as the players. I guess everybody's part of the show. My seat is occupied by a construction worker whose hobbies are body building and steroid abuse, so I take the nearest empty one instead. As I sit down, the action stops and very loud organ chords begin to play, ascending the scale like a B-movie or a bad panto.

The game starts again, then immediately stops. The score is 1:1, but I don't know if that's good or not. Right in front of me is a man with very long bright ginger hair tied back in a purple ponytail. You don't often see that. Across the aisle a young Japanese woman with plaits is clapping and cheering like a Jerry Springer fan while her boyfriend orders beer and popcorn from a waiter. Where I come from a beer and popcorn waiter at a sporting event, though theoretically possible, is beyond the wildest fringes of the imagination, like lobster for school dinner.

The British are supposed to be world leaders when it comes to irresponsible heavy drinking at sporting events; yet here in the spiritual home of AA, where alcohol, like pornography, must be concealed in brown paper bags, and the talk-shows and magazines would have you thinking that the whole nation is on detox, everyone I can see is holding a plastic container of beer. Many are slumped as if they're at home in a favourite armchair watching TV. They seem to be drunk, but not in the way that people are drunk in open-air sports stadiums from Sunderland to Sydney. This is an amiable, plastic-beakered, popcorn drunk, possibly induced by some social control additive in the rancidly sweet beer-type drink I have just purchased and discarded in disgust. It may also contain some kind of chemical cosh to persuade people to sit still for so long. Whenever play stops so does the clock, which means a twenty-minute quarter seems longer than a Ken Dodd show.

The players have just taken another break so that a load of new players can come on. I suppose the pauses suit the rhythm of TV ad breaks. The organ music is an almost constant soundtrack, as if this were a show rather than a match. One day all our lives will have background music, and possibly a commentary, to make them seem more real. There's some sort of trivia quiz going on now on a screen above the rink. They're playing 'Start Me Up' by the Stones, and showing a clip from *Chariots of Fire*. The answer is 1981, but I don't know what the question is. There are huge electronic sponsors' logos all round the ice which keep on changing: blink, and Footlocker turns into Bud Light turns into the Satanic Mind Control Resort and Casino in Atlantic City. Now the main screen is saying MAKE SOME *NOISE*, and the word *NOISE* is vibrating and drawing attention to itself. And now it says LET'S GO RANGERS, and everyone's started chanting 'Let's Go Rangers.' Why would they need a lyric sheet? It's hardly six verses of 'Abide With Me', is it?

All this wholesome, brightly lit neo-drunkenness is making me nostalgic for real, unsavoury drunkenness, and I'm beginning to feel paranoid. Perhaps my drink has been spiked. I decide to do the Wigan Walk: I will get up and leave before the end. I've got a story prepared in case the stewards give me a hard time for wasting a ticket that some deprived kid from the Bronx could have used, but they don't even give me a glance.

Walking to the subway through the deserted cross-town streets of the garment district I remember how edgy New York used to feel, but now all the bad guys seem to have gone somewhere else. I felt more threatened than this last week at closing time in Cheltenham. The rubbish is out for collection. On top of one pile of plastic sacks is a brand-new three-piece suite in peppermint-striped fabric. Maybe it looked better in the catalogue. As I get to the subway I realise that, though the snow has melted, my neck and head are cold. I've left my favourite scarf and hat behind at Madison Square Garden. This may be God's way of telling me not to sneer at games, and cultures, I don't understand.

The apartment I'm staying in is the home of an old pal from England who's been in New York for ten years. Once upon a time Phil used to play saxophone in a band and appear on *Top of the Pops*, but now he's got a job instead. One of his riffs is very famous and is still sung on football terraces. You probably wouldn't know what it's called, but you'd recognise it if you heard it. Der der der duh der, Der der der duh der. Yeah, that's the one.

We're in a bar in the East Village called St Dymphna's, who was the Irish patron saint of lunatics, or lunatic asylums, or something. A Mexican waiter is decanting HP Sauce from one bottle to another so slowly he looks like a sculpture. Van Morrison is on the stereo, and a couple on bar stools are kissing with tongues. Phil's telling me about the time the band supported the Jam on tour, for no money, staying in semi-derelict DSS bed and breakfasts and generally living like beasts. He and the guitar player were in a chip shop one night after the gig, surrounded by concert-goers who didn't recognise them, when the football crowd on the telly all started singing along to their hit. The chip-buying Jam fans all joined in. They took in their anonymous moment of superstardom, then ordered two bags of chips because they didn't have enough money for fish.

When they came over to play at CBGB's in New York Phil went missing with some people he met in a bar, and didn't reappear till the night of the show three days later. He still can't piece together quite what happened. At the time many of us took it as a sign that this was the city for him, and that's how it's turned out. He married a New Yorker, and now has two sons. One of them put a raisin up his nose recently and they couldn't get it out.

'It started to swell and turn back into a grape. We had to take him to emergency.'

Lucky it wasn't a prune.

He says he was amazed at the high standard of musicianship when he moved here. 'If you had your own van in Brighton you got to be the bass player.' He says they won't let you give blood in New York if you're from Britain, because we've all got mad cow disease and foot and mouth. This is the kind of crucial information you never find out unless you know someone who lives in a place. And he reckons there are so many dry-cleaners on the Upper East Side because washing machines are prohibited in most apartment blocks. There was a scandal in Phil's building recently when a man was found to have surreptitiously installed one, though how he got it past the doorman and the twenty-four-hour security cameras remains a mystery. Perhaps he dismantled it into small parts and smuggled it in bit by bit up his trouser leg, in a sort of reverse Colditz scenario. He was caught when the woman downstairs spotted telltale bubbles frothing up through her plughole. The doorman earned his $1,000 tip by hunting him down like a badger with TB, only without killing him, because he was a lawyer.

The extended happy hour with $3 Guinness comes to a sad conclusion and we get a cab to Rocky Sullivan's. On the way Phil tells me about the bar where all the beer is free during Monday night football on TV, until the first person has to go and take a leak. It could take years to recover from the mental trauma and bladder damage. I expect the real hardcore fans just wet themselves and front it out. If the bartender objected you could claim it was spillage.

Seanchai, I've discovered, is Gaelic for 'storyteller'. As we walk down the steps and pay our $10 to someone who looks like an off-duty cop, they launch into an Irish hip-hop version of the Beach Boys' 'Do It Again', which shows a commendably eclectic range of influences, but isn't quite what I'd been expecting. To be honest, I don't know what I'd been expecting.

I suppose I'd been hoping for a band and a bar that might serve as a symbol of what Irishness has become in the intense crucible of urban New York, and as I watch and listen it turns out that's exactly what I've got. There's a full-on rock-and-roll electric guitar player, a fey folky on mandolin, a teenage Brooklyn girl scratching the turntables, a tough-looking American guy rapping and playing the uillean pipes and the bodhran, and a young Irish woman with a pierced nose and a pure voice that soars over the whole rhythmic mix. She sings a spine-tingling version of 'Something Inside So Strong' accompanied by just the bodhran, then goes straight into a raucous 'Thirty Years On', a song about Bloody Sunday. 'Garvaghy Road' is about the Drumcree protest, and by now a pattern is emerging. I don't believe Dr Paisley would feel at home here; nor is it a place where Terence MacCarthy's theory of Ireland being an invention of the English would go down that well. The music is a rallying cry for nationalists and republicans. It's at times like this one has to face up to the confusing responsibilities of having an Irish Catholic mother and an English Protestant father. Celebrate and honour both traditions, and denounce injustice wherever you find it. And if they start hitting you with chair legs, try and cover your groin.

The set finishes with 'The Fields of Athenry', the song I heard warbled to death in Cobh. Tonight, though, it's transformed into an anthem of passion and beauty. This woman has a wonderful voice. The band go off, even though there's nowhere to go except stand next to the stage, then come back on for an encore.

> *Ten thousand fenian bastards pumpin their fists*
> *Not sayin they any better*
> *But ain't worse than any other*
> *Unrepentant yeah!*

The crowd goes wild. This is the band's calling card. The tough-looking guy has taken over on lead vocals, and you know he means it. Then the storm is over and they've gone. I ask Phil what he thinks, and he says, 'They'd sound great with a saxophone player.'

It's always intimidating to approach performers after a show, because some of them are arrogant bastards who would rather eat soil than speak to a member of the audience, but I decide to risk the humiliation. They're happy to talk. Rachel, the singer, is in her twenties and comes from Dublin. Chris, who sings and plays the pipes, is in his thirties, and also co-owns the bar. He grew up in Brooklyn but spent summers with family in Ireland where he learned to play traditional instruments. This has left him with a curious accent that sounds three parts Brooklyn to one part Donegal. What's even more curious is that he was a cop on the streets of New York until he got a record company advance to buy some studio time. He got it free from a friend, and spent the money on the bar instead.

'My buddy and I realised we had nowhere to drink any more because our favourite bar had been turned into a fuggin' Irish theme pub.'

'But isn't this place an Irish pub?'

He narrows his eyes as if I'm much more stupid than he'd realised. 'No. It ain't themed. It's a New York bar, but with an Irish influence. It's like the music. It couldn't come out of any place but this city.'

I tell him I'm booked to do a reading during St Patrick's week. There's a twinkle in his eye but I'm not sure what it means.

'So you're the guy. Have they warned you?'

'They have.'

He doesn't say anything, so I fill the gap. 'Do you think it'll be okay?'

'Maybe. Could go either way.'

We arrange to meet for a drink on Sunday night and discuss a strategy that will ensure my safety. Chicken wire would be an option, but it's probably too late to install it.

Back at the apartment I make a right turn out of the elevator, as usual, but Phil stops me.

'No, not that way. This way.'

He heads left. I could have sworn it was right, but he's been doing it for years, so I suppose he must know. Mind you, he looks a bit out of it, gazing around in confusion, as if his sax player's brain has been removed and replaced with a drummer's. Then he says, 'Are we in the right building?'

I confirm that we are. He walks right up to the wall and stares hard at a framed painting just beyond the end of his nose.

'Hey. This is all wrong!' The light of realisation is dawning on his face. 'This is the wrong picture! I know what they've done! They've changed the art! *They've changed all the art around* while we've been out.'

I explain they haven't changed the art, he's just walked in the wrong direction, and guide him to his apartment door. We open it as quietly as we can so as not to wake up the children, and wake up the children.

*

Next morning is Saturday. The kids are off school and Phil is in bed with no sign that his emergence is imminent. One of the boys looks at me quizzically.

'Why does Daddy drink so much beer when you're here?'

I explain that Daddy is a vegetarian, so beer is good for him because it's a meat substitute, but he doesn't seem to get it. I suppose you can't blame the boy. I think the school syllabus is different over here.

Phil still hasn't emerged when I head out for lunch.

I've decided it's time for some noodles. Less assertive than pasta, more comforting than the potato, they are the perfect food for the fragile solo traveller, and also make a nice change from toasted ham and cheese sandwiches. New York Noodle Town on the Bowery in Chinatown looks just the job. The tiny formica tables are crammed with people of all races, ages and states of mental health. There are two round communal tables for solo diners. I go and join a very old Chinese guy who's drinking tea, and a younger man in a leather jacket who is shouting into a mobile phone in a language I don't recognise. His aggrieved, indignant tone conveys a real sense of menace, as if he's speaking to a shop that just sold him a faulty electrical appliance, or berating a hit-man who's killed the wrong guy.

My roast duck and green vegetables with noodles is one of the bargains of world cuisine at $3.95, which includes tea and tax. I could have had a starter of cold jellyfish for an extra $3.50, but I didn't, because I've had it before. There's also an extensive and impressive porridge menu, all of it very competitively priced by international porridge standards. Pig's stomach porridge, for example, is only $2.95, while house special porridge is $9.95, though that does serve four, or more than four if they're not very keen on porridge. Shrimp porridge is $5.50, but for a dollar more you may as well go for the most expensive item on the menu, which is frog porridge. I picture a big pan of oatmeal, bubbling and spluttering on a fierce gas burner as scores of tiny frogs perform a desperate but doomed breaststroke in a heroic bid to escape the nutritious, all-consuming lava. We've got frogs in the garden. Maybe I should make some when I get home.

My pornographic frog reverie is interrupted by a gruff old Chinese lady who pushes past me to get at the old guy who's drinking tea. She sits down and starts shouting at him just like the old lady outside Café Central in Tangier except that, unlike the old Moroccan boy, the Chinese man starts shouting back. They go at it hammer and tongs for about five minutes, then break into loud laughter and move to a table for two that has just come free. As I finish my noodles, the guy in the leather jacket finishes his call. He looks pleased, as if the killing is back on for tonight. His meal arrives, a vivid and elaborate stew of the kind of unspeakable inner organs you wouldn't usually find outside a textbook or post-mortem. Looking round I can see that most of the other diners have also gone for variations on this lung and bile-duct special, their bowls brimming with shades of grey and brown rarely encountered in nature, or Tesco's. I may fancy myself as a cosmopolitan diner, but my noodles with recognisable mainstream animal are about as adventurous here as egg and chips. As I stump up my $3.95 at the counter in the corner I remember the most intimidating menu I ever saw, in Guangzhou, China. I still have it at home. Camel's Hump in Wonderful Taste. Boil Badger in Earthenware Pot. But a special place in my heart will always be saved for Corfu. 'Spleen Stuff,' it said, 'with salad of wild green things.' I believe we had the moussaka.

I'm walking to Canal Street subway, past traders selling gloves, pak choi, hats, durian, watches, luggage and giant crabs, when I spot a poster for Corona Beer in the window of a Chinese grocery store. The unique attraction of Mexican beer, as I've always understood it, is that you drink it from a bottle that has a slice of lime or lemon stuck in the neck, a concept about as attractive to the serious beer drinker as a pint of bitter with a banana in it. But here in the middle of Chinatown I've discovered a previously unimagined selling point for fruity Latin American lager. The face of a stereotypical Mexican bandit, swarthy and unshaven, framed by sombrero and poncho, leers out. Hanging from the sombrero are dozens of tiny shamrocks. 'Kiss me,' the bandit is saying, 'I'm Irish.'

I'm on the platform waiting for a downtown train when two seedy-looking men with grey complexions come through the barrier and start walking towards me. One pauses to look at a subway map, as if he's pretending to read it while keeping lookout, while the other walks towards me with an ominous sense of purpose, but no visible weapons. He's in his twenties, wearing a leather jacket that's too thin for the climate. By the time he reaches me and makes eye contact I've decided that he's some kind of low-level foot soldier from one of the ex-Soviet mafias, one of the ruthless thugs I've been reading about in the paper who are infiltrating the New York underworld. Cruel and very unscrupulous, by all accounts. I should be careful. The lookout is still by the map, cleverly blocking my way if I try to make a run for it. Stay calm. Don't do anything rash. Wait for help if you have to.

'Excuse me, how ya doin'?'

He's a tourist from Ireland. What the hell does he think he's doing going about the place pretending to be a Ukrainian pimp and scaring the shit out of everyone?

'Cold, isn't it? Look, we're trying to get to the Brooklyn Bridge but we can't work out which train to get. Do you know if this is the right platform?'

I tell him I'm a stranger myself.

'These maps'd do yer brain in, wouldn't they? Confusing, aren't they? Not like getting the tube.'

So we get talking and I ask if he's on holiday, and he says he's working here for a few weeks, and I wonder what kind of work, and he says he's in a play, him and his mate, but his mate sleeps all day so he's not here. So what play's that then?

'It's called *Howie the Rookie*.'

'What? The seventy-five-minute dramatic torpedo?'

'That's the fella.'

Now what are the odds, I'm wondering, against trying to book for a play, just the one play out of the dozens in New York, and it being sold out because it's such a hot ticket, and then one of the cast – half of the cast, for God's sake – walking up to me, out of all the people in the city, and asking me the way? I have to say, I'm impressed. It's almost enough to make you believe that our choices really are guided by some higher intelligence, and crop circles aren't made in the middle of the night by nutters with balls of string who are off their faces on scrumpy. I'm fascinated by this kind of stuff. I've always wanted to do some research on the meaning of coincidence, but I suppose deep down I've been waiting for a chance meeting with someone who could tell me all about it. Right now I'm about to have a chance meeting with the lookout, who's walked up to join us.

'This is Mark. He wrote the play. My name's Aidan, by the way.'

'Mark O'Rowe? Of the distinctive voice and the profane unsentimental prose?'

'The very man.'

I get off the train with a ticket for Sunday night's show.

Howie the Rookie is spellbinding. Two interlocking monologues describe a night of mayhem and violence in searing Dublin slang. Aidan is terrific, and so is Karl who sleeps all day. The audience of middle-aged Manhattan theatre-goers who've been lured to the down-at-heel performance space by the rave reviews seem awestruck rather than involved, like anthropologists examining specimens from a distant civilisation. At one point a mobile phone goes off in the audience. Karl, quick as a flash and emphatically in character, snarls, 'Turn that fucking thing off,' and the phonee finds himself on the wrong end of a brilliantly improvised stream of abuse which makes Karl's character more terrifying than he already is. Four Dubliners in the audience are laughing like drains at all the bits that are completely impenetrable to anyone who isn't from Dublin. As I leave after the show I hear one of them saying, 'That Pakistani doctor he was slaggin'. He's my feckin' doctor! The same guy! I can't believe he didn't even change his name.'

Actors and author join me in the Patron Saint of Lunatics Bar. The waiter is still decanting HP, but there's no sign of the snoggers. We talk about the play, which they're taking to San Francisco next, and about Mark's kidney stones, and then the three of them come with me in a cab to Rocky's, where I've arranged to meet Chris from Seanchai.

There's a handful of Sunday night customers, but no sign of Chris, so we take our pints and sit under the window that's like a screen. Mark's on fruit juice because of the kidney stones.

Aidan tells me about his friend from Dublin who's landed himself a job in New York as an art deliverer.

A what?

'He just takes really expensive paintings back and to for this super-rich collector. He went round the other day with a Van Gogh, and the guy told him to put it in the closet with the others. He hires 'em out at twenty grand a pop for dinner parties, so the lazy feckers have something to talk about.'

Karl and Mark have discovered the juke-box. I've told them about Seanchai and Karl keeps on playing their CDs. He seems very taken with Rachel's singing, and keeps saying, 'Jesus, but this girl's got a great voice, hasn't she?' So we carry on for an hour or two the way people who tour for a living always do, nattering away like best mates though this may be the only time in our lives we ever meet. By midnight it's clear that Chris isn't going to show and it seems time to call it a night. Karl puts Seanchai on for one last time – 'will ya listen to her voice!' – and Aidan and I are discussing how bizarre it was that he should ask me for directions like that, and wondering whether coincidence is a genuine power in our lives, when the door opens and Chris and Rachel walk down the stairs.

'Karl?' says Rachel.

'Rachel?' shouts Karl.

They only went to primary school together in Dublin, and have known each other since they were about eight years old. He's been playing her records all night without having a clue it was her. He didn't even know she was in New York. She didn't know he was the hottest ticket in town. When it's late at night and cold outside and you're a long way from home, it's comforting to discover that life has meaning after all. The situation clearly merits a quiet drink by way of celebration.

When you sit up all night talking, a spell is created whose magic is dissipated the moment you walk through the door and back into real time. There's a very particular feeling, half elation and half self-loathing, when you're going home after a night out and everyone else is going to work. I'm reminded of these things as I hit the street, hoarse, euphoric and already forgetting the stuff we've spent the last six hours gabbling about. I do recall that Karl and Aidan are marrying a pair of sisters, and I think one of the weddings might be happening in Mexico. And Rachel's parents nearly called her Vivien, 'which would have been a feckin' disaster', but changed their minds and called her Rachel instead. Rachel Vivien. And Mark of the profane prose and the kidney stones went back on the beer at about three in the morning; and isn't Chris suing a British TV station for millions of dollars for using his music without his permission in a film about terrorists? Something like that. The details are receding into the mental fog as I get into a taxi that's just dropped a security guard outside an office building. God, I feel rough. For years I've been telling myself I ought to go to the theatre more often, but perhaps it's not a good idea. It ought to carry a health warning.

Fifteen minutes later the driver wakes me outside the apartment building. I'm hoping to slip in incognito but the guy in the top hat and greatcoat makes a big fuss of opening the car door for me. I manage to get out without falling into the gutter and make it to the elevator without walking into a plate-glass door, though the bright lights are very distressing. I don't want to wake anyone before the alarm goes off at seven, which is in half an hour's time, so I take my shoes off and carry them into the apartment. Phil and his entire family are in the living-room, about to phone homicide to report me missing.

'Nobody goes out to the theatre at six o'clock on Sunday night and doesn't come home till seven on Monday morning. Especially in a place where they don't know anyone. What the hell happened?'

I tell him it was just a coincidence.

This morning I discovered that it's actually possible to be nervous while you're still asleep. I woke up filled with dread, my stomach churning even though for a moment I couldn't remember why. I must have been like that all night. No wonder I felt exhausted. And then the realisation came flooding in. Tonight's the night! With any luck this is as near as I'll ever get to waking in the condemned cell and hearing the key turn in the lock.

As I dressed I found myself thinking back many years to the first performance our newly formed theatre company ever gave outside the safety of our home enclave of Brighton. To the terror of some of the cast we had been booked by the Merseyside Arts Association to do a short tour of pubs in Liverpool, in an evangelical and potentially life-threatening initiative to take theatre to venues that had never experienced it before, and inflict the arts on people who didn't bloody well want them.

After a slow and depressing trip up the M6 – during which our most gifted performer, who was due to appear in women's clothing, tried to escape at Keele Services – we arrived in Halewood and started looking for the first night's venue. After ten minutes driving round bleak-looking tower blocks in a mood of escalating panic we pulled over at a bus shelter to ask directions. It wasn't until we stopped that we discovered the only person in the shelter was a Hell's Angel, a massive man in biker's leathers with terrifying tattoos all over his hands. A whimper of fear came from the back of the Transit as I rolled down the window.

' 'Scuse me, mate,' I said in a well-practised 'I'm not a woolly-back I'm a Scouser' accent. 'Do you know the way to a pub called the Heavy Bottle?'

'Er, yeah,' said the Angel. 'Do a U-ee back up the road, second left, first right, you're there.'

'Thanks, pal.'

'No problem.'

We were just about to pull away when he spoke again.

'I wouldn't go there if I was you though. It's really fuckin' rough.'

When we arrived the landlady told us that there'd been a murder in the public bar on Saturday night. 'Don't worry about that though, love. You're on in the lounge.'

And do you know what? They loved us. I've been trying to remind myself of that all day.

I had lunch with Phil in a hundred-year-old restaurant called Joe's Gay Nineties that recently acknowledged contemporary reality and changed its name to Joe's Nineties. While we ate he regaled me with more glamorous tales of life as a musician; like the time the out-of-control blues singer threw up on stage, a grotesque torrent of foaming red because she'd been drinking home-made wine that was still fermenting.

'I remember mopping it up with a towel on my foot while I was trying to persuade the promoter to book us again, and hoping he wouldn't notice.'

At the end of lunch he gave me a pep talk. 'Look 'em in the eye, never step backwards and turn up late like a punk rocker.'

*

I've already ignored his advice by turning up on time. As I came round the corner past Curry in a Hurry I heard the noise for the first time: a raucous Glaswegian rendition of 'You'll Never Walk Alone' that I knew wasn't coming from any of the vegetarian Indian restaurants. I'm standing in the doorway surveying the carnage, wondering whether to take the three steps down into the heart of the Fenian carnival or turn on my heel and flee. The FEB factor has gone right off the scale. I can't even see the picture of Cagney on account of all the Scotsmen draped in green, white and orange Irish flags jumping up and down and waving half-pints of whiskey in the air. They're dancing now, or at least some of them are, not kids but men in their thirties and forties, jigging on the spot and propping each other up with their heads like the poles of a drunken tepee. The TV is showing the video of the Celtic match they watched this afternoon, are watching again now, and will surely watch for a third time before the night is out, comas permitting.

Right. Here we go. I step down into the mêlée and try and push through the crowd, only without pushing. Directly in front of me is a huge guy with a little green-dyed shamrock of hair on the back of his otherwise shaven head. Big mistake. Skulls as lumpy as that should be kept hidden from view, especially when they have no neck. His head just seems to grow straight out of his chest and shoulders, like a massive tumour with a face painted on one side and a shamrock on the other. He'd have been better off sticking with a centre parting and split ends but who's going to be brave enough to tell him? Not me. 'Glasgow Celtic Supporters Club – TIMS On Tour', says a green lycra leisure top stretched tight as a lager and lime condom over the grotesque dome of his belly, giving him the alarming profile of a man who has recently swallowed Robbie Coltrane. He's only just arrived from Scotland, so it's possible that he has.

A frightening man who has just missed his mouth with his drink and has Irn Bru dripping from his chin seizes my arm. One side of his face is drooping in a way that suggests he may be suffering from Bell's palsy. I hadn't realised until now that it's named after the whisky.

I manage to worm my way undetected through the Caledonian frenzy to the far end of the room, where a tiny handful of bewildered New York literary types with no previous experience of our glorious sporting traditions are trapped between the stage and the mob without protection of water cannon. Surveying the scene with arms folded and a hint of a smile is Chris from Seanchai.

'So, Peter. Are you ready?'

I do my best to convey confident and nonchalant enthusiasm, but it comes out as a nod, a squeak and a wince, as if I've just heard that Brother Dermot is going to hit me with the leather strap again and I'm trying to pretend it won't hurt. Chris takes the mike and says a few words of welcome, but the decibel level doesn't drop. This is usually a bad sign. He ploughs on in his deep, Donegal-Brooklyn brogue, and eventually they start to notice he's there.

'I'd like to welcome all our visitors from Glasgow.'

There's a huge roar, as if the blade's dropped and another head's just fallen into the basket.

'So please, this is his first appearance in the United States, so I'm asking you to give a big New York City welcome to . . .'

Good. I've managed to get to the mike without collapsing. Okay. Loud and direct. Look 'em in the eye, don't go backwards, and don't leave any gaps for them to fill in.

'Thanks, Chris. It's good to be here.'

And then a voice calls out from in front and somewhere to my right. I think it might be the singer from the Celtic Supporters Club band who are on after my death.

My reading! After my reading!

'Hey, pal! You're fuckin' English!'

There are times when life seems hyper-vivid, super-real, and this is one of them. It's a special moment. Nerve ends are tingling. Never have I been more exhilaratingly aware of the fact that I am alive.

The only question is, for how long?

6

FAIRYTALE OF NEW YORK

One of the many great things about Billy Wilder's *Sunset Boulevard* is that it turns out the movie is being narrated by the corpse you see floating in the pool in the opening scene. Usually, of course, if a story is being told in the first person it's a cast-iron guarantee that the protagonist will survive whatever scrapes life puts in his way, because otherwise he wouldn't be there to tell the tale. I know it would be a great twist if I could say they stormed the stage and killed me, or just left me in a coma, but unfortunately it didn't happen.

In fact I owe those terrifying Glasgow drunks – there you are, I'm doing it again – an apology, because the fear was all of my own making. The deepest fears of death by audience are engendered by the most stereotypical and potentially extreme situations: kiddies' entertainer cornered by tiny evil-eyed *Lord of the Flies* psychopaths; southern ponce trying to elicit laughter from embittered redundant miners in northern working men's club; and, of course, that old favourite, FEB reading book to paralytic

Scottish football fans. But it's never as bad as you expect. After all, how could it be?

So the upshot is that, when you take into account the presence of a group of very jet-lagged men who'd had a huge amount to drink, had no interest in books and were not naturally predisposed to give an FEB the benefit of the doubt, it seems to have gone quite well. Shamrock Head just gave me a hug and said something I couldn't understand, so I smiled and nodded and said yes.

They've put the video of the match back on while the band set up their gear. I went over to Phil so he could congratulate me, but instead he laughed and said, 'You looked like you were going to die when you walked out there,' so I'm talking to Chris instead. In England you don't often get the chance to talk to an ex-policeman who's fronting a radical political hip-hop band.

'It ain't too usual here either. I did the job for eleven years and what a great blessing it was in life. But I don't like to talk about it too much, to use it as an angle for the music. I got too many friends who are still on it who would see it as transparent, you know what I'm saying? Hey, I left the cops because we got a record deal. What a fuckn' jerk-off I was.'

So how did he come to spend time in Ireland?

'A lot of kids my age got sent over in the seventies to get away from the heroin thing. I had a cousin with a small farm, a cow, a heifer and a TV that didn't start till six o'clock in the evening, and to be quite honest with ya I thought this was like absolute fuckn' purgatory. But now I can see it's the best thing that ever happened to me. On a Saturday night for something to do I used to cycle nine miles to learn from this other cousin, a blind flute player. He also played saxophone and if he walked into a hall and there was trad Irish playing in one room and jazz in the other he wouldn't know which way to go because he played both.'

He must be proud of the way Chris is mixing up the music.

'I don't think so, Peter.' He's starting to laugh. 'I think he'd be fuckn' disgusted to tell ya the truth. But I'll tell ya somethin' else. Ya know what the really cool thing is about playing the uillean pipes? Whatever shit you play they still sound like Ireland. You could be playing "Hava Nagila", you could mix it with soul beats, reggae, hip-hop beats, still sounds like Ireland. Even the fiddle can't do that.'

He says that the Troubles led to a big upsurge of interest in Irish politics. Now the war is over a lot of that energy is going into culture, but not the backward-looking, preserve-the-past-in-aspic sentimentality to which previous generations of Irish Americans adhered.

'It's like I was tellin' ya. Seanchai has an Irish element, but it couldn't come out of any city but New York. I wish people would do that in every city where Irish people are. Work with the local flavour and make somethin' new. I think our music is a lot more honest than standing on Fifth Avenue singing "The Mountains of Fuckn' Mourne". You know what I'm sayin'? Don't get me wrong. I love Ireland, but I couldn't get up on that stage and sing "The Old Bog Road". A lot of Americans used to feel that the more they read about Ireland, the more they travelled there, at some point in their life they would achieve the rank of being Irish. See, I don't aspire to that. I'm Irish American and I don't want to be them. I'm real happy being me.'

So in what sense is he an unrepentant Fenian bastard? Is it just a cheap shot to wind up the loyalists and the Brits?

'Absolutely not. It's the same thing as nigger, man. Fenian bastard, especially in Northern Ireland, was absolutely the equivalent of nigger. It was an insult I grew up with, same as a lot of these guys from Glasgow. Now I've got nephews, sixteen, seventeen years old, young Irish-American kids in Brooklyn and they say to their black friends "hey, nigger" and that's great. Once you put the word back in usage it takes all the sting out of it. I ain't saying we're Fenians, we bomb people and we're proud of it. I've been accused of that and that's completely missing the fuckn' point. My attitude is, yeah, I'm a fuckn' Fenian bastard, and I ain't apologising to no one about it.'

The band has started to play and the Celtic fans are going mental. I'd been expecting something with a bit of substance to it, maybe a Scottish equivalent of Seanchai's Brooklyn-Irish hip-hop, but this is just new words to tired old songs, football-terrace politics given the Barron Knights treatment. There's a marked lack of enthusiasm among some of the Irish-Americans in the crowd, so at least I know I'm not a minority of one. Now they're playing the old Lonnie Donegan song, 'My old man's a dustman', but they've changed the words to 'My old man's a provo'.

An American guy near me just turned to his girlfriend. 'This is sectarian garbage. I'm outta here.'

Chris says, 'You should see the banner they wanted to put up on the stage behind you. Irish tricolour, Pope in the middle, IRA slogans all over. That was too much, even for this place.'

The New York St Patrick's Day Parade has inspired many imitators all over the world, not least in Ireland itself, where until the 1970s the saint's day was celebrated by closing all the pubs so that a suitably pious and penitent mood might be observed. The only flicker of light at the end of the fun-free tunnel was provided by the Dublin Dog Show, traditionally held on the same day, which had a special dispensation to serve alcohol to the surprisingly large numbers of dog lovers who flocked to it each year.

The first New York parade was organised in 1766 by homesick expatriate Irishmen who were serving as soldiers in the British army, doing their bit to keep the colonies in their place. This delicious irony is not widely publicised these days, though the event's military origins are acknowledged by the presence of a unit of uniformed soldiers, the Fighting Sixty-Niners, at the head of the parade. In the eighteenth and early nineteenth centuries it was a simple, ad hoc affair, but in the 1850s the Ancient Order of Hibernians took control and an organising Grand Marshal was appointed. Floats were forbidden, to ensure a solemn and patriotic tone as the Irish marched through the poshest parts of town in a bid to establish their credentials as solid US citizens. Since then it's grown to include a plethora of Emerald, Irish language and Irish county societies, though the Ancient Ones have retained control of who gets to march and who doesn't.

Most notoriously, they have enforced a rigid No Feckin' Pooftas policy that ensures acrimonious protests every year from Irish gay groups angry at their exclusion. My research suggests that they are not alone in their belief that the Hibernians represent the past rather than the present, and certainly not the future, of Irish America.

In a radical departure from my usual methods of working, I have been conducting this research not through conversations with semi-coherent dipsos in public houses, but in the reference section of the New York Public Library. Writing is a solitary occupation, so the opportunity to work in a room full of other people qualifies as an exciting social event, and may also help defer the onset of madness. Being among other human beings acts as a civilising influence, providing a concrete reason for getting washed and dressed in the morning, and discouraging dubious literary habits like talking aloud to yourself, and eating tinned soup. If you tried either of those activities in here Security would have you out on your ear before you could say 'Shh! There are people trying to work!' Attendants in paramilitary uniform patrol the reading rooms on constant red alert for any sign of deviant behaviour. New York has made a conscious decision to distance itself from the liberal northern European tradition of public libraries being places where tramps and mad people can pop in for a sleep and a warm.

It feels good to take the handsome staircase up to the magnificent first-floor mezzanine, stroll through the room full of unstable-looking people staring at computer screens, and emerge into the gilt-embossed splendour of the reading room. Eight enormous chandeliers hang from a vaulted ceiling decorated with pink and grey clouds on a radiant blue sky. High arched windows look out on to the sides of gleaming skyscrapers. Each beautifully inlaid beechwood table has four pewter and brass reading lamps and eighteen chairs. I'm in my favourite seat today, number 703, to which I'm becoming so attached that if I ever come in and find it occupied I may have to feign Tourette's syndrome or pretend to be a Mormon missionary until the intruder sees sense and goes and sits somewhere else.

The level of concentration in here is fierce, and also highly contagious. I just looked up and realised that the elegant black woman who was sitting in 705 when I was counting the reading lamps has left and been replaced without my noticing by a cadaverous man with cruel lips who is probably here to read about embalming fluid. Though we've never met, he and I are now part of the same community. We understand the pleasures of collective silence and contemplation in a hallowed setting. If we ever bump into each other at the vegetable counter in Safeway, or at an S & M party in a rubber-walled dungeon, we'll be able to catch each other's eye and say, 'Don't I know you from the library?' The solitary life has a lot to commend it, but sometimes it's good to belong.

It's impossible to read about St Patrick's Day without delving into the wider history of the Irish in America, a massive subject of which I have an even more fragmentary knowledge than previously suspected. As the days go by I find myself gripped by accounts of the impoverished Irish who arrived from Cobh and other ports in the wake of the famine, settling in the overcrowded tenements of New York, Boston, Chicago and San Francisco. Drinking and fighting were not unknown. Many clawed their way up from society's basement through uncompromising careers in politics and law enforcement, professions to which they and their ancestors had traditionally been denied access back home. Others tried different routes: Billy the Kid, aka William Bonney but real name William McCarthy, was the son of Irish parents. Senator Joe McCarthy was another one who famously let the family down. I'm amazed to discover that 20,000 Irish died digging the New Basin Canal in New Orleans in the 1830s; and that a similar number of Irish once lived in a shanty town in what is now Central Park, where they raised goats and pigs. There are learned articles on how Irish music crossed the Atlantic and became country and western and bluegrass, and a passionately argued but borderline loony piece claiming that, when it comes down to it, all music is Celtic.

Rather more plausible is the assertion that Irish monks may have visited America as early as the sixth or seventh century, a theory supported by a Celtic inscription carved in symbols ten feet high on a cliff face in West Virginia. At the winter solstice – or Christmas, as the early Christians named it, in the first recorded instance of corporate rebranding – the rising sun illuminates the inscription exactly as it does the burial mound of New Grange in County Meath. So perhaps the boys from County Meath were the first Europeans to cross the Atlantic and get their hands on a much coveted green card. Maybe that's why it's called a green card in the first place.

I enjoy dropping in for a couple of hours, browsing from subject to subject and noticing how certain stories and names keep recurring. Prominent among them are those of Thomas Francis Meagher and John Mitchel, two of the Young Irelanders who were transported, along with the politician Smith O'Brien, to Van Diemen's Land in 1848 for inciting rebellion against the crown. This is the same John Mitchel who was brought to my attention by the Bishop Basher that afternoon in Cobh. After extraordinary adventures in the wilderness of Tasmania, Mitchel was eventually released, while Meagher escaped. As if to prove that Irish politics is never as straightforward as you think it's going to be, they both made their way to America, where they ended up on opposite sides in the Civil War.

The more you read about Irish America, the more you realise it's a heavily loaded term. Forty-four million Americans can claim some kind of Irish ancestry. Those who identify themselves as Irish Americans are overwhelmingly from the green, nationalist, Catholic tradition, yet at least half, possibly more, of the Irish who emigrated to the USA and Canada were Protestant. Many came over before the great migration of the famine. A greater religious and political affinity with the English meant they were quickly assimilated into the property-owning classes of the colony, and consequently were less inclined to maintain, romanticise or sing about their allegiances to the old country. Theirs is a tradition that will be absent from Saturday's parade, and you can't help feeling it's a big omission.

The library has rest rooms and phone booths, but no bar. This is a major historical oversight in libraries the world over. Who invented libraries anyway? The Greeks? The Romans? Irish monks? Whoever it was, I bet they had bars in them. It stands to reason. What could be more likely to illuminate your manuscript than a couple of drinks at the end of the day? Or in this instance, the middle. I decide to head outside for a breath of air. Better not leave my bag behind, though. Wouldn't want the Argentinian and Bolivian chapters that follow on from Tangier to go missing.

Launderettes. They should have bars as well.

The library's just a short walk from Grand Central Station, which is one of my favourite places in the city. I like to use it as a park or market or piazza, somewhere to walk and eat and watch the world go by. Once in a while I go down the ramp to the Oyster Bar and have half a dozen and a Guinness, but today I settle for a sandwich in the big food court underneath the tracks, then take a walk through the central concourse. This is one of the truly great public spaces, now restored to its full glory, with hazy light diffusing from high distant windows illuminating the stars and planets on the ceiling and the two palatial staircases at either end. It takes a moment or two for the true masterstroke to sink in; and then you see it. Or rather, you don't. There are no ads or retail outlets. They have all been put somewhere else. This is a Nike- and Burger King-free zone in the heart of the global advertising industry, where no brand or logo has been able to buy the right to clash with the surroundings. The huge detail-perfect period setting looks as if it were built yesterday. The only clues that it's the twenty-first century are the tiny individuals in modern clothes who cross and recross at pleasing intervals, though even they look like extras directed by Alfred Hitchcock. And it's so gleamingly clean that you could eat your dinner off the floor, unlike most stations, where it looks as though someone already has.

Twenty minutes later I'm back in my new hotel room.

The management of hotels don't get anxious if you aren't home till breakfast time, nor do they have innocent young children who may be scarred for life by their father's hangovers and inappropriate late-night behaviour, so for the sake of our continuing friendship I've moved out of Phil's apartment and into an hotel for a few days. It's a nice Italian-style place with marble floors, just a few blocks from where the parade begins. They've upgraded me to a mini-suite, which is a first, and can only be a case of mistaken identity. It won't be long before they cotton on and kick me out into a boxroom near the food-slop skips. There's a phone in the lavatory, and a TV next to the sinks so you can view while you shave. There's also a living room with a sofa, an enormous shrub and a small library compiled with the business traveller in mind, featuring books with titles such as *Retire Early with Rental Properties* and *How to Make a Fortune from Discounted Mortgages*. I search the shelves for copies of *Get Rich Quick by Embezzling Widows* or *Make Big Cash by Selling Orphans*, but they don't have them. I'll mention it when I fill in the questionnaire.

I finish unpacking, then put all the shower caps, sewing kits and shoe mitts in my empty case so they'll have to leave some more tomorrow. If everything else falls apart then one day I'll open a market stall. It won't just sell hotel tat either. There'll be aeroplane socks and blindfolds as well. And mint imperials from Chinese restaurants. While I'm at it I decide I may as well get my money's worth out of the room and stay in on my own for a couple of hours. Much as I've come to love the library, I do enjoy being free to talk out loud to myself. I think the effects of solitude probably get worse as time goes by. Next time you hear someone has published their seventeenth or eighteenth novel, imagine how barmy they must be.

I'd planned to spend the evening shaving and watching TV, but I soon get fed up with the adverts, and the cuts, so I go round to see Phil instead. The kids have just gone to bed, but the doorbell wakes them up. We have a drop of Jameson's, then go out to a Tex-Mex bar to see a guitar player who used to be in Commander Cody and his Lost Planet Airmen, because that's the kind of thing musos like to do. It's a sedate, polite crowd, though someone does try to sell us crack in the gents' after the show. It's late when we head home. I hope they haven't moved the art again. Phil could wander those corridors for days before the guy in the top hat finds him.

Like all right-minded people, I am an instinctive ideological opponent of globalisation. I had planned to support the cause by going to the last G12 summit, smashing up a few Mercedes and fire-bombing McDonald's, but the Sheraton and the Hilton were fully booked, so there wasn't anywhere to stay. But I can say, hand on heart, that I've never been inside a Starbucks.

Until now.

After one of those strange American breakfasts where you get sweet pancakes, meat and fried potatoes all on the same plate, I head down to Battery Park to get the ferry to Ellis Island. The next boat isn't for half an hour, and it's several degrees colder on the waterfront than it is in midtown. I think the buildings, as well as shielding you from the wind, must release delayed warmth, like giant storage heaters. Remember them? A neat metal casing as if they were proper heaters, but when you took them apart there was nothing in there but bricks. They kept the place hot all day while you were out at work, but then it was freezing in the evening when you got home, so you had to go out to the pub and spend the money you were saving by not having central heating. There's nowhere else to wait in the warm for the ferry, so I've abandoned what's left of my principles and come into Starbucks.

I can see the Statue of Liberty from here, a larger-than-life symbol of the spirit of free enterprise represented by the famous coffee I'm drinking. I can't see what all the fuss is about. It's just ordinary black coffee, served for some reason in a massive cardboard cup you could grow a cheeseplant in.

I'm just wondering why drinks in America are now pedantically known as beverages, which sounds like something a policeman giving evidence from his notebook would have consumed while proceeding in a northerly direction, when I notice a strange mini-drama being acted out in front of me. A woman in a tartan skirt 'n' coat ensemble that makes her resemble a tour guide or air-hostess, or Princess Anne opening a community centre – she's got quite a beak on her as well, which makes her look even more like the princess – comes in and sits at the table behind me, all the while speaking into her mobile phone. Then she gets up and starts peering out through the tall plate-glass window, walking along it past the doorway to the far corner of the café, still gazing through the glass as if at some mirage or vision.

Meanwhile a man, also on a mobile, has approached the café from outside. He peers in through the glass, yattering away, but sees only me. Then he walks to his left along the outside of the window as Princess Anne walks in the opposite direction along the inside. They pass at the doorway, the only place on the whole wall where they can't see each other, and end up once again in opposite corners. I'm just about to hold up a placard saying, YOU REPRESENT NON-COMMUNICATION IN A WORLD OF NEVER-ENDING TALK, but before I can get the felt-tip and the flashcard out of my coat pocket a waitress comes out from behind the counter, taps the princess on the shoulder and points to the man. The customers stop laughing and go back to their cardboard buckets of cappuccino, the guy comes inside, and the two of them purchase beverages and assume a sedentary position at a seating unit adjacent to my vicinity.

'Great awards ceremony last night,' he says.

'Yeah.' She laughs in what she believes to be a coquettish manner. 'Yeah, I was pleased to win again. Hey, you know David? The head of . . .'

I can't hear what David is head of because the milk frothing machine has just burst into life.

'. . . back at the hotel and he came on to me, like, really strong? Again? But you know, he's married and though it's flattering and very, well, like, tempting, hey! Do I really need those kinds of complications? I don't think so. But it was very gratifying to win. Again.'

My ferry's due and I get up to leave realising that I will never know which award she won last night. Again. Maybe if she wins next year she'll think what the hell, and give poor old David the kind of seeing-to that'll bring tears to his eyes many years from now, possibly when his kids are making speeches at his diamond wedding.

The ferry goes to the Statue of Liberty first, which I don't intend climbing, then on to Ellis Island. There's a grumpy fifty-something guy who never intended to end up in a job like this serving more beverages, snacks and souvenirs behind a counter in the centre of the boat. He seems pleased to be out of coffee, and can only offer tea or hot chocolate. The young couple on the wooden bench seat next to me are clutching their cardboard cups in heavily gloved hands, sipping tea through the little gob-gap in the plastic lid. The teabag's label and string dangle down the side of the cup like a tampon. They just don't get this tea thing, do they?

Two thirteen-year-old boys go up to Grumpy's Souvenir Emporium and say they want to buy Statue of Liberty lighters, big chunky things with a torch of freedom that bursts into flame and ignites your ciggie. He takes one down from the shelf, removes it from its presentation packaging and presses the lighter to test it. Once. Twice. Three times. No flame. With an air of profound resignation he takes a second one down and repeats the action. The same thing happens. He sighs, in silence, but with his whole body. You'd think the boys would realise this isn't a top-of-the-range gift item, but their youthful enthusiasm remains undeterred. The third lighter works at the second attempt. He puts it back in the box then into a brown paper bag, like a fifth of bourbon. The boys leave happy and he turns to put the two duds back on the shelf.

'Useless pieces a shit.'

It's always nice to see someone happy at his work.

The Registry Room on Ellis Island is a huge hall with a vaulted herringbone brick ceiling, three great chandeliers and massive arched windows that frame the Statue of Liberty on one side and the Empire State Building on the other. From its opening in 1892 every immigrant arriving in New York was processed through this room, up to 5,000 each day during the first quarter of the twentieth century. This was journey's end for all those who boarded in Cobh, and there's a statue of the first person to pass through here, Annie Moore of Cork, which is replicated on the waterfront in Cobh. But though America features large in the Irish story, Ellis Island reminds us that Ireland was only one of dozens of strands in America's narrative. There are photographs of people from Armenia, Hungary, Jamaica, Hiroshima,

Scotland, Belorussia, Greece, Assyria, Rumania and Lapland. A pair of women from Guadeloupe arriving in 1911 in spectacular frocks fix the camera with worldly-wise eyes staring out from beneath remarkable hats. The pictures help you see what happened here not as a process of mass immigration, which is the story the statistics tell, but as something experienced by individuals. It's so recent, yet at the same time so remote: they came, they did it, they've gone. A couple of hours wandering around leaves you aware of what little time we have in life to make an impression.

The buildings were abandoned in 1954 – around the same time that Cobh went into decline – and fell into disrepair until restoration began in 1982. Many damaged and decrepit artefacts are displayed in the condition in which they were found; a broken piano, a shattered children's picture, mangled crutches, a weighing machine, bedpans, scales, bed racks and hospital cots sit covered in dust, their paint peeling, eloquently evoking the fractured lives they once serviced. In a country that's never been backward about coming forward, there's a restraint about the way this story is told that is unexpectedly affecting.

A section devoted to popular song and entertainment gives an insight into the social niceties and racial attitudes of the era. There's sheet music of a Chinese person singing 'I No Washee Today' and another bearing the title 'I'm Going Back to the Land of Spaghetti'. 'Yonkel the Cowboy Jew' was a big hit for 'that Yiddish loafer Glen Burt', pre-dating by almost a century the satire of Kinky Friedman and the Texas Jew Boys and songs like 'They Ain't Making Jews like Jesus Any More'. 'Neighbourhood ethnic theatres were a cultural refuge for new arrivals,' explains the caption. 'On stage the players spoke a familiar language . . . [they] freely lampooned the foibles of ethnic Americans using ludicrous stereotypes that today would be considered insensitive and demeaning.' There's a song called 'Ireland Must be Heaven for my Mother Came from There' by my long-lost cousin Joe

McCarthy, but pride of place must go to 'Since Arrah Wanna Married Barney Carney', a moving tale of cross-cultural fertilisation. On the cover a Native American woman, as she would be now, or Red Indian squaw, as she'd have been then, is dressed as a bride for her marriage to a parody Paddy with a green top hat and a shamrock on his lapel. An Indian chief straight out of the comic books is bowing in front of them in the 'we are not worthy' position. With Celtic fusion music now sweeping the globe the time could be ripe for a revival of this number. Imagine the video.

Tucked away around a corner is a framed cartoon of a brawl featuring assorted Bolsheviks, Commies, Paddies and Micks. THE U.S. HOTEL BADLY NEEDS A BOUNCER, reads the text. NO BEGGARS OR LOAFERS ALLOWED IN THIS ESTABLISHMENT. NO BOMB THROWING. NO INCENDIARY TALK. NO COMMUNISM. NO FENIANISM. Another shows a man saying, 'Well, I came to America because I heard the streets were paved with gold. When I got here I found out three things. First the streets weren't paved with gold. Second they weren't paved at all. And third I was expected to pave them.'

The afternoon light is fading as I head back to the boat. I sit next to a young architect from Queens who's been working on Ellis Island. Without my asking, he tells me he's Jewish.

'But not fanatic, okay? When I'm in New York, I'm Jewish. Abroad, I'm American. Makes life easier.'

He tells me about a Jewish sect from central Europe who have managed to survive intact for over 2,500 years.

'And you know how? Because most of them live in Queens. So what's the big deal with Israel? It's just a patch of dirt. Give it up! Go to Queens. Everybody gets along.'

Paddy's Day breakfast is a big disappointment. I'd been hoping the hotel might make an effort – after all, if you dyed bacon green and put it next to a fried egg it would look like the Irish flag – but there isn't even an emerald cappuccino. You can't help feeling it's a missed opportunity.

Things buck up when I hit the street and the first thing I see is a nun setting her car alarm. This seems a fair indication that a colourful day lies in store. I know we live in a post-feminist society, but I can't quite shake off the feeling that there's something . . . well, unnatural about nuns driving cars. The current Pope is widely regarded as the most reactionary for a long time. He won't allow contraception or women priests, so you'd have thought you could rely on him to clamp down on heretical frivolities like nuns driving, and priests playing guitars. I blame the sixties. One minute everything was in reassuringly incomprehensible Latin and nuns had to trudge round the place frowning and dressed like Albanian widows, then along comes the Vatican Council and Swinging London and the next thing you know the nuns are all in light grey Mary Quant twinsets, grinning like Lulu, driving Minis to folk masses fronted by priests who think they're Crosby, Stills & Nash. And there was the Singing Nun. You don't hear much about her these days. Perhaps they found her floating face down in Keith Richards's swimming pool one morning. The Vatican is a very secretive organisation, so we may never know.

The nun walks up the street ahead of me with the confident stride of a pickpocket from the Bronx who has dressed this way before and is at ease with his femininity. She turns right underneath an advertising hoarding for Smiling Pumpkin Ale and disappears from view. I'm soon caught up in a tide of people heading east towards the junction with Fifth Avenue, where the parade is due to begin. I pass a man in an overcoat buttoned all the way to the top who says, 'Only the Lord Jesus has the power to transform your life,' and another in a black puffa jacket who says, 'Blow weed, Coke E,' which I think might be a quote from the storm scene in *King Lear*.

By the time I'm a block from Fifth the crowds are thick, milling back and forth in the search for the best vantage point, so I pause to consider my strategy. Next to me on the sidewalk a family of two stout parents and four big-boned children have paused at a vendor's stall while Mom buys an enormous submarine roll filled with onions, ketchup and flame-grilled roadkill. 'Aw, Mom,' says her daughter plaintively, 'don't pig out now! We're gonna be pigging out on the pasta buffet for lunch. You really gotta want it!' The family are all wearing white plastic bowler hats covered in Bud Light logos and shamrocks, which might at first glance look silly, but when you think about it are just like miniature versions of how St Patrick's coracle might have looked if he'd been sponsored by Budweiser to sail from Wales to Ireland, so in a way they're very authentic.

Here's my strategy.

I'm going to gatecrash the parade.

I'm not sure how, but it's got to be done. I haven't come all this way to stand and watch it go by. I want to stride up Fifth Avenue surrounded by bishops, drum majorettes and paramilitary fund-raisers while the crowds cheer. I want to know what it feels like. I want to understand what it's for. The problem is you have to be affiliated to an accredited organisation and, like the gays, the lesbians and Ian Paisley, I'm not. I've been trying my best to get affiliated, but it seems I just haven't got what it takes. I left a message at the County Cork Association explaining that Cork was the county of my mother and my ancestors, in the hope they'd offer to let me carry the banner, but no one even called back. I spoke to an Irish-American academic whose number I'd been given in Dublin and asked if he could help arrange it, but he said that, 'the whole day is a total frigging nightmare,' and that he 'wouldn't be found within a hundred frigging miles of the city. And Boston's even worse.' Chris said he could fix for me to march with the retired homicide detectives, which sounded cool, but his buddy who was going to square it for me fell sick and wasn't going to be there. 'Just turn up, say who you are and walk with them,' said Chris. 'There won't be a problem.' I kidded myself I might do that, but, frankly, I'm too intimidated.

In a tactic which may have been specifically designed to discourage gatecrashers, the Ancient Order of Hibernians have refused to publish the Order of Parade, so I've no way of knowing whether Cork will be up at the front or way back down the line. I'm wedged behind a crash barrier on the corner of Fifth, without a plan, when the twenty-deep throng in front of me start cheering and whistling, and over their heads and shoulders and Bud Light coracle hats I catch a glimpse of camouflage fatigues and bayonet tips going by: the Fighting Sixty-Niners. The parade has started, but I'm still dithering about with no notion of how I'm going to join it.

I head off into the side streets to try and escape the crowds, but they're all packed with bands and marchers lined up and ready to filter onto Fifth Avenue when their turn comes. The street I'm in has two banners: at the far end is County Dublin, and in front of them is County Mayo, assembled along the block at which I've entered the street. There's no sign of Cork. There must be dozens of streets like this. They could be anywhere. I don't know what to do. I'm going to miss it! I've wasted my chance. I've failed. I feel guilty. Forgive me, Father, for I have . . .

'You need some help there?'

A dour-looking man with spectacular ear and nostril hair has spotted me lurking in a suspicious manner. He's wearing a steward's armband, so he's probably authorised to shoot me if he finds out I'm not accredited. Shall I lie and tell him that I am? Or will that make it worse? What if I tell him I'm supposed to be meeting the cops? I know. I'll just smile and walk away. Oh, no. He's smiling back, and now he's walking with me!

'You looking for anyone in particular?'

'Cops.'

'Huh?'

'Cork! County Cork. Do you know where I'd find them?'

'Sorry. Not a chance in hell. Could be anywhere. This here is Mayo.'

He pauses for a moment, and I'm about to make my escape into the crowd when he says, 'You wanna walk with us?'

Ten minutes later I'm turning the corner onto Fifth Avenue, walking right up the middle of the street with half a dozen people either side of me, past the dignitaries' grandstand outside St Patrick's Cathedral, head held high, smiling and waving back to the politicians, the cardinals, the Kennedys, Michael Flatley's parents, Seamus Heaney's second cousins, whoever the hell it is sitting up there applauding us. Then the cathedral is behind us and we're passing the corner where a few minutes ago I was twenty people deep without a plan. All I could see then was the back of their heads, and now they're smiling and waving like I was a long-lost relative. This is fun. Doctors should prescribe it for patients who are lacking in self-esteem. You feel like you're the centre of attention, like you've won a football trophy or a minor war at the very least, plus you get to see Fifth Avenue in a way you've never seen it before, from the middle of the street, with no traffic. You can look up at the gorgeously ornate façades of the buildings, take in all the faux gargoyles and deco twiddly bits without being in fear of your life. Gucci, Elizabeth Arden, the names keep on coming, and now we're passing Gap and a woman walking next to me asks did I see the report about the guy with no legs who robbed the store in his wheelchair and stole ten pairs of trousers? She seems serious, but I can't be sure. It just goes to show it's true what they say. The British really don't understand the American sense of irony.

We pass a roadside protest against the exclusion of gay groups. There's some barracking, and a guy is holding a placard saying ANOTHER QUEER FROM IRELAND, which would make a cracking album title. And then everything comes to a halt and there's time to look around and take in the scene. I can see the banners for Dublin, and beyond them Donegal, and a great line of people stretching out into infinity, or at least twelve blocks. There's a marching band ahead and a pipe band somewhere behind, and a lot of austere-looking older men, walking up and down in sashes and top hats and taking it all very seriously indeed. The top hats must be the republican haberdashery industry's response to the much vilified bowlers of the Orangemen, which shows that each side in this futile argument can make themselves look as ridiculous as the other if they really put their minds to it. 'Hey, pal! You look a complete eejit in that stupid hat and sash! And you know why? Because they're slightly different from my hat and sash, you Fenian/Orange bastard.'

It's a mild day and as we begin walking again coats are unbuttoned, scarves loosened and there's a convivial buzz of conversation among the marchers. There are no actual Irish Irish people near me. Everyone is second, third or fourth generation, proud of where their family comes from, though enquiries suggest that most of them have been there maybe once or twice, or never, in their lives. And everyone is sober, which isn't quite what I'd expected. The city has banned street drinking at all parades, and the mood could almost be described as dignified. There's a woman who looks like she's storing nuts in her cheeks and has decorated them with a couple of glittery shamrocks, but for the most part there's less shillelagh-and-leprechaun Blarneyfication than I'd expected. As we get further uptown and the spectators begin to thin out it starts to feel like a local community event, with people calling out to their friends. 'We meet people on the same block every year,' says a lady next to me. 'There'll be some McCarthys at 98th Street. I'll introduce you.' And she does.

We reach the Metropolitan Museum of Art on Central Park South, and suddenly it's all over, less than an hour and a half after we started. I'm able to take some time to stand and watch the rest of the parade coming up behind me. There are majorettes in green, white and orange capes who can throw their batons so high they can turn a double cartwheel and still catch them on the way down. NORAID march past, a group of men, and a few women, who have perfected the art of looking so completely deadpan and normal that it's sinister. Their impact is diminished, however, by a thickset guy with a bushy moustache dyed green for the occasion, which suggests that he may not be quite the political heavyweight he imagines.

ENGLAND GET OUT OF IRELAND, says the County Derry Association banner, which is being carried by some polite-looking ladies in sensible coats, and has all the more impact for it. Close behind come the self-proclaimed Irish Freedom Committee in their uniform of sunglasses, dark berets, black trousers, black leather gloves and chunky cream sweaters with a cable pattern down the front. Andy Williams wore one on the cover of his Christmas album. The bizarre combination of paramilitary chic and yer granny's traditional hand-knit suggests bedroom revolutionaries whose mothers tolerate the black gear, but won't let them out of the house unless they're dressed up smart in that nice jumper they got for Christmas.

I walk away in search of lunch and a beer, thinking that it's all a lot of fun, but perhaps it's time for New York's big day to take on a more pluralistic vision reflecting the inclusive Ireland that a lot of people are working to create. You know what, though? There'll always be room for a nice cable-knit sweater. They look smart *and* casual at the same time and, whether you're a freedom fighter or just going for tea with Daniel O'Donnell, that's not a quality to be sneezed at.

There's a bunch of cops hanging round near the subway station as I make my way back downtown. The New York Police Department has traditionally been an Irish-dominated profession, but the gardai never looked like these guys. Their body language is spectacular. They have a way of walkin' – of loungin', of hangin', of chewin' and leanin' on the wall – that makes it look as if they're acting cool for the cameras, even when there's no camera there. Each of these guys thinks he's in his own TV series. They certainly know how to get the most dramatic impact out of a situation as straightforward as wearing a uniform. Americans are said to be so media savvy that you can stick a microphone in front of anyone and get an instant soundbite. Well, I reckon you could stick a camera on any group of NY cops and get a series. Mind you, they are just a touch on the roly-poly side. Okay, I know they're not all like that – there are the really super-fit ones you see patrolling Central Park on mountain bikes – but these guys, no mistake about it, have spent plenty of time in the squad car eating pizza and doughnuts while they wait for the bad guys to show up. It's not necessarily a disadvantage. Fitness is an overrated virtue in a law enforcement officer. In their way these guys are much more menacing. They're putting out a subliminal message: 'Don't run away. We can't chase you, so we'll have to shoot.'

I'm on a crowded platform waiting for the train when a mournful-looking Chinese man comes walking down the stairs wearing a long grey overcoat and carrying a large case. He chooses a busy spot near the foot of the stairwell, then carefully opens the case and takes out one of those curious Chinese string instruments that may be distantly related to the cello. He stands for a moment poised with bow in hand, then launches into a tender, heartfelt and authentically oriental rendition of 'Danny Boy'. Heads turn all along the platform. It's the best moment of the day.

I get off the train at 42nd Street but there's a hold-up as I try and walk across town to my hotel. Fifth Avenue is closed because the parade hasn't finished yet. It started at eleven o'clock, and now it's four thirty, which means – hold on while I count – it's taken five and a half hours to pass any one point, and it shows no sign of stopping. The hard nuts in the Aran sweaters will have been back in their bedrooms for a couple of hours now, doing their homework and posing in front of the mirror with their berets and leather gloves on. Any way you look at it, this is a long parade.

The cops eventually give in to the heckling and hold things up for thirty seconds to let us cross the street, then off it goes again. My last glimpse is of a band of African-American college kids dancing on the spot and waving their trumpets and saxophones in the air as they play the old Drifters' hit 'On Broadway'. I don't think the Drifters were Irish, but I suppose you can never be sure. One of them was called Ben O'King, wasn't he?

In the evening Phil comes round with a six-pack of Sam Adams beer from the grocery store so that we don't have to use the hotel mini-bar. We're running a bit late, but we stay and drink them because they're saving us so much money. Outside it's raining hard and there are no cabs, so we take the subway down to Greenwich Village.

In the 1980s a London Irish band called the Pogues reinvented Irish music, playing the traditional songs with punk frenzy and writing a clutch of classic new ones into the bargain. Their singer and songwriter Shane MacGowan was eventually sacked, or left the band, according to whom you believe, amid tales of alcoholic excess and worse. He's due to play in a Greenwich Village dance-hall tonight, presuming he's arrived in the country. He had a warm-up gig in New Jersey last night but didn't show, according to someone on the march today, so his new band, the Popes, played without him.

MacGowan seems determined to live out the role of terminally alcoholic Irish visionary in which he has cast himself, so there is always the added frisson these days that if he does turn up it may be the final show. A friend of mine saw him once in the latter days of the Pogues and thought it might be happening when he started bringing up green bile on stage – the full works, down the nose, catch it in a pint glass, the lot – but Nottingham is not a romantic place to croak, and it would have done little to enhance the myth. But to die live, as it were, on stage in Greenwich Village on St Patrick's Day, singing of drink, oppression and exile – now that really would be a fairytale of New York. As we splash through the streets south of Washington Square in search of the venue, I picture Shane in his dressing-room drinking pints of Martini while a priest gives him the last rites and the sound engineer gets ready to tape the show – *Live Death, The Album*.

Perhaps out of gratitude for not being thrown through the window of Rocky Sullivan's, Shane has invited Chris and Rachel to play and sing on some of the numbers tonight. They've promised to put us on the guest list, but as we walk up the steps I don't hold out much hope, rock-and-roll paperwork being a notoriously unreliable branch of bureaucracy. The safest bet used to be to try and read the list upside down and say you were someone who hadn't been crossed off yet. They must have wised up to that, because a woman in black lipstick looks in a drawer behind a screen, then smiles and gives us two plastic laminates. 'VIP', they say. 'Very Important Paddy.'

We pass through a couple of club rooms with cocktail bars and pool tables, head up a broad sweeping staircase, and go through an ornate double doorway. As we walk into the hall a huge roar fills the place. I look up and see people hanging over the packed balcony, waving to MacGowan and the band who have just walked on stage. He's clutching a glass and wearing a traditional black Irish drinking suit, which is like an ordinary black suit, only with more stains. As the barman pours black pints into plastic beakers I read the health warnings plastered on the wall. 'Smoking permitted – but breathing second-hand smoke can be harmful', says one, though it's done little to dampen the increasingly wild mood of the crowd, many of whom look as if they may have ingested second-hand smoke before. Next to it is a poster full of small print under the banner headline: PROCEDURE TO SAVE A CHOKING VICTIM. They probably stick these up wherever Shane plays these days, just to be on the safe side.

The sprung dance floor is bouncing up and down under our feet as he launches into 'The Irish Rover'. Plastic glasses arc through the air, the cascading beer dramatically lit by the stage lights as it soaks the audience in what is almost certainly a witty post-modern reference to St Patrick baptising the Irish. Teenagers, ageing punks and superannuated Greenwich Village hippies are careering into each other with wild abandon as the band crank through their repertoire of high-octane laments. Next to us a group of college boys have gone for a hokey-cokey formation.

'Awesome, dood!' shouts one.

'Excellent!' replies his friend.

'Say, man, this the dood used to be in U2? Far out!'

'Excellent!'

'Awesome!'

These guys make Beavis and Butthead sound like Germaine Greer and Tom Paulin. I remember the Ted Nugent conversation in Rocky's and decide to move before they throw up on my leg.

Chris comes on to play the pipes, but it's hard to hear him because all the other instruments are turned up to eleven. I spot one of the college kids apologising to a Neil Young lookalike for barfing on his back, and then Rachel is on stage, singing the achingly beautiful 'Fairytale of New York'. MacGowan is waltzing her round the stage and grinning, and the show's a triumph.

The rain has stopped so we decide to walk uptown to Rocky's. On the way we pop into a couple of bars, and pop straight back out. The day's festivities have taken their toll and the broken glasses, glazed eyes and incoherent shouting suggest terrible post-festive trauma, as if the place has been turned over by marines on shore leave.

Up at Rocky's a man is lying unconscious on a bench outside the toilet, like a carved knight on a medieval tomb, only poorlier-looking. The place is littered with crushed plastic glasses, and the floorboards are stickier than student union lino on a Pour the Free Baileys Over Your Head promotional night. All my life I've been a fan of seedy, chaotic bars, but this is so extreme that drinking Aqua Libra in an art gallery tea shop is beginning to look like an attractive proposition.

I get trapped in a corner for a while by a wild-eyed ginger man who wants to tell me that everyone who failed the eleven-plus in Derry was left-handed, so he does. I'm talking to the third homicide detective of the week, wondering why I've never met one in England, when Phil suggests we call it a night. It's almost three. 'Stay awhile,' says the cop. 'MacGowan will be here soon.'

'Tell him I'll see him another time.'

'I'll tell him,' says the cop, 'but I don't know he'll understand. Hey, take it easy out there.'

As we leave Rocky's a black Range Rover driven by two women with big hair pulls over to the kerb. 'Where are you going? You getting in?' shouts one of the women. We say no, because we are married, and because men with daggers will be lying on the floor in the back. A yellow cab driven by a jovial Russian picks us up. 'In Moscow everybody is drunk like St Patrick's Day all the time.'

In the silence of my room I notice I am suffering from rock-'n'-roll tinnitus, so I brush my teeth and turn on the miniature TV next to the bathroom sink to drown it out. 'Do you have an overactive bladder?' demands a nosy man on the screen, for no apparent reason.

I don't know, mate. I'll let you know in the morning.

As I fall asleep I realise I haven't seen a single pint of green beer all day.

I'm feeling a bit rough when I surface at eleven, on account of all the second-hand smoke. I'm too late for the hotel's complimentary pastry served with choice of beverage, so I'm sitting in a Greek diner reading *Be Cool* by Elmore Leonard and eating cinnamon toast.

There are padded counter stools, a few booths and a guy who shouts, 'You gaddit!' every time someone orders something. The door opens and an old guy in a corduroy hunting cap, checked shirt, stained tie and threadbare overcoat comes in and sits at the next but one counter stool. Yougaddit pours him a mug of black coffee and takes his breakfast order.

'Chicken salad on rye, lettuce and mayo, no tomayto.'

'You gaddit!'

Then to the person on the other side of the serving hatch, 'Chick-inn salad on whiskey, no tomayto!'

The Hunter looks across at me. 'That an Elmore Leonard thriller? Y'know he wrote some pretty good westerns in his time. That movie. *Apache*, was it? Burt Lancaster.'

He takes a sip of coffee.

'Gee, but books are expensive these days. Took a paperback to my brother in hospital last week. Eleven dollars. In the Depression they were twenty-five cents. Idea was anybody could have one. Not any more. Same with movies now. Ten dollars for a movie? Jeez! Say, where ya from? I thought so. I took a trip to the British Isles fifteen years ago with that Irish airline, Aer Lingus? Said they'd never lost a passenger, so that was good enough for me. Scared a flying, see. Made my life insurance out to my brother. Enjoyed Ireland. Wanted to see the Abbey Theatre, though, but didn't get to see it. Didn't see the zoo either. I like zoos. Liked Edinburrow too, but didn't get to see the Highlands. What they did, though, in the end of a meal in a castle, gave us haggis? In a sheep's stomach? Jeez. And I thought my grandmother's cooking was bad. And then . . .'

He pauses for a moment, suddenly distressed, as if he's suffering from haggis flashback; but it's worse than that.

'Then we went to Wales.'

He averts his gaze and stares into his cup. A deep sadness has clouded his face.

'Wales was . . . bleak.'

He has the mournful tone of a man whose heart has been pierced by an arrow of cold steel, or who has been served laver bread for breakfast. Whatever the horrors inflicted on him in the Principality, he can't bring himself to share them with me. There is a terrible silence as he sits for a moment contemplating Wales; then he shrugs off the memory and snaps back into life.

'Hey, gimme a refill, would ya?'

'You gaddit.'

'Hey, here's one you might like. About the Irish Catholic priest in Alaska? You know it? Bishop comes to visit him, asks him how are things.

'"Oh, okay I guess, but y'know it gets very cold and dark." The priest shudders. "Don't think I'd make it through, wasn't for my rosary and my martinis."

'And the bishop says, "Oh, I'm sorry to hear that."

'"Ah, not to worry," says the priest. "Say, would you like a martini?"

'"Why, thank you," says the bishop, "I do believe I would."

'So the priest shouts, "Rosary!" And this beautiful girl comes in. "Rosary, get this man a drink!"'

The place is filling up. A guy orders coffee to go then stares at two exhausted-looking yesterday's doughnuts in the clear plastic case on the counter.

'Are these the only doughnuts you have?'

'Yessir.'

He almost leaves but changes his mind.

'Ah, okay, I'll take 'em. And gimme a lo-fat creamer, and some sweetener.'

'You gaddit.'

He leaves, gets into the van he's parked right outside the window and drives off. Yougaddit waits till he's turned the corner, then reaches under the counter, takes out a pristine box of today's freshly baked doughnuts and lays them out in the plastic case. The Hunter is just finishing his sandwich. His lower teeth don't fit too well and slurps of mayo keep escaping, but he's managing to clean himself up okay with a napkin. He gets to thinking about air travel again.

'Did ya see that, what was it, Concorde? Jesus.'

A fifty-year-old woman in last night's make-up and clothes eating a Spanish omelette on the next stool to him takes this as her cue to join in.

'I worked on the Virgin account for a few years. I met Richard Branson once.'

'Really?'

'Uh-huh.'

She pauses to pursue some diced red pepper.

'People say he's an asshole, but he's not.'

It's nice here. Like being in a village. As I get up to leave I say to the Hunter, 'Hey,' because that's what they all used to say to each other in *NYPD Blue* when they were entering or leaving a room. 'Hey,' I say, remembering his threadbare coat, 'Better stay warm today.'

'Yeah,' he says. 'Throw another Irishman on the fire.'

I smile and slap him on the back, even though I haven't got a clue what he means.

7

THE DARK UNDERBELLY
AND THE TASTIEST CUT

A peculiar thing occurs the day I arrive in Van Diemen's Land.

'Welcome to Tasmania – home of Cadbury's', says a sign above the single luggage carousel in Hobart airport, right next to a clock that's thirty-four minutes slow, but that's not the peculiar thing.

I take delivery of the hire car outside the terminal under a fragrant gum tree full of red and green parrots, and drive into Hobart along a post-neutron-bomb deserted highway. The light is clear, the hills wooded, the harbour spectacular and as undeveloped as Sydney's might have been fifty years ago. I check into my hotel on a restored wharf on the waterfront, pausing to admire the French and Australian Antarctic exploration ships loading provisions outside my bedroom window, and set out to explore the city. Though I've been a frequent visitor to Australia over the years, this is my first time in Tasmania. I don't know a soul and I'm not sure what to expect. Mainland Australians, in their good-natured way, take great pleasure in mocking the island as an anachronistic backwater of inbred halfwits, particularly if they've never actually been there. They tell you about the

Tasmanian parents who wouldn't let their son marry the girl of his choice because she wasn't sleeping with her brothers or uncles. 'If she's not good enough for her own family, she's not good enough for you.'

It's a Saturday afternoon and there are hardly any people about, but maybe it's always like this. I wander along a pedestrianised shopping street, watching teenagers in up-to-the-minute Tasmanian hip-hop gear snog and punch each other. IT'S MOTHER'S DAY, says a sign in a bookshop window, above a display of appropriate titles, among them *The Floating Brothel*.

The shop, like the city and, I'm already beginning to suspect, the whole island, is almost deserted. I'm at the till paying for a map when a woman in her twenties comes and stands next to me, and places a paperback on the counter. I glance down, and am astounded to see it's a copy of *McCarthy's Bar*. I'm almost, but unfortunately not entirely, speechless. She notices me staring and catches my eye, so I say, 'What a coincidence, eh?'

'What?'

'The book.'

'What about it?'

I'm embarrassed now, but it's too late to turn back.

'Well – it's . . . it's . . . my book.'

She gives me a filthy look, then pulls the book along the counter towards her.

'No,' I burble, watching the situation deteriorate with each passing second, and powerless to do anything about it, 'I don't want it. I wrote it.'

She takes a second to consider the improbable nature of my claim.

'I don't believe you.'

'I did. Look – I'm wearing the same jacket that's on the cover.'

Tragically, I am. The truth of my life is laid bare in all its glamour-free squalor. It's possible I'm wearing the same socks as well, but I'm not going to risk telling her that as I can't see how it's going to improve the situation. She takes out a credit card and the bookseller gives her a pen to sign the receipt. She passes the pen and the book to me and says, 'Would you mind signing it for me?' Then smiles and adds, 'I'm real sorry, mate. I thought you were a fackn' loony.'

Welcome to Tasmania.

Before leaving Melbourne this morning I had fresh tuna kedgeree with avocado salsa for breakfast, which is all very well, but you try getting something as straightforward as a bowl of cornflakes or a fried egg in a Designer Boutique Hotel. The waiter with the black linen Nehru jacket and withering sneer would make sure you never ate breakfast in this town again. I was already in the doghouse for lowering the tone of the joint by wearing primary colours rather than black.

Melbourne has been one of my favourite cities ever since I spent two months working there in 1985 and wondered why everyone had been keeping it a secret. The food, the wrought iron, the bizarre weather, the reassuringly non-Aussie lack of decent beaches – I loved the place instantly and with a passion. In recent years the city has worked hard to conceal its rough edges, pouring money into new riverside developments and a gargantuan casino as it attempts to compete with Sydney in the glamour stakes. And now there's this new vogue for 'boutique' hotels.

What kind of nonsense is this? Boutique means 'shop', doesn't it? When I arrived yesterday I couldn't find my way in because the cutting-edge architect has cunningly disguised the door as part of the wall. I wandered up and down outside the front window like a mad person, or that guy trying to find Princess Anne in Starbucks in New York. 'Don't worry, everyone does that,' said the intimidatingly beautiful girl with black lipstick, or bubonic plague, behind the front desk. It's clearly a deliberate ploy to put the staff firmly in charge and new arrivals at the bottom of the food chain where they belong.

She checked me in to a room on the fourth floor, then said, 'There are no stairs to the fourth floor. They stop at the third so you'll have to use the lift. Okay?' On the way up in the lift there was a sign saying, 'In case of fire do not use lifts', which wasn't okay. On the table next to my pyrotechnically challenged bed, and I swear on St Dymphna's bones that I'm not making this up, was a pillow menu. Perhaps I don't need to try to convince you. It's possible that most people these days are au fait with boutique hotels and their invisible doors and pillow menus, and because I've always been a habitué of the scummier kind of accommodation I'm just out of touch.

This is what it said on the menu.

PILLOW MENU
Please call Reception to make your request

(1)   WOOL BLEND PILLOW
Natural support and feel of pure new Australian wool, combined with resilient polyester, for that softer feel

(2)   DELUXE POSTURE TRI-PILLOW
Ensures correct comfort and support. Non-allergenic. Suitable for reading and watching television.

(3)   EASY REST POSTURE PILLOW
Super posture sleep with a soft foam core, provides contoured head and neck support.

(4)   NON-ALLERGENIC PILLOW
Made from high resilience and long-life polyester. Ideal for asthma sufferers.

(5)   PILLOW FOR BITING
Made from natural outback leather with fashionable black rubber trim.
Ideal for face-down fun.

Okay, so there were only four, but it's no less deranged for that. It's almost enough to make you nostalgic for readers' wives' headboards and brushed nylon sheets.

Yesterday I visited a friend in the Melbourne suburbs, and outside several houses saw garden gnomes brandishing axes, daggers and chainsaws. The city's always had a well-developed sense of kitsch; it is, famously, the place that named a swimming pool after Harold Holt, a Prime Minister who drowned. In the afternoon I visited the Victoria State Parliament, where a statue of Queen Victoria is on display. Apparently she hated it so much she asked for it to be sent as far away as possible. Perhaps she didn't know about Tasmania.

I spent the evening and early part of the night at the Melbourne Celtic Club, a venerable institution founded in 1887 to serve Victoria's burgeoning Irish population. In the bar brash young Aussies rubbed shoulders with ageing well-weathered bachelors who looked as if they'd just dropped in after milking the cows in a shed in Connemara. In the toilets I met Diarmuid from Waterford, who told me about the little pub at home where the old lady's kitchen was on the way to the loo, and at Christmas everyone ate the turkey that was on the table because they didn't know it was her dinner and thought it was a buffet. 'Give it a few years and that kind of thing won't be happening any more. Everyone's mad to be modern at home these days. And rich. I'd sooner be here, to be honest with ya.'

Back out in the bar he told me – he just couldn't stop telling stories, this fella – about his friend who got a job as an air-hostess.

'A real hardcore Dub she is. Don't know how she got the job in the first place. So she's on a flight to the States, and this Yank businessman takes a shine to her, but she's not having any of it. Anyway the Yank keeps trying to catch her eye, and she keeps her head down, serving all the others. Then the Yank says, "Are you avoiding me?"

'"No," says she, and gets her friend to go and serve him.

' "No thanks," he says, "I want her." So she goes over. "I'd like a gin and tonic please, honey."

' "Look," says she, "I'm very busy, me friend'll serve ya."

' "Hey, I'm the customer. I want a gin and tonic and I want it from you."

' "*Well, why don't you feck off then?*" she says and all hell breaks loose.

'There's a row. Ya man is completely outraged and he complains to the purser and she takes my friend to the galley and she denies it, says he's exaggerating and she'd never dare think of such a thing, let alone say it. So the purser goes out to pour oil on troubled waters, says there must have been a misunderstanding, persuades him to forget it, and asks if he'd like anything to drink.

'And then he only sees my friend coming out of the galley and he says, "Yes please, miss. Like I said, I'd like a gin and tonic."

'And my friend says, "I thought I told you to feck off." ' '

I'd been invited to the club by Maureen and her partner. She comes from a Tasmanian Irish family, and joined me for breakfast at the Boutique to fill me in on what to expect. The kedgeree arrived before she did, and it was okay, but salsa is always a bit of a disappointment, isn't it? It sounds like it's going to be a complex, fiery, tropical concoction, spicy and sexy as the dance of the same name; but when it comes it's just raw stuff chopped up. It doesn't really deserve a name of its own. The catwalk creature in the black Nehru jacket eventually served me despite my yellow shirt, but forgot to put Stockhausen or the Velvet Underground on the stereo to intimidate us. Instead it was tuned to a commercial radio news channel. Though this jarred with the intended ambience of designer cool, it made for an entertaining start to the day.

'. . . And there are reports that a rogue crocodile has been spotted cruising just a hundred metres off the town's main beach. A conservation expert warns that the pressure of an increasing crocodile population since they became a protected species means they are more likely to venture into populated areas than they were ten or even five years ago. Asked if he had any advice for the terrified local population, a representative of the local council had this to say: "People had better get used to the buggers."'

Meanwhile, according to the same bulletin, the conference of the Australian College of Surgeons has been told by a senior tissue technician that breast implants could become redundant in five years because new technology 'could allow women to grow their own'.

You often hear stuff like this when you're a long way from home, but when you get back no one else has heard anything about it, and you never hear it mentioned again. Does each country have scriptwriters making weird stuff up so that news will maintain its audience share? Or is it true, but only here, so that just Australian women will be able to grow their own breasts? Maybe the minerals in the soil out here mean it's the only place that can produce the right kind of grow-bags. Things are possible in the Antipodes that could never be contemplated in Europe.

Maureen turned up with wild hair, dilated pupils and an intense expression, as if she were about to try and convert me to one of the less plausible branches of Satanism, but instead embarked on an impassioned and somewhat chilling account of her feelings about Tasmania.

'It can be a very overpowering place. If you're sensitive you'll feel a hostility in the landscape to European culture, which isn't to say Aboriginal culture is necessarily at home there either. They got stuck there like everybody else. I sense a hostility to all human life. A lot of Tasmanians think, why me? Why wasn't I born in Paris or Berlin? Why did I end up in this place? It's an existential problem. So we go away. But there's always something drawing us back. A bit like Ireland in that respect.'

I showed her a glossy brochure picturing blue skies and an

empty beach, promoting Tasmania as the most beautiful island in the world for two years running, according to recent polls.

'This Condé Nast glamour image is a big mistake. They should have concentrated on its metaphysical qualities – the deep, dark underbelly of the place.'

But it'd be hard, I said, to market a place on such a concept. Come to sunny Tasmania, hostile to all human life.

'It's a story of people struggling to overcome that hostility. It wasn't by chance that it became the most notorious prison in the British Empire. Hobart is a kind of prison too. It faces Antarctica. It is surrounded by the elements, mountains behind and the ocean in front. The only way out is by taking high risks. It's about islands within islands, prisons within prisons.'

'Not to mention the prison inside your own head,' I said, adopting an uncharacteristically gloomy tone that had sprung unbidden from some secret place.

Maureen seemed pleased. 'Yeah, you've got the idea. I think you might have a good time in Tazzy. Just don't expect it to be like the good times you've had anywhere else.'

Tasmania is 200 kilometres off the coast of Victoria. It's about the same size as Ireland, but with a population of only 470,000. Aboriginal tribes lived here for more than 25,000 years before Europeans ever saw the place. These original inhabitants crossed from mainland Australia on a land bridge and achieved the status of islanders when it was washed away by melting glaciers at the end of the Ice Age. In 1642 the Dutch explorer Abel Tasman stumbled across it when he came looking for Australia, which he somehow missed. He named the island Van Diemen's Land, in honour of his patron, but it was never occupied by Europeans until it was settled as a penal colony by the British in 1803. After the cessation of convict transportation in 1853 the name – by now a byword for heinous crime and even crueller punishments, and known as Damn Demon's Land by the convicts – was

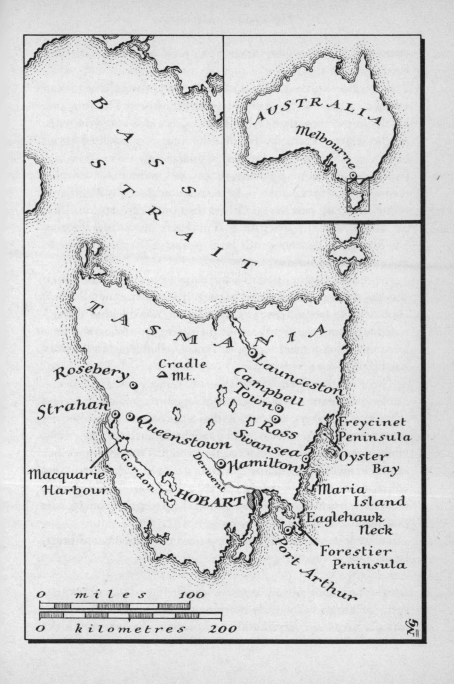

BASS STRAIT

AUSTRALIA

Melbourne

TASMANIA

Rosebery

Cradle
Mt.

Launceston

Campbell
Town

Strahan

Queenstown

Ross

Swansea

Freycinet
Peninsula

Oyster
Bay

Macquarie
Harbour

Gordon

Derwent

Hamilton

HOBART

Maria
Island

Eaglehawk
Neck

Port Arthur

Forestier
Peninsula

0   miles   100

0   kilometres   200

N

changed to Tasmania, in a marketing ploy designed to attract a better class of settler.

More than 65,000 British and Irish convicts were sent to Van Diemen's Land – 40 per cent of all those transported to Australia. It's not known how many Aborigines were wiped out in the wake of the white settlement, because no one ever counted them; but twenty-five thousand years of indigenous occupation was obliterated in less than a hundred. In 1828 martial law was proclaimed giving soldiers the right to shoot on sight any Aboriginal found in a 'European' area. Others died of disease, malnutrition or simply despair. The Australian historian Robert Hughes has described what happened here as 'the only true genocide in English colonial history'.

For convicts transported to Van Diemen's land, the island itself was the prison. Assigned to a master or landowner in a licensed form of slave labour, convicts were free to move within a designated area until they worked out their sentence and earned their freedom. Among them were the Young Irelanders, whose story has brought me here.

There was a problem though: what to do with repeat offenders. Or for that matter with absconders, agitators, malcontents and other troublemakers. A prison within a prison was deemed necessary, where incorrigibles might be taught the error of their ways, while providing some service for the crown. The most notorious of these was at Macquarie Harbour, on the wild unexplored western side of the island. When the settlement opened in 1822 it could be reached only by a hazardous boat journey from Hobart that took several days.

Today it's a single day's drive, across the unpopulated heartland of the island.

It's the beginning of the southern winter, grey and cool with a spray of drizzle in the early morning air as I leave Hobart. Australians have been very skilful in projecting an image of a lucky country of perpetual sunshine where winter never happens, because they know it makes us unhappy, and it's important for them to know that the Poms are miserable. Winter in Melbourne, however, can be a bleak experience, and here in Tasmania, with nothing but 2,000 miles of southern ocean to separate it from Antarctica, they say it can get quite draughty.

The trick, of course, is to leave Britain in mid-winter and arrive down here at the height of summer, which always feels like a miracle however many times you do it. This time I've opted for the miracle in reverse. After an apocalyptic winter of floods, foot and mouth and other disasters, followed by a complete absence of spring, hot summer days appeared without warning just as I was about to leave. No matter. That was always the plan. Like every other half-decent place in the world, Tasmania is experiencing a significant rise in the number of tourists, drawn here, it is believed, by promises of clean air, unspoiled beaches and wilderness hiking, rather than the allure of its deep, dark underbelly and hostility to all human life. I understand what Maureen was getting at, and metaphysical tourism is an interesting idea, but I can't honestly see they'd generate the same kind of income by gearing their image to the Fred West/Charles Manson niche market. I've chosen my month deliberately. I've come out of season, the visitors long gone, in the hope of getting closer to the great empty heart and the dark secret soul of the island; and if I can't manage that, at least it'll be easier to get a drink in the evenings.

It's early morning rush hour, and the radio's on as I drive out of town.

'You know what it's like, you're at the footie on a Saturday afternoon and someone steals your lawn mower from your shed . . .'

I'm in no rush and no one else seems to be either. Traffic is light, though for all I know this may qualify as gridlock in Hobart. It feels quite unlike the centre of a capital city. Water keeps appearing in unexpected places, which is one of the best things about being in a harbour town, and goes some way to making up for the presence of all those yachties. I find myself looking at the other drivers and envying their lives in such an unpressured environment. 'Australia's Natural State' proclaim the licence plates, a reference to the wilderness which covers half of the landmass. The state also lays claim to the freshest air in the world. Everywhere in my hotel was non-smoking, even the balconies. One day Tasmania could become the world's first non-smoking island, and smokers will have to get the ferry to Melbourne if they want to stand in a doorway and have a fag.

The old weatherboard houses are giving way to new exclusive developments of Executive Homes – do they refuse to sell you one if you work in a factory or a shop? – as I reach the outer fringes of the city. I'm by the water again, and beyond it there are gum trees and empty hillsides as the road splits and I take the left fork to Strahan and the west. The drizzle has stopped but ahead of me I can see a wall of mist. Seconds later I'm enveloped in it. The mist, or cloud – or alien life form disguised as mist or cloud – is an opaque and eerie yellow in the muted sun. It rises in swirls from the surface of the lake or swamp, or alien life form's mother disguised as lake or swamp. Gnarled branches reach out of the water like drowned men's arms. It's as if I've been transported into an episode of *The Twilight Zone*.

Half an hour from Hobart it's dark as nightfall under a low, low sky. Annie Lennox is on the radio singing 'Here Comes the Rain Again' and you have the feeling it probably gets a lot of radio play. I saw her once on a deserted beach near Perth in Western Australia, sunbathing in a gold bikini surrounded by half a dozen minders. Annie, not me. I fell asleep in the sun and burned because when you're travelling on your own there's no one to put sunblock on your back. It peeled like clingfilm. They've changed the record now.

He's got the dirtiest shoes I've ever seen
He wipes his butt with a magazine.

Catchy.

A sign says I'm in the Central Highlands, and the town of Gretna. I pass the Gretna Green Hotel on my left. A sign outside a shop says: MRS MACK'S FAMOUS BEEF PIES. A couple of hundred yards up the road a woman appears out of the science-fiction mist, walking along the side of the road towards me. She's wearing a light blue tracksuit top, a long black pleated skirt and trainers, and is carrying a pie on a silver tray. What can it mean? Is it Mrs Mack herself, in training for the Central Highlands pie marathon? The atmosphere is getting denser, as if the director has turned the smoke machine on again, and by the time I reach Hamilton the place is completely shrouded in Hammer Horror fog. Through the gloom I can see beautiful old sandstone buildings with roofs of corrugated iron, a discordantly un-European detail that makes me feel as if I'm dreaming them. The mist rises for a moment, and I catch sight of the Highland Pie Shop. What's going on with all these pies? I remember *Titus Andronicus* and *Sweeney Todd*, and remember they have always been a traditional method of disposing of bodies.

This is the only road from east to west of the island but there are hardly any vehicles, apart from the occasional logging truck. As the non-existent traffic becomes even more sparse, so the roadkill grows increasingly abundant. Furry casualties litter the road in oozing piles. Enormous orange-eyed birds stand defiantly astride the corpses, pecking out the tasty bits. I pass no other vehicle for ten minutes, yet count more than a dozen dead animals. That's a hell of a strike rate. It seems statistically impossible. How can there be more roadkill than cars? Do people take detours to chase them and drive them down deliberately? Or are the beasts depressed and prone to suicide? Neither seems likely. It's more probable that an evil genius is holed up in a big house in the forest conducting unspeakable experiments on wildlife, then ordering his minions to dump the bodies on the roads before the blood congeals. I read a magazine article in the hotel that reckoned Tasmanian hippies – ferals they call them out here – are so vegetarian *they make their shoes from the skin of roadkill.* How messy would that be? I wonder what they use for laces or socks? What if you needed wellies, or something you could tap-dance in? I can't honestly see it as a humane answer to the global footwear shortage. I turn a bend, negotiate the brow of a hill and disappear from view, knowing that as soon as I'm gone a bare-footed crustie will emerge from the bush and try a dead marsupial on for size.

There are few of the Aboriginal place names you find in the other states of Australia. Instead there are plenty of direct transpositions from Britain and Ireland: Bracknell, Lewisham, Glenelg, Kilorran. Other names are original and wonderfully subjective: Cape Grim, Snug, Mistaken Cape, Creepy Crawly Walk. I cross Black Bob's Rivulet, named after that clever dog in the *Dandy*. By the time I reach Derwent Forest there's no traffic, people or signs of habitation. Tall straight trees and ferns bigger than a big man line the roadside. Thick mists shroud the tops of the trees, and it's pouring with rain. That'll be why it's called the rainforest then. People don't always twig. They say they're going on holiday to the rainforest in Costa Rica or Queensland or Brazil, which seems epic and glamorous, but then grumble when you ask what it was like.

'We didn't get much of a tan. It rained all the time. It was horrible actually.'

That's the time to tell them it's been sunny at home, even if it hasn't.

Radio reception is getting fainter but I can still pick up the lunchtime news. There's a good alcohol-deterrent item, straight from the Australian College of Surgeons' breast-growing school of reporting: 'A Korean woman who cut off her husband's penis with a kitchen knife while he was in a drunken stupor has admitted flushing it down the toilet so he couldn't rush to hospital and have it sewn back on.'

Under the circumstances it's hard to imagine him rushing anywhere. The report doesn't explain why the woman might have done it. Perhaps it was a Saturday, he'd been to the footie, went for a few beers, got home late, someone had stolen the lawn mower from the shed while he was out and she decided *she'd just had enough*!

I now seem to have been transported from *The Twilight Zone* into an episode of *The X Files*. The mist has partially lifted and I can see two huge silver tubes running up a hillside to two tall towers at the top. All that's missing is the Smoking Man leaning against a tree, watching as government agents in protective suits run out, drug me and take me off to a bunker for interrogation. The road continues to rise and I can see five more of the sinister silver pipes running away across the increasingly bizarre landscape into infinity. Down in a gorge there's a lot of electrical-generational pluggy gadgety-type stuff that, as you can see from this description, is a mystery to me. Then without warning the cloud lifts completely to reveal a blue sky and I'm alongside a crystal-clear deep blue high mountain lake. You certainly get your money's worth in this place.

SURVEYOR'S MONUMENT – 500 metres, says a sign. It sounds ominous, at least for the surveyor. A little further on there's an arrow pointing off the road. POWER STATION MUSEUM, it says. I haven't seen a tour bus or even another tourist all day, so it's unlikely to be crowded, but I think I'll give it a miss all the same. Here's another one. BRONTE PARK, it claims. MORNING AND AFTERNOON TEAS. God knows where. It's just wide-open wilderness in every direction. Perhaps you're meant to sit by the sign and the emergency services will helicopter in the scones and cream and jam. Maybe there are flares for you to set off to place your order, colour-coded according to the kind of jam you'd prefer. You probably wouldn't want to be too fussy.

The Laughing Jack Lagoon is behind me and Fourteen Mile Road is also history as I reach Derwent Bridge, which appears to be a small settlement of chalets, but no people. Ah, no, hang on. Two bemused-looking hitch-hikers in quilted jackets and hats with comedy earflaps are standing outside the Wilderness Hotel holding a sign that says, 'Hobart'. I don't know if such a condition is recognised by the medical profession, but they appear to be suffering from Traffic Deprivation. They look as if they've been there so long they might have made the sign after Christmas dinner. I'd say their chances of being picked up by a vehicle before they're picked clean by the wildlife are less than evens.

The clouds are back and it's raining again as I pass a sign that says, 'Welcome to the West Coast', which seems a peculiar claim to make in a forest on top of a mountain with no imminent prospect of beach, pier or catch of the day. Bill's Creek, Cardigan River, Raglan Creek, Snake Creek and the landscape is getting more and more unsettling the further west we get. There are hundreds of dead trees on either side of the road. It looks like the scene of an epic battle, where some of the more vulnerable and sensitive trees have been picked on by the others. According to the map we're not far from Queenstown.

It's a dramatic arrival that doesn't feel like driving into town so much as coming in to land. 'Queenstown', says the sign. 'Mining since 1880.' There's a solitary derelict building – a gaunt burned-out shell still bearing the legend '1910 Royal Hotel T Kelly' – then the road snakes up the stark ravaged mountain behind the hotel past what look like three or four prospectors' cabins. It's like the opening shot of a bleak and violent movie set in a nineteenth-century mining claim in the Wild West. There's a ninety-degree bend at the top of the mountain and there, far below, is a cluster of wooden buildings, dwarfed by the devastated and barren landscape, like a gold-rush town on the dark and jagged side of the moon.

The sensation of making a landing is enhanced by the fact that

I'm descending through clouds as I zigzag down the mountainside. Golden yellow ore, shiny from the rain, gleams through the rock that borders the road. I'm hoping for lunch, but Australia's celebrated Pacific Rim fusion cuisine may not have made it this far, and I may have to settle for a sausage. A sign on a garage says, 'Enter At Own Risk'; but does it mean the garage, or the town?

I park outside the Empire Hotel, a Victorian confection with an ornate arched balcony. There's a view up a single street of run-down wooden buildings; where the street ends, and instinct tells you the dust and red rocks of Arizona should begin, is a mountain shrouded in cloud. A sign advertises a chairlift, but you'd be lucky to see your own feet today.

Across the street an elderly beaten-up white Valiant is parked at the kerbside. Stretched across the front seat with his feet on the dashboard, a tough-looking man in his thirties sits staring at me. He's unshaven and covered with so much dirt that I'm only guessing about him being unshaven. As I walk past his windscreen I feel as inconspicuous as Kirk and Spock beaming down in Dodge City.

The street's deserted, as if today's gunfight is due at any moment. A shop on the corner doubles as the Tourist Information office, but a sign says it's closed till four. Perhaps that's when they get the daily rush. There are some rocks in the window and a notice headed THINGS TO DO IN TOWN. Item four is 'Walk Round the Town', so I do.

The Paragon Theatre has a yellow and pink art deco façade and a corrugated roof. A man with what appear to be plaits in his beard, but I don't like to look too closely, is standing outside with the two most frightening dogs I've ever seen, enormous, wolf-hyena hybrids with Mike Tyson shoulders and fangs dripping with drool. The three of them look strangely alert, scanning the street as if they have an appointment to keep. Maybe the guy with his feet on the car dashboard is waiting for the clock to strike the hour, when he will come round the corner and stand in the middle of the street. Plaitbeard and the hyenas will step out to block his way, and the shooting will begin. Or perhaps they'll use flame-throwers, or crossbows. Anxious not to get caught in the crossfire I head on up the street past Axel's Takeaway, a café offering souvlaki, kangaroo steaks and Internet access. 'Business For Sale', it says in the window. 'Genuine Enquiries Only.'

Across the street is Hunters Hotel – 1898, another ornate wrought-iron and balustraded job that looks as if it's been boarded up for years. Even the 'For Sale' sign looks worn out. 'Lifelike Plants', reads a card in the supermarket window. Another advertises 'Miner's Cottage – Original character. Two Bedrooms. Partly Furnished. Previous owner – miner. $18,000.' I'm hungry, but not hungry enough for kangaroo or souvlaki, so I decide to settle for a sandwich and a beer if I can find a pub before they put it on the market.

'Counter Lunches', claims a sign in the pub window, misleadingly as it turns out, because according to the guy behind the counter they don't do food. He's been perfectly cast. He looks like Jim Broadbent playing the part of a barman in a run-down Tasmanian mining pub that advertises food but doesn't serve it. I order a low-alcohol beer in an English accent, a potentially hazardous act from which I emerge unscathed. There's a pool table at one end of the room on which no one is playing. Above the bar a TV screen is showing what seems to be the gambling channel, rows of numbers interrupted at intervals by the announcement of prizes. Five men sit at five stools along the bar, beers in hand, gazing up at the screen. They look tough but vacant, willing but broken in spirit. After a while one of them gets up and takes the two paces to the poker machine, and begins to play. The other four swivel in unison to watch. He has a couple of wins, but keeps going until he's put all the money back in. Then he returns to his seat, the guys spin round and everyone watches the gambling channel again. As I get up to leave the man on the end of the row gives me a gentle nod and a warm smile, which is cheering. I smile back, but I'd be lying if I didn't admit that something's bothering me.

In the fifteen minutes I've been in here no one has spoken.

In 1815 a twenty-four-year-old ship's captain called James Kelly – a convict's son from Parramatta in New South Wales – set out from Hobart in an open whale boat propelled by four oarsmen in an attempt to circumnavigate Van Diemen's Land, a feat that had not previously been achieved in the twelve years of the colony's existence. On the unexplored and unknown west coast, hemmed in by impenetrable rainforest and unforgiving mountains, and situated in the wettest place in Australia, he discovered a harbour bigger than Sydney's. He named it in honour of the then governor of New South Wales. Within ten years Macquarie Harbour was home to the most dreaded penal settlement in the southern hemisphere. The rainfall, though prodigious, would probably have come low down the list of the inmates' complaints.

The place of punishment was a low point almost levil with the sea . . . in the center stands the Triangles to which a man is tied with his side towards the platform on which the Commandant and the Doctor walked so that they could see the man's face and back alternately.

It was their costome to walk one hundred yards between each lash; consequently those who received one hundred lashes were tied up from one hour to one hour and a quarter – and the moment it was over . . . he was immediately sent to work, his back like Bullock's Liver and most likely his shoes full of Blood, and not permitted to go to the Hospital until next morning when his back would be washed by the Doctor's Mate and a little Hog's Lard spread on . . . it often happened that the same man would be flogged the following day for Neglect of Work.

So wrote a convict called Davies, Christian name unknown, whose account of his experiences has survived. I'd say it made quite an impression on him. I'm going to remember the back like Bullock's Liver all my life, and I wasn't even there.

The settlement was to be the destination of repeat offenders – those convicts who had failed to observe the terms of their original sentence, and so were deemed to require further punishment than the standard slave labour and 13,000-mile banishment from home. Though characterised as the worst of the worst these supposed incorrigibles were, according to the testimony of the prison surgeon, guilty of such crimes as 'disobedience of orders to their masters, neglect of duty, absence from the farm without permission' and – a particular favourite this one – 'drunkenness'. Convicts were pressed into service as guards, guaranteeing a never-ending cycle of resentment and recrimination. So harsh was the system that prisoners would prearrange vicious assaults on each other so they might be guaranteed the trip to Hobart to stand trial or give evidence. Others sought more permanent escape, and committed murder for no reason other than to secure their own execution. But why not commit suicide rather than kill another man? asked the chaplain of one such murderer, according to the account of the prison storekeeper.

'If I kill myself I shall immediately descend to the bottomless pit, but if I kill another I will be sent to Hobart Town and tried for my life; if found guilty the parson would attend me and then I would be sure of going to heaven.'

Macquarie Harbour was chosen because of its total isolation. To cross the mountainous interior of the island and reach it on foot from Hobart was impossible, and a hazardous sea voyage was required in order to arrive or depart. Sole entrance to the thirty-mile-long harbour was through a bottleneck opening known as Hell's Gates, beyond which the Roaring Forties could cause the Pacific Ocean to foam and swell, stranding ships at sea for days before they could enter and reach the prison island within.

Sarah Island, deep inside the harbour, was named, in the words of Captain Kelly, 'in honor of Mrs Birch, wife of Thos. William Birch Esq. of Hobart Town'. Even today this is an isolated island near a larger isolated island off the shore of an isolated continent. The nearest settlement – one of only a handful on the whole west coast of Tasmania, much of which is still as untouched as it was in Kelly's day – is the tiny town of Strahan. This is where I'll be staying tonight, before visiting the island named in honour of Mrs Birch first thing tomorrow morning.

'Mate, all you need is some hessian, a piece of string and a can of petrol.'

I've driven in from Queenstown, checked in to the converted stable block in my colonial-style B&B, been to see a play and now I'm in a pub on the Strahan waterfront, picking up handy hints from a miner on how to quick-chill a beer.

'Wrap the beer in the hessian, tie it to the string, soak the hessian with the petrol, then swing it round ya head. The petrol evaporates and the beer gets real cold.'

I'm picturing hundreds of people all doing this on Brighton beach one scorching August bank holiday Monday when he says, 'Where ya from anyway, mate? Jeez, ya poor bahstard.'

The pub's busy. There are half a dozen other tourists all tucking into $10 T-bone steak dinners. I recognise them from the audience at the play. *The Ship That Never Was* is performed each evening in a little purpose-built amphitheatre on the waterfront, and tells the story of the *Frederick*, the last ship to be built in the convict shipyard on Sarah Island. It was hijacked by ten bof the convicts who built it, then managed to sail it all the way to Chile. When two of them were tried for piracy they mounted the ingenious defence that as they had stolen the vessel before it was commissioned, technically it was not a ship, but a collection of boards, canvas and rope; they were therefore guilty of theft, not piracy. And they won. All ten survived to live eventually as free men.

It was a high-energy performance involving the piece-by-piece construction of the *Frederick* on stage, and as good a night out as a cold, lonely, slightly spooked visitor could wish for, with the added bonus of discovering that one of the escapees, John Barker, was a gunsmith and watchmaker from my own home town of Warrington. When you come from somewhere that rarely gets a mention, it's always nice to feel included.

Halfway through the performance a young Japanese couple in expensive designer clothes made a late and noisy arrival, standing in the aisle and conducting an animated argument in Japanese before exiting sharpish the way they had come, pursued by ad libs from the cast. At the moment they're sitting silently in the corner.

The audience aren't the only customers in the pub. The clientèle are mostly men, thirty or forty of them, local fellas with big arms bulging from polo tops and rugby shirts, and they're a lot more forthcoming than the melancholy defeated-looking guys I saw in Queenstown. One of them sees me looking at the T-bones, which provokes further mirth at the thought of living in a dump like the UK.

'I'll bet y'll have a few good feeds of steak while ya here, knowing it won't rot ya brain.'

'Y'll be breathing deep, will ya, taking as much fresh air as ya can?'

It's a big bar, and out of tourist season, so I'd presumed the crowd was down to the after-work rush. Turns out I was right, though not in the way I'd expected.

'They're here to drown their sorrows,' confides a guy with a ZZ Top beard and bushy eyebrows that meet in the middle, as if two caterpillars have gone to sleep on his face. 'I'm one of the lucky ones. They announced it today. Forty more redundancies.

Screw you when you're working, and they screw you when you're not.'

I head back to the B&B for dinner. Perhaps it'll be a good feed of steak. Or bullock's liver.

I've wanted to come to Macquarie Harbour since I first read *The Fatal Shore*, Robert Hughes's epic account of the convict settlement of Australia. One story has stayed vividly with me for more than a decade, and I've just come across it again in a local magazine I'm reading at dinner. I'm trying not to listen to the guy in the purple polo neck and goatee beard at the next table telling his sister in the black linen two-piece and designer tortoiseshell glasses about the intricacies of his love life.

'He has the most gorgeous brown eyes ever. And he's saying to me, "You're perfect, do you know that, the most perfect person ever?" So I just had to tell him, well, I don't feel the same way about you, honey. Mind you, he is one terr-iffic root.'

My chargrilled octopus has just arrived, along with their starter of prawns as big as a baby's arm. Australians are admirably forthright people, and he's going into explicit detail as he eats. I block out their conversation by propping up the magazine on my bottle of inky Cabernet Sauvignon and immersing myself in the strange tale of Edward Pearce, as I nibble the firm, pink-suckered slivers of octopus flesh and hope I'll be able to keep them down.

Pearce was a native of County Monaghan, sentenced to seven years transportation at Armagh Assizes for stealing six pairs of shoes. He arrived in Van Diemen's Land in 1820 and was assigned to work as a servant, but was frequently drunk and absent from work, and in 1822 was sent to Sarah Island for forging a £2 money order. In September of that year, along with seven other convicts, he seized a boat from the shore, crossed to the other side of the harbour and headed off east into the interior with the unlikely intention of commandeering a schooner and sailing it back to Europe. Unfortunately for everybody concerned, it didn't quite work out like that.

They were hideously unprepared for the dense rainforest and jagged mountain gorges which, even today, are scarcely explored. They lasted a week before their rations were gone, then began to consider alternative sources of nourishment. 'There were four of us for a feast,' confessed Pearce later. 'Bob said that he had seen the like done before and that it eat much like a little pork.' They settled on one of their company, on the grounds that he had been a flogger on Sarah Island, though this remains unproven. After killing him, according to Pearce: 'We cut off his clothes, and tore out his inside, and cut off his head; then [others] put his heart and liver on the fire and eat it before it was right warm; they asked the rest would they have any but they would not have any that night.'

'Are you finished with that, sir?'

There's one tentacle left. I say I'll need a couple of minutes longer. My neighbours say they're ready for their mains. I pour another glass of red wine as Pearce's gang decide to split the flesh seven ways and – this was way before clingfilm, remember – put it in their pockets and set off in search of a schooner. But two ran away and died of exposure, and then there were five.

Then four.

Then three.

Then two.

I've finished the octopus.

Having killed and eaten the others one by one, Pearce found himself alone with Robert Greenhill, a sailor from Middlesex. Fuelled by their strict high-protein diet, they had successfully crossed the worst of the terrain and found themselves among fields and woodlands in a landscape that might have reminded them of home. Greenhill was beginning to flag; but though Pearce had the stamina, Greenhill had the axe. Both knew that one of them would be eaten when supplies of the last of their comrades ran out. They walked a distance apart, watching constantly and avoiding sleep. For two nights they sat and stared at each other across the campfire. Just before dawn poor Greenhill fell asleep. By late morning Pearce was on his way, whistling as he strode out across the undulating meadows, his pockets well stocked with prime Middlesex arm and thigh.

'Your main course, sir.'

'Thank you.'

I've ordered noisettes of lamb, rare, in a rosemary Shiraz jus, and I really wish I hadn't; because a few days later a convict shepherd called McGuire caught Pearce in the act of dismembering a lamb and eating it raw. McGuire, who was unaware of Pearce's special dietary requirements, wasn't inclined to dob in a fellow Irishman, and hid him for several weeks. Pearce fell in with a couple of outlaws living in the outback, and in January, almost four months after his escape, the three were arrested by soldiers and taken to Hobart, where Pearce confessed.

The lamb is very tender but also rather rich, and I have to confess I'm finding it a tad cloying, especially on top of the octopus. They've finished eating at the next table, and now he's lifting up the purple sweater to show her a tattoo or piercing or something right near his nipple. I can't see what it is without being obvious and leaning across.

'Oh, wow!'

'Cute, isn't it?'

'It's gross. Are you going to show Mum?'

The authorities didn't believe Pearce's story and thought he was just covering for his mates who were still roaming free in the bush. Only a criminal, they reckoned, could come up with so deranged an account. So they sent him back to Macquarie Harbour, where he was flogged and put back on the chain gang, and treated as a celebrity by his fellow prisoners. He was, after all, living proof that escape was possible, provided you had the right supplies.

*

Next morning at breakfast I decide to read something a little lighter. A story in the paper under the headline SPORTS NEWS catches my eye.

A top rugby player, who shall remain nameless in case our paths should ever cross, has put his career in jeopardy, 'after yet another unsavoury incident'. Last year he was fined for being involved in a drunken brawl, and a week later had to be fined again 'for being drunk and abusive at training'. Skip forward another couple of months and this time the charges related to another drunken brawl, this time on a beach. And now less than six months later one of the club's major sponsors is threatening to withdraw financial support, 'after the winger brought the club and the game into disrepute for sticking his fingers up three opposing players' backsides'. Fingers, mind, not finger. The offended sponsor funds the players' shorts.

The Strahan waterfront is a pleasing collection of old wooden buildings facing a few small wharfs and piers. In the 1890s it became the busiest port in Tasmania, servicing the prospectors and mining fields around Zeehan and Queenstown. Horses, machinery and miners arrived by sea, and the ore left by the same route. The mining boom is long over, though as I discovered last night, there's enough of it left for it still to be in decline. The new industry on which economic hopes are pinned, as it is everywhere else in the world, is tourism. Today there are just thirty or forty of us gathered on the quayside waiting to board the boat that will take us first to Edward Pearce's alma mater, Sarah Island, then up the Gordon River into the rainforest. This has the makings of a memorable day, a fact that's not been lost on the couple next to me in the queue to board.

'The buffet's included in the price, and Annette says it's reely, reely excellent. She says remember to take piles and piles of smoked salmon. Don't worry about the people behind you. They bring out more when it's all gone. And they serve it in the down-stairs lounge, so don't hang around on the top deck looking at the trees and get stuck at the back of the queue. We don't want to miss out on the salmon.'

'I thought you said they put more out if it all—'

'Look, I don't want to fight about this! Do you think you could just do what I'm asking? Thank you! Some day out this is turning out to be. And the Chardonnay's extra but Annette says it's worth it. You'll have to queue separately for that.'

It's a comfortable modern catamaran with plenty of room to move about until the feeding frenzy starts. Daunting mountains rise up to port as we head out into the harbour towards the ocean. The waters are an eerie shade of browny-black, with an orange foam of a distinctly urinous tinge – not pollution, but natural tannins and minerals.

The boat takes us out past thick blue gum forests – 'the only source of blue gum in the whole of 'Stralia' according to the commentary – to Hell's Gates, then for a few minutes into the unforgiving ocean beyond. The harbour mouth is fifty or sixty metres wide, with jagged rocks and treacherous sandbanks on which many vessels have foundered. Despite a biting wind conditions are calm today, and our precious cargo of smoked salmon is safe enough. We come through the Gates and head back into the harbour beyond Strahan, following the route that the convict ships would have taken. Pearce, of course, made the trip twice.

The island's macabre atmosphere is inevitably diminished by arriving as part of a multinational taskforce in a dozen shades of Gore-tex. Many of my co-passengers are fully psyched- and tooled-up for the first hint of a photo opportunity, while others seem to be just killing time until the buffet. The Japanese couple from last night are sitting on the jetty eating chocolate and ignoring each other. I'm resigning myself to an imperfect tourism experience when proceedings take on an altogether rosier hue.

Richard, our guide, turns out to be the author of last night's play, an itinerant actor/manager/author who has spent his life performing his way around Australia, America, Mexico, Europe, Egypt and other places I can't remember because the wind is cold and starting to hurt my ears. He brought *The Ship That Never Was* to Strahan for a short run which grew to seven years, during which time he's been investigating and documenting the history of Sarah Island. Dressed in full-length waxed coat, riding boots, leather hat and *Raiders of the Lost Ark* Nazi spectacles, he cuts an imposing figure, working the crowd with passion and skill as we tour the brick and timber ruins.

There was another prison offshore for those deemed too troublesome even for Sarah Island. Grummet Island is visible a few hundred yards across the water, a bare rock on which men were dumped in chains and sodden clothing to spend the night in the teeth of the elements. I have to keep reminding myself that these events are not some wild Gothic fiction, but as real as the jailhouse bricks beneath my feet, and more recent than the house in which I live.

As we shuffle from the site of one horror to another Richard offers a constant barrage of insights into how things might have been, none of which I found in any of the mainstream published accounts of life on the island. 'These guys weren't master criminals but the long-term unemployed – long-term self-employed I prefer to call them.' The Suffolk oven we see at the bakery, he says, produced 400 loaves a day. A substance called ergot was added to the bread so it would quickly go mouldy and couldn't be saved for escape attempts. Ergot, however, also has similar hallucinogenic properties to LSD. 'Add it to the natural amphetamine in the sassafras trees and the large magic mushrooms that grow here, and you have a powerful chemical cocktail.' I suppose this could explain the extreme behaviour of Pearce and the others as a severe attack of the munchies.

Rather than a place of subjugation and passive acceptance, says Richard, the island would have been 'a battleground', where prisoners fought for their identity and their souls. There were also Irish politicals and English trade unionists here, and there are records of men being flogged for organising strikes from forced labour. Homosexuality was a way of life – it's sometimes cited as one of the reasons for the closure of the settlement – and prisoners 'openly flaunted homosexual marriages,' claims Davey, 'because they knew that the authorities didn't like it and it showed that whatever they did to them they could never truly control them'. Other proclivities flourished even among the forces of law and order. On one celebrated occasion a soldier was caught in flagrante with the chaplain's goat. No doubt there was a bit of good-natured ribbing in the barrack-room that night, after which it would have been quietly forgotten.

Our tour is reaching its climax, but a baffled-looking couple in jogging suits fashioned from by-products of the Soviet space programme have had enough.

'C'mon, let's go back to the boat and get a cup of tea. We can find out this kind of stuff in a book.'

They turn and go. Richard, standing among trees by a sharp drop at the water's edge, removes his hat and unbuttons his long coat. Still talking, this time about the shipyard that produced the *Frederick* and more than a hundred other ships, he strips off his boots, shirt and trousers to give a brief glimpse of the wetsuit he must have been wearing since he got up this morning. Then he leaps over the restraining fence and disappears beneath the icy black-brown water. Several uneasy seconds pass – has the bloody island finally sent him over the edge and made him top himself? – before he pops up like a cork, glasses still in position, and starts walking on, or at least just below, the water. It's a great coup de théâtre, his way of demonstrating that just below the surface the shipbuilders' slip yard put in place in the 1820s is still intact. 'Huon pine,' says Richard, 'no other timber like it in the world.'

'He was a strange chap, wasn't he?' says a woman from Adelaide in a poplin mac as we walk back to the boat, 'because there was really no need to jump into the water like that.'

As our party re-embarks, increasingly tense at the prospect of the almost imminent buffet, Richard waves us off from the water's edge. Tonight, as he often does, he will sleep rough and alone on the island. Fair play to him. If it's possible for a place to be haunted, then this one surely is.

On Kelly's voyage of discovery he noted: 'We also found Plenty of Huon Pine growing on the Banks of the Harbour.'

Huon is found only in Tasmania. A fine-grained white pine, it is light, durable, easy to work and, because of its natural oils, impervious to rot. It was much sought after in the early days of the colony as a boat-building material. Thirty thousand were cut by convicts between 1822 and 1833. Unfortunately the Huon pine takes 500 years to grow to maturity. Many of those felled were more than 2,000 years old. They would be much in demand now, if there were any left.

The lunch stampede is over – I saw him, and, boy, did he take piles and piles, and piles of smoked salmon – and we're cruising upstream on what's billed as 'The Last Wild River in Australia'. It's a big attraction. Not everybody comes here for the cannibalism stories. Most are drawn by the prospect of gliding up one of the last pristine river systems to see the rainforest and photograph its famously perfect reflection in the still, tannin-dark waters. Unfortunately it's clouded over, and there's no reflection today.

Eco-tourism wasn't quite so in vogue in 1975, when loggers were photographed cutting down a 2,200-year-old Huon pine. Its demise was imminent due to a planned hydroelectric scheme that would have changed the face of this corner of Tasmania. Strahan became the battleground for the most bitter conservation protest in Australian history as hundreds of 'greenies' moved into the town to confront the authorities. SAVE TREES – USE GREENIES

FOR WOODCHIP, says one woman's T-shirt in a photo taken at the height of the protest. The issue split families and ended lifelong friendships. In 1983 the High Court stopped the development. The hydroelectric jobs never came; but the water, undammed, has continued to bring the town a living.

We're the only boat on the river, and whenever the engines are turned off there's an unsettling silence. There's no birdsong because the forest is able to reproduce without birds carrying seeds on its behalf. Does this mean it is an autonomous living being? This would be the perfect location to speculate about Gaia theory and the earth itself being a living organism, but a tour party isn't the best company in which to speculate on the metaphysics of the universe.

'There, look, those two are.'

We've stopped for a brief walk into the forest along a wooden platform. A man and a woman who don't seem to know each other are arguing about whether any of the trees are Huons. We know there's some new growth in here, centuries away from maturity; we just don't know which ones.

'No, they're not actually.'

'Yeah? So whadda you know? Do ya wanna bet? Come on, I'll bet ya.'

He's going a bit red and has a mad glint in his eye. A small crowd is forming around them.

'Come on, come on! I'll bet ya! Those two are!'

An elderly lady steps forward brandishing some manner of *I Spy Huon Pine* book. 'No,' she says, 'the lady's right. They're not. Look.'

Everybody looks and nods. He's furious and embarrassed as well now, getting redder all the time. The bloody women are ganging up on him! What's the bloody world coming to? They're only bloody trees after all!

'Yeah, well, I only had $10 in me wallet anyway.'

He strides off along the walkway chuntering to himself, and I decide I really ought to give the wilderness another crack while I'm here. On my own this time. See what it's like when it doesn't come with a buffet.

I drive north-east from Strahan in beautiful afternoon sunshine through forested hills. In an hour I see just one house. Two kids are playing on a swing in the garden. I try and imagine what their life must be like, and fail. In the tiny settlement of Rosebery two men are coming out of Kirkpatrick's Bar. Both have huge beards, just like the guy I was speaking to in Strahan. Either it's the accepted facial hair code for miners, or there's a ZZ Top convention on.

The quiet A-road becomes an extremely quiet B-road which I follow for a while before turning sharp right on to an utterly deserted C-road. I consult the map, but there aren't any D-roads. I've been climbing all afternoon and I'm on high ground, a wild and empty sparsely wooded plateau, when the giant razor-backed silhouette of Cradle Mountain looms on the horizon. As I get closer to the mountain the ground is littered with dead, bleached-white trees. A tall, thin, metallic windmill stands alone among them. The emptiness is beautiful, but also menacing on both physical (how would you survive?) and spiritual (what can it all mean?) levels. The island's cruel history lurks always in the background. Have I overdone it and filled my head with too much horror? Or does the past live on in the landscape, speaking out whether you want it to or not?

There are two people ahead of me at the desk as I check in to the Cradle Mountain Lodge. It's the Japanese couple from Strahan. I'm assigned a cabin a few hundred yards from the main building. It's comfortable, spacious and wooden, with a huge pile of logs outside the door, and a cast-iron wood-burning stove that dominates the room and encourages the feeling that you're living like a pioneer, which of course you are. It's just that there's a five-page wine list.

Unidentifiable twilight noises are emanating from the dense bush that touches my veranda as I walk down to the lodge in the darkness. On the edge of the car park I bump into a litterbin, which grunts and turns out to be a wombat. I arrive at the lodge just in time for the early evening wildlife slide show, and go straight to the bar instead. Slides might be an anticlimax after actually bumping into the wildlife, and I'm in no mood for disappointment.

The bar has a big lounge with a huge log fire and stone chimney in the middle. A tree trunk supports the roof. A well-fed Australian woman in her forties is holding court in the corner. She's decided against the no-frills, I've-just-walked-five-miles-up-a-mountain clothing favoured by everybody else, and has opted instead for the crisp coiffure and gold and chiffon trim of a bookmaker's wife on a Russian cruise ship who's hoping to get off with the captain. She's shouting a conversation at a fit-looking old geezer sitting on his own on the other side of the room, whom she seems just to have met. A man her own age, who I take to be her husband, is sitting next to her looking on in silence.

'Graham's from the Gold Coast but I'm a Sydneysider born and bred.' She takes a glug from what looks like a vase of white wine. 'Still, at least you get a bit of exercise up here so you feel justified about having a few drinks, a feed and a bit of fun in the evening.'

'Well, I'm seventy-two years old and I don't need to feel justified. I can have fifteen meals a day if I like. I never put on any weight.'

As they talk she's absentmindedly peeling the bark off the tree that's keeping the roof up. The fit old guy wants to stop her but doesn't know what to say. He half gestures with one finger raised from the arm of his chair.

'Er . . .'

'Ah, don't worry. It isn't real. I think it's been stuck on.' She peels away a big length of bark and dumps it in the hearth.

'It is real,' says the old guy. 'It's called pencil pine.'

'Hey,' she says, 'did you ever do the Gordon River cruise?'

'No,' he says.

'Oh, you really should. We've done it twice. You have to go to this horrible island but it's worth it. The lunch is just' – she's rolling her eyes to heaven now – 'out of this world. Serve yourself, take as much as you like. You should do it. Hey! Liddle tip. Take piles and piles of smoked salmon. They always bring out more.'

While she's been talking the barman has walked across and whispered in Graham's ear. Graham waits patiently for her to draw breath, then claps both hands down on his knees with cheery finality and says, 'C'mon, Annette. Our table's ready.'

During dinner I notice that Annette and Graham have acquired a twenty-five-year-old man from somewhere. I saw him standing near their table chatting earlier, and now he's sitting with them. He's saying something to Graham over the pudding, but I can't make out what it is. Perhaps it's, 'Will you be filming, or just watching?'

This morning I plan to walk up the mountain. I haven't done any hiking for months, as the English countryside's been closed due to the foot and mouth epidemic, and I'm not sure how I'll cope. My boots are in good nick though, cleaner than the Gordon River thanks to the quarantine department at Sydney airport. Any new arrival from Britain or other contagious third world countries had to go and stand in one of the Obnoxious Disease queues and wait to be examined. A stern young woman made me raise my feet and show her the soles of my shoes, like a horse being examined by a farrier. I owned up to the South Downs-encrusted boots in my bag before she found them and had me put in a detention camp. She took a close look, then popped them in a sterile forensic evidence bag and took them off to the nuclear cleansing sheds to be zapped. They came back cleaner than any boots I've ever seen, even in a shop. I don't know what they do with all the polluted soil. Squads of government-funded Aussie backpackers may already be flying incognito to Gatwick and Heathrow to dump it all in the corners of filthy London pubs, where it will lie undetected for years.

My fire was still glowing when I woke this morning, which was just as well, because the temperature had dropped to five below in the night. Halfway through breakfast a water pipe burst and we all had to evacuate the building and shiver in the car park under a clear blue sky. There's frost and ice on the path as I set out along the track that follows the shore of the lake at the foot of the mountain. It's completely still and totally, unnaturally silent. The stark mountain and azure sky are reflected so perfectly in the water that when I get the photos back I won't know which way up to hold them. I hit a good walking rhythm, revelling in the solitude as the trek takes me over massive boulders, through an enchanted forest and past a gushing waterfall.

I'm taking a rest just above Wombat Pool when I hear sounds in the distance, a bird-like yakkering and screeching that's getting closer with each passing minute. And then I see them on the track below: six hikers carrying enormous packs and talking and shouting to each other non-stop. I decide to wait and let them pass. Five men and a woman go by with cursory grunts of recognition. They are all in their twenties, kitted out in pukka hiking gear: map pouches, ski poles, stretch fabric shorts worn pervily over thermal tights, all that kind of caper. 'We're the real thing, tourist,' say their scientifically engineered fibres to my jeans and woollen lumber jacket. They're all talking at maximum volume, apart from the guy at the back. As he passes I hear the tinnitus rhythms I associate with the London underground, and see that he is, unbelievably, listening to techno music on a set of headphones. He's staring at the path as he walks, rather than bouncing along waving his arms in the air, so maybe he's still waiting for the Es to kick in.

Hiking alone offers different therapy from walking as part of a group. With friends or family you conform to a communal rhythm and subsume your own thoughts to the conversation of the group. Alone, it's a more primal experience. The walk sets the rhythm for what's going on inside your head. It's even better if you're in a place you've never been before. Away from the influence of favourite walks and landscapes, thoughts spring unexpectedly from nowhere. Your mind can wander free over concerns, worries, ambitions, loves. Key moments from your past spring uninvited into focus. Strong emotions are stirred up and then, without realising, you're where I am now, standing on top of the world.

I've scrambled over the last few boulders to find myself on a summit plateau, looking down on three lakes. Across to my right mountains and dense forest stretch away as far as the eye can see. To my left the six noisy hikers are standing staring at a camera balanced precariously on a rock. 'Okay? Grin!' shouts one of the guys, but before the time switch activates itself the camera blows off the rock and disappears over the edge. 'Oh, no,' they chorus, but it's only caught on a ledge and is quickly retrieved.

'Would you mind taking it this time?'

Of course I wouldn't. They explain how the camera works, but I already know. You just line up that white square you can see through the viewfinder so that their bodies are in it but their heads are just outside it, then *click*.

'Thanks, mate.'

'No worries.'

When they've gone I stand and gaze out at the 360-degree wilderness. It's astonishing to think I'm looking at places where no man has ever trodden; but even as I stand here admiring it in glorious sunshine and a cutting breeze, I find my thoughts straying against my will to the comforting man-designed land-scape of home. There's something about the way that fields and churches and orchards and houses and dry-stone walls have been

artfully arranged over the centuries that nourishes our inner life
and calms the human psyche; wilderness, on the other hand, is
just saying 'Woooaaahhh!' I don't think you'd want too much
of it, or you might end up like Jack in *The Shining*. As I begin
my descent I find myself thinking, and not for the first time,
just how useful wilderness must be when it comes to burying a
troublesome relative, or a complete stranger.

Or eating them.

A few months after he was shipped back from Hobart to Macquarie, Edward Pearce escaped again, this time with just the one
companion, everyone else presumably having got doctors' notes
for sore throats and bad backs that prevented them from travelling with him. According to Pearce's own account, a newly
arrived young labourer called Cox kept pestering him to escape
again, and this time take him along. It's a very cinematic moment,
I think: the naïve young man saying, 'Let's go off into the bush,
Mr Pearce, just me and you,' and the camera lingering on the
reaction shot, a barely perceptible 'All right, it was your idea but
don't say I didn't warn you' glint in Pearce's terrible flesh-hungry
eyes. And then the glint vanishes and Pearce is smiling at the
prospect of the outing.

'Ah, sure, why not? Come on, Coxie Boy, let's find ourselves
a boat.'

They escaped on 16 November. Pearce began eating him on
the 19th. He was picked up two days later by a convict ship.
This time the authorities believed Pearce's story, possibly because
he still had half a pound of Cox in his pockets, taken from the
thick part of the arm, which he reckoned was the tastiest cut.
The authorities concluded that Pearce had acquired a taste for
human flesh on his previous adventures, and couldn't resist
coming back for more. Pearce himself disagreed. Though not
denying he'd killed and eaten the lad, he said he'd only done it
because he was annoyed when they came to cross a river and he

found out that Cox couldn't swim. Thank God it didn't turn out the kid was afraid of heights or couldn't climb trees, or he'd have ended up in real trouble.

Pearce was hanged in Hobart in July 1824. They took out his brain, boiled his head and donated it to an American phrenologist for a collection called American Golgotha. They tell me it's in a glass cabinet in a museum in Philadelphia.

8

YOUNG IRELAND IN
DAMN DEMON'S LAND

I'm on the sixteenth floor of a casino in a room made of prefabricated concrete slabs watching a British TV detective show starring that actor who's always a bit blank behind the eyes, as if he's taken a nasty knock on the head. Somebody's just been murdered with an antique chest of drawers, which is fine if you're watching in England, but seems hopelessly arch and pouffy on a windy Saturday night in Van Diemen's Land. I missed the first quarter of an hour because the hotel had hidden the telly inside a great big cupboard and I presumed I didn't have one, but I think I'm up to speed with the plot now. I reckon the posh alcoholic who runs the post office did it. Her, or the heterosexual vicar. I hope Tasmanians don't think England's really like this.

I had hoped that a sudden transition from rainforest wilderness to urban jungle might prove stimulating, and Hobart Casino seemed like my best, indeed only, option. An evening or two rubbing shoulders with a few high-rolling movers and shakers might exorcise the ghosts of Sarah Island and the spirits of the roadkill before I head off into the wilds again in search of the Young Irelanders; but the sudden jerk-around from where I was then to where I am now was unwise in the extreme, and I've taken refuge in my room to nurse my damaged psyche.

It was already dark when I got here. A man in a uniform flagged me down outside the main entrance. I thought he was going to tell me to clear off, but instead he took my car keys and drove it off to park it for me in some secret place. I thought that kind of thing only happened in movies. Valet parking, like pillow menus, has never previously featured in my life, and it looks like I'll be heading home a more sophisticated man-about-the-world than when I arrived.

As I was checking in I took a daily paper from the free pile on the desk. 'Hang on, mate,' said the desk clerk, 'I'll give you a better one than that,' and produced a different paper from underneath the counter. Nice touch, I thought. He's spotted that I'm an upmarket, erudite kind of guy who merits a better class of journo. It was only when I stumbled upon the telly in the cupboard and couldn't find any of the programmes in the listings that I looked at the date and realised he'd given me yesterday's paper. Why did he do that? Is he part of some campaign being waged by the Tasmanian authorities, an artful and knowing programme of pranks and stunts designed to send up their clichéd image of being seriously behind the times? First there was the slow clock at the airport carousel; now this. I think it has to be deliberate.

I took the elevator downstairs for a slice of Saturday night action and there it was again: on the menu on the wall of the lift, among the starters, above the drizzled this and coulised that, right where you'd expect to find the soup of the day. *Soupe d'hier*, it said, followed by the translation: soup of yesterday. 'As it should be, made the day before,' read the explanation. Well, that's as maybe, mate, I thought, but you don't fool me. This caught-in-the-past routine? A façade, probably the brainchild of

an expensive image consultancy, designed to appeal to the subliminal nostalgic in all of us.

Though I don't gamble myself, I've always found it exciting
to watch reckless card-sharps dressed in the kind of clothes
Americans wear at weddings standing at green baize tables
displaying more courage and élan than I'll ever have. But as I
walked out of the elevator into the heart of Saturday night the
four card tables and two roulette wheels had no takers. Instead
rows and rows of people as badly dressed as me were standing
round the bars, staring at the gambling games on the TV screens
like the broken-spirited miners of Queenstown, only with more
aftershave. Fat men, thin women, shrill girls and punky boys
with gelled hair were pouring their hard-earned into the machines
until they were sure it wasn't coming back. Of all the choices
available to them tonight they had decided to do this with their
lives.

And so had I.

I needed to get out, so I took a walk to an oriental noodle
place I'd spotted up the street. I got there at five past nine. It
closed at nine. Purveyors of ethnic food in Australia don't seem
to have latched on to the British idea that they're supposed to
work eighteen-hour days for the convenience of the locals. So
now I'm hiding back in my room watching the Detective. I must
be homesick, because there's no other reason for watching it.
He's interviewing a suspect now, but giving the impression he's
thinking of something else while he's doing it. You can forget
the postmistress though. I reckon the clever money's got to be
on the pub landlord. He's hiding something, mark my word. I
bet it turns out that he never was in the Parachute Regiment in
the first place. They never are, are they? It usually turns out they
were only using that as a cover story to hide the fact they'd been
doing time for sexually assaulting a hot-dog vendor or a circus
clown or something. Next thing you know, they're killing people
with chests of drawers.

Room service has arrived: Thai chicken caesar salad with nan bread. This fusion-combination fast food is getting out of hand. It started when they put pineapple on pizzas, but where will it end? Sweet and sour Cajun blackened bar-b-q Thai chicken tikka masala caesar salad pizza fajitas? Deep-fried sweet and . . . wait, the ads are on. I missed the ending. They must have revealed the killer while I was signing for the food. That's nearly an hour of my life squandered; more if you add on the trip to the restaurant that was closed. When I'm on my deathbed I'll remember this night and think, What a waste of a life. I could have had two more hours.

I'm woken in the night by high-spirited screaming and shouting in the corridor outside my room, which is traditional in Australian hotels on weekend nights, especially if there's a big sports event on, which there always is.

During my visit to Cobh the Bishop Basher had drawn my attention to the political prisoner John Mitchel, who had been imprisoned on Spike Island in Cork Harbour. Until then I knew little of the extraordinary story of Mitchel, his compatriots Francis Meagher and William Smith O'Brien, and the Young Irelanders' Rebellion of 1848, which culminated in the Battle of Widow McCormack's Cabbage Patch in a back garden in Tipperary. If it weren't for the widow's cabbages, I wouldn't be in Tasmania today.

In the early 1840s Mitchel, Meagher and O'Brien were driving forces in the Repeal movement, a political campaign to liberate Ireland from British rule. Most people today would see this dispute as fairly clear-cut: Catholics are nationalists, and Protestants are loyal to the British crown. What drew me to the story of the Young Irelanders is that many of the key players, like Wolfe Tone before them, were Protestants. It's good to be reminded that political ideals have not always split along sectarian lines, as some would have us believe.

John Mitchel was a lawyer, born in Derry in 1815 to a prosperous Protestant family. By 1845 he was editor of the *Irish Nation*, a Dublin-based campaigning newspaper. Francis Thomas Meagher, born a Catholic in 1823 in Waterford, was a flamboyant and gifted orator, a dashing, romantic figure who, unlike his abstemious Protestant colleagues, was fond of the odd drink. William Smith O'Brien was a pillar of the Protestant establishment who none the less campaigned passionately for Irish independence. He was born in County Clare in 1803, a descendant of the eleventh-century Irish king Brian Boru. Unlike your average Irishman, he was educated at Harrow and Trinity College Cambridge, and by 1828 had a seat in the House of Commons. Despite being a landowner he campaigned on behalf of the impoverished Irish peasantry, and brought to public attention the scandalously exploitative behaviour of absentee landlords.

By the summer of 1843 Repeal was gaining momentum, and huge public rallies were held all over Ireland. If millions of people showed support, the thinking went, they would achieve freedom without resort to physical force. The biggest rally was planned for October at Clontarf, near Dublin, a symbolic location where in 1014 Brian Boru had died defending his country against Danish invaders. Steamers were chartered to bring expatriate supporters home from England, Wales and Scotland; but they weren't the only ships in the Irish Sea. British warships gathered off the Dublin coast, the city was packed with troops, and the rally declared illegal. Repeal supporters dispersed without a fight.

It was during 1843 that O'Brien – a respected MP, and widely perceived to be a man of principle – joined Repeal, driven by the unacceptable levels of poverty in Ireland which the government seemed to be doing nothing to alleviate. This new alliance of politicians, orators, journalists, poets and landowners was christened Young Ireland; though a unionist paper in the north jibed that O'Brien, a generation older than most of his comrades, should be known as 'Middle-aged Ireland'.

In 1845 the potato crop failed for the first time and the country was devastated by famine. The following year O'Brien spent long hours in the House of Commons trying to disrupt the Coercion Bill, a measure designed to give landlords even greater powers over their troublesome half-starved tenants. For his pains O'Brien was asked to serve on the Parliamentary Select Committee on Scottish railways, which he refused to do until Ireland's calamitous problems were addressed. He was imprisoned for a month by order of his fellow MPs; Meagher and Mitchel visited him in jail.

The situation deteriorated over the next two years. The potato crop failed repeatedly, landlords evicted starving tenants, and there was a mass exodus of impoverished Irish to Liverpool, Manchester and the USA. The mood turned inevitably towards armed uprising. Meagher spoke in admiration of America's War of Independence against British rule. Pressed by conservative elements in Repeal and in the Church to renounce violence, he instead praised the sword as 'a sacred weapon'. In the years to come he would be known – in Ireland, and in distant places of which he had not yet dreamed – as Meagher of the Sword.

By 1848 Mitchel was predicting imminent revolution. He wrote an open letter to his fellow Ulster Protestants saying that 'popery and papists' were not the problem, but 'tenure of the land'. He made increasingly fiery attacks on the British government, in a deliberate attempt to provoke them into retaliation. Troops were sent to Dublin, and Mitchel, Meagher and O'Brien were arrested on charges of seditious libel. O'Brien and Meagher were tried in Dublin and acquitted; at which point the British government came up with Plan B. A new law, the Treason-Felony Act, was rushed through parliament, making it an offence even to express the opinion that the British crown might one day relinquish power in Ireland. Mitchel was convicted and sentenced to fourteen years transportation. On 28 May he was taken to Cobh, where he spent four days on Spike Island, and signed autographs for the locals.

On 1 June he embarked for Bermuda, en route to Van Diemen's Land.

Britain suspended the Act of Habeas Corpus in Ireland. With warrants out for their arrest, Meagher and O'Brien went on the run. O'Brien, however, was not temperamentally suited to armed struggle. Arriving at a country police station one night with a few supporters, he demanded that the five officers inside give up their arms. 'But if we surrender to so small a force,' pleaded the officer in charge, 'we will surely be dismissed and our families will starve.' Unwilling to condemn fellow Irishmen to such a fate, O'Brien agreed to go away and come back later with thirty men. 'That wouldn't look so bad for us,' said the constable. O'Brien returned to an empty police station.

Matters came to a head in the village of Ballingarry, near Clonmel in South Tipperary, on 29 July. O'Brien was behind a barricade with a crowd of about 200 people when a column of police approached, then disappeared into the back lanes. Word came back that they had commandeered a cottage belonging to the Widow McCormack and had barricaded themselves in. The Young Irelanders surrounded the cottage, with the five children who lived there still inside. When the widow returned from an ill-timed errand to find guns pointing out through her cottage windows, O'Brien escorted her through the cabbage patch to a window so she could ask after the kids. 'Give up your arms,' he told the police, 'we will not hurt you.' Policemen shook his hands through the window; but then stones were thrown from the rebels' side, shots were fired in response, and two rebels lay dead.

O'Brien was ridiculed in the London press for 'creeping away among the cabbages'. Disguised, though not very convincingly, in an old cloak, he was arrested on Thurles station by a railway guard. When police tried to take him to Dublin the train driver refused to start up the engine, and had to be persuaded to do so by an officer holding a gun to his head. Meagher, who had not been present at Widow McCormack's, was arrested a week later.

The men were charged with high treason. Along with a number of their colleagues they were tried in Clonmel. Senior parliamentarians and a British army officer appeared for O'Brien as character witnesses, but to no avail. He, Meagher and two others were sentenced to be hanged, drawn and quartered.

The sentences were greeted with uproar and widespread outrage. In June 1849 they were commuted to transportation for life. The men arrived in Hobart at the end of October, and O'Brien was loaded on to another boat bound for his destination. 'The outline of this coast resembles much some parts of the Highlands of Scotland and the mountain regions of Ireland,' he wrote of his arrival on Maria Island, off the east coast of Van Diemen's Land.

These days it's just a two-hour drive from Hobart.

I wake at eight, open the curtains and immediately feel bad for writing unkind things about the casino last night. I arrived in the dark, unaware that the view from my window is possibly the most spectacular I've enjoyed from any hotel in the world. The whole harbour is spread out before me, sunshine glinting off the water to dazzle the early morning sailors on the yachts heading out the Derwent Estuary towards Storm Bay. As I watch, a seaplane lands at the water's edge sixteen floors below. I'm glad I came to the Casino. It offers an extreme mix of sublime natural beauty and darkness of the human soul that perfectly encapsulates the Tasmanian experience, with the added advantage of room service.

In the corridor a maid is clearing up last night's trays and empties of sparkling wine. 'Lovely morning,' I say.

'Well . . . yeah. It's okay, I suppose,' she says, looking at me as if I've still got the electrodes taped to my forehead. In the lift on the way down to breakfast a couple in their thirties get in at the tenth floor. They have authentic rural Australian haircuts – mullet for him, Suzi Quatro for her – which are still glistening wet from the shower. As the doors slide shut the tiny space is filled with the heady scent of complimentary unguents and herbal shampoos, with an underlying but unmistakable fragrance of yesterday's forty-proof alcohol. The three of us are halfway to the ground floor when he turns grimly to the well-scrubbed long-suffering beauty and says, 'Gee, I only had a few drinks last night, and I'm still off me fakken head.'

She smiles indulgently, because she knows that this is his way of saying he loves her.

Patsy Cline is singing 'Crazy' on the radio as I cross the harbour bridge and head north-east towards Louisville and the ferry to Maria. 'Ah, mate,' says the DJ, with what may be a genuine tear in his eye, 'I wish she was still alive.' Then he introduces the news. It includes the first mention of Britain I've caught since I've been here. One in three Britons, it seems, is kept awake at night by their partner's snoring. London is worst of all, with everybody who lives there being woken at night by their next-door neighbour's snoring. Some sort of chain reaction, I suppose, ricocheting along those depressing Victorian terraces in which the poor Poms have to live. This isn't a snoring story, of course, but one of those 'Jeez, it must be bloody awful to live in the UK' stories which the Aussie media use to pep up the feelgood factor and foster national unity. It's a particularly effective one, as there doesn't seem to be a snoring problem here. I took a walk around the residential streets of Battery Point, the oldest part of Hobart, last weekend, and at nine p.m. there was total silence. No stereos, TV, talking, shouting, cooking, playing, driving, walking, barking – not even a bit of snoring to liven things up. What do these people do in the evenings? Is it in any way connected to roadkill?

The journey, though less eerie than the drive to Strahan, is once again devastatingly beautiful: pasture, woodland, hills and rivers dotted with wood-frame houses and stone churches.

Break-me-neck Hill is my favourite place name so far. It's certainly better than the Legs 'N' Breasts Chicken Shop, a cringeingly blokish nudge-nudge choice of name that makes you fear the Tits 'N' Ass Pie Shop can't be far behind.

There's nearly an hour to wait for the ferry as I leave the car in a near-deserted car park that probably holds upwards of a hundred vehicles in high season. Two birds straight out of a children's colouring book, with bright red heads, yellow midriffs and green tail feathers, are sitting in a tree outside the café/bar/ticket office. As I walk past admiring them, their profiles go red yellow green, like two sets of traffic lights.

I get my ticket and settle at a table looking out across the white-topped water to the mountains of the island. This morning's paper says that a new survey shows that many butter-substitute olive oil and vegetable spreads are far more harmful than butter, and some should come with a health warning attached. Another report says that too much vitamin C messes up your genes and gives you cancer. I feel strangely comforted, as I did when I heard that the guy who invented jogging had died while he was out jogging.

I share the small boat with a dozen over-excited schoolboys and their hairy-kneed teacher, a khaki-clad outward-bounder of indeterminate sex. The skipper operates the steering wheel with his feet while reading the paper. It's an enjoyable crossing, choppy enough to make you wonder how rough the four-month crossing from Cobh might have been. O'Brien was right about the view. Looking back to the mountains across the deep blue water, it would be easy to believe you were in the west of Ireland. As we come ashore at a jetty by a white sandy bay there's a sudden flurry of rain. A perfect rainbow, a dense ground-to-ground canopy connecting the beach to the forested mountainside, envelops the island.

As the schoolboys head off along the track I go into the former Commissariat stores, now an unmanned information centre near the jetty. The island isn't yet part of the tourist mainstream, and only has 13,000 visitors each year. There's a visitors' book which I open at random at what I presume must be the record of a school visit like today's. 'Totally awesome,' wrote one kid, though opinion was divided on the merits of the place. 'Neat.' 'Cool.' 'Okay.' 'Boring island.' 'Too many walks.' 'Sorta okay and sorta sucks.' 'Never seen so much kangaroo shit in my life. Fantastic.'

When O'Brien, Meagher and the others arrived at Hobart they were offered terms under which they could enjoy a high degree of liberty within the confines of Van Diemen's Land. Earl Grey, the Secretary of State for Colonial Affairs, had ordered that they 'should be punished for their crimes, but with consideration of their superior rank in society . . . for such men banishment and forfeiture of property and station is an extremely heavy infliction and probably punishment enough.' Attitudes within the government had clearly mellowed since that first heady rush for hanging, drawing and quartering. Nor was forced labour – the fate of most convicts – on the agenda for the Irish politicals. The deal offered was that each man would be assigned a separate district in which he was free to move. They would report once a month to the authorities, be home by nine at night, and not leave their district nor have contact with each other. In return, they had to give a promise not to escape – their 'parole'. After some negotiations, all agreed these terms except O'Brien, who was ordered to be confined on Maria Island. The others were free, within certain boundaries, to socialise, ride horses and go to the pub.

The island today is a national park. Endangered species of wallaby, kangaroo and Cape Barren geese have been introduced and seals, dolphins and whales flourish in the protected off-shore waters. The convict settlement was at Darlington, a ten-minute walk from the jetty. The schoolboys have vanished and I seem to have the island to myself. As I approach the settlement the hairs are standing on the back of my neck in a thrill of anticipation. Having stumbled across this story in Cobh and read so much about it since, it has taken on the feel of a folk-tale or legend. And now, after all these miles, here's the real thing. This place feels impossibly remote even today; it's hard to conceive how far removed from their own world the prisoners must have felt.

In contrast to the ruins of Sarah Island, Darlington is pretty much intact, a cluster of cottages and bunkhouses in which the schoolboys and the Khaki Hermaphrodite are installing themselves for an overnight stay. O'Brien's white-painted cottage is the middle one of three, where he lived flanked by the assistant superintendent and the Catholic chaplain. He may have had terrific sea views, but when he arrived he didn't even know how to light his own fire.

'If Maria were placed near the coast of Ireland I should be quite contented to make it my abode so long as I was surrounded by my children,' he wrote. 'I find myself much less fitted for the life of a Robinson Crusoe than I believed myself to be.'

I walk inside into a two-roomed cottage with a fireplace on each side. The attic where he wrote a secret diary has been exposed. At the back is a small garden. O'Brien was allowed to move within a 200-yard radius of the cottage, but was kept apart from the other prisoners. Sir William Dennison, the governor of Tasmania who regarded penal reform as 'maudlin sentimentality', wrote that O'Brien expected to be 'the centre of attraction to a wondering and admiring multitude. He finds that at Maria Island he is not known nor cared for, and he is bitterly disappointed.'

The cottage is stark and simple, and serves as a moving record of O'Brien's time here. There are details I haven't previously come across, including mocking quotes from the London press at the time of his conviction. *The Times* derided him as a fool 'of unsound intellect . . . who wanted to be Smith the First, King of Munster'. *Punch* said: 'The courage of Mr Smith O'Brien in slinking among the cabbages in Widow McCormack's garden may be questioned; but it must be remembered that the hero, if he crept out of the way of the bullets, betrayed no fear of the slugs.' That'll teach him to go round suggesting that Catholics and Protestants should go to the same schools, a belief that also upset his fiercely loyalist mother, who wrote to Maria Island warning him against 'the deceitful delusion of Popery . . . those cunningly devised fables'. I suppose it's unlikely to be still there now, but I find myself wishing I'd tried to find the widow's cabbage patch when I was last in Ireland.

One detail catches my eye. A letter home has two sets of writing to the page, one across the other at right angles, exactly as Louie had written the letter about poor Bert that I read at Vince's house in Cobh. It must have been common practice. It's a precise, very human detail that links O'Brien and her together in the same era, and the same fate of separation by the seas. There's also evidence that O'Brien's solitude drove him to that most extreme refuge of the truly desperate: poetry.

> *When patriots' stomachs yearn for food*
> *Withhold their usual fare*
> *For bread with butter if imbued*
> *Will tempt the soul to dare*
>
> *Let not of curried rice the heart*
> *Fire to the veins impart*
> *Nor coffee's essence, strong and sweet*
> *Uplift the sinking heart*
>
> *For such is the system of control*
> *In Mary's isle applied*
> *Thus the controller daunts the soul*
> *And tames a rebel's pride*

Outside with a banana and a bar of chocolate I sit on a stone looking down towards the sea and try to piece together the locations of the most farcical, and most notorious, incident of O'Brien's sojourn on Maria.

The superintendent of the island, Mr Lapham, came from Kildare. He and O'Brien seem to have had a cordial relationship from the start, and Lapham gradually relaxed the terms of his famous prisoner's confinement, even going so far as to allow him to speak with some of the officers and their families. The Lapham family house was close to O'Brien's cottage – I'm sitting next to it as I eat – and he shared an interest in botany with the superintendent's youngest daughter Susan. He was soon to wish that he hadn't. On 18 July he was with Miss Lapham in her garden, not knowing they were being watched by three men with a telescope. Constable William Rogerson takes up the story:

I saw him reclining on the garden seat . . . saw Smith O'Brien take Miss Susan Lapham by the hand. He pulled her towards him and threw his cloak partially round and round. She was leaning over him . . . her hand had disappeared with his under his clothes. It appeared to be in his trousers. I saw her clothes move as if his hand was under them.

O'Brien's cloaks weren't doing him a lot of favours; it isn't clear whether this was the same one that let him down on Thurles railway station. The constable certainly seems to have been in possession of a top-notch telescope. One of his colleagues took a turn next. 'I saw O'Brien's trousers open in front and I saw Miss Susan's hand in his trousers. I could see the button [!] on his trousers and I saw Miss Lapham take her hand from his trousers . . .'

Considering the nature of the alleged offence it seems strange no action was taken against O'Brien. It's possible the allegations were covered up from Lapham, though his wife certainly knew. O'Brien dismissed them as 'the reports of a mischief-maker, who states that he saw with a telescope doings that he could not have seen had he been within ten yards'. Whatever the truth of the matter, surveillance of O'Brien was stepped up. In Hobart, Meagher, acting in collaboration with an Irish doctor called McCarthy and with support from Irish nationalists in New York, organised a ship to rescue O'Brien, who had never given his parole not to escape. Like many of O'Brien's grand gestures, the attempt ended in farce. O'Brien was apprehended splashing about in the water by one of the constables who had manned the telescope during the alleged groping of Miss Lapham. Shortly afterwards O'Brien was told he was to be transferred to the feared penal colony of Port Arthur, south of Hobart. In a letter to his sister he wrote: 'I have been told that Port Arthur is as near a realisation of Hell upon earth as can be found in any part of the British Dominions.'

He had been on Maria Island for two years, during which time parliament had passed a bill granting representative government to Van Diemen's Land. No such proposal had been made for Ireland.

The haze has lifted and the sun has come out, lighting up the wooded mountains and the white tops on the Mediterranean-blue sea. I walk back to the Commissariat stores, then up the hill behind it. According to the map, the island's cemetery is on a hill up here; beyond it are spectacular fossil-encrusted cliffs.

At the top of the hill is a convict-built brick barn full of decaying farm tools and four wooden-shafted pony carts with rusted steel wheel rims. Everything is covered in feathers and droppings. There's no sign of any chickens, so I suppose it must be down to the geese. It says on the map that Cape Barren geese were in danger of extinction in the 1950s and are still one of the rarest breeds in the world, with just 16,000 remaining. A hundred of them are here, eating grass and laying eggs. 'Each pair of geese establishes a territory in autumn, prepares a nest site and defends it noisily and determinedly against other geese.' It doesn't say anything about them being aggressive to humans, but in my experience you can never be too careful. A pub I know used to have a guard goose to keep burglars away. Vicious bastard, according to the brute who owned the place, and he should know.

I can see about a dozen of them as I head across the tussocky grass towards the cemetery, which is silhouetted against the ocean and mountains of the mainland. They've got pretty grey plumage and vivid pink legs, and each one looks about big enough to feed a family of ten. I'm just passing a big red boulder that's protruding from the grass when two geese pop up about thirty or forty yards in front of me, directly between me and the cemetery. My track record with wild animals, or domestic ones for that matter, isn't good, and as a general rule I think it's best always to be afraid of them unless you have good reason not to be; yet these guys don't look at all menacing, and I'm finding it exhilarating to walk among such rare creatures in so dramatic a setting while breathing the cleanest air in the world.

Hang on though. One of them has just done a couple of funny little hops; and now it's flying close to the ground like a smart missile or low-level bomber, flying fast and straight and true, and directly at me, its suddenly vicious beak aimed at my throat like a feathery bayonet as it lets rip a banshee screech. Look, I didn't mean it about the family of ten; these thoughts just pop into my head and I don't have any control over them. I'm sorry. It was in very poor taste. It's landed now, digging its evil-looking heels into the turf like the roadrunner trying to slow down, but it's still coming at me on foot, and I'm thinking you wouldn't want a peck in the groin from the bugger, beak like teak I expect, with all that foraging. They say swans can break your arm, don't they; so there's no knowing what this evil fecker might do. Forget the cemetery. Sod the fossils. I'm going back to the jetty.

I turn on my heel, blindly trusting that an endangered goose must be a liberal at heart who supports other good causes and so wouldn't be sneaky enough to attack a man from behind, when I notice something strange about the red boulder.

It appears to be trying to stand up.

It's on its back legs now, and it's as big as me. *At least* as big as me. I'm caught in a pincer movement between a psychotic goose and a kangaroo whose sleep has just been disturbed, and I'm not sure of the survival etiquette. The kangaroo is just standing there trying to stare me out, and I'm looking at him, imagining him with boxing gloves on. I'm shocked at their ingratitude, ganging up on a human after all we've done for them. I've often thought that conservation is wasted on animals. You wouldn't mind so much if they showed some sign of appreciating it. The goose has stopped advancing now, and the three of us are just standing here like chess pieces, waiting for someone to make the next move. It'll have to be me. Tasmania's been freaking me out enough already without being on the wrong end of a good pecking and thumping. I take two steps back. They don't do anything. Two more. Nothing. Good. Anyway, seen one graveyard, seen them all really, and fossils are just very old. I turn and walk back towards the barn.

A couple of hundred yards away the schoolboys are marching breezily towards the fossil cliffs. I hope the Khaki Hermaphrodite knows what he/she's doing. I wouldn't like to be the one having to face the parents and tell them that little Daryl has been maimed by an endangered species.

Back at the car park on the other side of the water I'm still rattled, and spend five minutes trying to unlock the wrong hire car. I don't think anyone notices. I wouldn't want people to think I'm not fit to be let out on my own.

The Freycinet Peninsula is supposed to be one of the most spectacular places in Tasmania, and as it's only a couple of hours' drive up the coast I figure I might as well take a look.

The drive alone is worth the trip. The road hugs the coastline, and as you head north the views of Mariá give way to the open spaces of the Tasman Sea before the peninsula appears like a distant island on the other side of Great Oyster Bay. This is the most beautiful landscape – to the European eye at least – I've seen so far, less brooding and threatening than the west and without all that rather worrying forest. I love the place names on the signs: Old Man Creek, Spiky Beach, Horse Poo, though the last one turns out not to be a place but produce for sale at the entrance to a stud farm.

On a lonely stretch of road I slam on the brakes and go into reverse so I can check if I've seen what I think I've seen. Hanging by laces and baler twine on a wire fence at the edge of a rolling meadow are fifty or sixty shoes: a lime-green jelly sandal, two non-matching wellies, a ski boot, three assorted kids' trainers, a range of flip-flops, plain shoes, shoes like dead pigs' noses, a hush puppy, a green Doc Marten, a brown Blundstone boot, a fur-lined pink slipper and a rubber wader impaled upside down on a fence post. There are more shoes than I've seen people all day. Just when you think Tasmania has calmed down and stopped being weird, something like this happens to unsettle you. There's no explanation, no acknowledgement, no sign of human life or habitation in any direction. Who's done it? What can it mean? Is it in any way connected to the mystery of the roadkill?

A little further on, completely on its own in the middle of a field, is a square brick bungalow with neatly pruned ornamental roses and bedding plants growing along a suburban garden wall. It looks even weirder than the shoes.

'Come and enjoy the English Gardens and Cream Teas', says a sign in the town of Swansea. I get out of the car to phone ahead and book accommodation, and to use the local cashpoint. 'Glamorgan Community Centre and War Memorial Museum', says another sign. 'Come in and see our Historic Billiard Table.' I book a room, but there's no cashpoint. I'd love to see the Historic Billiard Table – there are two Historic Billiard Tables in the oddball Fijian town of Levuka, and it's one of my favourite places in the world – but I have to press on. I don't want to be late for dinner, because when you're travelling on your own a lonely and depressing dinner for one is a highpoint of the day. It gives your life focus.

I'm passing a field full of strange spiky clumps of grass that look like Mohican haircuts, as if someone has buried a couple of hundred punks – perhaps that was a roadside shrine and those were their shoes – when I see a guy hitch-hiking. He isn't carrying any visible weapons and looks nothing like the pictures of Edward Pearce, so I pull over and pick him up. He's a nineteen-year-old German called Andreas, and he makes me feel like an old fart in a hire car. Andreas is cycling around Australia. He's been doing it for four months, camping every night in a little tent on his own, unless he's lying and he goes to orgies in the campsite table-tennis room with all the other cyclists. Something's not quite right though.

He hasn't got a bicycle.

'I do not like to cycle the same road two times. So if I must go one more time on this road, I hide the bicycle in the bush and hitch-hike. Since two days now I am hiding the bike.'

It isn't easy meeting people in a place as empty as Tasmania, and there have been times when I've felt the loneliness getting to me. 'You must meet a lot of people,' I say to Andreas, enviously.

'Yes,' he says. 'Canadians.'

I rephrase the question because I think he must have misheard, but get the same reply.

'Always in Australia I am meeting Canadians. More times I meet Canadians than Australians. Even Canadians are telling me, they are meeting more Canadians here than in Canada.' He pauses to consider. 'I think they have very long winter.'

He asks me to stop on the edge of a wood where he's hidden the bike. I wonder if he's ever afraid the bike might be stolen.

'I think people in Tasmania are very honest.'

'Well,' I joke, 'perhaps that's because they're descended from convicts.'

'Yes,' he agrees, and shakes my hand. 'Thank you. Goodbye.'

At the Freycinet Lodge I have a gorgeous cabin overlooking a twilit beach on which a spherical woman in leggings is doing exercises that look like a cross between t'ai chi and semaphore. It's possible she may be signalling to another civilisation that isn't visible to the human eye. I get changed for dinner, which is just as well, because there's a sign on the door of the lodge.

THIS IS A SMOKE-FREE ZONE. DRESS RULES APPLY. EVENING ATTIRE: COLLARS, NEAT CASUAL FULL-LENGTH PANTS. FOOT-WEAR MUST BE WORN. NO THONGS.

Despite their nation's casual and carefree image, Aussie bars and restaurants seem very big on drumming dress sense into the population. Standards vary according to the location. In Margaret River in Western Australia, near one of the world's greatest surf beaches, I once saw a sign on a pub door that said: NO BARE FEET OR CHESTS — SINGLETS AND THONGS MUST BE WORN. Inside, a herd of bare-chested surfies with nothing on their feet were playing pool, watched by a clutch of tattooed teenage girls with babies on their laps. One guy sported a Long John Silver broomstick leg from the knee down, where a shark had bitten off the original. I doubt if there were any shirts or footwear within a twenty-mile radius, but at least the landlord was trying to make a difference. Next time I go they might all be wearing lightweight two-piece Armani suits and suede loafers. NO TWO-PIECE SUITS OR LOAFERS, the sign will say. WAISTCOATS AND LACE-UP BOOTS MUST BE WORN.

In the last twenty years Australian cuisine has won worldwide acclaim, and rightly so. There are signs, though, that it's started to go to their heads. Any Australian menu now contains at least one word that you've never seen before in your life. The res-taurants must be employing experimental linguists to compile them. Tonight's menu features smoked salmon with a lemon pepper lavroche, oysters with a mango brunoise, and beef served with pommes anna. The fresh catch comes with potato chats accompanied by a gribiche sauce, while the ravioli has a capsicum brunoise. I order a starter of seared scallops instead. They are sensational, the best I've ever eaten, so I order them for my main course as well. 'Boogie Woogie Bugle Boy from Company B' is on the stereo, and the waiter comes round with a pepper grinder as big as Ronnie Corbett. If you're ever in the area, pop in. Trust me. You won't be disappointed.

There's another sad lonely bastard at the next table, an older guy with a beard who's eating rare fillet steak bluto with a bora-bora grenouille papadoc lino and a side order of watutsi hucklebuck limedervish splat. It looks good, if a little plain. He picks up on my accent as I'm ordering more scallops for pudding, and immediately strikes up a conversation.

'So who do you think will win Super League? Wigan or the Bradford Bulls?'

There's surely no other country where a stranger in a fancy restaurant would break the ice by talking about rugby league, and I find it heart-warming. I grew up with the game. When Warrington played St Helens in the Lancashire Cup on a Wednesday afternoon because floodlights hadn't been invented, at least not in Warrington, the Brothers gave everyone time off to watch the game while they put in a few extra hours in the gym on the heavy punchbag. When St Helens won the Challenge Cup at Wembley on Saturday afternoon, the trophy was on the stage at Monday morning assembly so we could give thanks to God and renounce Satan and all his works and pomps, which were based at Twickenham. So Patrick from Sydney and I chat about sport, as men do when what they really want to say is 'Help, I'm lonely.' As I'm signing my scallop account Patrick pours me a glass of the wine he's been drinking, a chunky-looking red. 'Give this a bit of a go,' he says. 'Tell me what you think.' I try it, and tell him it's the best red wine I've ever tasted, because it is. 'Good on ya,' he says. 'Penfolds Bin 389. Best wine in Australia, bar none. Nice talking to ya. G'night.'

As I peer into the darkness from my balcony, trying to see if the woman in leggings is still signalling to the aliens, I'm thinking how much I've enjoyed the chat and the human contact. Tasmania is conspicuously emptier than Manhattan, and meeting people isn't as easy as it is in Rocky Sullivan's. Normally if you're travelling on your own in an alcohol-oriented culture you can rely on pubs for a convivial time, but in recent years many Aussie pubs have been hijacked by the gambling industry, which doesn't encourage conversation. A friend in Sydney who has always taken great pride in his city's pubs was telling me that he barely visits them these days because so many have turned into betting shops with small bar attached.

Someone has decided to package drink along with another vice to raise taxes, and sociability no longer gets a look in. KENO. TAB. OASIS. GAMING ROOM, said the signs outside a pub I was in the other day. 'The management of this venue is pleased to promote responsible gambling for Tasmanians', said a notice in the gents'. 'Gambling problems? If you have a gambling problem in your life, call Gambling Helpline Tasmania, twenty-four hours a day. Press "One" for recorded info, "Two" to speak to an operator, and "Three" if you'd like to have a bit of a bet.'

I'm up bright and early for breakfast. It's just a few miles to Wine Glass Bay, a classic curve of sand that's on all the postcards, but is unlikely to look like paradise in this drizzle. Never mind. I could do with the walk. I head uphill through shrouded forest, striding out over massive pink granite boulders, and quickly develop chest pains and pins and needles in my head. I expect it's indigestion. Can't be the wine. Red wine combats heart problems, doesn't it? I was reading that the French have actually put the contents of red wine in a pill so they can sell it to health fanatics in America who want it because they know it's good for them, but won't drink it because they know it's bad for them.

Apparently the pink granite is unique to Tasmania, and very beautiful it is too. There are gradations as you climb, like steps, so you feel like you're in the atrium of a very expensive Italian hotel. As I reach the top the boulders are massive, as big as houses, and have gnarled trees with bark like ivory growing out of them. It's like a fantasy fairy place from a kid's storybook, with secret hiding places and strange shapes and weird images, as if your subconscious has come to life around you. On an outcrop high above, shaped in the rock, is the perfect form – head, eye, arched back – of a giant iguana gazing down.

I continue the last few yards to the lookout point, and there it is far below me: turquoise water, white sand, wooded hills, one of the great beaches in the world; and all of it completely invisible because of the mist. I can't see a thing. I head back to the car and go looking for Mitchel and Meagher.

While O'Brien was under house arrest on Maria Island, Meagher and Mitchel were enjoying the life of Reilly, Reilly himself being in Mountjoy Jail at the time. Having undertaken not to try and escape, they were free to move at will within their designated areas. They were able to go riding and hunting, rent rooms in hotels and, in Meagher's case especially, go to the pub. 'I must say,' wrote Mitchel, 'that the English government, since our conviction, has treated us in a frank, mild, honourable spirit.' Political activism could continue unimpeded, provided it went unseen by the authorities.

Meagher was assigned the area around Campbell Town and Ross, two central inland towns north of Hobart and west of Swansea and the Freycinet Peninsula. Today Campbell Town straddles the main north–south Launceston–Hobart road, which was built by convict labour. As I approach it from the east I crest a ridge and see the little town on the flatlands below, the sinister mountains of the west looming on the far horizon. There's a working sawmill, a few rough and ready single-storey wooden houses and a cluster of unkempt goats. It's all pleasingly ramshackle till you reach the main street, which is far more proper. The Campbell Town Inn is an elegant sandstone building dating from 1840. The big attraction is the bridge, which was constructed by the transportees in 1838 from bricks they manufactured on site. It was designed to cope with horse traffic but has never required major repairs, even though it now takes 1.2 million vehicles a year, at least according to the statistics. That's a hell of a lot of cars for such an empty island. I must only have seen about twenty or thirty of them since I got here. I wonder where they're hiding all the others?

There's a tiny museum where, as is now traditional, I am the only visitor. This was once a predominantly Gaelic-speaking area. 'The early log splitters – mainly Irish – would come down into town and go on wild drunken sprees,' it says on the wall, 'usually accompanied by their women.' There's something very ominous-sounding in that final phrase, though I can't quite put my finger on it. One woman, it appears, was so drunk that she had to be 'carried to Bridge Street Jail in a sedan box'. For some reason Meagher didn't like it here and after a few days moved south to Ross. I decide to follow his example.

Unlike Campbell Town, Ross is now bypassed. 'Tasmania's Finest Heritage Village', claims the sign. It certainly looks picture-book pretty as I drive in along an avenue of autumnal yellow trees. Behind them are discreet rows of nineteenth-century houses built in timber or mellow, beautifully weathered sandstone. I park outside the Tasmanian Scottish Centre and take a few minutes to admire its impressive stock of Scottish sweeties, Edinburgh Rock and Irn Bru. In the window is a cardboard cut-out of a man in a kilt with an orange beard and mad staring eyes. I can't be sure, but I think he may have been at my reading in Rocky Sullivan's.

A map in the Campbell Town museum showed Meagher's

house standing at the junction of Bond and High Streets in Ross. You'd think it'd be the kind of thing a heritage village would make a fuss about, but there don't seem to be any signs or plaques. I stroll round to the junction of the two streets and find a pair of simple cottages. One of them has broken windows. Ravaged-looking toys litter the porch. It looks derelict, but maybe the kids just play rough. Unless he lived in one of the 1960s brick bungalows across the street, one or other of them must have been his home, but nothing's marked, and there's no one to ask because there isn't a soul in sight. Maybe they've all nipped up to Campbell Town for the afternoon to drive back and to across the bridge and keep the statistics up to scratch.

Back in the heart of downtown Ross I go into a shop to buy the picnic I've been planning for weeks. I'm expecting to be served by one of those slick twenty-first-century tourism operatives with anxious smiles that you find everywhere these days, but instead I get a nineteenth-century shepherd with tree-trunk arms and a *Cold Comfort Farm* haircut. I select a straightforward meat pie from the lengthy pie menu. Instead of wrapping it up, Cold Comfort seizes a plastic squirty bottle of tomato ketchup. He's about to inject the red stuff into my pie like a builder squirting insulation into a wall when I spot what he's up to and ask him to desist. He's clearly alarmed by my eccentricity, and by the time I leave town word will be out that there's a weird pie-eater on the loose.

Pies are a cornerstone of Australian life. Gastronomy may be the new national pastime, but away from the epicurean heartlands you'll still find plenty of people whose idea of a seven-course meal is a six-pack and a pie. In the Sydney resort of Manly I once stood and admired the Manly Pie Shop, its subliminal promise of meat and testosterone making it one of the finest business names you could ever dream up. In Adelaide they favour the pie floater, an ugly liaison between a pie and a gallon of green liquid distantly related to mushy peas that even has most other Australians heaving at the prospect. And in the Tasmanian daily paper this week I read that 'the good old Australian pie is about to hit the menu at fast-food chain McDonalds . . . if a trial proves popular the great Australian snack could go international.' A spokesman for the pie manufacturers said: 'Soon they'll be saying, "Do you want pies with that?"'

I put the pie into the car, fasten its seat belt and drive the few miles south to Tunbridge.

Meagher had been given strict instructions by the supervising magistrate that his area of liberty ended at Blackman's River, beyond which he could not pass. The other Young Irelanders had all been allotted different districts to prevent any possibility of their meeting up and plotting further mischief. Meagher however realised that his colleague Kevin O'Doherty – a trainee surgeon with the nickname Saint Kevin – had been allotted a district to the south of Ross which had as its northern boundary the same Blackman's River. The village of Tunbridge straddled the river. Meagher arranged for the landlord of a local pub to set up a table on the very centre of the bridge over the river along with two chairs, one either side of the boundary. Each Monday he and O'Doherty would meet there for lunch, each sitting just inside his own district. As well as poking fun at the British officials this gave Meagher the chance to be Tasmania's first Irish nationalist restaurant reviewer.

'To be sure, the passage through the air, for upwards of five hundred yards or so, condensed the steam of the potatoes and solidified the gravy somewhat; but the inn was not to blame for that. The Home Office spoiled the cooking.'

It seems only right to commemorate this flamboyant stunt while I'm in the area.

Tunbridge is bypassed by the main road and I find the bridge straight away. There's nothing to mark it out as the scene of a major historical practical joke, but there is a sign identifying the river. The bridge is clearly the Victorian original, with five stone balustrades so you can calculate precisely where the table would have been placed. I put the pie on the wall, exactly at the centre, and begin to unwrap it. As I'm doing so an old man crosses the bridge pushing a wheelbarrow full of pig shit. He winks and smiles and gives a cheery 'G'day' as he passes.

I bite into the pie in a conscious act of communion with the men whose story has brought me to the other side of the world. The pastry's fine – but God in heaven, what's this stuff inside it? Meagher's congealed gravy had nothing on this evil black slurry. It reeks of something deeply unpleasant, a carrion stench that makes me gag even as I swallow. I daren't take a second mouthful, because there's a serious risk that as it's on its way down the first one might be on its way back up. What a stinker! What a rotter! I can't eat it, and I'm certainly not letting it back in the car. I check that no one's watching, then drop it into the river, where it lands with a sickening plop. I'm instantly overwhelmed by guilt and regret. I may just have poisoned Tasmania's pristine river system. The fumes could also taint the air and kill the rainforest. Too late now. The pie is caught between two stones on the riverbed, like a sealed nuclear container waiting to surprise a future generation. I feel ashamed. I'm going to get out of here before anyone realises what I've done. As I walk back to the car I remember the old man with the wheelbarrow. Perhaps he was smiling and winking because he's the guy who puts the filling in the pies.

Leaving Hobart is becoming a habit. I'm heading south this time, crossing a causeway called Pitt Bluff. There's shimmering water on either side. Gum trees rise above the hilltops, silhouetted against the skyline as they are in early colonial paintings. I'm feeling rather sad and blue. This may just be the potent combination of homesickness and travelling alone that always makes its presence felt at some point in a trip; but I can't help feeling that it's something to do with the landscape. And it's not as if I'm still in the wilderness. I just passed a garden centre and now I'm in an incongruous hamlet of dour redbrick bungalows, none of which seems to have quite enough windows. There's an obsessive neatness about them which looks deeply peculiar in this environment. A few have ornamental flamingos and garden gnomes, though without the ironic weaponry I saw in Melbourne. They look as if they were modelled on England in the 1950s, and tell of a nostalgia for the life the ten-quid tourists left behind. There are fields and cows and more gum trees now, and another bungalow all on its own at the top of a paddock. I think I know why I'm feeling blue. It's because it's just like home, except it's not.

To the European eye something is slightly wrong. All the elements are here – houses, trees, birds, fields, churches – but things have been rearranged and re-emphasised, as if in a dream. Sometimes you can wake from a dream that isn't a nightmare feeling, if not disturbed, then possessed by a sense of disquiet. I think that's what's happening here. I'm experiencing familiar things, but not as I know they should be.

It's getting wilder the further we get from Hobart and I can't get a clear reception on the radio any more. The last thing I heard was an ad for Serious Chainsaws. I don't think you have your logs delivered round here. Pick-up trucks and four-wheel drives with roo bars look as if they belong, in a way they don't when you see them in England with women with streaked blonde hair parking on double yellows to drop off tiny kids in Just William school uniforms outside expensive prep schools run by child molesters with no educational qualifications. The solid brick bungalows have given way to more ramshackle clapperboard-and-corrugated efforts where nothing is for ornament and everything is for function: an ancient pick-up truck, a pile of logs, pieces of dead machinery. Many have hand-painted signs outside. 'Cockatiels for Sale', says one, whatever they are. 'Chicky Poo –

$2.50 a LARGE bag!' Work shirts and dungarees are drying on a porch behind a wire mesh fence on which is fixed the legend: LeAVe THe DOg ALone!!! I'm more than happy to comply.

At the end of the Forestier Peninsula I stop to admire the sea views over Pirate's Bay. There's one of those official Tourist Attraction signs pointing to the Tessellated Pavement. I haven't a clue what it is, but I know I've got to go. This is what tourists do all over the world. You see a sign for something you've never heard of and probably wouldn't cross the road to see at home, and, bang, you're there. And then people tell you about other things you ought to go and see. Once you're in a small obscure area that the rest of the world knows nothing about someone will say, 'Our big attraction is Satan's Drain. You really should go.' So you do. And you develop an interest in geological features and sea levels and all sorts of other stuff you've never cared about before; and then you go and see the Perpendicular Forest, where someone tells you about the Pointy-Headed Sparrow, and so it goes on until you've seen everything, and are really none the wiser.

The Tessellated Pavement is a sort of tiny version of the Giant's Causeway, paving stone and loaf-of-bread-shaped rocks sitting at the water's edge. There's just one other sightseer, a man in a car coat and grey shoes who walks off without a word when I turn up and spoil his day. Like the attraction itself, the information on the sign is geological, and I can't pretend I understand. What exactly occurred when the 'Tectonic plates separated'? What would have happened if you'd been standing on them at the time? I suppose you'd have been tessellated too. How can they be sure the plates separated anyway? Was someone there taking notes? I mean, are we really expected to believe that rivers and mountains were formed by glaciers? You never see it happening on the news. Geologists? Bunch of fantasists. Sometimes you come to a place like the Tessellated Pavement, and you have to say that God seems like a much more plausible explanation.

It's starting to drizzle and the mist's coming down as I get back to the car and cross from the Forestier to the Tasman Peninsula, still heading south. Fields are hemmed in by forest whose treetops are shrouded in cloud, which makes for a sombre, brooding atmosphere. If you'd been sent here from a Victorian city, with little previous experience of fields or trees, it must have come as a terrible shock, especially on top of a fourteen-year sentence. First the boat journey, then Nature; then being flogged half to death for stealing a turnip. You can see how it would change your outlook on life.

The Good Onya Café is the last bastion of no-nonsense matey Aussieness before the theme of crime and punishment takes over; first the Convict Country Bakery, then a bar called Escapes. Maybe there'll be a restaurant called Banged Up. And then a sign next to a brick wall with a barred window says, 'Welcome to Port Arthur'. I park next to a maroon four-wheel drive with a bumper sticker that says, 'Eat Potatoes and Love Longer'. I'm in a spooky remote place with people who think that potatoes are an aphrodisiac. It's hard not to feel a shudder of apprehension.

After the closure of Macquarie Harbour and Sarah Island in 1830, the new destination for convict recidivists was Port Arthur. Colonel George Arthur, governor of Van Diemen's Land, had a vision of a penal system that in the wake of the Industrial Revolution would be like a machine 'grinding rogues to free'. With this in mind he experimented with a new, supposedly scientific approach to punishment that would work hand in hand with traditional methods like a bloody good hiding. Advancement and progress through the system was a possibility; increasingly harsh punishment for those who reoffended was an inevitability. The site was chosen for both its accessibility and its inaccessibility. Port Arthur is at the very foot of the Tasman Peninsula. It's a short and straightforward journey by boat across Storm Bay from Hobart, which is how both prisoners and supplies got here. To escape on foot, however, was a near impossibility. To leave the Tasman Peninsula the escapee would have to cross Eaglehawk Neck, a tiny strip of land less than a hundred yards wide just south of the Tessellated Pavement. The Neck was guarded by a tethered line of eighteen vicious dogs through which any escapee would have to pass. More dogs were placed on platforms projecting into the water, to discourage swimmers and waders. Slaughterhouse waste was put into the water to attract sharks, just to be on the safe side. Despite this there were regular escape attempts. The guards at Eaglehawk Neck looked forward to them. 'It takes on the aspect of a hunt,' wrote one.

Port Arthur closed in 1874. In forty-four years, despite the horrific brutalities inflicted on the inmates, no one was ever executed here. But in 1996 this remote, sparsely populated place became the scene of one of the greatest mass murders in history, when a lone gunman shot thirty-five people dead.

As I step into the brightly lit visitor centre I'm in the grip of an emotion I don't recall feeling at a mainstream tourist attraction.

Dread.

Much of the original penal complex remains intact, giant Victorian industrial structures on the banks of a beautiful natural harbour. A church and a host of smaller colonial-style structures are dotted around the partially wooded hillsides. Dominating the view is the three-storey stone-built penitentiary situated close to the wharfs. This must be one of the few dockside Victorian buildings in the world that hasn't yet been converted into luxury loft-style apartments with stripped wood floors, a health club and designer kitchens that nobody cooks in.

'Very picturesque,' was Smith O'Brien's verdict on Port Arthur. 'Surrounded on every side by wooded hills and looks more like a pretty village.' When he arrived here, unshackled, on a boat from Maria Island – a voyage he shared, bizarrely, with Superintendent Lapham, his wife and daughters – he was assigned a two-bedroom cottage with a fifty-yard garden from which he was forbidden to stray. Unlike his cottage on Maria Island it was detached, though this didn't mean he'd gone up in the world. He was segregated from other prisoners and saw nothing of Lapham and his controversial daughters, who were in any case dismissed from the settlement not long after they arrived. On 9 November 1850, after receiving a petition signed by hundreds of his supporters in Hobart, O'Brien gave his word that he wouldn't attempt to escape and was licensed for release into the wider prison of Van Diemen's Land. On 18 November he left for Hobart not by ship, but by railway. In a macabre detail that couldn't be dreamed up by the Coen Brothers, Port Arthur's railway carriages were propelled not by locomotives, but by four convicts running and pushing, with the perk of being able to jump on board for the downhill stretches. It was said to be arduous in the extreme, but a soft option in comparison with some of the other pastimes on offer.

But the cottage doesn't thrill me the way the house on Maria did. There, O'Brien was the main act; here, he was a barely significant sideshow. What of the thousands of others who were sent here, more than a quarter of them O'Brien's fellow Irishmen? Their fate was unlikely to be a detached cottage with a private garden.

Leaves crunch underfoot and there's a fragrance of unfamiliar vegetation as I wander round the massive site. There's so much space I hardly notice the other visitors. Detail after detail hits home with sickening impact. Men who passed out during flogging were doused in salt water in the revival room, and the punishment continued when they regained consciousness. Formal gardens were laid out for the officers' wives, though while they strolled in them they could still hear the sounds of the beatings. On Point Puer – the island prison for juveniles aged ten and up – the white rocks were the traditional place of suicide for the boys. Convicts assigned to the coalmines were kept in underground cells. An Irishman called William Derracourt sang 'If I had a donkey and couldn't make it go' while receiving fifty lashes. There were 13,253 books in the library, from which the literate prisoners read aloud to the illiterate. A stained-glass chapel window was 'the work of a felon lunatic during his lucid periods'. English trees were planted in the garden of the commandant's house to make him feel at home. By lunchtime I'm reeling, but there's worse to come in the afternoon.

I walk into the Model Prison and feel a chill descend on my heart. 'We are offering you the opportunity to contemplate your past misdeeds,' those incarcerated here were told. 'You may meditate upon these.' If you offended again within Van Diemen's Land you were sent to Port Arthur; offend within Port Arthur, and you were sentenced to time in here.

The block of sixty solitary cells, all under constant surveillance, operated a system of 'silent and separate' treatment. No prisoner was allowed to see, speak or in any way communicate with another. Silence was total. The stone floors were covered with matting, and warders wore padded slippers. Those who broke the rules were confined to one of the 'dumb cells' situated off the tiny exercise yard.

I pass through four heavy doors hanging at right angles to each other. When I reach the central chamber a guide closes them behind me. I'm in a place of total silence and utter, impenetrable darkness, all the dreadful details I have learned today ricocheting around inside my head. For a moment I'm overcome with panic, even though I know I'll be in here for a minute or less. Men were left here for days at a time. The shape of the room is slightly asymmetrical, and meals were delivered at irregular intervals, so the person inside would lose all sense of time and space. One man is said to have kept his sanity by ripping the buttons off his clothing and repeatedly throwing them in the air. Hunt the button, he called it. Thirty days was the maximum sentence, though they say that three or four was enough to break the toughest man. This is truly the Russian doll of penitentiaries, a prison within a prison within a prison within the prison island of Van Diemen's Land.

Inmates of the Model Prison were only allowed to utter any sound on Sundays. Covered by hooded masks, they were taken in silence to the Model Chapel. At one end of the room pews rise in tiers, like a lecture theatre. Each row is divided into separate booths with doors. The prisoners would enter, the doors closed behind them and at a signal all masks would be removed. Once unmasked, the prisoner could see no one but the minister, who could see all of them. Booths were allocated each week by random ballot, so a prisoner could never know who might be his neighbour. All communication was forbidden, and no sound permitted until the time came to join in with the hymns. Participation in the singing is said to have been vigorous and enthusiastic.

I'm struggling to take it all in when I see a notice next to the wall.

'The Separate Principle of quiet and solitary confinement was an advanced concept for its day, and in substituting silence for the lash, teaching useful trades, and subjecting convicts to the moralising influences of religion was considered a model of instruction and reformation.'

This chapel is the most terrible place I have visited in my life. I leave and walk out into dazzling sunshine feeling physically ill. Handily situated a short walk away is the prison asylum.

I'm walking down the hill in the direction of the visitor centre when ahead of me and off to my right I see a more modern ruin. To one side of it a woman is laying a small bouquet on the ground. She leaves as I arrive. This is the café where the first killings took place in the massacre of 28 April 1996. By now my nerve ends are jangling, and I feel I can't take on board any more grief. I go into the centre and find somewhere quiet to sit while I contemplate my fellow countrymen, both English and Irish, who conceived, staffed and populated this dreadful place, while

George Eliot was at home writing *Middlemarch*. Remarkable people, the Victorians.

I've been mooching about in the bookshop, tea room and museum when I notice a small crowd gathering by the ticket desk. 'Any more for tonight's ghost tour?' asks a guide. All over the world these days every tourist attraction worth its salt has a ghost tour. I've seen them pass, but never actually been on one. It doesn't seem like a good idea, given the dark history of this place, but I suppose they must know what they're doing. And after all, I am here, and it's not as if there's a lot else to do at the far end of the Tasman Peninsula on a dark night at onset of winter. I could sit on my own thinking melancholy, disturbing thoughts, I suppose; but I'll be able to do that later anyway. I put my hand up. Minutes later we're retracing some of my steps from this afternoon, but this time in the dark.

She's not the most charismatic of guides, but it isn't her fault that a couple have decided to bring along a three-year-old girl. 'I'm scared,' she keeps saying outside the haunted officer's house. 'This is scary.'

'No, it's not,' says her dad, grinning like a vigilante. 'Here, get out of the buggy. Come and sit on my shoulders.'

'But this lady's scaring me.'

'No, she's not.'

Things reach a head in the autopsy room, a cheery spot close to the flogging yard. We file in by torchlight, to be confronted by a mortuary table made of four stone slabs. 'That was to make cutting through the body easier, and it also allowed the blood and body fluids to drain away on to the floor.'

'I want to go!'

'This would not have been a place for the squeamish.'

'Please, Daddy!'

'The senior medical officer lived upstairs. He liked to bring his work home with him.'

'I'll have bad dreams, Daddy!'

'The stone gutter round the perimeter of the room was to drain away the escaping . . .'

Her voice echoes down the corridor as I slip away unnoticed. FELONS' RESTAURANT – THERE'S NO ESCAPING QUALITY, says the sign outside the à la carte restaurant next to the now-closed cafeteria. It's way past dark, I'm very hungry, and it's unlikely that anywhere's still open in the outside world. I really should have something to eat.

I take a table, order some fish and admire the logo – a set of manacles – on the cover of the menu. I'm disappointed they haven't gone all the way with the theme. There's no bullock's liver, no steak flogged within an inch of its life, no soundproofed darkened dining-room available for private hire. Port Arthur has made a huge, visceral impression on me, but you sense there have been some uneasy compromises made here between the historians and the businessmen, the forces of public service and free-market enterprise. The historians have done a fantastic job, but I'd say the businessmen won out when it came to Felons.

I finish my meal, buy a bottle of Autopsy Room red to take away, then go out into the pitch-black silent night to look for the only car in the car park.

I'm booked in for the night in a former Victorian probation station somewhere in the back of beyond, only more remote. I phoned at lunchtime to ask for directions.

'Carry on going as far as the sign for the Tasmanian Devil Park. When you reach it you'll know you've gone too far.'

I drive for half an hour and don't see a single vehicle. 'You should try bush walking at night,' one of the ex-miners told me that night in the pub in Strahan. 'It's as dark as the inside of a cow.' The road tonight is darker than the inside of a cow that's been stitched inside another cow and put inside a black velvet sack in an underground cave. I reach the Devil Park, turn back, drive for a while, turn round, reach the Devil Park again, turn back, and spot a self-effacing sign in the scrub directing me up a track past a derelict building labelled CELL BLOCK, to a terrace of three single-storey Victorian brick cottages. I'm in the one at the far end. I park so close I'm almost touching it, because if I strayed more than three feet away I wouldn't be able to see it any more and might get lost. I get out of the car. Somewhere a dog is howling. Mind you, I can't hear one, so it can't be anywhere near here. It's as silent as a blade of grass in an egg box inside a cow in a quilt in a grave.

The key's been left under a brick on the doorstep, possibly by a psychopathic shaven-headed Victorian warder who spends his night-times mutilating his arm with a bread knife as he weeps for the unspeakable brutalities he's inflicted on his fellow creatures. That's the kind of cheery vibe this place has. It's colder inside the cottage than out. There's a living-room-cum-kitchen with an open fireplace, a pretty bedroom with an antique bed and multicoloured quilt, and a shower room as cold as Pingu's fridge. I light the log fire that the psychopath has set for me, and wonder how best to have some fun.

There's a small wooden dresser in the corner. Propped up in pride of place on the middle shelf is a plate with a picture of the *Mona Lisa* on it that has been broken into three pieces and glued back together. On the back of the plate it says, 'Made in England'. A chipped 1937 coronation cup bears the legend 'Long May They Reign'. Another plate portraying a hunting scene has been shattered into more than twenty pieces and also glued back together. The plates feel like evidence of some unknown crime.

An information sheet tells me I'm in the officers' quarters of a convict work station. On a table is a laminated copy of an official report by a Quaker who visited in 1853. 'The air is so close it makes me feel faint and sickly,' he wrote of the solitary cells here, where men were confined in forty-pound chains. He met a prisoner called Hart, 'transported ten years for felony' who absconded sixteen times, had 291 lashes, 311 days' solitary and five thirty-day stints in a darkened cell.

'His gloomy countenance and knit brow relaxed after a little conversation. He showed us a book in which he had been copying out some verses and learning "Oft The Happy Shepherds." He repeated them to us of his own accord . . . my soul mourned . . . there was nothing forbidding or ferocious here, quite the contrary. A cheerful pleasant smile would play over Hart's features . . . in the evening the prisoners were assembled in the chapel. They were very quiet and orderly.'

The laminated card isn't sharp enough to slit my wrists, so I turn the tiny portable TV on instead in the hope of an Aussie soap or some one-day cricket, or anything with lots of bright sunshine. Reception is poor, and there are just two fuzzy channels. On the first they're trailing the programme that's on after the ads, a documentary about an Australian hairdresser who wants to date a millionaire. There's a clip of her putting on her bra and pouting at the camera and saying, 'I'm desperate.' The second channel is showing the Eurovision Song Contest. 'We are very excited,' claim the Swedish co-hosts, with the relaxed joie-de-vivre of a couple of poker-playing funeral directors from a small town near Malmö. 'Yes, you look it,' says a familiar Irish voice, heckling the hosts on behalf of the viewers. In my melancholy dungeon at the bottom of the world I can now sit back and listen to the voice of Terry Wogan. I have been in solitary confinement for less than half an hour, and already I fear I may be losing my grip on reality.

Much has been made in recent years of Australia's dynamic new home-grown culture and its escape from the cultural cringe that made it defer to all things European, so I'm surprised that our greatest annual kitschfest has been given airtime. Do they really care about this stuff in Darwin and Alice Springs – or in the Tasman Peninsula, for that matter? Would the Pacific Rim

Song Contest get airtime in the UK? I suppose Channel 4 might show it if they could guarantee some surgically enhanced lady-boys and a crew of priapic dwarves. They're very keen on cultural diversity.

In between songs TV Tas cuts away from the BBC coverage to a studio in Melbourne, where a panel of celebs and comedians are giving Wogan marks out of ten for how well he's doing at subverting the coverage. Melbourne has always had faith in the comedic power of tongue-in-cheek retro-fashion, and there's a lot of pink and blue hair, diamanté glasses and charity shop frocks in the studio, especially on the men. There's a parody Greek TV presenter and a performance by a parody techno singer, but it's always a doom-laden enterprise to try and satirise an event that's already doing that to itself.

Back in the Eurodome Estonia is declared the winner, and their contestant steps forward to say a few words on behalf of this dignified, long-suffering nation that's spent so much of the last century fighting against overwhelming odds to retain its unique cultural identity. 'Yeah!' he shouts. 'Arright! Lemme hear you say yeah!'

I go to bed, where I am plagued by nightmares.

I wake next morning feeling exhausted and distressed. The warder has laid on eggs, bacon, bread and an eco-friendly butter-style spread, so I cook some breakfast and thank God for inventing daylight. What a terrific idea that was. My night's rest has scored *nul points*. Though the air was cold, the bed was warm and comfortable; yet despite the reassuring presence of a Swiss army knife under the pillow and a chair against the door handle, I did not slip easily into gentle oblivion. Convicts, Irishmen, Eurovision and roadkill populated my dreams, and I returned with grim monotony to that dreadful chapel. Once I was woken by a loud noise, a clang of metal or the slam of a door. I opened the curtains, but was still inside the cow. I must have dreamed the noise. It can happen. You dream a noise and it wakes you up.

While I'm eating I take a look through the visitors' book.

'Did the hair on the back of your head creep when you entered? Mine did.'

'All quiet on the Western Front until about 4 a.m., when we heard a lot of loud noises, a distant clanging of chains ... we had a great time, but not much sleep.'

'The night-time noises add to the uniqueness. Thanks for a great stay.'

'No pillow menu,' I write. 'Estonia won. Beware the dark brooding underbelly.'

I go outside and discover that the cottage looks out on to a lovely unspoiled bay. Cormorants are paddling in the shallows along a thickly forested shoreline. A man waves and walks down to meet me – not a psychopathic warder after all, but the gentle young man who owns the place. He asks did I sleep well, though he already knows the answer.

'It's weird. People have no problems in the other two. Just in your one. We tell people, "Don't worry, you're okay, that's the one that seems to be haunted." It's fun though, isn't it?'

His great-grandfather bought the place when the convict days came to an end, and installed a hydroelectric system to power the nearby village. When he retired at night he would lean out of his bedroom window and pull a rope to turn off the power, plunging the whole village into darkness. Crazy place, crazy guy.

We walk over to a barn that's being converted into a museum. There's some old machinery and a photograph of the 1907 footie team with the captain in the middle holding the ball and smoking a fag. On the grass outside the barn there's a large empty cauldron.

'We used to have a whale's head in here, but someone came in the night and stole it.'

The old mess hall is still intact. He tells me you can hire it along with the accommodation for weddings and parties. I can see how that might be fun. Hundreds of friends would be very comforting. I'd say it would be an exciting place for couples to stay as well. Romantic. Well, atmospheric. Lots of cuddles in the dark. But on your own? It might be worth trying to pick someone up in Felons on your way through. You might be glad of the company.

I had other plans, but I can't resist going back to Port Arthur. I'm haunted by so many of the images I found there, and for all I know I may never stray this far south again. I just want a little time to let the enormity of it all settle in, and to see if I can in any way comprehend how it must have been when it was a teeming community of brutalised souls, some of them here for no more than a handkerchief in Shoreditch or a loaf of bread in Galway.

I leave the Model Chapel for the second time and head down to the 28 April memorial. All I remember of that day is the international news coverage of another terrible thing happening in a faraway place. I never imagined I'd ever be here. The tragedy is referred to only obliquely on the site. Discreet notices request visitors not to ask staff about their involvement on the day. The fact of such an event occurring in a place already so emotionally charged is almost inconceivable. I feel obliged to inform myself about what happened. I go to the bookshop, buy a couple of books and sit down in a quiet corner for a long time. I'd come for Smith O'Brien, but his story was immediately superseded by the scale of the narrative I found here: that in its turn is now all but obliterated by what happened in 1996. I cannot bring myself to write a full account. Thirty-five people died. The image of the gunman hunting down a five-year-old girl and shooting her where she hid behind a tree will stay with me for the rest of my life. I cannot dignify the perpetrator by naming him. The shock of Port

Arthur has been that, like prisons within prisons, one story has been eclipsed by a greater horror, and that in its turn by the greatest horror of all.

Why this place, on all the planet?

On the drive back to Hobart I stop at Eaglehawk Neck just after dusk. There's meant to be some sort of sculpted mock dog to represent the sabre-toothed halitoxics who once guarded it, but it's almost dark when I arrive, and there's no one to ask because the shop's shut. I stumble about a bit in the fading light, but in a place where people once avoided the dogs, I can't find one. Defeated, I return to the car. I bought a gloomy-looking Hank Williams CD the other day, and it seems like the right choice for a gradual, mournful readjustment to life outside a prison colony. I turn on the ignition, drive to the edge of the car park and insert the CD into the player before pulling out on to the road.

Nothing. Silence.

I press EJECT.

Still nothing.

I turn the overhead light on and press EJECT again. NO DISC reads the display. Where's the bloody CD then? I lean forward, and there it is, its edge just visible beyond the rim of the plastic. The problem is, it isn't in the CD slot. With astonishing aim I've somehow managed to shove it into a gap in the plastic moulded dashboard where two prefabricated sections meet, just a couple of inches above where it should have gone. First the trauma overload of the last two days, now this. Gently, ever so gently, I pinch my thumb and forefinger together, reach for the CD, and nudge it further into the gap. One more grab, and it disappears entirely into the fabric of the vehicle. Gone. Consumed. Vanished. Digested. The car has eaten Hank Williams. My life is turning into a Stephen King story.

*

In the last couple of weeks I've slept in more beds than I can count without taking my shoes and socks off. More than once I've woken in the night with no idea of where I am and lain there in the dark, trying not to panic, until the realisation dawns. I found it strangely comforting to check back into the hotel on the pier in Hobart today. The Antarctic exploration ships were still at their moorings, so in a way it's almost like coming home. It's strange how quickly you can become used to the unfamiliar. Perhaps I will get back to England and feel disoriented by the absence of a brutal convict history in the South Downs.

I managed the drive back without having to feed the car again, but I have to say that the CD incident has left me rattled. Technology, like nature and wildlife, can never resist an opportunity to laugh in my face. The hire car has now taken on some of the menace of the Tasmanian landscape, possibly through a kind of quasi-mystical osmosis. At any moment the central locking could snap shut of its own accord, leaving the airbag free to smother me to a Hank Williams soundtrack while the hazard lights flash. If the good Lord's willing and the creek don't rise, I think I'll keep the driving to a minimum until I fly home in a couple of days.

It wasn't late when I got in last night, but Hobart was already closed. The lady on reception knew a Thai restaurant she thought might still be open, so I called a cab. The driver told me I shouldn't be going there.

'Thai food's shiddouse, mate.'

He said he would have refused to take me and made me go to his favourite Chinese instead, but that was already closed.

'We always have the banquet. It's such a big feed you take more away in bags than you can eat. And it's got bugs in.'

I think he meant Moreton Bay bugs, which are a kind of Aussie langoustine, but I couldn't be sure.

'Where you from, mate? Really? Jeez, that must be rough. Y'been anywhere else in Oz?'

Sydney, I tell him.

'Sydney?' I can see his eyes in the rear-view mirror, and he's incredulous. I'm about to tell him that in Europe Sydney's regarded as one of the more glamorous cities on the planet, but then realise there's no point.

'Bloody Sydney. Why would anybody want to go there?'

He gives the matter some thought.

'I suppose all that smog would make you feel at home. Where else y'been, mate?'

Melbourne.

'Melbourne? What a shiddouse place! Full of wogs. Where else, mate?'

Well, I was in Perth once. And Adelaide. Alice Springs?

'Shiddouse, the whole fakken lot of 'em. Y'know the place to be, mate? Here.'

What – Tasmania?

'Not just Tasmania, mate. Don't wanna be out in the sticks shaggin' sheep. Hobart! The big city! This is the place to be. How's yer hotel?'

I tell him it's great.

'They've fakken ruined the centre of town, mate. It's all over. Finished.'

By the time we reach the restaurant we've established that his street, in his newly built suburb on the very edge of town, is the only place in the world you'd want to be.

I order pad Thai and chilli prawns. I was worried they might be shiddouse, but they're actually very good.

I spend a restful long weekend mooching around Hobart before heading for home. It's a delightful place, more like a country town than a capital city, as everyone is keen to point out. The casino's the only high-rise in town. Houses wind up the hills that enclose the harbour, giving the impression that everyone must have a view of the water. I decide to risk the drive to the top of ·

Mount Wellington. It's a clear day and I can look out over the city, the harbour and large parts of the landscape through which I've been travelling. It's stunning. Maureen was right about the dark underbelly, but that's only added to the attraction. I could quite happily come and live here. Mind you, I say that about four or five places every year.

I decide to stick with the malevolent car for as long as it takes to drive the few miles to Richmond. The road takes me through valleys and vineyards, and past a turning called Malcolm's Hut Road. I bet when Malcolm built his hut he never imagined it would give him immortality.

Richmond's a pretty little town, slightly disfigured by a proliferation of tourist-industry signposts and placards. There's a famous jail, but I'm a bit jailed-out. And the oldest bridge in Tasmania, which is everything you hope it might be. 'Antiques and collectibles', says a sign on a shop. 'Please keep off the grass. No prams. No pushchairs. No food. No drinks. No lollipops. No ice creams. No sharks. No earth-moving equipment. No military dictatorships.' Just inside the door is a chest of drawers: $7,000, says the tag. Huon pine, you see. You could buy a small house near Queenstown for that.

In the nineteenth century Richmond was a vibrantly Irish town, where the pubs were segregated along religious lines. What was once the most notoriously boisterous Irish pub in town is now a sweetie and lolly shop. As I stand outside admiring the original pub balcony an old-style ocker in a bush hat is coming through the door, telling his wife he'll be waiting outside. He fixes me with a conspiratorial leer.

'Bloody woman's paradise in there, mate.'

Francis Meagher's infant son is buried in the churchyard.

In Ross, Meagher had married Katherine Bennett, the daughter of an Irish highwayman. He was already plotting his escape from Van Diemen's Land, a plan from which he did not deviate even when his wife fell pregnant. In a typically flamboyant gesture which seems absurdly romantic today, and probably did even then, he announced to the police that he was renouncing his parole with the intention of escaping, and it was their responsibility to try and catch him.

With the help of British settlers sympathetic to his cause he made his way to an island in the Bass Strait, where he spent ten days waiting to rendezvous with a boat that was to take him to America. For some of the time he was unexpectedly joined by a rowing boat of escaped convicts who were heading for the gold rush in Victoria. They cooked Meagher seafood stew on the beach. He eventually made it to New York via Brazil, and was greeted with a hero's welcome. His adventures were only just beginning.

Katherine made plans to go to America and join him, but before she could do so the four-month-old son he had never seen died and was buried here in Richmond.

In 1853 an old friend of Meagher's, the wonderfully named Pat 'Nicaragua' Smyth, turned up in Hobart on behalf of the Irish Directory, a New York-based 'secret' organisation that everyone seems to have known about. His mission was to arrange the escapes of Mitchel and O'Brien. O'Brien was reluctant to go, knowing that it would mean he would never be able to return to Ireland. Mitchel made his bid for freedom in an outrageous escapade straight out of a *Boys' Own* comic.

Accompanied by Nicaragua, who had a gun under his coat, Mitchel went to a police station and gave notice that he was withdrawing his parole. The two of them galloped away on horseback pursued by police, while kids on the corner offered odds on who would win the race. It turned out to be Mitchel. He went into hiding for a while in an Irishman's attic; the ladder he used to climb in and out is still put on display every St Patrick's Day. He was sheltered after that by Tasmanian and English settlers. Disguised as a Catholic priest, but with a weapon under his cassock, Mitchel the Protestant travelled across Van Diemen's

Land by stagecoach, and came through a police inspection without being recognised. Disguised once again, this time as Mr Wright, he openly boarded a ship bound for Sydney on which Nicaragua and Mitchel's wife and family – who had joined him from Ireland – were among the fare-paying passengers. From Sydney the Mitchels travelled via Tahiti, San Francisco, Nicaragua, Costa Rica and Cuba to New York. His arrival in Brooklyn was greeted with the official thirty-one-gun salute traditionally reserved for visiting heads of state.

Poor old O'Brien had a rather dull time by comparison. Before he could escape he was conditionally pardoned by the British government, with the proviso that he lived anywhere except Britain. After staying for a while in the presbytery here in Richmond he sailed to Melbourne, where a lavish dinner was held in his honour by the Irish community. He subsequently went to live in Brussels, was reunited with his family and died not in New York or Nicaragua or Costa Rica, but in Bangor, North Wales, in 1864.

Despite the shared ideals that drove them to rebellion, Mitchel and Meagher ended up fighting on opposite sides in the American Civil War. Meagher finished his days as governor of Montana, where a statue of him stands to this day.

Salamanca Place in Hobart is a row of dockside industrial buildings that have been converted into shops, cafés, galleries and apartments in a very laid-back, not-in-your-face Tasmanian way. The Saturday market is a focal point for the island's alternative community. On a street corner a hippy is dancing barefoot – you just can't get the roadkill these days – eyes shut and waving and twisting his arms imploringly to heaven, like an archive clip from the 1969 Isle of Wight festival, while the Bolivian pan pipe band from *The Fast Show* play an old Simon and Garfunkel tune to encourage him. 'Home-made Curried Scallop Pies', says a sign on a stall. I run like the wind and go to a restaurant instead, where I have Singapore Laksa at a pavement table. The Tunbridge Stinker may mean it's over for good between me and the pies.

In the afternoon there's an Irish music session in the New Sydney Tavern, a Victorian pub with no poker machines, a roaring fire and a wonderful atmosphere. There are about ten musicians: fiddles and pipes, a guitar and a bodhran, and also the first suzaphone player I've ever seen at an Irish session. His inclusion seems to be a subject of controversy among some purists in the corner. The conversation flows and I could almost forget all the time I've been spending muttering to myself in weird and lonely places. I get talking to George, a harp player and artist from Belfast who's been here for decades. One of his prints adorns the pub chimney. He tells me about the local Irish Association, and how he doesn't think there should be one, as it divides rather than integrates. He has, however, been voted on to the executive, on which he'll now be able to sit as he argues that it should be abolished.

As afternoon turns to evening I realise how much I've been missing the simple pleasures of conversation during my solitary wonderings. 'Tasmania is the diamond pendant around the neck of Australia,' a woman in a velvet skirt tells me. 'After all, it's shaped like a heart.'

'Map of Tassie,' the guy beside her tells me. 'That's Aussie slang for a woman's pubes.'

'Bush walkers have accidents, go missing, they die. Everybody knows that. But the reason they're never found' – the man takes a swig of Guinness, narrows his eyes, but keeps them fixed on mine – 'is the devils. A Tasmanian devil will consume everything. Grind bone till there's nothing left.'

As evening turns to night a bunch of us end up in an Indian restaurant. We've ordered the food when the man next to me starts telling me how he feels about Tasmania, and everyone else goes quiet.

'I love this island. I was born here and could never wish to live anywhere else. You must remember, though, that this is the arsehole of the universe. There is no reason for our being here, and this can make us a little pensive and withdrawn. The population of Australia is increasing, but Tasmania's is in constant decline.' He takes a pause. 'Ours is a disappearing voice.'

And then everyone starts talking at once.

The clock's still slow at Hobart airport as I hand back the keys to the woman at the car rental desk. 'There was just one little problem,' I say. 'I don't know if they might be able to sort it out when they're servicing it. And maybe send it on to me. You see I had this Hank Williams CD . . .'

Two hours later as we're crossing the southern coast of Australia I'm still cringing with embarrassment at the conversation, especially once the mechanic showed up and joined in. Here's a tip. If you ever happen to insert a CD deep into the body of a hire car by mistake, don't bother telling them about it when you take it back. Go out and buy another CD instead. So I have a couple of drinks to help me forget, and then they bring the meal, and some wine, then there's a movie, and then I fall asleep. And when I wake up five hours later I look out of the window, and we're still flying over Australia.

9

VICTORY WON AND PARADISE LOST

There's always a lot riding on your first pint in Dublin.

I've had a couple of hours to let a thirst incubate, and now I'm ready. The barman seems to be pouring it carefully enough, in the sense that he's walked off and is doing nothing while it settles, but he's unlikely to smooth off the head with a kitchen knife the way they used to, probably because of some new nit-picking health regulation prohibiting bar staff from putting breakfast cutlery in customers' drinks. They had those ivory-coloured spatula jobs for a while, custom-designed for stout-smoothing, but I think the government must have organised an amnesty and had them all handed in and put beyond use, because you don't see them much any more. It seems a pity. Innovation has its place, but not when it comes to the serving of a pint of stout.

For years now informal research among friends, family and mad people I meet on buses and trains has suggested that there are two main reasons why – despite the family links that mean more English people visit Ireland each year than any other nationality – some English people still refuse point-blank ever to cross the Irish Sea. Either they think that it's so close that it will be just the same as home; or they imagine they'll be blown up for having an English accent. I think we can safely add a third reason to that list. For many generations, certainly for longer than anyone now living can remember, people in the UK have been intimidated by the daunting reputation of the Irish pint. For many people, the prospect of visiting a country where people go out for a drink just so they can discuss the quality of the drink they are currently drinking is simply too much to bear, so they go to Corfu and have retsina instead.

The question I'm asked most frequently by people who've never visited is, 'Is it true what they say about an Irish pint of stout?' Actually, I'm being coy here. Despite the undeniable achievements of the good people at Murphy's and Beamish, the thing people really ask is, 'Is it true what they say about Irish Guinness? Is it really that much better?' This is like being asked by a five-year-old if Father Christmas really exists. You can't let them down. In fact you could tell these people anything. That you can stand a spoon up in it, slice chunks off it, and drink twenty without getting full up or suffering from a hangover. It's so creamy it just slides down, you see, which is why it improves your singing voice, and cures tonsillitis. It's so thick you can shave with it, so dense you can lay bricks with it, and the complex bouquet and long nose means I'm getting blackcurrants, cherries, vanilla, Jerusalem artichokes, charcoal and cream, spuds and buttermilk, Shane MacGowan's trousers, peat soot, testosterone, nectar, Fungi the Dolphin . . . the water's different, you see. Something to do with all those dead nuns in the Liffey. No, there's no comparison between your British and your Irish pints.

Once upon a time all this was true. The gulf between a pint in Ireland and the one you'd get anywhere else in the world was massive. As a teenager I remember my uncle from Cork looking on in horror as the barman in a church social club in Warrington did the honours. 'What is that eejit doing?' he enquired, as the lad clicked on the tap, then clicked it off again when the glass was full of what looked like Coca-Cola with a scum on top. In those days bar staff knew no better. If you weren't careful they'd put a glacé cherry on top as well. There was certainly no concept of allowing it to settle. As far as they knew, it required the same technique as pouring keg cider, or urinating into a bucket. Bosh – you started, and then you finished. Yet in Ireland I would gaze in fascination as a wizened old lady took four or five minutes to pour a pint, longer if it clashed with the Angelus. One taste confirmed that this was indeed a different substance entirely.

But since then something has happened. It's a combination of factors. The stuff that's brewed in Britain has improved. British bar staff, many of whom come from Australia, New Zealand and South Africa, have been taught how to pour. But it also seems to me – and here comes the treasonous bit – that, with occasional spoon-standing, peat-tasting, bricklaying exceptions, the stuff in your glass in Ireland is not quite what it was. Oh, it's still pretty marvellous all right. Look, I like it, I like it a lot. But no doubt about it, the gap has narrowed.

At the heart of the matter is the chill factor. It used to be served at cellar temperature, but these days they ask if you want 'extra cold' or, dear God help us all, 'regular'. Even the regular is almost frozen. This has been done to target a youth market weaned on Bacardi Breezers, Bailey's with a KitKat in, and other fun drinks, who can't be doing with the strong, bitter tastes associated with smelly auld bachelors with string round their waists and shit on their shoes. Low, low temperatures, as well as conveying a quite literally cool image, mean that the dark peat taste is muted. Consequently there has been a levelling-out of standards, in which Ireland loses, while everybody else gains.

These days there's also a strong whiff of the global brand about what used to be the homely stuff that old Mrs Herlihy used to fetch from some hidden scullery out the back. All those brilliant adverts that have swept the world, the waves and horses and squirrels and swimmers that have replaced the toucans and the fella carrying the girder, have taken their toll. As a fully qualified amateur psychologist, it's my belief that one's inner knowledge of these gleaming tools of modernity can trigger a negative psychic reaction that adversely affects the taste; the flashy ads are spoiling the flavour.

I can't prove it, but I have reason to believe that economics may also be involved. Thirty years ago Ireland was a very poor country with a world-class pint, while the UK was very much richer, but with a dreadful pint. As Ireland has enjoyed unprecedented economic growth, so has the pint – slowly, barely perceptibly, possibly metaphysically – gone into decline; yet over in the UK, not nearly so rich as before, the drink in your glass has improved. All the evidence suggests that if the Irish economy continues to boom, the pint will really go down the tubes. If, however, the oft-predicted collapse of the Celtic Tiger does occur, pints look set to return to 1969 quality, and the economic dark cloud will have a creamy head for all discerning drinkers.

In the last year sales of Guinness in Ireland were down 4 per cent. This calamitous statistic required a response from the brewers, who duly came up with one, though it probably wasn't what their devotees had been hoping for. The chief executive announced that they are developing new technology that will deliver a pint in fifteen seconds because the traditional pouring-time 'is not relevant to our consumers today'. I'm going to be charitable here, and hope he was pissed when he said it. Look, I'm on their side. I love this drink. But cold and fast is not the way to go. And before anyone in Marketing suggests it, they shouldn't start serving fries with it either.

So, though a gulf the width of the Irish Sea no longer exists, this is still a pretty decent pint standing in front of me. Not a pint so ambrosial that had it been placed on a rock off the coast of Amalfi it would have lured Ulysses and the lads to their doom, but it's perfectly okay for a Thursday night, especially for a tourist trap pub in Temple Bar. IRISH MUSIC, says an emerald-green neon sign in the street outside, but even though it's Kool and the Gang on the maximum-volume sound system, no one's asking for their money back. Maybe he was really called Finn MacKool, and Kool was just a stage name.

While the pint was being poured MacKool segued to a disco compilation, then to Marc Almond and Gene Pitney singing 'Something's Gotten Hold of my Heart', proving that the roots of Irish music stretch much further than any of us previously imagined. I saw Marc a few months ago doing an after-dinner cabaret, the final act on one of the most unlikely triple bills ever assembled. First Anita Roddick discussed new-age loofahs and the ecologically sustainable mascaras of amphibious matriarchal tribes; then Ann Widdecombe discussed herself, and problems arising; then Marc came on in plastic trousers and a puff of smoke belting out 'Tainted Love', as camp as Liza Minnelli at Dale Winton's wedding. Hats off to whoever booked them. You could run a national cash prize competition on the back of John-son's Baby Oil bottles and still not come up with a running order as bizarre as that.

I came in from the airport this afternoon in a taxi whose driver had one of those accents that make you start wondering where Dublin ends and Liverpool begins. Dun Laoghaire, I suppose, some time in 1845. We were stuck in traffic so he turned on the radio. 'Let's hear what Bin Laden's been up to today,' he said, but all we got was an account of a traffic incident somewhere in the centre of the city. A reporter was out on the street getting eye-witness statements from market traders and passers-by. 'They've terrible Dub accents, some of these fellas,' said the driver. 'I'd say you'll have a hard time understanding them.' I think that's what he said, but I couldn't really be sure because of his accent. It seems someone had driven a car through a pedestrianised street at sixty miles an hour, sending shoppers and stall-holders diving for their lives and injuring more than a dozen people. Amazingly, there were no fatalities. What was it like? enquired the reporter of a woman who ran a flower stall. There was a brief pause as she considered her reply.

' 'Twas like Hillstreetfuckinblues.'

I'm in Dublin for the Ireland v England Rugby Union International on Saturday. I've come because I don't know who to support, and I'm hoping being there may help me find out. At the moment I'm only short of two things to make sure it's a great weekend: somewhere to stay, and a ticket for the match. I've contacted all the people I can think of who might be able to help on either score: hotel agencies, ticket bureaux, tourist boards, breweries, publishers, actors I have met in Rocky Sullivan's, an old primary school friend with contacts, RTE journalists, the press officer of the Irish RFU, touts, policemen and a priest. So far, nothing. It's not been made any easier by the fact I don't own a mobile and haven't got a hotel room where people can leave messages, such as where I can find a hotel room.

Consequently I had a few hours to kill before the pub rendezvous time I agreed with my various contacts. I was mooching around in a bookshop earlier, looking in tourist guides and noting down the phone numbers of vegetarian B&Bs and Buddhist hostels that might not already have been booked out by supporters over for the match, when an elderly lady came in, collared the woman who was restocking the Irish history section and said, 'Excuse me.'

'Can I help you?'

'Do ye have a flask?'

'A flask?'

'A small flask, for a child to take to school?'

'It's . . . er . . . it's a bookshop.'

'I know. Just one. For a small girl.'

'No. I'm afraid we don't.'

'All right so. Will I try across the street?'

'It's a shoe shop.'

'I know. God bless now.'

As she went I exchanged a sympathetic smile with the bookseller, who smiled back and cleared off sharpish before I could enquire about the availability of Tupperware. I decided to take a look at the history section, in case it could help me decide where my allegiance should lie this weekend. *To Hell or Barbados: The ethnic cleansing of Ireland* by Sean O'Callaghan was the first title to catch my eye. It sounded like it might come in handy. I paid and went off to look for a phone box so I could call Shambala, 'a multi-denominational guest-house and healing centre for group and individual retreats', and see if I could persuade them to let me have a room. I'd just have to hide the Jameson's and go somewhere else for breakfast. As I left the shop I saw Flask Lady coming out of a computer shop across the street.

It turned out to be no go at Shambala, who could only offer me a room from Sunday, the day after the match, which was presumably when the rugby fans would be checking out, having unbalanced everybody's chakras, disturbed their auras, and reduced the meditation room to alcohol-impregnated stripped pine matchwood. But then a final despairing call to Tourist Information miraculously came up trumps. The last available hotel room in Dublin was mine, close to Merrion Square, not far from Stephen's Green, and just a short walk from the stadium at Lansdowne Road.

I was delighted to find a row of elegant Georgian townhouses, tastefully converted and painted inside in rich terracottas and blues. Period oil paintings hung on the walls, and there was an award-winning restaurant. Unfortunately my room was only seven feet long and there wasn't enough space to put a suitcase on the floor and open it. It was probably used normally for storing stationery and bottles of shampoo, but I wasn't about to complain, as I only planned to use it for sleeping. I suppose there might be a problem if I tripped and fell when I opened the door, because I might hit the far wall with my forehead and get wedged. They'd left a form to fill in for room service breakfast, which seemed a bit optimistic, as they'd never get a tray through the door with me in there at the same time, especially if I was in a coma at an angle of forty-five degrees.

I've got myself trapped in a corner of the pub now by a tour party of Belgians drinking Gaelic coffee, so I'll take a break and come back later in case anyone turns up with a grandstand seat or a reservation for the presidential suite at the Shelbourne. A hundred yards up the street is the Palace, an atmospheric old-style bar in which no one is drinking Gaelic coffee. With the hopeless inevitability of fish swept up in a drift net, tourists in Temple Bar who want to go to an authentic Irish pub are trawled up by the fake, newly designed ones that have been created just to entrap them, while places like the Palace, untouched for decades, remain exclusion zones populated almost entirely by Dubliners. There's a fierce buzz of chat and I'm the only person with no one to talk to, so I lean on the bar and read the paper, pausing occasionally to look at my wrist as if I'm expecting somebody to arrive at any moment and engage me in a conversation that'll be just as good as the ones they're all having. Unfortunately I'm not wearing a watch, so I probably look as if I'm checking whether the skin infection is getting any worse, which would explain why I'm on my own in the first place.

There's an article bemoaning the fact that the big Irish family is now a thing of the past, and that if you take children into a restaurant in the capital 'the staff look at you like you're a freak and the other diners can barely conceal their contempt'. Social attitudes tend to trickle down from Dublin, so if this is true it may be the way the rest of the country will go in a few years' time. Elsewhere in the paper, however, there is reassuring evidence that out in the countryside many traditional attitudes remain unchanged. 'A Leitrim man told a garda to "stick his torch up his arse",' the court was told. When the officer asked him to calm down, 'he started to grunt like a pig.' The man claimed not to remember the incident, and said he had been out celebrating his son's exam results.

I finish my drink and head back to MacKool's, where a few pessimists are waiting to meet me. All have the same story: they've managed to get a ticket for the match, just the one like, for themselves but not for me. Like gold dust, apparently. No matter. We make a night of it, and end up in a restaurant that seems horribly modish until the teriyaki sea bass with buckwheat noodles arrives, accompanied by a big bowl of roast spuds. In the street as we leave a tout is offering £1,000 for any pair of seats for the match. Things aren't looking good, especially once I get back to my room. To negotiate the narrow corridor that leads from bed to bathroom requires the skill of a tightrope walker. I focus until I feel centred and in the zone, but still manage to break the wall light with my shoulder.

The room has a Perspex skylight at the far end – well, seven feet from the door, which is as far as you can get – through which they probably used to dump nutty slack in the days when it was still a coal hole. I'm woken in the night by rain pelting against it, and am immediately overwhelmed by claustrophobia as I lie there in the darkness. There seems barely enough air to breathe. But what if it gets worse? What if the ceiling and walls start pressing down on me? I saw it happen once in *Flash Gordon* when I was a kid. I'm not going to be able to get back to sleep now. I may as well turn on the light and read. Maybe have a look at that Barbados book I bought today. I grope round in the darkness until I find the bedside switch for the other light, the one I haven't broken. I flick it on, and the light bulb pops.

There are two envelopes waiting for me at reception after breakfast. One contains a message from a friend who has a friend at an alcohol corporation who are one of the sponsors of the game.

Tickets are scarcer than scarce, he says, and unfortunately there's no chance. Sorry.

The other is from the alcohol corporation itself, and contains a compliment slip and a ticket for the game. Obviously there's been some kind of mix-up, but I'm not about to ask any questions. I now have a room in a hotel and a seat for the match, both of them approximately the same size. The lads from Shambala would take this to be a good omen. The pressure's off and the day is my own. I think I'll spend it reading. First I'll go for a walk, though, because I could really do with the exercise. If I stride out I could be in the bar of the Shelbourne in less than ten minutes.

Sean O'Callaghan died in August 2000 at the age of eighty-two, just as *To Hell or Barbados* – his fifteenth book – was going to press. It's a terrible shame, because the tale he has to tell is astonishing, especially if, like me, you went to school in England. Most of us growing up in half-Irish families picked up a rudimentary grasp of Irish history, but as I discovered in Tasmania, the greater part remained undiscovered. I suspect O'Callaghan's story might also be news to many native-born Irish, not to mention a few people in Bridgetown.

The bar of the Shelbourne Hotel makes an excellent reading room but is also a major meeting place on international match weekends, and as late morning heads reluctantly towards lunchtime it starts to fill up. My equilibrium is disturbed by a party of posh buffoons in their fifties, England fans on a corporate jolly, kitted out in leisurewear that would have been best left on the mannequins in the window of the Pringle shop. They are playing a noisy drinking game which involves whacking glasses of expensive claret down in one. I decide to adjourn to Doheny & Nesbitt, a pub just up the road with a strong literary tradition, in the sense that many writers have drunk themselves to a standstill there over the years. When they needed to extend it they built a back bar that is an exact replica of the front one. I install myself in a corner with the intention of carrying on reading until I'm in need of solids or a lie down, whichever comes first.

In the wake of the execution of Charles I in 1649 Oliver Cromwell feared revolution, and possibly invasion, from Ireland, which he perceived as a hotbed of support for the royalist cause. The history of our islands echoes with such ironies and contradictions. Oliver's army, 20,000 strong, crossed the Irish Sea and laid waste the countryside, carrying out a series of brutal massacres with the aim of terrorising Ireland into submission. Drogheda, in 1649, remains the most notorious. Cromwell gave orders that no man, woman or child be spared, and the slaughter went on for four days. 'I am persuaded that this is a righteous judgement of God upon these barbarous wretches,' wrote Cromwell as he surveyed the carnage. A grotesquely Pythonesque detail comes in the account of the death of Sir Arthur Aston, a Catholic from Cheshire who was officer in command of the Drogheda defences, and was believed by Cromwell's men to be concealing gold inside his wooden leg. When the leg turned out to be empty, they beat him to death with it.

English propaganda at the time depicts the Irish as, in O'Callaghan's words, 'a lower race . . . a subhuman species'. He quotes a Puritan pamphlet describing them as 'the very offal of men, dregs of mankind, the bots that crawl on the beast's tail . . . cursed be he that maketh not his sword drunk with Irish blood.' In the wake of Cromwell's victory, the Protector famously ordered that Irish Catholics be banished 'to hell or Connaught'. As well as authorising the execution of 200 Irish chiefs at Kilkenny, the wittily titled Act of Good Affection of 1652 decreed that all lands in Ulster, Munster and Leinster be forfeit and reserved for the British; the Irish were to be removed to the barren lands of Connaught in the west, except for those parts of Galway and Clare where the land was good, which were handed over to Cromwell's soldiers. Many British troops didn't want the land they had been gifted, and sold or gambled it away, which is how many huge estates were assembled.

By 1654 three-quarters of the population had been moved to one-quarter of the land. Those who refused to go were subject to execution or transportation. Guerrilla fighters who took to the forests and mountains were known as Tories. Private bounty hunters, and organised hunts with dogs, pursued those who did not comply. The population declined from just over 1½ million to barely 1 million. These events have been part of the historical record in Ireland for generations, but they come as a hell of a bloody shock if you grew up studying English history. It's also a dreadful wrench trying to come to terms with them if, like me, you're half and half. Reading about them is also rather an extreme preparation for a sporting contest between the two nations, and despite the early hour I think I may need another drink. It's strange reading this kind of stuff while the people next to you are discussing whether Brian O'Driscoll is going to 'massacre the English defence' tomorrow.

It's during the next pint that O'Callaghan drops his bombshell. In the wake of the Cromwellian conquest, he alleges, 50,000 Irish men, women and children were forcibly transported to work in the plantations of the West Indies. Some went as indentured servants, able eventually to earn their freedom; but the majority, according to O'Callaghan's researches, were sold as slaves. 'Fifty thousand or sixty thousand was a drop in the ocean compared to the eleven million African slaves,' he writes, 'but a slave is a slave, no matter what the colour of the skin.'

Some were prisoners of war, though more were the families and dependants of those killed during the Cromwellian campaign. Others were simply rounded up from the countryside, kidnapped and loaded on to the same Bristol- and London-based slave ships used previously to remove Africans from their homelands. As well as labour for the tobacco and sugar plantations, young women were also much in demand as the planters, according to

Cromwell's son Henry, 'had only Negresses and Maroon women to solace them'. The going rate paid to those who could deliver a young woman was £4 10s, no questions asked, for transportation from the Cork ports of Cobh, Bantry, Youghal and Kinsale.

The English language was even adapted to describe their fate, as a letter-writer in 1655 makes clear: 'A terrible Protector this ... very apt "to Barbadoes" an unruly man ... so that we have made an active verb of it: "Barbadoes You".'

But Barbados was not the only destination for those exiled by Cromwell.

Others ended up in Montserrat.

Life's too short to fit in everything you'd like to do, so I skipped lunch and settled for a nap instead. I've just edged my way out of the permanent dusk of the Coal Hole in search of natural light and a cheese and ham toastie, only to be diverted from my mission by an enigmatic message at reception asking me to attend a certain hotel at a particular hour this evening if I wish to learn more about the case of the MacCarthy Mór. Though I've never made it public, the sender of the message is clearly aware of my visit to Tangier. My match weekend has suddenly taken on an unexpected cloak-and-dagger aspect, not to mention a sour aftertaste of Cromwellian massacre. To be honest, I'd been hoping for more of a party atmosphere.

The survivors of the claret drinking game are still in the bar of the Shelbourne when I roll up to meet my friend Seamus, who's agreed to accompany me to my clandestine rendezvous. Four businessmen in cashmere golf sweaters and nasty slacks are swaying and lurching like stage drunks on Mogadon, shouting incomprehensible bollocks in terribly expensive accents. A table of women who have convened for their Friday after-work drink are monitoring the drunks' spectacular decline and starting to panic at the prospect of ending up with vomit in their hair.

It's a fine night and the bars are busy, with an overspill of rugby fans on the pavements as we head for the designated meeting place.

We arrive a little early for my appointment. 'You've just missed Marianne Faithfull,' says a sixty-year-old man with a ponytail. Isn't it always the way? You go down the pub for a few beers, and Bob Dylan's just been in. Nip round the corner for a curry, and the blonde one out of Abba just left in a minicab. I once got talking to a scruffy old bloke propping up a bar in Chelsea, but by the time I realised it was Laurie Lee it was time for him to go, so really it was just as bad as missing him in the first place.

Apparently there was a famine relief fashion show or some such nightmare event this afternoon, and the tail-end of Dublin's bohemian-aristocratic avant-garde have adjourned to the lounge where I'm waiting to meet a man about a Mór. The hotel has gone for expensive antiques, oil paintings and a décor themed on Old Money rather than the Celtic Tiger Nouveau Riche favoured in many circles these days. Seamus introduces me to someone he says is an Austrian count, though it's possible I may have misheard him. I fear I'm not making much of an impression and may be coming across as someone who's spent a large part of the day in Doheny & Nesbitts, then fallen asleep in his clothes.

My MacCarthy Mór informant turns out himself to be a claimant to an ancient Irish title. He arrives in the company of two glamorous young men and immediately embarks on a brutal denunciation of our man in Morocco. Whatever the truth of the matter, Terence clearly has the ability to inflame strong passions. Within a few minutes I feel much as I did on several occasions in Tangier with Conor and Tommy, bombarded with historical and genealogical detail I find impossible to absorb or evaluate, and which leaves me feeling punch-drunk. As he talks I find myself wondering not only whether what he alleges is true, but also where his motives lie. Is he what he seems, or am I being set up to do someone else's dirty work?

I have no axe to grind because of my own scepticism about

the whole notion of hereditary clan titles – a feeling I know is shared by many Irish people, to whom this is a closed and increasingly irrelevant world. I went to Tangier because I was attracted to the baroque and fanciful nature of the story and the personalities involved. Terence is a colourful figure, and I like his brothers. Some of their ideas appealed to the Celtophile in me, but I also have to face the possibility that Terence may be a fraud. On the other hand, so might the man sitting opposite me now. As he proposes to leave, he hands me a bound manuscript hundreds of pages long.

'These documents are not in the public domain. They were secretly photocopied in Irish government departments. If asked, I will deny they came from me.'

I look at the heading: THE FILES CONCERNING THE ACTIVITY OF MR TERENCE MACCARTHY FROM THE DUNMURRY ESTATE IN BELFAST DURING THE YEARS 1977 AND 1995. VOLUME I.

'Here's my number if you need it. Who do you think will win tomorrow? Should be a great game.'

Seamus says he knows a nice little bar, which turns out to be Doheny & Nesbitt. It's filled up since lunchtime, and nobody's here to read. They're three deep at the bar, and that's just on the serving side. It's unseasonably warm and the pavement outside is packed with people in shirt sleeves, some English, some Irish, all happy. It's one of those easy evenings when strangers start talking and you get invited round for Irish stew tomorrow lunchtime, and then bump into someone you once worked with and lose them in the crowd, and pints are passed over your head but nobody spills one on you, and everything seems right with the world. It's getting near closing time, which is observed in most Dublin pubs with a rigour that would horrify those brought up on Irish rural flexitime. I decline all offers to go on to a restaurant or a club, because tomorrow is a big day and I want to be feeling good.

Everyone gets into cabs without me and immediately I regret

it, but it's too late now. Another potential life experience has disappeared for ever, unrepeatable, and there's nothing for it but to head back to the Coal Hole on my lonesome in the certain knowledge that nothing exciting is going to happen tonight. It's amazing how bad you can make yourself feel for trying to get an early night, especially when it's nearly one o'clock in the morning.

My room feels much smaller because, as well as me and a suitcase, it now contains a bulky file of illicit Irish government documents which takes up most of the remaining space. I put the chain on the door and check my miniature bathroom for tiny Special Branch agents who may have been sent to recover the dossier. Satisfied that I'm alone, I prop myself up on the divan and begin to read.

Within minutes the sheer weight of references to Srugrena Abbey, King Zog of Albania, the Niadh Nask, primogeniture, fires and explosions, frauds and counter-frauds, the Prince of Lipp and Colonel Gayre of Gayre & Nigg has, as they say in heraldic circles, done my brain in, and I put it to one side. For the moment I have other priorities. The historic conflict between Ireland and England will be acted out in ritual form at Lansdowne Road tomorrow afternoon, and I still haven't decided which side I'm on; petty infighting between ancient chiefs, or modern charlatans, will have to take a back seat for a while. And besides, *The Producers* is about to start on the tiny TV someone has thoughtfully bolted to the wall.

I pour a small Jameson's, watch the opening sequence of the film, then wake up an hour and a half later as the end credits are rolling. Clutched in my hand, not a drop spilled, is the untouched drink. I may not be able to tell a real Gaelic clan chief from a pair of vacuum-packed kippers, but there are some instincts you just can't put a price on.

Match day dawns sunny and bright, though I have to say I feel guilty for not going out on the tear last night and waking up feeling wretched. Feeling bad at breakfast because you don't have a hangover is evidence of a complex emotional life it can take many years to perfect. As I tackle the black pudding, my mood is improved by a piece in the paper alleging that 'Cootehill, County Cavan is becoming overrun with "bonking" dogs in the streets and alleyways, night, noon and morning.' 'We've sexy dogs around Cootehill all right,' claims a proud-sounding Commissioner, though there's no mention what he's commissioner of. Another non-specific commissioner takes a contrary view, complaining that 'the dogs seem to go out of their way to engage in anti-social behaviour when visitors are in the town.' As Cootehill is not known to be one of Ireland's tourism hotspots, it seems possible the dogs' passions are being ignited by some kind of supernatural sex force that's triggered on the rare occasions a tourist hits town. Perhaps they should consider a no-holds-barred Inquisition-style canine exorcism, so that in future in Cavan, the dogs' bollix will be a holy relic, and not an expression of admiration.

The morning papers are full of speculation about the game. All reach the same conclusion, namely that Ireland are going to have the living daylights kicked out of them by a flamboyant, well-drilled, highly professional England side. This comes close to taking all the fun out of the occasion. I was rather enjoying the moral and genetic dilemma of trying to choose between the two nations. Whoever I picked, it was going to feel like I was betraying half of my family to the secret police, which was giving the situation a certain frisson. Now it looks like being business as usual: bully-boy England to trample plucky downtrodden paddies into the auld sod in a re-enactment of the historical events of the last 900 years. It's like being a kid again, with my poor mum sitting on the sofa surrounded by triumphal English accents as she fights to hold back the tears. And that was just during *Top of the Pops*. Looks like the decision's already been made for me then. C'mon Ireland! I have to say, though, it doesn't feel quite right. Why couldn't the two of them just join forces for the afternoon and play against Wales?

I've been going to the Shelbourne Hotel quite a lot this week, and this morning's no exception. I may not be staying here, but I wish I was. I developed a taste for it three or four years ago, while recording some programmes for Radio 4 in Dublin thanks to a classic piece of BBC management insanity. It was a comedy quiz show, recorded with a live audience, and was one of those programmes that are contracted out to independent production companies staffed by people to whom the Beeb has recently made large redundancy payments. We'd recorded the first series in-house, at the BBC Radio Theatre in Portland Place, but for this series – and this is the really clever bit – the production company's budget on which to make the programmes had been frozen (major victory for BBC accountants), but massive increases had been made to the cost of hiring the Radio Theatre (another accounting triumph). So high was the rise that the budget was no longer sufficient to hire the theatre, which would now remain empty, generating no income whatsoever. Instead of going back to the BBC, the production money would now go to an outside organisation. To another country, in fact; because there was enough money to fly cast and technicians to Dublin, hire a theatre in Temple Bar, and put us all up in the Shelbourne. We even had a conference room to rehearse in, and a Mrs Doyle look-alike wheeled in urns of tea and too many sandwiches.

So I've a soft spot for the Shelbourne, which has a seductive aura of old-time hotel despite an updated bar and bistro. I can sit here at quarter past eleven on Saturday morning and view the changing economic fortunes of Ireland, or at least of certain postal districts of Dublin. A woman with a mahogany-brown suntan wearing some manner of lace and leopard-skin cape just parked a BMW coupé outside the front doors and gave the keys to a flunky in a top hat with whom she was on first name terms.

Two ruthless-looking sods with deep voices and Cuban cigars, who look as though they could buy, sell and get the bailiffs in to Charlie Haughey before breakfast, are discussing enormous sums of money over early morning brandy and coffee. There are also a few fragile-looking England fans nursing a range of hangover cures, none of which will work until just before kick-off when the adrenaline kicks in and their bodies forget. I'm here to pick up a message I know won't arrive, but I said I'd be here, so I am. Ten more minutes and I'm off. Hang on. The message has just walked in.

I met George last year in a pub at the Kilkenny Festival. In a bar full of bookish types and wide-eyed culchies his expensive casual clothes and carefully considered haircut marked him out as an urban wide boy. Fifty years old but looking barely forty, he's an archetypal King's Road cockney, very Minder, very Alfie, very Venables. Come midnight we were eating Singapore noodles in one of those Chinese restaurants that appear to be staffed entirely by Irish people. Also in the company were his wife, a delightful, well-spoken woman about half his age, and her mother, a sixties beauty of aristocratic manner with a permanent smile of how on earth did this happen? on her lips. Never in her wildest dreams had she anticipated George entering her life when she was an art dealer to the Queen Mother. To keep her on her toes George rolled a Kilkenny Carrot on the table, spilled the contents on the floor before he could light it, then blew his nose on the tablecloth for an encore. Afterwards the bouncers outside the hotel at which I was staying refused to let us in, accusing me of aiding and abetting non-residents to use their late-night bar facilities. We found a service entrance instead, and made extensive use of the late-night bar facilities until George fell asleep in a wing-backed chair.

At the time he was living in County Carlow in a big house in a field, making a living from a little bit of this and a little bit of that. Since then he's moved back to Fulham, where he grew up.

His parents, both from Galway, ran 'a pub full of villains and Irish labourers' where an impressionable George spent his formative years. I rang him a couple of weeks ago as part of my desperate trawl for tickets, realising there was a chance he'd been best man for many of London's top ticket touts. 'Don't think I'll be going myself,' he said, 'but I'll have a word with . . .' – at this point he namedropped an England rugby international, one of the most celebrated the country has ever produced – 'and see what he can do.'

I presumed that in George's circles people mention assorted Rolling Stones and supermodels and boxers and footballers all the time, go round to parties at Chris Evans's gaff and Jonathan Ross's place, crash Stephen Fry launches at the Groucho and Eddie Izzard first-night parties without ever really knowing any of these people. I was being fobbed off, and tried to take it gracefully. I'd be in the Shelbourne on match morning just in case, I said, and they could page me in case George wanted to leave a message, or a ticket.

And now here he is in person, grinning like Martin Kemp and saying, ''Ello, mate, drink up, car waiting, someone to meet.' So off we go to the Clarence, the Temple Bar hotel owned by U2, where the rugby legend himself is waiting with a ticket for the match, which means I've got two now. The spare is passed on to someone who's been waiting on the off-chance. What about George? 'Press box. I'll be the one without a typewriter. I'll say I'm with the *Sporting Life*.'

Before he leaves I ask the Legend how he thinks it'll go today. 'They're a good side,' he concedes, eyes impassive. 'But I think we're going to kick the shit out of them.' C'mon Ireland.

We fall in with some people and set out to walk to the ground in the warm sunshine, past Trinity College and the Shelbourne. I always feel it's best to get familiar with a small area of a city rather than trying to spread yourself too thin, so we stop outside Doheny & Nesbitt for just the one. Two men dressed as pints of Guinness are dancing on the pavement to the accompaniment of an experimental drum ensemble.

We're getting close to the stadium when a jaunting-car passes us, pulled by a big black horse and carrying four inebriated English management consultants who have put the weekend down to expenses. In most countries a vehicle like this would be driven by a man with a moustache wearing a bottle-green great-coat with epaulettes and some kind of Prussian military hat, but this one's in the charge of a ginger-haired teenage lad in a blue nylon tracksuit who looks as if he lives in a skip. Suddenly he's standing up shouting 'whoah!' and slamming on the brakes, or whatever you do to stop a horse that's travelling at high speed towards a solid object. The horse digs all four hooves into the road and goes into a spectacular, spark-spraying skid as the four guys in the back stand up in terror and wait for the collision.

Thirty yards ahead a minibus taxi, impatient with waiting for a gap in the traffic, has pulled out of a side street trying to turn right, and is now directly in the horse's path, blocking the carriageway. The crowd streaming towards the game have stopped and are watching in awe as the horse continues its cartoon skid, head back, nostrils flared, eyes lit, like Tom careering across a frozen lake bang on target for the ten-ton weight that Jerry has just slid into place. The result is as inevitable as today's England victory. We're already wincing in anticipation of the impact when the horse, heroically, finds that little bit of extra purchase and slithers to a halt four feet from the barely continent taxi driver, shaking his head nonchalantly as if to say, 'Hey, what did you expect? I'm a horse from a council estate who dodges traffic for a living.'

The kid stands up to his full four feet ten, whip in hand, face contorted in anger, his hair much redder than it was twenty seconds ago. 'You fuckn' wanker!' he screams at the taxi driver, and everybody bursts into spontaneous applause. If we see anything on the pitch today to equal this we're in for a cracking afternoon. The two of them then launch into a bitter tirade of high-octane abuse. The cabby's about a foot and a half taller than the Ginger Skid, but there's a slightly hesitant quality to his use of obscenities that doesn't really convince, as if he realises he's in the wrong and knows that some time in the wee small hours the kid is going to break into his home through the letter-box and perforate his kidneys with a rusty Philips screwdriver.

As we reach the ground George and I go our separate ways, agreeing to meet back in the bar of the Clarence at seven. 'It's going to be wild. Official banquet, England party, Ireland party, then see where we end up after that. My flight's at eight in the morning, so I doubt I'll be doing a lot of sleeping.'

I pass through the turnstile to be confronted by a sign saying HOT POWERS – not a fundamentalist preacher proclaiming the miraculous abilities of the Irish team, but a stall selling hot whiskey. Hot whiskey! Imagine the carnage if you sold that to football fans. There are even paper towels in the gents', which isn't something I ever recall seeing at Warrington versus Wigan. There's an interesting variation on 'I'm on the train' when the guy next to me answers his mobile and says, 'Oi'm havin' a piss at Lansdowne Road.'

I can see sunshine on mountains as I take my seat in the stand. I'm quickly involved in a discussion about my allegiance dilemma with the couple in front of me. He's Irish, she's English, and they live in Edinburgh. The two teams run out and three national anthems are played, which takes a while. First there's 'God Save the Queen', which isn't the ugly experience you might expect given the history of the last 900 years; then there's 'The Soldier's Song', anthem of the Republic; and finally a new all-Ireland sporting anthem, 'written by the eejit who did the feckin' Wombles' according to the man on my left, 'because the RUC lads in the team said they couldn't be singing that Fenian shite any longer'. The Irish rugby team, uniquely, has included both North and South since long before any of the recent cross-border initiatives were introduced. But it's hard to make out the words of the new song. Everyone bellows out the chorus line, 'Ireland, Ireland!' but there's a kind of collective choral muttering on the next lines, as if not everyone's on top of the words just yet. I'm only guessing, but it sounds like:

> *Ireland, Ireland*
> *A bit mixed up*
> *But we'll sing it just the same*
> *Ireland, Ireland*
> *Here come the Brits*
> *But this time it's just a game*

The match kicks off, and within five minutes one thing is crystal clear: if anyone's going to be on the wrong end of a kicking this afternoon, it's England. Despite being offered at an absurd four to one on to win at the bookies next to Hot Powers, they are badly rattled by the unexpected ferocity of the Irish. This can only end one way. It's just started, but already it's all over. This presents me with a serious philosophical problem. Although I'm not totally at ease supporting either side against the other, I've decided it's only fair to go with the underdog, which until now has been Ireland. However, with seventy-five of the eighty minutes still to play, it's clear that England are now the undisputed whipping boys – so should I be shouting for them? Is it possible to be four to one on, yet still be underdogs? This is hopeless. I might as well be watching Poland versus Cambodia for all the commitment I can muster. The Irish fans are singing 'The Fields of Athenry' now – how can anyone be expected to beat a team who have three bloody anthems? – and the English are busting a gut trying to catch up, but there's not a soul in the stadium believes it's going to happen. There's an injury break while someone has his head put back together with vinegar and brown paper, and I ask the guy who didn't think much of the Wombles if I can borrow his binoculars. I train them on the press box, and there, true to his word, in the middle of the front row, no typewriter in sight, is George. Watch out for him the next time you see the Trooping of the Colour, or the Oscars. Like Zelig or Forrest Gump, he'll be in there somewhere.

The game ends, and the whole stadium erupts into 'In the Name of Love' by U2. Four anthems? This is getting out of control. I'm delighted that the Irish underdogs have won, but sorry that the English underdogs have lost. And now a very bizarre thing is happening. Though England have lost the game, they're the overall winners of the Six Nations Tournament that also includes Wales, Scotland, France and Italy. They're having to stand in a line, their abject faces projected on to a giant screen, and be presented with the Cromwell Memorial Cup, or whatever the thing is called, while the Irish players stand a few feet away ripping the piss out of them. I expect they're all good friends after the game.

It's midnight and I'm back in the Coal Hole after the most miserable and anticlimactic night you could imagine. Seven o'clock turned to eight turned to half past as I sat in the bar of the Clarence with no sign of George, who was presumably out sipping champagne with the stars, but without me. Realising he wasn't going to turn up I phoned everyone I could think of, but it was half past bloody eight on the night of a famous Irish victory and everyone was out celebrating with their friends. Except me. It's lonely enough trudging through the Tasmanian wilderness all on your tod except for a few vicious geese, but it's even lonelier hanging around the edges of a city-sized party hoping someone will invite you in. It's a small town really, I told myself, just get out there and it'll be like last night: you'll have just missed Marianne Faithfull but never mind, you'll soon be bumping into old friends and hospitable strangers and next thing you know you'll meet up with George and the Legend and half the Irish team and Peter O'Toole at a party round at Ronnie Wood's place, with Van singing 'Raglan Road' while Elvis Costello plays the accordion and Sinead O'Connor does a weird dance in the corner of the kitchen. Nothing doing, I'm afraid. Even Doheny & Nesbitt let me down when I turned up, the crowds that had welcomed me in last night this time only forcing me to the outer fringes.

Standing on the street outside the pub, surrounded by euphoric Irishmen and over-affectionate couples, a decidedly non-classic plastic container of stout in my hand, I realised I was famished as well as depressed. FAST FOOD – ISMAIL KEBAP, said a neon sign across the street. In the alleyway next to it a fat man in a white jacket, luridly lit in red, was devouring a kebab. As he finished he sucked the grease off each finger in turn, like Wimpy in a Popeye cartoon. I may be at the bottom of the barrel, I thought, but I can do better than this. Turns out I was wrong.

'Sorry. No table,' said the waiter at the Indian restaurant round the corner from my hotel.

I looked in despair at the crowded room of exuberant friends, carefree lovers and amiable drunks in green rugby shirts, and spotted a tiny table covered in pilau rice, nan crusts and filthy plates, situated almost, but not quite, inside the toilets. 'How about there?' I said.

Bastard's spotted it, thought the waiter, smiling and saying, 'Of course.'

The mess was cleared up by a young man only marginally less bitter and twisted than I was. The menu was ludicrous. 'Recommended Exquisite Choices From Poultry Farm.' I'll have a sag chicken, and a pint of whatever you've got.

'Sorry, sir, no beer.'

You what?

'No beer. Beer finished.'

Finished? Just when you think things can't get any . . .

'You like red wine? Gin? Dubonnet?'

I hate wine with curry, but this was a desperate situation. I knew, however, that after living on black pudding and Guinness for three days, a curry with red wine at midnight would be a serious error, especially in a room that might contract and squash me in the night.

'I suppose it'll have to be wine then.'

'Certainly, sir.'

'May as well put some gin and Dubonnet in it while you're at it.'

In fact I had water, from the tap, in a jug, as the evening reached its lowest ebb. How am I going to explain this to people back home who'll want to be told they missed a first-class night out? I'll have to find a credible way of explaining that in a place where the whole city was the party, I couldn't find it. There's more to life than going out partying, I'll say. And rugby's only a game. Dear God, I'm getting desperate now.

It's at times like this you have to rely on your inner resources. You know. Satellite TV. A self-pitying phone call. The miniatures of Drambuie you stocked up with on the flight back from Hobart. And then the world starts to look like not such a bad place after all, especially in such a confined space, where it's hard to have any real concept of the world anyway. And I often find that if you focus hard on one thing – like how badly the taste of half-digested lime pickle goes with Drambuie – then other thoughts will spring unbidden from some secret source. And so it is that against all the odds I find the day is leaving me with the warmest of glows. On the most basic level, it's so long since I've been to a big international sporting event that I'd quite forgotten just how vivid and uplifting an experience it is to be part of such a huge communal occasion. Television can't even hint at it.

But best of all I've seen the way an adversarial contest has managed to bring out what the two nations have in common, rather than what keeps them apart. I've seen no nationalistic hostility anywhere in the city. The occasion has been marked by generosity of spirit, and has been a reminder of how many of us are connected by family and friendships that span the generations and the Irish Sea. My God, this Drambuie's good, isn't it? I think I'll have another. I fumble in my bag for a miniature, and tucked behind the MacCarthy Mór dossier is *To Hell or Barbados*. On an impulse I pick it out and flick through the index looking for Montserrat. I'd known about a light-hearted Irish connection, shamrocks in the Caribbean, a Paddy Day's party, all that carry-on, but it wasn't until yesterday that I was aware of a darker Cromwellian story.

I wonder if you can fly direct to Montserrat from London?

Three months later George's wife phones me. She's been waiting for him to make the call himself, but he's too embarrassed. He got back to the Clarence at six and was so tired from the day's exertions he went upstairs to the Legend's room – directly above the bar, just a few vertical feet from where I was sitting waiting for him – for a quick nap.

He didn't wake up till two in the morning. Couldn't understand why I hadn't given him a knock.

And no, you can't fly direct.

SEVENTH DAY ADVENTISTS BELIEVE, says a sign in the window of the first taxi in the queue at Antigua airport. It's commendably honest, but not very snappy. MORMONS DO IT ON THE DOORSTEP – that's the kind of thing you need to get people's attention these days. METHODISTS DO IT ON THEIR KNEES. JEHOVAH'S WITNESSES DO IT WHETHER YOU WANT THEM TO OR NOT. CATHOLICS DO IT, BUT SAY THEY'RE SORRY AFTERWARDS. I could stand here all day making this stuff up. I may have to. I don't seem to be going anywhere else. My negative hotel charisma has gone into overdrive this time.

I was at home packing at eight o'clock last night when I discovered my ticket was for yesterday morning's flight, the one that had left twelve hours earlier, and not today's. Confronting your personal incompetence head-on like this plunges you so deep into existential angst that you feel physically sick. My mood of despair went further into freefall as I spent twenty-five minutes in the airline's telephone queue, listening to a trauma-inducing loop of jingles and marketing messages that would have snapped the Taliban like twigs if they'd piped it into the cages of Guantánamo Bay.

By the time Craig informed me that this was the airline and it was he who was speaking, then enquired how he might help me, I was beyond weeping and into a terrifying mental zone of white light and involuntary guttural noises that will be familiar to anyone who's ever tried to phone IKEA and tell them a shelf part is missing. Luckily Craig was more than man enough for the task. Within seconds he had talked me down from the ledge and put me on the next day's flight, even though he and I both knew it was a non-changeable ticket. 'Well, why not?' he said. 'The office is closed now, and you'll be in the air before they open in the morning. Have a good flight.' But I knew, and I'm sure he suspected, that this wouldn't be the end of it.

At check-in this morning the woman told me there were three P. McCarthys on this flight, two of them called Peter, an ominous piece of news that suggested the potential for chaos was limitless. I presumed this was just a preamble to her refusing to let me on the plane, but she smiled and surrendered a boarding card without any show of resistance.

As I turned away I saw a prematurely aged man with incomplete teeth and a 1970s physics teacher's suit talking into a mobile phone the size of a brick. PARADISE RESORTS ANTIGUA said the clipboard under his arm. I couldn't believe my luck. I waited for his conversation to end then said, 'Excuse me, I wonder if you could help me?'

This rattled him. 'What do you mean?' he blurted, as if I'd asked him if he was still seeing much of Samantha now that Big Vinnie was out of Broadmoor.

I explained that I was a customer of Paradise Resorts, who were supposed to be meeting me in Antigua, but they'd been expecting me last night, not tonight. Perhaps he could let them know at the Caribbean end that I was running a day late?

He looked at me, then at the floor, then licked his lips, like a burglar wondering whether to give the copper the right address, then said, 'Well, the thing is, there are two Paradise Resorts in Antigua.' Now he'd said it he almost believed it himself. 'Yes, that's right! Two. We're long-established and respectable, and now this other mob have come along, and started using the same name.'

This was clearly so far-fetched as to be risible, but that wasn't going to stop him. 'So it might not even be us that you're staying with, in which case there's not a lot I can do. You see my problem?'

We talked for a while, and he eventually conceded there was a 50 per cent chance I might be booked with them, so he called someone up on the brick, but couldn't get a reply, possibly because it was only a pretend phone. As I walked off to departures I made him promise to do all in his power to pass on the information. 'Don't worry,' he said. 'Leave it with me.' And at that moment we both knew there would be no one to meet me in Antigua. Our eyes met and I saw deep into his soul, and realised that he'd bought the clipboard in a Sue Ryder shop, and came to the airport every morning for a bit of company.

So now I'm at Antigua airport at five in the afternoon with nowhere to stay. Drawing on all the experience accumulated during a lifetime's travel, augmented by the survival techniques I've picked up from countless TV series of *Ray Mears Cooks a Squirrel and Lives in a Bush*, I have worked out the most effective way of dealing with this situation. I will approach the Paradise Resorts desk, and explain my dilemma to the rep.

Of course she denies all knowledge of me. I was actually due yesterday, I say. No you weren't, she says. But it's paid for, I say. Prove it, she says. Look, here's the contact phone number they gave me, I say. That's not a proper number, she says. It doesn't exist. Before she can add, 'And neither do you,' I change my line of attack and start pleading in the most pitiful manner I can manage for her to find me a room. Somewhere close to the Montserrat ferry would be perfect, as it leaves at six thirty in the morning. She finds room in a resort as far away from the ferry as you can get without leaving the island. I immediately agree to pay even more than has already been pre-paid for the one they say they know nothing about, and also to pay my own taxi fare instead of being collected by the courtesy minibus, which is busy ferrying more important customers around the island. What a result! Ray Mears couldn't have done better himself, though he might have been able to use a boy scout magnifying glass to set her hands on fire.

My room has a view of the Caribbean, which is full of well-basted all-inclusive couples groping each other below the water-line while they watch the sunset. The pool was empty as I went past carrying the porter's luggage, so I decide to have a swim there even though it's already in the shade. Unfortunately it's now also surrounded by twenty-five lithe West Indian men in chefs' costumes setting tables and laying out the buffet for the poolside barbecue, and the prospect of exposing my porridge-coloured skin and splashing about in front of them like a lonely sod who's just got off the plane and wants his money's worth is too terrible to contemplate. I go back to my room for a shower, then turn on the TV for company and a bit of local colour. It's showing a studio debate about incest in trailer parks in Tennessee.

There's a 'manager's cocktail reception for all guests' at the pool bar before the barbecue, but even the prospect of limitless free rum punch can't sugar the pill of listening to red-nosed couples discussing property prices in Sutton Coldfield and United's chances in the Champion's League.

There's another bar up on the terrace where I spend a pleasant couple of hours reading, paying for beer, and watching people at candlelit poolside tables squirting lobster juice down their shirt fronts. I go to bed at twenty-five past nine, and wake at ten past eleven to the sound of a steel band playing 'Hey Jude' while everybody sings along. Prices start at £2,135 per week, which includes windsurfing and a voyage on a pirate ship.

My taxi is already waiting as I check out next morning at ten past five. The charming young man behind the desk has a smooth line in patter, delivered in a half Caribbean, half African-American patois.

'You going to Montserrat? For St Patrick's Day?'

'That's right.'

'Yeah, I hear it is a big deal over there. Now you remember – in Montserrat always stay to the left.'

'What, when I'm driving?'

'No, man – so the volcano don't get you.'

10

EMERALD ISLE OF THE CARIBBEAN

Montserrat is one of the few remaining possessions of the British Empire, now referred to not as a colony but as an overseas territory. It is one of the Leeward Islands, discovered in 1493 by Columbus, who didn't land there, but just sailed past and named it after a monastery near Barcelona. It is pear – or perhaps pearl – shaped, eleven miles by seven at its widest point, green and mountainous, washed by warm tropical waters and cooled by the trade winds. Though volcanic in origin, there had been no volcanic activity there since long before Columbus's day until 1995, when the Soufrière Hills started belching out gases and debris. Plymouth, the handsome old capital situated below the mountain at the water's edge, was evacuated. In 1997 a series of devastating eruptions and pyroclastic avalanches buried Plymouth under metres of ash and rock, and wiped the airport and the villages of Kinsale and St Patrick's off the map for ever. The southern half of the island was declared an exclusion zone and the population was reduced from 11,000 to fewer than 4,000, as families fled to Britain and the USA. You probably saw it on

the news. Clare Short, the British government minister responsible for aid to the disaster zone, said that the homeless islanders
'would be asking for golden elephants next'. It's a line that didn't
play too well in the Caribbean, and has remained lodged in the
popular memory.

Montserrat is also the only country in the world, apart from
Ireland, where St Patrick's Day is a public holiday. ✱

Three enormous cruise ships full of people in sun visors with
turn-ups on their shorts are queuing to get into Antigua as the
six thirty ferry leaves port, and I remember that a warm sea
breeze on bare arms is one of the greatest sensations in the world.
We had to check in by five thirty on account of a lot of carbon
paper being involved, even though there are just thirteen of us
on the 300-seater catamaran. Montserrat hasn't had much of a
tourist industry since the ash began to fall. Even Clare Short
hasn't been over for a holiday.

The journey's only an hour, but everybody soon gets to know
each other. There are three returning residents, a French film
crew from Guadeloupe come to shoot inside the exclusion zone,
and half a dozen day-trippers from resorts in Antigua. A mournful-looking American in his sixties is wearing a T-shirt bearing a picture of fire-fighters hosing down the Twin Towers
above the legend UNITED WE STAND UNITED WE PRAY. Outrageous slogans on frivolous leisurewear are a traditional part
of tropical holidays, but it's hard to know how we're expected
to react to this, especially at half past six in the morning.
A pigeon-chested Englishman in a pale blue Millett's polo shirt
has struck up a conversation with him. They are discussing
television.

'Been watching the BBC on satellite,' says United-We-Pray.
'Something called *Ground Force*?'

His speech has a monotone, automaton quality that's clearly
struck a chord with Millett, who says, 'Oh.'

'Yeah. Real good. Gardening.' He looks Millett straight in the eye with a gaze of utmost gravity, as if he's just told him his mother's dead. Now his wife is joining in, eager to explain the concept of the programme.

'They come home and they're like, oh wow, you've changed the colour!'

'We rented a videotape once, from the library back home. Kew Gardens? That was neat.'

'So where is home?'

'Ohio. Not very exciting. I have a place, makes steel parts for the railroad.'

Millett extricates himself from the conversation before the excitement gets too much to bear and comes and joins me at the stern. He's from Caterham, and is very knowledgeable on the subject of cheap booze warehouses in Copenhagen that cater for people who've driven over from Sweden on the bridge. Part of the bridge is a tunnel, apparently. As we talk he's swigging from a cold can of fizzy orange, which I'm eyeing jealously. I haven't had a drink since I brushed my teeth this morning, which seems about half a lifetime ago. I was too early for breakfast at the hotel, there wasn't a shop at the ferry port, and the cafeteria on the boat is closed because there are only thirteen of us. Millett has come prepared. He probably bought the can in Asda in Caterham, and has been keeping it cold in his mini-bar at the resort's expense until he needed it. I wish he'd give me a swig. But no, he's draining the can now, and shaking it in his hand to make sure it's empty as we approach the cliffs of northern Montserrat and the mooring jetty, and now he's – my God, I could have stopped him, I could have jumped on him, but it all happened so quickly – *THROWN THE CAN OVER HIS SHOULDER INTO THE CARIBBEAN!*

'Ah, well. Nice talking to you, old son. Places to go. Volcanoes to see. Don't do anything I wouldn't do.'

The boat passes a small sandy beach, rounds a point and we're entering a U-shaped harbour with a single jetty and minimal infrastructure. A wall of palm trees and green hillside is framed between the blues of the sea and sky. A few brightly painted wooden houses add variety to the relentless blues and greens. Immigration and Customs is a tiny, pristine wooden building, painted pale blue, with shuttered windows and ceiling fans. A sign on the wall says:

WELCOME TO MONTSERRAT
The Emerald Isle

A single vehicle is parked outside with its bonnet up. Two men are tinkering with the engine. It's not a taxi, but an ancient black estate car that's been converted into a hearse. IRISH'S FUNERAL HOME says the lettering on the side. 'Looks like he's broken down,' I say to one of the West Indian guys who was on the boat.

'Yeah,' he says. 'I tink de engine die.'

In 1668 Lord William Willoughby, governor of Barbados, described Montserrat as 'almost an Irish colony'. The census of 1678 supported his claim, showing a population of 761 English, 52 Scots and 992 Africans – but 1,869 Irish, more than the other three groups put together. Yet the island was a British possession; so how did the Irish become so predominant that even today the national symbol is Erin on a harp, and passports are stamped with a green shamrock?

Montserrat was first populated by Arawak and Carib Indians who were deprived of their lands in the traditional manner by forces of the British Empire. It was settled in 1632, largely by English and Irish Catholics who were unwelcome in other colonies because of their religion. While Catholicism wasn't encouraged – it's recorded that Father Stritch of Limerick used to disguise himself as a woodcutter and say Mass in the jungle – it was tolerated, and the Irish population began to swell. Crom-

MONTSERRAT

Antigua 38km
Tipperary 6,720km

C A R I B B E A N   S E A

Ferry port
The Quiet Spot
• Observatory
Pentecostal Church •

CENTRE
HILLS

Former
airport

Salem
•
Vue Pointe
Hotel

EXCLUSION ZONE

SOUFRIERE

Tar
River

VOLCANO

PLYMOUTH

HILLS

Kinsale

St. Patrick's

ATLANTIC OCEAN

Montserrat

SOUTH AMERICA

O   m i l e s   4

O   kilometres   6

well helped by transporting some of the survivors of Drogheda and other massacres to Montserrat as well as to Barbados. Indentured Irish servants who had served their contracted time on Barbados, and others who had escaped, made their way to Montserrat to find work among their countrymen.

It seems to have been an uneasy tropical alliance between English and Irish. One English settler wrote: 'These two nations accord not upon this island. The Irish are most malicious against the English.'

In the late seventeenth and early eighteenth centuries the French had designs on Montserrat and its booming sugar economy, and launched a series of invasion attempts. The Irish residents of the island, resentful of religious and economic discrimination, were happy to assist. In 1665 they helped the French land at Kinsale, an Irish enclave in the south-west of the island named after the port in County Cork that in 1602 was the scene of one of the definitive battles in the fight for Irish independence, when the English won a famous victory. In Kinsale, Montserrat, however, the French came out on top and laid waste to English possessions, leaving the Irish untouched. Two years later crown forces once again took control, but it was clear the Irish were not to be trusted, and sectarian tensions remained close to the surface.

In 1668 legislation was passed 'to restrain several odious distinctions used by the English, Scots and Irish reflecting on each other (English Dog, Scots Dog, Cavalier, Roundhead and many other opprobrious, scandalous disgraceful terms)'. The Act made no mention of the African population.

Slaves stolen from their homes in Africa began to arrive shortly after the Irish. What resulted was a three-tiered colonial society. The British owned the island, and ran it for their own financial interests. Shrewdly they appointed a series of Irish governors who were also Protestants, and so had one foot in either camp. On the second tier were the bulk of the settlers, Irish Catholics who were forbidden land grants and the subsequent ownership of large plantations because of their religion; they became a white underclass engaged in fishing and subsistence farming, occupations in which they would have received a good grounding under British rule in Ireland. In Montserrat they found themselves in the unaccustomed situation of not being at the bottom of the British-dominated pile, because at the next level down came the Africans: 'the slaves of slaves' as the Montserrat poet and historian Howard Fergus has described them.

Although the Irish had themselves suffered under the heel of oppression, there is no reason to assume that the treatment of slaves in Montserrat was any less brutal than in other colonies. Irish and Africans lived in close proximity, but this might have been due as much to topography and economic necessity as to solidarity between the races. What is certain, however, is the savagery of the punishment meted out to black slaves. The cutting off of ears and burning with hot irons were commonplace; so were executions by hanging and dismembering, and also by burning 'at the usual place in Plymouth', as in the case of a slave burned to death in 1695 for stealing a cow. The slave's owner received £3,500 of sugar from public funds as compensation for his loss.

In 1768 the slaves planned a rebellion. The day chosen was 17 March, St Patrick's Day. Though Irish Catholics still did not enjoy equal status, weight of numbers meant that their national feast was always celebrated. During the festivities the slaves inside Government House would seize their masters' swords while their fellows launched an attack from outside. Their plans were overheard and they were betrayed 'by a white seamstress noted for drunkenness' according to Howard Fergus, or 'by a drunken old prostitute from Liverpool', according to a guy I met in a rum shop last night. Either way, the rebellion was suppressed and its nine ringleaders publicly executed. This week's St Patrick's Day celebrations are therefore a two-edged sword, celebrating both the island's Irish heritage and the attempted overthrow of white rule by slaves now hailed as freedom fighters by many of their descendants. The Irish have always enjoyed a good argument, so the embodiment of two conflicting traditions in one St Patrick's Day celebration seems entirely apposite.

I've been studying Montserrat's history for the day and a half since I arrived. I've established an office at a table in the shade of a mango tree, with the unrealistically blue Caribbean to my right and the volcano constantly belching smoke and ash away to my left. It's an office in the sense that, as well as a chair, there's a small table piled with books, and a bottle of cold Carib beer. Behind me is an empty swimming pool, because I am the only tourist. The only other guest is a civil servant from Clare Short's Department for International Development, DFID, here to help referee the contentious distribution of funds.

The Vue Pointe is a hotel with an air of Ian Fleming chic. It is the Caribbean before it got Michael Winnered and Del Boyed, before All-Inclusives and Couples-Onlys and Kidz-Klubz. There's just an open-sided lobby and bar opening on to a pool, and eighteen little cottages set in a huge tropical garden that slopes down to the sea. It used to slope down to Montserrat's only golf club as well, but that's now just a scar on the landscape, the fairway buried under millions of tons of mud and ash. The dark grey beach I can see below me is twenty yards wider than it was five years ago, due to the build-up of volcanic material.

As well as books, my office is equipped with the official programme of the St Patrick's Day Week of Activities.

12 March	St Patrick's Lecture. Pentecostal Church, 8 p.m. Also results for Schools' Quiz.
13 March	Around the Island Boat Trip.
14 March	Storytelling. Good Life Restaurant, 6.30 p.m.
15 March	Freedom Jam and Bingo. Cricket Pitch, 5 p.m. until.

16 March	St Patrick's Day Dinner. Vue Pointe Hotel, 6 p.m.
17 March	Church Service, 9 a.m. Junior Calypso Competition, 7 p.m.
18 March	Freedom Run, 6 a.m. Slave Feast. Festival Village, 2 p.m. until.

I think I'll go to them all.

Except the Freedom Run.

Among the books in my alfresco library is a copy of the Montserrat telephone directory, a slim volume that's got a lot slimmer since 1997. When I asked for one this morning, the woman at reception told me about her friend who finds it hard to look up a phone number without crying. 'The book is so thin now, it reminds her of everybody who's gone.' A quick flick through the pages reveals some familiar surnames: Carty, Cavanagh, Collins, Daley, Farrell, Fergus, Halloran, Hogan, Macnamara, O'Garro, Osborne, Riley, Ryan – lots of Ryans – Sullivan, Sweeney and Tuitt. There are also some Paddys, and twenty-one families called Irish. This may prove nothing about genetic make-up – though it's hardly credible that the Irish, and also the English and Scots, didn't intermarry with African slaves and their descendants – but establishes beyond any doubt a significant Irish cultural connection among the West Indian population.

The names are a confirmation of the whole unlikely story. When I'd told friends in Ireland about a Caribbean island where they stamped your passport with a shamrock, the dark-skinned locals were called Paddy and Irish, and they had a calypso competition on St Patrick's Day, I was variously accused of being a Celto-Fantasist, of plotting the script for an Irish Ealing comedy, and of falling for one of those rumours in which we'd all like to believe, like the one about the tribe in grass skirts who worship the Duke of Edinburgh as a god. That one's true as well, by the way. They've got a volcano too. They believe Prince Philip to be the son of the deities who inhabit it. And it's only the women who wear grass skirts. The men wear penis gourds, as I believe they're known in Limerick.

As well as the names, I've unearthed various supposed Celtic connections that I hope to investigate while I'm here. Chief among them is the accent, which according to some linguists, and many casual observers, has distinct Irish influences, among them a proclivity for ending sentences with the expression 'at all at all'. On the face of it this sounds ridiculous, though there's a story that's been in circulation locally for many generations concerning the settler who came over from Ireland, and chatted to the first black man he met on the beach. 'Jaysus, paddy,' he said, feeling at home with the familiar accent, 'haven't you got yerself a fierce tan while ye've been here.'

Other alleged Irish influences include a percussion instrument related to the bodhran, a wind instrument descended from the tin whistle, and a heel-and-toe dance called Bam-check-a-lay Chuga Foot Myer that is said to be related to Irish step dancing, and predates *Riverdance* by centuries. In addition, an academic from Ohio University claims to have traced the recipe for the national dish of goat stew to Connemara. The Roman Catholic religion is thriving, and there is said to be a flexible, Irish-style approach to the concept of time. I am looking forward to a week of rigorous anthropological research. First, though, I will have another cold Carib, and a siesta. Reading in the tropics can be a very gruelling business, especially when there's a volcano at the end of the garden.

The radio is on in the taxi as I head north in the dark on the island's only road on my way to the Pentecostal church. My limited experience so far suggests that the radio is always on in Montserrat, broadcasting a continuous output of upbeat, feel-good island music, soca, jump-up, calypso and reggae. There's no trace of the gangsta rap and machine-made music that has swamped other radio stations across the world. Unlike young whites in England, black Montserratians don't seem to want to pretend they're black New Yorkers. The song that's on at the moment has a fiendishly catchy riff, and a chorus that goes:

> *Ants ants ants*
> *Beware of de flying ants*

I've just decided to buy the CD and take it back home when the song ends and I realise it was a public health announcement. As we pull up outside the church, it's followed by another ad: 'Come to St Patrick's Day at Festival Village. Enjoy yourself, Irish stylee!'

It's not yet five to eight as I enter the church, but the event has already begun. I'd been warned that nothing ever begins on time, but hadn't realised they meant it might start early. Still, at least it's unpunctual, and that's the main thing; it's always good to be reminded that you are time's master, and not vice versa. Howard Fergus – who is a professor, and also now a Sir, so I'm not quite sure how to refer to him, because they don't seem big on formality over here – is reading one of his poems about the volcano, 'Irish Landfill': 'For St Patrick's Day,' he says.

> *Montserrat was their Plymouth Rock*
> *Their Botany Bay . . .*
> *When emancipation broke*
> *The Irish beached on the first wave*
> *And mercy slowly trickled down*
> *From smiling eyes to slave*

When he finishes, he hands over to Chedmond Brown, who will give tonight's lecture, which is also being broadcast on radio here and in some of the neighbouring islands. Brown is a slim man with luxuriant, gently curling greying hair and light brown skin. The introduction says he is an elected representative to the island's government, and makes it clear that he has a reputation as a bit of a firebrand and a radical. His text this evening concerns race, religion, conflict and culture, and is an impassioned plea to turn away from Montserrat's colonial, Eurocentric and white heritage, and embrace its people's African roots. I'm intrigued. I'm also aware that mine is the only white face in the room, apart from a couple sitting in the pew at the front, well-dressed, in their fifties, who must be tourists as well. It's only when Mr Brown makes direct reference to them that I realise it's the British governor and his wife. As Chedmond warms to his task, the governor's body language becomes increasingly agitated. He's grinning at Cheddie in a we're-all-colleagues-here-even-if-we-don't-always-agree kind of a way, but looks as if he could do with a stiff G and T. I can't find fault with most of what Chedmond has to say, particularly the way he's encouraging people to read the history of their island and understand where they come from.

Hang on, though. He's just said that the whole Irish thing is an invention of the tourist industry. If it is, it's not a very successful invention, as I'm the only tourist here; but in any case, the facts don't support him. Erin and the harp were on Montserrat's stamps in 1903, long before any such industry existed; and the facts of the numbers of Irish settlers, and the names in the phone book, are indisputable. All the brown and black people in the room may not have Irish blood; but it's likely some of them have. One day someone will check the DNA, and then we'll know. There's a lot of guff talked about blood and race and purity anyway. Most of us come from far more mixed-up backgrounds than we ever dream or admit to, particularly in the British and Irish Isles. The notion of Anglo-Saxons being 'swamped' by foreigners always raises a chuckle among those of us who aren't ashamed of our Celtic-Roman-Saxon-Viking-Norman racial purity.

At the end of the lecture Dr Professor Sir Fergus asks for questions and comments from the audience. Someone makes the point that the slaves might have been encouraged to rebel by the example of the perennially rebellious Irish, but Chedmond isn't convinced. Someone else asks who St Patrick was anyway. Chedmond tells him, and then it all goes quiet. The guy from the radio with the headphones on looks anxious. There's still eight more minutes of airtime to fill. 'Any more questions?' Doesn't look like it. He is in trouble here, and must be rescued from the ignominy of dead airtime. I reach the microphone in the centre of the aisle, and feel all eyes in the room upon me. My forehead is sweating. All I need now is a question.

'Er . . . this is my first time in Montserrat. I've barely been here a day, and, er . . .'

Up at the front Chedmond is scrutinising me. The governor has stopped wiggling and appears to have settled down.

'Er . . . I've come here, really, to try and make sense of the things Mr Brown has been talking about, you know, the Irish, and, er, er . . . slaves . . . and . . .'

Seven minutes to go. Come on. Think of a bloody question. 'The thing is . . .'

Mind you, no one said the question had to be addressed to Mr Brown, did they?

'Er . . . the thing is, I'd really like to know what the British governor made of Mr Brown's speech.'

Uproar. Everybody's clapping. A lot of them are screeching with laughter as well, which suggests I may have dropped the governor in the shit here. Perhaps it wouldn't normally be protocol for him to speak at an event like this. Tough. He'll have to now. They're still clapping, and clearly have no intention of stopping until he gets to the microphone, which he just has. I give him a winsome smile, as if to say, 'Sorry.' He gives me a knowing frown, as if to say, 'You're dead, pal.'

He starts off well, with uncontroversial, conciliatory-sounding expressions that mean whatever people want them to mean and will bring the broadcast to a gentle, terribly British conclusion. And then he says, 'To be honest, I don't know a great deal about Caribbean history.'

There's a pause, a split-second hiatus in which we all think, What? What did he just say? Looks are exchanged, a mouth drops open, and then he continues.

'But I have spent many years in Russia, where I learned . . .' I survey the crowd, and get the distinct feeling that Russia, in Montserrat, in St Patrick's week, is an extremely remote concept. He finishes, and the Schools' Quiz results are announced. Through the open church door I see my taxi driver waiting outside.

I decide to leave before the governor finds out where I live, in case he has retired SAS men on his staff who are at a loose end for something to do in the evenings. The guy who's made the point about the rebellious Irish inspiring the slaves shakes my hand at the door as I leave, asks me my name, and says that he's called Cecil. I get into the cab thinking that from now on I'll try to keep a lower profile. There are 4,000 people on this island, almost all of whom are Afro-Caribbean. You never know. Maybe I'll just blend in.

I pour a tumbler of Barbados rum and switch on the TV before I go to bed, to try and take my mind off my embarrassing diplomatic faux pas. That actress who used to be in *The Golden Girls* is on screen, saying, 'Clean your closet and your conscience by donating your fur to the needy.' I switch channels, and find a news story claiming that Muhammad Ali's grandfather was an Irishman.

I go to sleep with the windows open and the mosquito screens down. When I wake halfway through the night the wind is blowing the curtains horizontally into the room, as if Dracula is about to come sliding down the wall at any moment.

Or the governor.

'Good morning. Would you care to join me? My name is Cedric.'

In a deliciously warm breeze, over tea, poached eggs and home-made lime marmalade – Montserrat was the source of the limes that earned English sailors the nickname 'limeys' – I make the acquaintance of Cedric Osborne. Though his surname is Irish, he's a sixth-generation Montserratian whose father built the Vue Pointe in 1961, which explains the Flemingesque ambiance. Until that year, he says, there were hardly any hotels, even in Barbados and Antigua; then Castro made a hostile takeover of Batista's tourism assets, and the Cuban overspill started to look for new destinations. He's a warm, genial man in his sixties, clearly besotted with his island. He says a friend of his, who like many of the islanders emigrated to the UK in the early sixties, came back recently and couldn't believe that people still parked their cars with the keys in the ignition. 'The only time anything bad happened was when someone banged my car one night, left bits of their brake light in the ground. There were only three repair shops on the island, so I just phoned round and found out who did it.'

We're joined by his wife Carol, who looks as if she could be one of my aunties. Perhaps she is. Her grandparents came from Skibbereen, a West Cork village seven miles from my mother's home, before emigrating to Boston, Massachusetts. Her grandfather was in the IRA: 'You know, the old IRA. The good IRA!' Every generation says that about the previous IRA. Her accent is a hybrid of Irish, American and Caribbean, and the chat just flows. It's like sitting in the kitchen of a bed and breakfast in Mayo, apart from the pool. And the palm trees. And the volcano. Cedric says he's been to Ireland many times. On his first visit he went to a Rotary Club meeting in Limerick. His arrival caused quite a stir. 'Everybody wanted to know what part of Africa I was from. So I told them I was from an Irish colony.

'"An Irish colony?" they said, amazed.

'"That's right," I said. "Just comin' back to claim what's mine."'

He has fond memories of a combined sweetshop, funeral

parlour and bar in Skibereen. 'Everybody's interested in you, wants to talk. Just like bein' in Montserrat.'

After breakfast I sit in the shade for a while, because you really don't want to go rushing at the day in a place like this. I'm reading the story in the *Montserrat Reporter* ('Montserrat Distorter,' someone told me yesterday) – PROSTITUTION IN MONTSERRAT BECOMING A FUN ACTIVITY – when Cordela, the bar manager, comes across. 'Look,' she says. A huge, vertical jet of sunlit, dense brown ash is shooting upwards from the top of the volcano with tremendous power. Clouds of lethal white smoke are jetting out horizontally from lower down the peak, as if it's sprung a leak. 'A good puff, eh?' says Cordela, with a relaxed smile.

'Yes,' I say. 'Very good puff.' Best since I've been here, actually. Hope the puffs don't get any better.

If you were solar-powered, the drive up the island from the Vue Pointe would charge you up for a month. Two fluffy white clouds have been artfully arranged against the royal-blue sky to stop it from looking monotonous. At every bend new, more startling vistas of the Caribbean are revealed. Bright blooms of frangipani illuminate the bush. Chickens run into the road. Goats for whom stew time is looming scrabble up hillsides. Like everyone else, Bob the taxi driver hoots his horn whenever he sees someone he knows. So horns hoot constantly, because everyone knows everybody else. Bob is pointing at houses. 'That one, George Martin's house. That one, where Paul McCartney stayed when he came to record. Air Studios. Many rock stars come here. Boy George. Sting. Rolling Stones. Other one. With rehab clinic on Antigua. Yeah, Clapton. Nobody knows who they are, nobody cares. Not like they Bob Marley.'

I ask what the rock stars did to relax.

'Drink rum. In Plymouth one night, my friend says, you wanna come to the rum shop? Stevie Wonder playing piano in there. He came here to record *Ebony and Ivory*.'

I suppose we'll just have to try and forgive Montserrat for that one.

Bob is a big, big man who was a security guard at the airport, and had to run for his life when the sky started falling in. His two colleagues were among the seventeen dead. All his family have gone to live in England, even his mum and dad. I ask him where. 'Kilburn. Mum and Dad both sick. I don't think they like the winter. Can't get used to that dark.' Neither can most of the rest of us, Bob.

Down at the jetty cars are parked with the windows open and the keys in. The boat for the round the island trip is the ferry that brought us over from Antigua. The deck is packed with local people, some resident expats, and a handful of day-trippers from Antigua. The island is so small that I'm already recognising faces. We head south out of port, anti-clockwise around the island, passing the new police and fire stations on the clifftop. I have no real notion of what to expect. I also have no cold beer, and there is no bar. Many of the locals anticipated this and have brought their own chilled bottles, which they are openly consuming in front of me. Later in the trip we've been promised 'refreshments', a euphemism the world over for drab sandwiches, a chocolate-style biscuit, and a resolutely non-intoxicating beverage. Can't wait.

The sea's calm as we head down the west coast. We pass Vue Pointe and gawp at the ex-golf course, but nothing's prepared me for what lies in wait as we round the next headland and see the remains of Plymouth. It's a scene of biblical devastation, a monochrome swathe of ash and rubble sweeping down the mountainside, entombing the town and stifling its once bright colours. Roofs and top-storey balconies crane their necks to look out over the devastation. Further south the villages of Kinsale and St Patrick's, once the hub of the saint's day festivities, have disappeared from the face of the earth. The Tar River valley, which still experiences daily rock and mud flows, is a post-apocalyptic moonscape. When the pyroclastic flow hit the sea here, the waters boiled. It's hard to reconcile these other-worldly sights with the mangoes and flowers, the churches and rum shops, just four or five miles away.

As we round the island's southern tip the sea is crashing into itself from half a dozen directions, and rises suddenly in a frightening swell. No one can stand without clutching a rail. Eyes are averted stoically towards the deck, their owner's mouths set in tense concentration. This is a very good time not to have been drinking beer. A voice announces that refreshments are now being served on the lower deck, then adds, 'However, as nobody can get downstairs at the moment, we'll stop and serve them just before we get back to harbour.'

As we head north up the east side, past the fragment of control tower where the airport used to be, the waters start to calm and people are talking again. A Rasta-looking guy tells me he ran away that day, even though he knew that if you were in its path no person or vehicle could outrun it: the pyroclastic flow moved at hundreds of kilometres an hour, and went from mountain top to water's edge in fifty-five seconds. 'Me house is gone, but me still gat four years to pay mi mortgage.' He could have taken the rescue package and gone to Britain, but chose to stay where his heart is, trapped in a post-disaster, post-colonial world. We go down for our refreshments, which are marginally more depressing than expected. Neither of us can face them, and we settle for a bottle of water each instead. It's very good. I must try it more often.

Back on bone-dry land I've got wind of an event that wasn't on the official programme, and scrounge a lift with Richard and Jennifer, who are not tourists even though they come from Doncaster. Jennifer is a tall, slender nineteen-year-old who has been out here almost seven months, accumulating proposals of marriage and offers to convert her to multiple denominations of Christianity while she works as a volunteer in one of the island's three primary schools. Richard is her dad, a lifelong primary school teacher who jacked it in a couple of years ago, jaded by the new management and logo and mission-statement culture. He's here to spend a couple of weeks with his daughter, for whom I am full of admiration. In a culture where gap years and travelling the world have come to mean going off with your boyfriend or girlfriend to meet up with a bunch of your other mates and do drugs and get dysentery on a beach where the locals get no financial or cultural benefit from your presence, her altruistic choice is heart-warming. We arrive at the cricket pitch just up the hill from the Vue Pointe, and she is besieged by small children, still eager to stroke her long straight hair and touch her skin in fascination after all these months.

If you ever have a choice of when to visit a small tropical island, try and go when the primary school sports are on. The whole culture of the place is laid out before you. In Fiji I once saw twelve schools from twelve villages build twelve palm-frond pavilions for the elders, then run themselves to a standstill under a jungle-covered mountain. One barefoot little boy wore a yellow T-shirt that said: ALL AUSTRALIANS LOOK THE SAME. Today the smoky smell of fried chicken hangs heavy on the reggae that booms around the playing field where not so long ago, according to a man in a rude boy trilby, the touring Springboks played a West Indian XI at cricket, and the players were reacquainted with their breakfasts on the boat back to Antigua. A tiny concrete grandstand is packed with mums and toddlers sheltering from the late afternoon sun, and echoes with laughter and a shrill of hyperanimated conversation. Other parents stand round the perimeter of the field under colourful sun umbrellas, or squat in the shadow of the sightscreens. A lady cop swings a giant Mag-Lite like a cheerleader's baton. Trousers are flared, headscarves vivid, halter-tops spangly, hats unrestrained and polka dots large. The girls' under-eleven 800 metres in 85° of sun is so brutal it gives me chest cramps just watching it. Ryan won the last race, and O'Garro the one before. 'Fathers' race next,' announces the island's top DJ. 'Then mothers' race, umbrella race, and politicians' race. Take your places now for small boys' relay.' It is happily, gleefully, sociably competitive.

Afterwards Richard and Jennifer drive me to the Vue Pointe and we walk down the hill to Jumping Jack's, a ramshackle beach bar on the edge of the devastated golf course. It's run by Margaret from Sunderland and her husband Danny Sweeney, a Montserratian fisherman. The beer is ferociously cold, the grilled tuna and waloo have been caught by Danny, and the mood is marginally more relaxed than falling asleep in a hammock. Within minutes I have mentally elevated it to the top ten of world bars.

Richard keeps me entertained with terrifying tales of life as a primary teacher once management mania and its theories and jargons and best practice bollocks descended on that profession. He was drinking a bottle of whisky a week, and gave up the day he left teaching. I tell him of the old-style professorial grammar school English teacher I once knew, who kept a bottle in the drawer of his classroom desk. 'It never came to that,' he says, 'but in the final months I did need a miniature of vodka in my orange juice to get through a staff meeting.' He shudders at the recollection. 'They were awful events. Like something out of Kafka.'

This glimpse into the pedagogic abyss is profoundly depressing, and a nightcap seems a good idea when Jack's closes and the two of them head back to the family home where Jennifer is lodging. Up at the Vue Pointe bar I sit under a ceiling fan and gaze out at the orange glow of the volcano in the night sky. A dozen elderly Canadians, Americans and Brits are playing a board game in the far corner.

'Expats,' says the waiter as he puts my beer down on a shamrock beer-mat. 'They have villas on the hill.' He points in what appears to be the direction of the volcano. 'Others go away, but they stay. Every week they come here one evening.'

I ask what they are playing.
'Tribute.'
Tribute?
'Yes. Tribute pursuit.'

Next morning I go up a dusty lane to the little house that's all that's left of the University of the West Indies in Montserrat. The warm, expansive Dr Fergus I saw in the church the other night has been replaced by a tight-lipped, defensive academic who doesn't seem that pleased to see me. Perhaps he has had his fill of halfwits who've come looking for black leprechauns. But he relaxes as we talk, particularly after I've mentioned five or six times how much I like his poetry, and speaks passionately about the commemoration of the St Patrick's Day rebellion on what used to be the white man's feast day.

'We secularised it, Africanised it, or at least indigenised it. In an attempt to build a counterculture in the face of still being a colony, we are seizing on an event that gives some measure of pride or self-respect. Emancipation didn't come about without resistance.'

I ask if he believes Fergus to be an Irish name.

'It is,' he says. 'But please remember there was really no comparison between the horrors of black slavery and the discrimination against the Irish.'

Afterwards I put in a good session at my office under the mango tree. I'd never have thought I was suited to an office job, but I'm starting to come round to the idea. Being able to have a swim and a beer whenever you feel like it is a big plus, and in the interests of productivity and job satisfaction should be introduced to all industries as soon as possible if we are to continue to compete in global markets.

I'm winding down from the stress by taking a short power nap at my desk when I'm woken by voices. 'Oi have a shuvil up dere a'ready. An' a pick.' It's the West Indian gardener talking to his assistant on the lawn below the pool. Maybe it's because I've been dreaming, but for a moment there he sounded just like Danny Dean who used to work on my Uncle Jack's farm in West Cork.

At the end of the day disaster strikes.

I take a walk along the volcanic beach to watch the sunset. Two ladies in 1950s Christian bathing suits with those funny little skirt fronts are about to go in for a dip, and a man is fishing with his son from the end of the jetty. Two enormous cows are rooting around in the lava by the eleventh hole, a sight that will be replicated all over the world when nature finally reasserts herself and deals once and for all with the golf problem. As the sun sinks rapidly into the sea I'm watching as closely as I can without melting my retinas. I'm hoping to see the Green Flash, a burst of emerald on the horizon that is said to occur on clear evenings right after sunset and is unique to Montserrat, unless they've made it up because I seem like a gullible fool and they're all hiding behind bushes pointing and laughing. The sun disappears, and then there's ... it sort of ... I'm pretty sure ... yeah, definitely, unless I imagined it ... I think it did. I'm as certain as I was about the gardener's accent.

Over at Jumping Jack's the power is off and the light is fading fast. If it doesn't come back on soon they'll have to close. Within minutes word arrives of what's gone wrong. This is a small island thing. Bob has told Cecil has told Paddy has told Maria has told Cordela has told Cedric who calls Danny who tells us that a lorry driver delivering pylon parts to the electricity generating plant has parked on a hill, the brakes have failed and the truck has gone crashing into the most crucial bit of kit on the site, blacking out the whole island. In fridges all over Montserrat, the beers that are an essential part of the psychological battle against volcanic ash are already beginning to go warm. And there's worse to come.

The storytelling evening has been cancelled because it needs lights and a PA.

This is calamitous news that poses a serious threat to my mental stability. There is so little actually to do on Montserrat that anything in any way resembling an event takes on disproportionate significance. Don't get me wrong here. The lack of things to do is one of the island's greatest charms; it enables you just to be. In particular the lack of things for tourists to do – casinoey, mini-mokeish, water-ski and shopping-type things, I mean, as opposed to sitting under mango trees, or going to lectures in the Pentecostal church – has been crucial in keeping the place like itself, rather than making it like everywhere else. But when something is scheduled to happen, like the storytelling, it becomes the centre of your mental landscape.

I feel like a fifteen-year-old standing outside the youth club staring at his watch and realising that the hot date he's been looking forward to all week isn't going to turn up because she's gone to a pop festival for the weekend with a lad that's left school and has got his own car. What am I meant to do for the next six hours till bedtime? Sit in the dark and remember stuff? Why do they need a PA and lights anyway? Why can't they shout, and hold up lighters? I think Margaret must have noticed me sobbing and banging my head on the counter because she just gave me a sympathetic look and said, 'They're got their own generator up at Vue Pointe, you know.'

Seconds later I'm heading up the grassy hill in the direction of the bar, picking my way through the nocturnal wildlife. A marvellous thing happens each evening just after the Green Flash. The hotel gardens are suddenly festooned with toads the size of handbags. I make it to the pool without standing on one, thinking all the time about what happened at primary school the day someone put a toad down the back of Margaret Houghton's dress and slapped her, and the nuns found out.

The Vue Pointe bar is a classically shaped beauty in polished hardwood, with a brass footrail and a row of swivel-top wicker-backed bar stools. On the wall behind the bar are two large cabinets in the same polished wood, in which an impressive collection of liquor is secured. I arrive just in time to see Mr Wilson opening the bar. Like Louis XIV getting up in the morning, this is the kind of ceremony to which people would feel privileged to be invited.

Mr Wilson is a tall, slim, dark-skinned man of conspicuous happiness, who is employed to do every job known to the hotel industry. At various times of day and night you'll see him in singlet and shorts pushing a wheelbarrow, in a business shirt answering the phone at reception, or as he is now, in a short-sleeved tropical-island shirt that means he's a cocktail barman. He is also standing on top of the bar holding a rope. Throwing it like a gaucho, he deftly lassoes a hook on the bar cabinet, yanks the rope as if he's hoisting a mainsail, and a flap door rises to reveal the booze within. Lashing the rope to an overhead beam he moves along the bartop, lassoes the second door, and repeats the operation. I have witnessed the opening of many bars in my time, but nothing to compare with this. For the rest of my life cupboards with doors that you open by hand will look like a soft option.

Four of last night's Tribute Pursuiters have come back for a game of bridge. I spend the evening chatting with the only other people to have ventured out in search of light, a charming couple from Scunthorpe. I remember them from the boat trip. They had their own beers. One is a civil engineer, the other an ex-policewoman turned gardener. The engineer has been coming to Montserrat since she was a child, staying in her parents' holiday villa. One night in the eighties, when Air Studios was in full swing, her mum came back from a restaurant and said, 'There was a man playing the piano in the restaurant tonight, love. Quite good. John somebody, he said his name was.'

'Not Elton?'

'Yes, that's him. John Elton. He seemed quite lively.'

There are thirty-eight satellite channels on my TV, but by far the most compelling is number 3, which brings you the picture from one channel, but the sound from another. It's fuzzier than the other stations, but it's worth it for the excitement generated by the random juxtaposition of sound and vision. Tonight, like men in cafés all over Tangier, I'm watching an old episode of *Cheers*, the one where Sammy starts dating a glamorous local politician. Over these classic comedy images I can hear Henry Kissinger trying to explain why he isn't a war criminal. This is a tremendous idea, with unlimited potential. Imagine a dinosaur documentary with *EastEnders'* dialogue. Or *Songs of Praise*, with the words from *Eurotrash*. Or the other way round. You could enter it for the Turner Prize.

At breakfast Mr Wilson is busy with the decorations for to-morrow night's St Patrick's Day dinner. The centrepiece is a display of palms he has cut with a machete from the trees in the garden. In the middle hangs a banner saying: 'Céad Míle Fáilte – A hundred thousand welcomes'. The words are flanked by two huge shamrocks. The shamrocks are flanked by the palms. I am eating coconut, and the volcano is erupting. The Chieftains are on the stereo, and Mr Wilson is dancing a jig. My friends in Ireland were right. I am in a McEaling comedy.

The national dish alleged to be descended from Irish stew is called goat water, and its most celebrated exponent is Mrs Morgan. Her goat water emporium is at the northern end of the island. 'But she does not always have goat water,' somebody tells me. 'First you must phone. But Friday is a good day. Pay day. Probably she will have it.' So I phone Mrs Morgan, and yes she does have it. She may also have it tomorrow, she says, but then again she may not, and anyway she hasn't decided yet whether or not she'll open tomorrow, so it would be better if I came today, then I can be certain. Unless she changes her mind before I get there.

WELCOME TO MORGAN'S SPOT LIGHT BAR AND RESTAURANT, says a hyperbolic sign on a pastel-blue wooden hut with a corrugated roof. There are two stools at a tiny counter just inside the door, one of them occupied by a shaven-headed builder drinking a cold bottle of Guinness 7.5 per cent overseas overstrength stout. Round the corner is a small room with three tables, plastic floral tablecloths and bare wooden benches. A cockerel is crowing stridently just outside the unglassed window, through which I can see goats and donkeys. Four local labourers and a handful of expat retirees are eating from bowls of dark brown lumpy liquid that looks like the curries we used to get in the front rooms of converted terraced houses in Bradford. There is no menu, just an elderly West Indian woman in a yellow polo shirt and knee-length yellow combat shorts who comes across and says, 'Goat water?' It seems a good system. I suppose if you didn't want any you wouldn't be there in the first place. In seconds she's back with my bowl, a beer, some bread, and a mysterious plate covered in tinfoil that I don't remember ordering. Maybe it had been implied in her original enquiry.

The goat water is full of chunks of goat meat cooked on the bone. It looks and tastes dark brown, and immediately brings to mind the mutton stew I remember eating as a kid. Whatever happened to mutton? Perhaps they phased it out along with pound notes and string vests, because you don't see a lot of it these days.

As I eat, a Canadian lady tells me their daughter phoned to say they'd had to cut the grass in Ontario in February, and we agree that this is conclusive proof of, well, any climate theory you care to mention really.

Though I've only known them for three minutes, some posh English ladies invite me round for drinks on Monday night. There's something in the air on this island that makes it easier to talk to strangers than anywhere I've ever been.

'What are you doing over here?' asks one of the PELs.

Very little, I tell her.

'Oh, but I am so curious, because hardly anybody comes here any more. Feel free to tell me if I'm being nosy.'

'You're being nosy,' I say, and she seems delighted.

Everyone's left by the time I unveil the tinfoil to reveal coconut pie and ice cream. The pie is excellent but the ice cream is the consistency of gravy, having been languishing under tinfoil in a hot room for three-quarters of an hour. As I'm finishing the pie, and pretending the ice cream is sauce, a tall, distinguished-looking lady with her head wrapped in a beautiful white, pink and lilac headscarf comes out from the kitchen. This is Ann Morgan, proprietor of the Spot Light Bar and purveyor of goat water to all social classes. 'It's nice havin' you,' she says, shaking my hand and seeming to mean it. Montserrat seems to encourage warmth and spontaneity. My two previous experiences of the Caribbean were disappointingly negative encounters with voracious tourist industries. Almost drowning didn't help, nor did the arrival three weeks later at my home of a mini-bar bill for the alleged consumption of a Toblerone and three non-alcoholic lagers, a ridiculous charge that would never have stood up in court. This island, though, is restoring my faith. If they can keep the jet-skis out they might just be all right.

The building next door is called Pete's Bakery and Mini Mart. I'm about to go in when a car stops, a big four-wheel drive. 'I'm just going down the hill,' says the driver. 'Hello, Peter.' It's Cecil, who I met at the Pentecostal church the other night, the one who asked whether the slaves had been influenced by the rebellious Irish. He's just telling me how he works for the government, something to do with the environment, I think, except that I don't quite catch it because he's turned the radio up so loud it's shaking the foundations of the house on the corner. 'Hear that?' It's the Irish-stylee St Patrick's Day ad. 'That's me. The voice-over.'

So he's a radio artiste as well as a civil servant?

'Yeah. And some other things too.'

He drops me outside the Tropical Mansions, the only other hotel on the island. I stick my thumb out, and the first car stops. The driver is Chedmond Brown. 'Oh, hello,' I say. 'I was at your lecture the other night.'

He shows no sign of remembering me, even though I ganged up on the governor for him; and then he says, 'You know what they do? They give these governorships out like a prize. You want to find out the truth about these islands? Check out my website.'

He gives me a card, and I don't like to tell him I haven't got a computer.

Mr Brown takes me a mile or so, which is as far as he's going, then pops into a crowded roadside rum shop to find me a taxi. A man emerges carrying a bottle of beer, and we get into his car. He's clearly very safety-conscious, because he wedges the beer between his thighs before driving off. As we head south, honking the horn at his friends and relatives every five or six seconds, he tells me how most of his friends and relatives emigrated after the eruption. He must have done a tremendous amount of honking when they were still around. There wasn't time to feel afraid the day the ash came and they had to run away, he says; but when he went back by boat to look for his things three days later, and realised everything was either buried or vaporised, 'I started shaking, and felt afraid for mi life.' As he drops me at the Vue Pointe he leans out of the window and says, 'You tell them we down, but we not out.'

There's another clap of thunder in the darkness, and the rain rattles the bar's corrugated roof like a tropical marching band. We edge further under the shelter of the veranda, and Bob the ex-lawyer makes his contribution to our discussion of places that are so small everybody knows everybody else's business.

'Listen, I'll tell you how small this place is. I was in Ram's supermarket one afternoon, checking out with a cartful of groceries. Ram's checking some of the stuff through the till for payment, but he's putting other stuff in a separate pile. When he's finished, he just asks me to pay for the things he's been ringing up. So what about the other stuff? I said.

'"Oh," he said, "your wife was in this morning, and she already bought those things."'

This evening I'd been planning to go to the intriguing-sounding Freedom Jam and Bingo up at the cricket ground where they held the school sports, but I've been trapped in Jumping Jack's by some serious rain. I could make a long list of less pleasant places to be trapped. Haywards Heath station on a Sunday night while you're waiting for the bus that will take you round the engineering works, for one. Every now and then the rain stops and the sound system comes through on the breeze just long enough for me to think I'll finish this beer and then wander up; but then it rains again, someone buys another round, and you try and persuade yourself that bingo might not be very interesting, even in somewhere as off-the-wall as Montserrat. 'I think you'll enjoy it,' says Bob. 'Everybody likes to play bingo here. This must be the only place in the world where guys in trainers and gold chains who really want to be cool just love to play bingo.'

Friday night is traditionally the busiest night at Jack's, when anyone from the fishermen to the governor might drop in. I hope he doesn't pop in tonight. A surprising number of people seem to have heard the lecture on the radio, and the consensus is that he won't have been thrilled to have been put on the spot by an uppity tourist.

Bob is from New York and took early retirement a few years ago, at the age of about thirty by the looks of him, and moved to Montserrat with his wife, another retired lawyer, and their young family. I've met them because I'm sitting with John and Bridget, who live half the year in a house on stilts in the jungle of Montserrat, and the other half in Wigan, unstilted and jungle-free. Also with us is Gary, who has a rum shop up the road in Salem that is known as Gary's Wide-Awake, because Gary has a day job as a plumber and is usually asleep behind the counter.

Some bars are blessed with a mood that allows strangers to meet as equals, and stories to be told, and Jumping Jack's tonight is that kind of place. The conversation moves on to car theft not happening in Montserrat, due to there being just the one road, so that anyone . . . you get the idea.

John tells us what happened one night in Wigan.

'I was in the house cooking dinner when I heard my car start up in the drive outside. I ran out and there was a lad trying to drive it away. He panicked when he saw me, and stalled as he was reversing. I ran and pulled the door open, and tried to drag him out, but he wouldn't budge. He was either very strong or very scared. I couldn't think what to do, so I got in and sat on top of him. We live up a lonely lane and there was no one about, and I couldn't sit there like that all night. So I turned on the ignition, and drove up the road to the pub. He didn't struggle much. There was a bloke coming out of the pub, so I shouted for help. Turned out he was a solicitor. The kid was so shocked he just sat there till the police came.'

I want to ask him if the solicitor invoiced him, but the grilled waloo arrives and I'm so excited by the bottle of chilli banana ketchup that it slips my mind. He's lucky the kid stayed around, though, and it didn't go to an ID parade. 'I can't be absolutely certain, Officer. Could I sit on number 3 again, please?'

The rain's stopped, the bass is still booming, and it's eyes down for a full house as I trudge wearily up the hill to my bungalow, wondering what would happen if the mountain blew in the middle of the night. I've met a lot of people this evening. In many places I've been, expat is a perjorative term for a right-wing throwback who likes the idea of having native servants. I've been impressed by the Brits and Americans and Canadians – no Irish, strangely enough – who've chosen to live here. They give freely of time and financial and engineering expertise, grow orchids and keep bees and coach tennis, and clearly love the place with the passion you must need to buy a house in the shadow of a volcano. Some of them seem quite well connected. Perhaps they could persuade the British government to send some of those golden elephants. It's never too late. Just two or three would come in handy.

These toads are really very impressive. A Tasmanian hippy would be spoiled for choice if he wanted to knock up a pair of slingbacks.

Next morning everywhere looks like it hasn't been dusted for five years. My feet make footprints on the tiles. Someone has drawn a shamrock in the dust on a poolside table. I was woken twice in the night by the rain – you don't get to be an emerald isle through drought – but with the rain came volcanic dust and ash. When the sun's at the right angle, you can see the particles hanging in the air like midges at sunset. I'm writing these words sitting out at the office, but my shirt is covered with a grey film and my pen is crunching on the page, as if I'm trying to write on a gravel path. The air tastes like emptying the ash pan the morning after you've had a coal fire. For the first time since I've been here I'm going to have to shelter indoors in daylight. Mind you, I'd rather have a bit of volcanic ash at the poolside than an aerobics class.

I click on the TV to catch up on some international news, and hit upon the live coverage of the New York St Patrick's Day Parade, which is where I was this time last year. It looks a lot cheesier on screen than it did in the flesh. They're singing the songs that Middle America thinks are Irish, but you never hear in Ireland any more. A young man in a green tie is standing on a podium warbling 'Danny Boy' in a voice that could empty an Arndale Centre in twenty seconds. He's just done that awful holding-a-long-note thing, like the needle's stuck. 'Yes I'll be *heeeeeeeeeeeeeearrrre . . .*' He's also wearing a tweed cap. He's being watched admiringly by fat-faced triplets in Aran sweaters and bonnets, each one draped in a green ribbon, like prize parsnips at a country show. There's really no excuse for this kind of carry-on.

There's a commercial break, and the American advertising industry has an opportunity to restore some sanity to proceedings. 'Totally make over your entire body in six weeks,' says a woman who appears to have been assembled from parts of other people that have been stretched to maximum tension. 'Eat more, exercise less. Worth $400, but yours for only $59.99.' I can't work out what she's selling, but it doesn't matter, because the next ad has started, and this is $59.99 as well. Maybe it's a figure with mystical numerological significance. A couple of career chip-eaters are sitting on a sofa smiling in a self-congratulatory manner as they strap Walkman-sized devices around the wibbly folds and flaps of their velour-tracksuited stomachs. 'Wear this energiser system while you watch TV,' says the voice-over, 'and lose three inches off your waist in a week without exercising.' Perhaps it's packed with maggots, or a Tasmanian devil.

Watching this kind of dross fills you with a deep sense of shame – partly for belonging to the human race, partly for watching TV without wearing an energiser – so I flip channels, to be confronted by a troupe of puke-cute eight-year-olds in pigtails and shorts and dungarees and ra-ra skirts doing Osmondesque dance routines in a hay barn, jiggling and grinning and shaking their booty and doing the backstroke. It appears to be some kind of God channel. 'Just take my hand, we'll find the door. Together we'll find strength in the Lord,' they sing, through stage-school grins that make Bonnie Langford look like Samuel Beckett. 'It's a good thing God's my friend, he'll stay with me till the end!' 'Uh-huh! Oh yeah! Walk with Jesus!' Then they all do the splits. It's disturbing to watch this stuff when there's no one to share the experience. I feel like the guy who sees a UFO when he's on his own and knows that no one's going to believe him. They're clapping their hands now, and shimmying like jelly on a plate, while two grown-ups watch from behind a hay bale.

Back on Fifth Avenue the commentator's having a shocker. 'Welcome back to the 248th St Patrick's Day Parade in New York,' she simpers. 'I love saying that. It makes me feel so historic.' The camera cuts to a close-up of a woman with twenty or thirty shamrocks on her sweater. 'Say, will you look at all those clovers.' You'd have to ask serious questions about the selection procedure that landed her this gig. 'Sixty-Fourth Street would be the place to come if you'd like to hear the minute of silence. By the way, I've been imported from LA for the occasion, but I understand that if you're really into it here in the Big Apple, you start the day with a green bagel – isn't that right, See-mus?'

'Er, that's pronounced Seamus,' says Seamus bitterly, as his big day disintegrates like a dried-up clover.

She falters for a moment, then earns my eternal admiration as she delivers, without a hint of humour or irony, a line that you could spend your entire career as a broadcaster honing and perfecting, yet never get a chance to use. 'The cardinal,' she says, 'looks very comfortable in that golf cart.'

The advert says six, the tickets say seven, so the dinner begins at six thirty. Two hundred people fill the open-plan bar and lobby of the Vue Pointe, spilling out to the poolside to admire the glow of the volcanic fireworks that are more spectacular than usual tonight. The Céad Míle Fáilte banner is fluttering in the breeze of a ceiling fan. John from Wigan is helping out behind the bar with the overworked Mr Wilson, who is decked out in a previously unseen bow tie for the occasion. Two black ladies from Montserrat and a white lady from Lancashire are singing 'The Mountains of Mourne' and I'm propping up the bar with a British ex-pat. 'Clare Short sends out thirty-five-year-old women in Laura Ashley skirts and sandals to sort the place out,' he says. 'The local lads can't wait to get stuck in.'

The first arrivals tonight were the snowbirds, the handful of silver-haired Canadians and North Americans who still winter here despite the acts of God. Determined to get full value from the buffet, they took their seats at six o'clock, teeth poised and sharpened on the tablecloth beside them. After them the place quickly filled up with white men in Hawaiian shirts, black men with silver beards, glamorous young local couples in skin-tight trousers and spangly tops, English lesbians, sensible West Indian mums in spectacles, kids, clergy, aid workers, an estate agent in a floor-length tie-dyed gown, and a Japanese architect. It is the most good-natured, spectacularly cosmopolitan and deeply weird St Patrick's Day gathering at which you could ever wish to be present. An elderly English lady with a cut-glass accent tells me about her days working among 'the bog Irish' in Liverpool. A West Indian man asks me what's Irish and stays outside all summer? 'Paddy O'Furniture.'

Dinner is a buffet that everyone has prepared at home and donated: baked fish, jerk chicken, sweet potato pie, pumpkin fritters, peas and beans. I'm sitting eating with Ian, a British civil servant, and Atsumi, a Japanese architect working for the United Nations, when the ad hoc multinational singing combo who've just been murdering 'When Irish Eyes Are Smiling' finish, and Ian and Atsumi get up to take their place. Ian begins playing one of those Yamaha keyboards that produce squelchy wah-wah chords and a cabaret drum backing track. In his white shirt and droopy black bow tie, his hair slicked back and a sandy moustache perched on his lip, he looks like a cruise ship entertainer from the days before rock-'n'-roll. The fact that he is a senior British government official adds a strange, Graham Greene-ish quality to proceedings, as does the presence of Atsumi on vocals. She's a slim woman in her thirties who has just designed Montserrat's new police station, but is now crooning 'The Look of Love' in a Japanese accent, while Ian crouches over the keyboard like Dr John and vamps away behind her. They finish with 'There Will Never Be Another You', then just when I think I've got the measure of proceedings, Ian whips out a clarinet and plays Acker Bilk's 'Stranger on the Shore', before leaving the podium to applause, followed by a heartfelt Caribbean singalong of 'It's a Long Way to Tipperary'. I check the reading on my strange-ometer, but it has exploded.

Just as I'm thinking that all that's missing is an Irish Irish person, you know, from Ireland, someone introduces me to Simon Sweeney, a young man who lives in a lighthouse in Mayo but is currently crewing a yacht that has just sailed from Cork to Antigua. He bumped into Danny Sweeney from Jumping Jack's, who invited him to come and stay because his name was Sweeney. They're heading up to Gary Wide-Awake's rum shop, and offer me a ride. In the interests of research, I reluctantly agree.

Gary's is a pretty pale blue wooden bar, with a big sound system and TV, and shelves stacked with tins of meat and fish, toilet paper and cooking oil. I'm disappointed to find that Mr Wide-Awake isn't asleep behind the bar, but delighted to hear that he used to play in the Montserrat golf team with a man whose nickname was Sleepy. We get some drinks, and Danny tells me how he taught Sting to windsurf.

'It was early in the eighties, and I was down on the beach, trying to teach this wrong-shaped Englishman whose arse stick a long way out how to windsurf. Day after day he keeps falling off the board, and I'm saying, "Keep your bloody arse in, man." Sting and the band are all on the beach laughing. One day George Martin comes across, and says, "Look, it's not very polite to keep saying arse like that. Don't you realise that man is the Attorney-General of Great Britain? Perhaps you could say bum instead." Next day he gets his right honourable arse, bum, what-ever into gear, keeps it in, windsurfs out to sea, turns and comes back. That's when Sting said, "You can teach him, you can teach anybody. I want you to teach me to windsurf."'

It's after eleven and somebody has just told me that the Dire Straits song 'Walk of Life' was actually written about Danny, when I see Wide-Awake smile and wave a greeting to a couple who are framed in the open doorway.

It's the governor and his wife.

They come in, buy some drinks, and join the company. I pull my mouth into a strange shape and cover my face with my hand, hoping I'll either become invisible or they'll think I'm someone else. I'm just starting to think I've got away with it when I realise his wife has me fixed in a sideways stare, and I know that I haven't. I develop a twitch to throw her off track. The Gov, meanwhile, has asked Gary to play the video of the Albert Hall Concert for Montserrat that was held after the disaster, and Paul McCartney, Sting, Eric Clapton, Mark Knopfler and John Elton are singing 'Hey Jude', just like the steel band in Antigua last week. Suddenly he turns to me.

'It's Kansas City next.'

What's he on about? Does he mean that's where the Foreign Office or the Queen or whoever organises these things is sending him? To Kansas? What's the poor sod done to deserve that?

'I'll bet you'd prefer to stay here.'

He looks down at me like a Latin master at a failed conjugater, and we both know I am pond life.

'Kansas City. The old rock-'n'-roll song. You should hear Elton play piano on it. Just listen to this. Sshh!'

So with the British governor calling for quiet for Sir Elton in a rum shop in the Caribbean, another St Patrick's Day dinner drifts to its predictable conclusion. The Gov's clicking his fingers now, and doing a little boogie-woogie thing with one foot while maintaining his dignity with the other. He hasn't had a go at me. Perhaps he doesn't remember.

'By the way, thanks for dropping me in it the other night.'

Oh, God, no. What am I going to say? This is like being a naughty kid. Stop being so soft! Stand up to him.

'I was just, er, just genuinely interested, you know. I didn't mean to drop you in it.'

'Of course you bloody did.'

He's right. Good judge of character, then. Just what we need in a governor. I know. I'll engage him in conversation.

'What do you think's going to happen in Montserrat? Are we going to be able to keep funding it?'

He doesn't answer but instead turns and walks off to join his wife in the corner. I'm not holding my breath for a Christmas card.

The world is divided into places where strangers say hello to you, and places where they don't. Montserrat is near the top of the league table in the former category, especially on quiet lanes and beaches, and emphatically so at church on Sunday morning. Though the dinner and the New York Parade took place yesterday, the feast day falls today, and there's an awful lot of hugging, handshaking, halloing and hallelujahing going on down at the back of the church. I arrived late, sneaked in past the half-dozen n'er-do-wells lurking outside the door, and managed to get the last seat in the house as a very old lady in a knitted hat and green sash came up to give me a hug and wish me a happy St Patrick's Day.

There's a band with guitar, congas and percussion, and choir and congregation are clapping and swaying and singing 'Ain't gonna study war no more'. The mood is gleeful, celebratory and welcoming. People have dressed up big-time, and the place is a riot of tropical colours. A two-year-old girl is wandering up and down the aisle in a fluorescent pink satin dress with black velvet trim and matching hair decorations. It's such a joyful, tumultuous scene that it takes me a while to notice the best detail of all: people are wearing shamrocks made from lime leaves. The singing stops, and we all settle down for the parish announcements. This is usually the dull bit, but the layman reading them out is Cedric Osborne, and he knows how to work a crowd.

'If anyone would like to come along, there's going to be a discussion group considering such issues as, should the chief minister and the legislative council be given greater powers?'

He pauses just for a beat, then answers the question himself. 'No.'

The church rocks with gales of laughter, interrupted by Cedric asking if anyone's had a birthday this week. Two hands go up, they're asked to stand, and the entire congregation sings for them. Any wedding anniversary? A white man and a black woman stand up. We all sing to them, wishing them many more years. Any politicians, or people who work for the government? Eight people stand and we sing to them, and then the band strikes up again and everyone's clapping, not just on the beat but across the rhythms, marching towards the door except for one woman in the corner on her own, rocking and swaying and shouting, 'Thank you Jesus!' as she raises her arms to heaven. Somebody notices me looking, and says, 'They asked her to stop going to the Anglican church for being too noisy, so now she comes here instead.' I don't remember Mass in West Cork or Warrington being like this.

Sunday is a witheringly hot day, the warmest so far. Three people in their seventies, two women in whites and a man in a Taoist T-shirt, are playing tennis in direct sun on the court next to Jumping Jack's. I fear one of them may die before I finish my lunch. Danny Sweeney is recovering from last night in time-honoured fashion, by sleeping under a tree. This afternoon I am moving house so I can sample another side of the island. Conveniently situated next to one of my top ten bars and top three volcanoes, the Vue Pointe is now established as a favourite hotel, and I know I will keep returning. I won't be able to get in, though, if people hear how good it is and start booking it out, so it's probably best if you take what I've said with a pinch of salt. It's not everything I've cracked it up to be. You'd probably be a lot happier in a Paradise Resort. It includes a ride on a pirate ship, remember, and you really can't put a price on that.

At four o'clock Lou comes and collects me and takes me to the little house he shares with his wife Shirley. It's surrounded by dense tropical foliage, and has a small pool and a view of the sea. There are two old-style rooms for guests, with ceiling fan and fridge and shower, and a dust mask reassuringly placed in the top drawer in case it all kicks off again. Lou is from Wisconsin and Shirley is Trinidadian. He has a beard, and she sings opera arias in the shower. They are talkative and hospitable and a little eccentric, and I'm glad I've come. I explain that I've had a late lunch and anyway I don't have much appetite in this heat, then Lou barbecues some huge steaks. As we eat looking out over the Caribbean, Shirley explains how to fight back against someone who's doing you wrong, like the person who keeps stealing from her. 'Write your name in red ink on the inside of your shoe. That way, you walk on them all day. Soon they'll feel the pressure.'

I've been wondering how to get to the Junior Calypso Competition, but haven't put a lot of energy into organising anything. As we finish dinner, Shirley says, 'I'm a judge at the calypso competition tonight. Would you like to come?'

They've built a stage in the parking lot at the back of the Tropical Mansions, and the whole island seems to have turned out. Cecil who does the voice-overs and works for the government is also in the band.

The contestants are aged from seven to fifteen, with names like Calypso Tina and Prince Andrew, and perform with ecstatic support from the crowd, and their mums. Whenever any of them attempts a particularly adult mannerism or a knowing bump-and-grind, the women all shriek with laughter, then burst into applause. With the backing of the very pro-sounding band, they each have to perform two songs that they've written, one on an ecological theme, one making some other kind of social comment. The standard is astonishingly high, especially for such a tiny island:

> *I'm a tree, don't put plastic bag on me*
> *I'm a tree, don't need no accessory*
> *Plastic bag is not de national flower*

'Free at last' sings seven-year-old Prince Andrew, getting big cheers every time he smiles. I'm presuming it's a liberation politics song until his backing singer produces a placard bearing a picture of a sheep and the slogan 'Keep Out That Nasty Tick', and I realise he's celebrating Montserrat's tick-free status. As he finishes, the leg on my fragile plastic chair collapses and I crash to the ground in a flurry of arms, legs, and Carib beer, to the massive amusement of everyone sitting nearby, to whom I represent the continuation of the centuries-old tradition of colonials drinking until they fall over.

It's clearly going to be a close-run thing between two of the girls, both hugely confident performers who move like stars and look the audience in the eye. I'm much taken with 'Just Like Me Daddy', in which the girl dreams of growing up to be like her dad.

> *Cos when I become a woman*
> *Jus get meself a husban*
> *I want to be just like you*
> *Me husban mus make me dinna*
> *While me out here drinkin liquor*
> *Just like me daddy*
> *If me husban start to complain*
> *Goin to leave the house again*
> *Just like me daddy*
> *Have no time to look*
> *In me children's homework book*
> *Just like me daddy*

It's sung to a jaunty, catchy beat. She's strutting with a beer bottle, thrusting her hips, and some of the men at the back have gone a bit quiet.

Even harder-hitting is 'Bring 'em In', an upbeat song about domestic violence, child abuse and pornography. Dressed as a magistrate, with an onstage cast of law enforcement officers and low-life criminals, the singer strides the stage in tremendous style, extolling a policy of zero tolerance for all abuse and violence in the home.

> *Bring 'em in, bring 'em in*
> *Bring all of 'em in*
> *If they black, white*
> *Chinese, Asian*
> *Bring all of 'em in*

The judges have been deliberating for almost three-quarters of an hour when Lou appears at my side. 'C'mon,' he says, 'we gotta go right now.'

But we won't know who's won, I say. We have to know the winner.

'That's the whole point,' he says. 'Shirley has to get out of here before they announce the winner. Some of these parents get very angry when their kid don't win. They like to blame the judges.'

We slip through a side gate, and make our escape down a road as dark as the inside of two cows.

Back at the house I sit up for a while with Shirley. She's an articulate, vivacious woman, and has me enthralled as she speaks of one of the theories circulating on the island about the cause of the volcanic devastation.

In 1995 archaeologists discovered the remains of a Native American settlement more than 2,000 years old, not far from Montserrat's airport. Tools, ceramics, and human skeletons were found, rare evidence of an ancient Caribbean society that could be crucial to understanding the history of these islands. Samples of the artefacts, including skeletons, were sent to the United States for analysis. Three weeks later the volcano erupted for the first time since Montserrat was settled by the British.

'For many people, the connection is clear,' says Shirley. 'A Native American chief came over from the States and stayed with us. He sat at this table and spoke of the natural world's connection to the spirit world. He said that the mountain would not sleep until the bones had been returned.'

And have they?

'They were supposed to come back, but they never did. And of course the mountain is still angry.'

To get to my room I have to walk across their veranda and go down half a dozen steps near the pool. It's lucky that I've been looking out for toads at night, otherwise I might have put my bare foot down on the land crab that is guarding the top step like a sentry. It's heavily armoured, and bigger than a dinner plate, but my confrontations with macaques and endangered geese have given me a new-found inner strength. I will walk briskly by without giving it another thought. As I attempt to pass, it rears up on its hind legs – claws, nippers, whatever the horrible things are – and starts flailing its front ones in my direction like a drunk with a broken bottle. If it could hiss, it would. My inner strength evaporates, and I leap backwards faster than a step dancer on hot coals. Lou and Shirley come out to see what the commotion's about.

'My God,' says Lou, 'it's enormous,' clattering it down the steps and into the dense bush with a couple of deft swings of an old-fashioned broomstick. 'Hell, maybe I shouldn't have done that. Maybe I should have kept it for lunch.'

Do they get them every night?

'First one I've seen in three years here,' he says, as I tiptoe to my room to check under the pillow and the toilet seat.

Next morning at breakfast all the songs from the calypso competition are playing on the radio. They got the kids into the studio a couple of weeks ago to record the CD, and now the whole island is moving to their music. 'Bring 'em In' was the winner. The news carries no reports of parental rioting.

Today is Monday, and because St Patrick's Day fell on a Sunday, it's also a public holiday, and there's a definite scent of carnival in the air. Before going to the Festival Village where the Slave Feast will take place I head to the north of the island, beyond Morgan's Spot Light Bar. When Plymouth still existed and was the focal point of island life the north was poor and sparsely populated, 'where the barefoot people lived' according to my taxi driver. Now people from the south have been re-housed up here and it's a bit more mainstream, though still not very.

'The Quiet Spot', says a sign on a shack that looks like it's about to collapse. 'Licensed to sell liquor by retail plus groceries etc. – M. Roacher'. Cricket stumps are painted on a wall opposite. A man in a knitted cap is opening young green coconuts in the street with a machete. An old man in a trilby is leaning in the doorway talking to an imaginary friend. I go in for a cold beer, and am made to feel as welcome as if I were returning to the place where I was born. The bar is tiny, the size of a large garden shed, a random jumble of vegetables, groceries, sacks, cardboard boxes and alcohol. Apart from the mangoes, it looks much as I imagine a bar in a poor part of the west of Ireland might have looked a century or two ago. 'Brother' Roacher, as he's known, is eighty-eight years old and a convivial host, and my beer is soon augmented by the Paddy's Day special, rum with coconut milk straight from the shell. There are three other customers, so the place is packed. I talk about accents and influences with a Rasta in his fifties. His name is Joseph Ryan, and he says his great-grandfather was from Ireland.

Primed by my lunchtime livener – after all, it is a bank holiday, so I don't need to go to the office – I head down to Festival

Village. It turns out to be rows of food and drink stalls on three sides of a coconut grove next to the beach, with a temporary stage on the fourth. Sound systems are throbbing, but the place is only just starting to fill up. It's fiercely hot, so I find a seat in the shade. 'Ah, begorra,' says a stage-ham Irish brogue, 'and are ya having a marvellous holiday at all at all?' I look up and see a black man in his sixties wearing knee-length shorts and a T-shirt that says ANTIGUA. 'You from Ireland or UK?' he asks, so I tell him. He lives in Streatham, and is a ticket inspector on the London–Brighton line. 'We come back every year for a holiday,' he says. 'Building a house for when I retire.'

He introduces me to Charles, a West Indian man of similar age dressed in long trousers, a floral-patterned flat cap, and a paisley shirt. In Ireland, I tell him, a paisley shirt is one that has NO written all over it. He tells me his grandfather was from County Cork. In fact, he does more than that. He rolls the r in Cork, pronouncing it Corrrk, exactly as Cork people do. I tell him this, and he says, 'County Corrrk, so. That's the only way I know how to say it.' The word 'so' is often found at the end of a Corkman's sentence.

I meet more people in the course of the afternoon and evening than I've met in the last year. This seems to be a culture where anyone can talk to anyone else without any prior connection. A man who was born in London with one black and one white parent tells me he feels more comfortable living here than anywhere he's been. 'In England, they'd shout "Black man" at me. In Jamaica they shouted "White man".' I ask him what they shout on Montserrat. 'Hey, English!'

Paul the Policeman is an exuberant Mancunian on secondment from the Met. He's been here over two years, and his eyes have the happy gleam of a man who may never return to Europe. I noticed him at church on Sunday. He's a charismatic figure on the island, constantly mobbed by kids and hugged by adults. He runs youth clubs, keep fit classes, and has started a women's football team. I've been told he's the only white man in the island's famous vocal group, the Emerald Singers, and is renowned for his on-stage impression of a white guy trying to dance like a black guy. He also coaches the Montserrat men's football team, who are ranked 245th out of 245 in the FIFA world rankings. 'Bhutan are ranked 244th. We're playing them away on the same day as the World Cup Final.' I've rarely met a man who exudes such contentment with his life.

Someone spots me talking to him and tells me about the policewoman who took out a mortgage on a new house two months before the volcano hit. She'll be paying it off for the next twenty years, even though it no longer exists. 'It's a government mortgage, so they stop it from her pay cheque. Not much left.'

But couldn't the government just wipe out such debts?

'She had two medals, one for long service, both buried by the volcano. They asked her to pay for them, cos they been lost through negligence.'

I overhear a British expat say he went to Gibraltar last summer, and my ears prick up. What was it like?

'It was nice. But my God – those Barbary Apes. Vicious bastards they are. There was this couple, walking up the Rock' – yep, I can just picture it – 'and apparently she had some peanuts in a bag zipped inside her bumbag. But the apes seemed to know this. Surrounded her, started grabbing at her and scratching her, so her boyfriend jumped in, and they bit lumps out of him. Had to go to hospital.'

I feel strangely vindicated.

So the afternoon is spent consuming cold beer and jerk pork and yams, and gradually the heat starts to fade from the sun. The high spot of the day is a series of promenade performances by the Masquerade Dancers. Dressed in masks, tall hats, brightly coloured ribbons, and carrying whips, they perform a strange and rather eerie hybrid of Morris, Irish, and African tribal dance.

It's a satire on slave owners. The masks are pink, to represent a white face. The ribbons represent the flowing tailcoats of the plantation owners. The hat is a cross between a gentleman's and a bishop's. The slave-driver's whip is cracked repeatedly, ferociously. And the music is played on a whistle or fife, very Celtic sounding, with supporting percussion and drums. At one point in late afternoon I look across the festival site and through the billowing clouds of dust glimpse Simon Sweeney, the only Irishman on the island, dancing like a maniac in the middle of the Masqueraders. He's wearing a green, white and orange Viking fur hat.

I get back late. The crab is there again, poised, waiting, looking at its watch and thinking, What time do you call this then? It looks very angry. Lou appears from nowhere, and whacks it with the broom one more time. 'Don't understand it,' he says. 'Never usually see 'em. Maybe you got some strange aura for wildlife.' Maybe.

As I walk down the steps I step on something crunchy. One of the crab's legs has become detached in the mêlée. It may try and limp back tomorrow night with some of its mates to sort me out, but by then I'll be gone.

On my last morning I visit the Volcanic Observatory. It's staffed by four British geologists and seismologists who are monitoring the mountain's every move, of which there are plenty. They show me pictures taken the morning after it grew a new ninety-metre pinnacle during the night. 'What we're seeing here is a new mountain being formed.' It is their job to give daily safety reports, and they have to respond to every threatening blip of activity, day and night. They look exhausted, as if they all have newly-born triplets at home. The British government is trying to cut costs, and may even discontinue their work later in the year if they can contract it out to someone who will do it cheaper. 'They think we should be raising revenue. Making money. You know, volcano tours and souvenirs. We had to come up with a business plan. We're bloody seismologists.'

I'm down at the harbour waiting for the evening ferry to Antigua. Moose's Bar is hosting its regular afternoon game of dominoes. Moose's wife Idabella is serving drinks and food. She is also the Minister for Education and the Environment. I get chatting to Eddie, a Montserratian who has lived in Ipswich for the last thirty years and is here on a day trip from his resort holiday in Antigua. He's a lorry driver, and also a coach to the British junior sprint team. His wife is from Suffolk, and Eddie can speak Suffolk or Caribbean, as the company requires. We're chatting away when a man creeps up behind Eddie and covers his eyes. There are howls of laughter, and massive hugs. They used to share a flat together in Ipswich, and haven't seen each other for fourteen years. We have a couple of convivial rounds, and the guys chat about friends who've died early, as men of a certain age will.

A man in a dark corner of the bar is beckoning me over. It's Moose. He asks me to sit down, then takes a silver ring off his finger. He pushes it on to the third finger of my right hand, and says, 'In the name of St Peter, name of St Paul,' followed by something I can't quite make out. Then he repeats the prayer. 'This is my old grandfather's ring. Kind of a voodoo type of thing, you know?' And then he tells me about something that's going to happen to me, but that I can't share with anyone for two or three years.

The last person I speak to before I leave is one of the British civil servants I've got to know. There aren't very many of them, and I've been impressed by their commitment and the compassion they clearly feel for the island and its people. They are, however, implementing a series of budget cuts imposed in Westminster that will drastically reduce British spending here over the next three years. But surely, I say, with empire comes responsibility.

'Of course. But we can't go on subsidising them ad infinitum.

Apart from anything else, how would we justify it to the British taxpayer?'

'I'm a British taxpayer,' I say. 'I think we should give them as much as they need.'

11

FROM BEARA
TO BUTTE

'Coming up next: a veterinarian will be here to give us some tips on dog toy safety. Is your dog playing with toys that could be dangerous for him? Could be. So stick around and learn how to perform the Heimlich manoeuvre on your pooch, after these messages.'

American breakfast TV is distressing enough at the best of times; but when you've just woken up in a $38 hotel room in Butte, Montana, feeling like a patient with a chronic personality disorder whose medication should have been topped up three hours ago, it is almost too much to bear. Outside my window the snow is still cascading down, unless I'm imagining it and it's a mental blizzard causing white-out in my brain, in which case it won't be long before I start to hear the voices. Hang on. I'm hearing them already.

'Gratitude! Pass it on. Just say thank you.' Two old ladies are on screen, helping a Hell's Angel across the road to a soundtrack of Steppenwolf's 'Born to be Wild'. 'A message from the Foundation for a Better Life,' says an oleaginous Hollywood voice. If the nurse doesn't come soon with the chemical cosh, I may start chewing my pillow.

This morning I am without any shadow of a doubt the most jet-lagged person in Montana. This is partly because there are hardly any people in Montana, a state that judging from the map is about the size of China and Australia combined, yet has a population of just 800,000; but mainly because of yesterday's journey. As I shave in the bathroom mirror – a haphazard, casually violent process, during which I cut my nose twice – I try and remind myself that I've only been travelling since yesterday morning. My brain rejects this information, and tells me that the trip began many years ago, possibly when I was still at primary school. This is exactly the kind of ordeal the nuns would have put us through to build our character and purge our sins. I ought to rest up today, but instead I am due to have lunch with a priest. Perhaps there's a psychology department at the local university that will give me $20 if I let them attach wires to my forehead while I tell them about my day.

The ten-hour journey from Heathrow to Seattle wasn't a problem. A flight of that length gives you an exhausted yet somehow euphoric lead-in-the-veins feeling that can be turned to your advantage once you realise it is a form of natural high. Lots of people would have no scruples about stealing the Christmas money their children got from the grandparents and spending it on Dutch superskunk or Taiwanese greyhound tranquillisers, if they thought it would make them feel like this. There's no point fighting it; just embrace the dislocation and enjoy the fact that the little things that surround you are suddenly different – look, there's a twenty-five-stone woman over there ordering a low-fat latte and a muffin as big as her head – while trying to stay awake until the local bedtime. My tried and tested method of passive acceptance, however, was rendered ineffective by the cruel five-hour wait for a connection from Seattle to Butte, a place two and a half hours and one time zone back in the direction from which I'd already come. I thought that two or three pints of Mac and Jack's African Ale in the airport bar would help, but they didn't. They just made me bitter. How can a Seattle–Butte round trip cost nearly twice as much as London to Seattle and back? Is Butte so desirable it merits a surcharge? Apparently not, according to the guy at immigration. 'Why would you wanna go there?' he asked. 'And hey, if you're going, you should know we pronounce it "Butte".' That's how I pronounced it, didn't I? Am I going mad? 'Little tip, buddy. You go to a place, then you better know how to say it.' I'll bear that in mind, I thought, in case I ever bump into you in Warwick, or Worcestershire.

Seattle airport is everything you hope it might be. There's a meditation room, a stall where you can get a massage for $19 a quarter-hour, and an easy-listening muzak version of 'Living in the Past' by Jethro Tull with the flute part played on a trombone. I sat in the bar until I was repulsed by the thought of more beer, then went out into the concourse to check departures. 'Medford', said the board. 'Yakima. Pullman. Kelowna. Pasco. Bellingham.' It was like reading Esperanto. I lived in this country for a year. How can there be so many flights to places I've never heard of? Then: 'Bozeman Butte. Weather Advisory'.

'Yeah,' said the woman at the check-in desk. 'It's snowing down there in Butte.'

That's as may be, I thought, but what does Bozeman mean?

'I been there once already today, got sent all the way back. Six hours round trip,' said a badly rattled Harry Dean Stanton lookalike behind me, who probably looked like Brad Pitt when he got up that morning.

'We're gonna go to Butte, and if it's still snowing and we can't land, we'll come back to Seattle,' said the check-in woman.

Harry Dean whimpered at the prospect of spending another six hours of his life flying around in hazardous conditions without actually going anywhere, and I believe we all felt a little older.

There were twenty-six of us on a seventy-seater twin-propeller plane. Before we left, the stewardess walked up and down the aisle, asking people to move seats. 'It's for the aircraft's stability,' she said comfortingly.

'Is this, like, when everyone on a bus jumps at the same time, and turns it over?' asked Harry Dean, who by now was on the brink of hysteria.

I passed the time until they served drinks watching the propellers go round and imagining them getting clogged up with snow. Then I read for a while – *The Falls* by Ian Rankin – until I fell asleep and *The Falls* fell on my gin and tonic, which fell on my leg, and made me wake up shouting like a mad person. 'Daytime drinking is special,' began the paragraph I'd been reading, but as I no longer knew whether it was day or night, there was no way of telling whether I agreed.

After a couple of hours we landed at Bozeman, which confirmed my suspicion that it must be a place. Nineteen people got off, which left me, Harry Dean, and five other ghouls. I found a map in the in-flight magazine, and saw that Bozeman was eighty miles east of Butte. This meant I'd already passed my destination twice today, once going in each direction, which is a very psychologically disturbing way to get somewhere. It makes you feel like some kind of airborne sheepdog, cutting down your destination's options before closing in on it. 'We need three-mile visibility to land, but right now they only have two,' announced the pilot, 'so we're gonna head on over to Butte, see what happens.' Great. What happened was, we locked into a holding pattern, going round and round in the middle of the turbulence waiting for the weather to break, just the seven of us, bumping and rattling and lit by the flashing light on the wing like characters in a melodrama, the atheists and agnostics all praying just as hard as the Christians. From where I was sitting you couldn't see three inches, never mind three miles, but suddenly we were down, bouncing twice before skidding along enough runway snow to have Gatwick closed till July. Ten past one in the morning, said the clock.

I could have got to Auckland quicker. There'd have been no point, though, because Larry McCarthy, the head of the North American Clan McCarthy Association wouldn't have been in New Zealand.

Turned out he wasn't in Butte either. He'd been taken ill, and was at home 200 miles away. So had my journey been wasted? Not at all, said the Irish-American welcome committee who'd heroically waited half the night in his place. You'll have a grand time. Father Sarsfield is expecting you for lunch tomorrow. And with that they brought me through the deserted, blizzard-lashed streets to my hotel. 'Will you be going out again tonight, sir, or will I lock the door?' asked the guy on the desk as I checked in at ten to two. Resisting the lure of the nightlife, or the temptation to take a walk to Bozeman, I headed for my room, poured a nightcap and watched another old episode of *Cheers*. It wasn't the episode I'd watched in Montserrat, which was the best piece of luck I'd had all day.

And now it's daylight, or at least as light as it will get today, and I'm expected for lunch in a little over two hours. I'd better go and have some breakfast first.

I wipe off the last flecks of shaving foam and take a look in the mirror. Not bad, considering. Like a cross between Bill Wyman and Beryl Bainbridge. Little bit of moisturiser and I'll be fine.

Butte began life in 1864 as a gold-rush town, but huge deposits of copper were soon discovered on what came to be known as 'the richest hill on earth'. Situated more than 5,000 feet above sea level, and riddled with shafts and tunnels, the city boasted that it was a mile deep as well as a mile high. The story goes that in the heyday of Irish immigration Gaelic-speakers who had no English would arrive in Boston or New York wearing a label that said: 'Send me to Butte, Montana.' The census of 1900 shows Butte to have been the most predominantly Irish city in the United

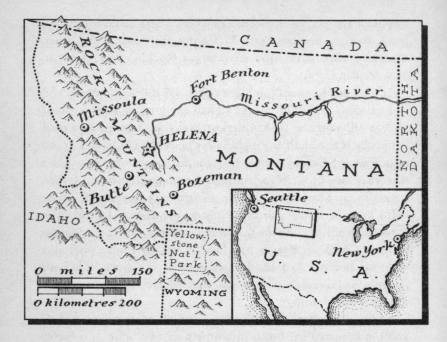

States, Boston included. Thousands of Cornishmen also came as the tin mines of Cornwall went into decline, along with Welsh and Scots, Italians, Scandinavians, Chinese, Germans, Poles, Native Americans, Serbs and Croats, many of whom are said to have learned English with an Irish accent. The rich ethnic mix, pioneering spirit and high wage levels made for a lively town. Saloon doors were manufactured without locks, because the bars – among them Dublin Dan's Hobo Retreat, the Bucket of Blood, and the Cesspool – never closed.

The town worked and played twenty-four hours a day. Whiskeys called 'Coming Off Shift Special', 'All Day Special', 'Good Night Special' and 'Morning After Special' were on sale. Like the ones marked 'Wakes, Weddings, Births and Holidays', the bottles all contained the same stuff. The mules in the mines learned to chew tobacco, the ice-cream maker got his ice from the mortuary, and two professional boxers once stopped fighting so they could watch the brawls in the crowd. Mining devastated the landscape, and Butte won a reputation as one of the ugliest towns in America, albeit with a heart of gold.

Walking along Broadway to Main Street this morning, though, it strikes me as a pretty good-looking place. The last mines closed in 2001, but they had been in decline for decades, so that Butte – like Cobh, where many emigrants bound for Montana boarded ship – could never afford a modern makeover. The few down-town blocks consist mostly of imposing nineteenth-century brick buildings that bring to mind the older and more atmospheric parts of New York and San Francisco, only without traffic or people. My hotel, the Finlen, is a gem. Built in 1923, it offers authentic Prohibition-era ambience for virtually no money. JFK and Nixon both stayed here, and there are photos in the lobby to prove it. An antique brochure by the door of the bar promotes the hotel as a 'crossroads for the wise of the earth. Men gather in the lobby or lounge in the bar, telling tall tales to men who think of taller tales of their own. Music from the lounge, faint as a valley wind, beckons youths and sweeter maidens. Young salesmen dabble in their dreams . . .'

There are few sights on earth more captivating than young salesmen dabbling in their dreams, but unfortunately the Finlen, despite its many admirable qualities, does not serve food. Conse-quently I've come out in the snow looking for breakfast to stabil-ise my system before it's time to go for lunch. A street-level art deco façade on a nineteenth-century building catches my eye. M & M, says the sign. I step inside and find myself in American low-life heaven. To my right is a long breakfast counter; to my left, a very long and well-stocked bar; ahead of me, half a dozen card tables and a handful of poker machines. There are more customers eating breakfast than drinking liquor or gambling, but only just. They are the people you've seen sitting at diner counters in every blue-collar American movie you've ever watched: hunting jackets, baseball caps, plaid shirts, heavy boots, visible weapons. The men look pretty tough as well.

I take a seat and do my best to look as if I live in a trailer park married to my cousin and like to shoot mountain lions for fun. 'Coffee,' I growl, in the most bronchial miner's rumble I can muster.

'Are you the guy from Ireland?' asks the waitress, effortlessly picking up on my shrill European warble. 'I hear you're having lunch with Father Sarsfield today.'

News travels fast in a small town, and it's clear I've as much chance of being inconspicuous here as if I were wearing a cheetah-print Versace halter-top with wet-look culottes and platform soles full of goldfish. And I'm a little concerned that she's called me 'the guy from Ireland'. I am, of course, the guy from England with an Irish mum, which takes a bit longer to explain. Irish Americans have a reputation for unwavering hatred of anything emanating from Cromwell's fair land, and I couldn't help noticing when I arrived last night and mentioned my flight from London that one guy's face dropped. 'You don't want to be going near that place,' he said. No doubt his feelings were politically moti-vated, though it's possible he once stumped up a couple of grand to see the Changing of the Guard and Sherlock Holmes's house and go to a medieval banquet at a Beefeater steakhouse near Heathrow, and may still be scarred by the experience.

It's that classic American breakfast again: eggs over easy, home fries, wholewheat toast, piss-poor coffee. Despite what you'd imagine from watching the coffee fetishism of *Friends* and *Frasier*, stewed sludge in a Cona jug is still standard in the heartlands. I feel bad for even noticing, because the waitress, a formidable woman of confident charm, is delightful, bringing iced water and chatting away to make me feel at home, and I do. American service as spontaneous as this has no equal, and those who dis-pense it should be decorated by their government, or win holidays in Hawaii. She tells me the M & M was named after Martin and

Mosby, the two guys who started it in the 1890s as a saloon, eatery and gambling parlour for the miners, a trade it has been plying uninterrupted ever since. I've always loved this kind of timeless Americana. Butte's ancient history may be very recent, but that's part of its appeal. In a room like this you can almost reach out and touch it.

The cook working at the griddle is a star. With a ponytail poking through his baseball cap, sunken cheeks, and pallid, cadaverous skin, he looks like Iggy Pop when he was scary but not yet really terrifying. His sinewy arms look powerful, not showy gym muscle but lean and taut, strength that he uses every day. He moves with speed and grace along the range, cooking six or seven orders at once, beating eggs with half a dozen flicks of his left hand as he shapes sizzling grated potato into hash browns with his right, breaking away to flip two eggs over in a pan with the barest suspicion of a wrist movement, then throws an omelette, turns a steak, and spins on the spot to retrieve bacon from an enormous glass-fronted fridge. It's like watching a class variety act: you're waiting for the spinning plates to fall, the house of cards to tumble, but they never do. These days some gourmet chefs in big cities will let you pay a premium to dine at a table in the kitchen so you can watch them in action. Go to Butte instead, and see this guy for free.

On your first day in a new place there are so many options that it can be difficult to know where to begin. By the time I've finished breakfast it's only half an hour till lunch, so there's that one taken care of. It's stopped snowing and visibility has improved, and I can see huge mountains at the end of the street. Somewhere up there on the edge of town is the continental divide, the point at which water stops flowing west to the Pacific and instead runs east to the Atlantic. Bozeman, I realised this morning when I looked at the map, is on the other side of the divide. I'm glad I hadn't imagined such a fearsome landscape when I was careering around just above it in the dark last night.

HARRINGTON SURGICAL SUPPLY 1890, says the lettering above a warehouse and shopfront across the street from the Finlen, where I'm waiting for my lift to lunch. It confirms the very specific nature of Butte's Irish antecedents. Harrington is a West Cork name from the Beara peninsula, the sliver of land that protrudes into the Atlantic beyond Bantry and Glengarriff and below the Ring of Kerry. As in Montserrat, a glance at the phone book confirms the historical connections. Sullivans and O'Sullivans, Murphys, Crowleys, Lynchs and McCarthys, all of them near-ubiquitous in County Cork, proliferate among the surnames. This is largely the result of a very specific link between Butte and Cork, and in particular the Beara peninsula town of Castletownbere – the home of McCarthy's Bar and Grocery, possibly the best pub in the world – and the outlying parishes of Eyeries and Allihies.

The Atlantic-pounded clifftops of Allihies were home in the eighteenth and nineteenth centuries to the richest copper mines in Europe. When they went into decline in the late 1800s, the miners headed west. Many of the Irish emigrating to America were unskilled labourers from agricultural backgrounds, but the Beara miners had specialised skills that were much in demand in the mining camps of the west. Butte rapidly became the biggest camp of them all. According to Professor David Emmons, author of the definitive study of the history of the Irish in the town, 90 per cent of the mineworkers in turn-of-the-century Butte were from Ireland. So strong are the connections that even today it's hard to find a family in Beara who do not have relatives in Montana, though they may have no one in more obvious places such as New York, Boston, or even Dublin.

It's strange to think that the Irish capital would have seemed a more remote place to those emigrants than a hill in Montana where friends and family were waiting. They would also have felt at ease with the Cornish miners who worked alongside them, despite differences of language, religion and political allegiance, because 'the Cornish were more Celtic than the average Dubliner.'

This, at any rate, is Father Sarsfield O'Sullivan's take on things. He's a genial, articulate man in his late seventies, the unofficial curator of the oral history of Butte. The blizzard was blowing again as I pulled up outside, but that wasn't going to prevent his sister Vernie from running the Irish tricolour and the stars and stripes up the two poles on their veranda, as she does every day.

We've just dined on split pea and ham soup, which was fine once I'd persuaded myself it was another breakfast course, rather than my second meal in an hour. We're in a drawing-room full of antiques, oil paintings and ecclesiastical memorabilia, waiting for the arrival of the cake and coffee that may blast me asunder before Father Sarsfield can administer the last rites. He's been telling me about a priest from San Francisco – 'a great man, helped Caesar Chavez start the farmworkers' union' – who had a smattering of Gaelic from his parents. On a visit to County Kerry he addressed a large lunch gathering, concluding with the traditional Gaelic toast that translates to English as 'The goat is on the spit'. Unfortunately his accent wasn't quite up to it. 'The Gaelic for "goat" is only a hair's-breadth removed from the word for the male organs,' says Father Sarsfield. 'You can imagine how shocked the good ladies of the parish were to hear this American priest proclaiming, "My balls are on fire." "I'll be dead for years," he said, "and that's all they'll remember me for in Ballyferriter."'

Sarsfield is one of the last of a generation that links us with the old west. 'My father was born in 1882,' he says. 'Geronimo was killed in 1884.' He says their father's grandfather built the first house on the tiny island of Inishfernard, off the coast of Beara, in 1823; his grandparents and the other remaining inhabitants were brought off the island in 1923, the year before he was born in Butte. His father had a ranch just outside town, and as a kid he remembers him giving work to Irishmen who were on the run from the latest round of the Troubles.

His Irish-American brogue reminds me of Chris Byrne and his rebel hip-hop thousands of miles away in New York. Listening to these men helps deconstruct the American accent. In Massachusetts and Vermont you can still hear a burr of West Country England that arrived with the pilgrims; with these guys you hear a heightened version of the Irish tones and rhythms that are now an integral part of the mainstream American dialect. As I listen to him talk, I remember as a kid hearing Jimmy Cagney saying 'youse guys', and wondering where it came from. Well, now I know, because I've followed the trail and heard it with my own ears.

'There was a Protestant man died in town, a lonely bachelor with no friends. The undertaker, a guy called Larry Duggan, went out looking for mourners, and found some of the Catholic guys on the corner. 'Come on, Dennie,' says he, 'help see the poor soul on his way.'

" 'Our shift starts in an hour,' says Dennie.

" 'Ah, it's just a short service,' says Duggan. So they carry the coffin into the chapel, and the minister starts up and says, 'Dear Lord, we commend this soul to you as he makes the journey across the great divide.'

" 'C'mon, boys, let's get out of here,' says Dennie. 'They're burying the bastard in Bozeman.' ' "

The cake's been and gone and I'm worried a party-sized platter of sandwiches might be next. If I don't eat myself to death I could be listening to this man's tales for days. In a town divided by religion, he says, the first true acts of Christian unity came about because of Prohibition. 'The best bootlegger in town was an Irish Protestant called Mike McKeown. Mike was no bigot. Each time he made a batch, he'd send a gallon to every priest in town. And the priests would send some on to the German Lutheran pastor. The pastor returned the favour, so when the Lutherans made booze, the priests would have a party.'

'He had very strict quality control,' says Vernie, a tiny, bird-like woman with bohemian clothes and a beautiful smile. 'If he wasn't sure about a batch, he'd use it as anti-freeze. I have a vivid memory of our father's car, a 1929 Ford, that in winter always smelled like brandy.'

We talk for another hour, then Sarsfield tells me someone else is expecting me. 'An older guy,' he says with a smile. Before I leave he tells me about his trip to a mission station in the Arizona desert in 1939 to see how the priest did things out there. When he arrived the Native Americans, or Indians as they still were back then, laid on a display of dancing. 'I felt uplifted, because the Church stands accused of destroying indigenous cultures all over the world,' he says. 'At last, I thought, a place where local rituals have been respected. So I congratulated the priest on what he had achieved, and he said, "Well, thank you, but it's really nothing to do with me, and anyway, all is not what it appears." And he told me that in the 1860s a priest went out there – he asked me not to give his name, so we'll call him Father Sweeney – to work with the Indians. And he was surprised, and a bit disappointed, because the ones he met didn't have any dances. He'd been expecting great things, but these people didn't dance at all. So Father Sweeney decided he'd teach them himself. "I can dance a few steps," said Sweeney, "but when you think about it, how many ways are there to put one foot in front of the other?" So he taught the Indians to dance. And when Hollywood came out to Arizona to make the westerns, where do you think they came to learn the authentic Indian dances? To these guys, who'd learned them from an Irishman.'

John 'The Yank' Harrington is one hundred years old next birthday. He made his first solo CD when he was ninety-six, and still plays live dates around Butte with the Dublin Gulch Band. I'm sitting in his snug ground-floor apartment. There's a tricolour on the wall, copies of the *Irish Echo* on the floor, and I can see snow fluttering down through the venetian blinds as he laughs and chats and plays his button accordion. He can remember how all the tunes go, but can't remember all the ones he knows, so it helps if you suggest titles. So far we've had 'Skibbereen' and 'Dear Old Donegal', and now it's 'Napoleon Crossing the Alps'.

John is American, a Butte man, so it's a reasonable first reaction to be puzzled that he's known throughout the city as the Yank. Curiouser still is the fact that the Yank speaks American with a pronounced west of Ireland accent. His father, John, was a nineteenth-century emigrant from Allihies who married another Harrington, Katie, a neighbour from Beara, and raised a family in Butte. When John died of a miner's lung condition, quickly followed by Katie, of influenza, John was adopted by his Uncle Dan. In 1919 the two of them emigrated back to Beara, where the teenage John acquired his nickname. In the 1920s he worked at the last copper mine in Allihies, and by night fished for mackerel using the local seine nets. 'I learned to repair the nets, because some of them there were too lazy to do it themselves. We'd watch for the mackerel in the moonlight. You wouldn't want to cast the net unless you could see 300 fish,' he tells me, as I listen to his life unfold like an epic saga of twentieth-century migration and dislocation. He stayed eight years in Beara, learned the Irish language and music, then re-emigrated to New York, where he was a labourer on the construction of the Eighth Avenue subway. Back in Butte he worked as a porter at the Finlen, and was reunited with his four sisters, who all lived into their nineties as well. Perhaps there's longevity in the genes, or the mackerel.

While he's been playing we've been joined by Terry, a recent arrival from Castletownbere who teaches Irish language classes here and in Helena, the state capital. Their conversation flits between English and Gaelic as they discuss families they both know back in Beara, even though the Yank left for New York in 1926. 'You know Sullivan there, from the back of Eyeries?' asks John. 'Well, a friend of mine is courting his granddaughter.' The Yank puts the ancient squeeze-box back in its case, and goes through to his bedroom. He comes back with a CD for me. 'Will you come back next year?' he asks. 'I have a big birthday. A week before St Patrick's Day. There'll be a party.' I imagine there will. I think I might.

DRINK HABIT

Thousands of wives, mothers and sisters are enthusiastic in their praise of Orrine, because it has cured their loved ones of the 'drink habit' and thereby brought happiness to their homes. Narbro Drug Co, 109 North Main Street, Butte. $1 a box. CAN BE GIVEN SECRETLY.

I'm reading an edition of the local paper, the *Butte Miner*, from 1914. The drugstore's advert is a neat snapshot of how things were in a town where clandestine anti-alcohol remedies were on sale, but the bars had no locks on the doors. Old papers often give unexpected insights into stories you didn't know you were looking for. Here's another one:

BUILDING OF ENGLISH CHANNEL TUNNEL MAY BE UNDER WAY WITHIN THE COURSE OF A YEAR

If red tape unwinds at a fair rate the railway tunnel under the English Channel between England and France may be in process of construction by a year this autumn.

It's morning and I'm sitting at a huge window framing nine-teenth-century rooftops, and beyond them the snowy mountains, in what used to be the firemen's dormitory, but is now the local archive's reading room. There are iron pillars, original radiators, and no microfilm or computers. Instead the shelves are lined with bound originals of Butte's newspapers, going back as far as the town itself. I've just had breakfast at M & M's again, as I believe I would every morning of my life if I lived here. Mind you, I think it would change me. I'd be buying shotguns, drinking Wild Turkey and sleeping in a baseball cap within a few days. I had steak for breakfast this morning. I don't know why I did that. I haven't had steak in England for twenty years. I don't eat steak.

It was just there on the menu. 'Steak and eggs', it said, and I thought, 'Yep, that's me. Pioneer in a mining town, horse tethered outside, prospector's pan on my saddle and I'm wearing a poncho. Better have some steak and eggs.' I expect a guy in a waistcoat will slide a bottle of whiskey along the bar towards me in a minute, and after that I might have a game of poker and shoot someone.

The lady on the next breakfast stool grew up in Butte, but has lived in San Francisco for thirty years. She comes back to visit, but is sick of motels and her sister's sofa, so she'd just bought a two-bedroom miner's cottage on the fringes of the old Irish district of Corktown for $7,000. Even by Tasmanian standards this seems something of a bargain.

'It's a great town, Peter,' Terry the Gaelic teacher told me last night. 'Would you ever think of living here?' I told him I think of living everywhere I visit. We were in Moloney's for a few beers after his class, where he explained his theory that the Young Irelander, Thomas Francis Meagher, while governor of Montana, had exaggerated the threat posed by the Indians so that he had an excuse for raising an army. His real intention was to seize Canada and trade it with the British for Irish independence. 'He may have been an American hero, but at heart he was still an unrepentant fenian bastard.'

Afterwards a few of us went to a Chinese restaurant up some stairs above a shop, where the seating was in wooden booths in two rows either side of a central aisle. The red-haired waitress hadn't been within ten thousand miles of China in her life, another Irish tradition that has survived intact in Butte. The food, like the town, was rugged and idiosyncratic, and not a little baffling. Everything we ordered consisted primarily of celery, augmented by some pork or shrimp or noodle or whatever it was we thought we'd ordered, and was submerged in a viscous, dark grey liquid that tasted like a single man's laundry. Most Chinese food is cooked quickly, but these mysterious concoctions had been stewed for a very long time, possibly since before the onset of winter, by someone with a deep celery psychosis who should seek professional help. 'Best Chinese food in town,' said the local Irish step-dancing teacher, clearing her plate. I tried to nod in agreement but it came out as an involuntary shudder, because I'd just chewed on a tough bit and was thinking it might be a Band-aid, or a toenail. I couldn't bring myself to tell her I'd never eaten worse, and I speak as someone who once ate chop suey in Hong's in Merthyr Tydfil after midnight on a Saturday during the 1970s. Take my advice. If you're ever in Butte, have the steak and eggs.

Come to think of it, there was a fried egg on top of the chop suey in Merthyr.

One of the women in the bar last night is curator of the city archive, which is why I'm here this morning. When I arrived I took a look at the pictures of all the ex-mayors displayed on the wall. 'Jeremiah H. McCarthy', said the caption under one. 'Alderman, Fire Chief, and liquor dealer.' An election-day cartoon also caught my eye. 'I'm voting for the liar.' said one man to another. 'He promises more.' Butte has a political stature that belies its size. The history of organised labour in America was kick-started by the town's mining unions, who were operating effectively here earlier than anywhere in the country. Sometimes things got a little rough, as they did at the Miners' Day parade of 1914, according to the report in the paper.

Alderman Frank Curran, socialist member of the city council and acting mayor, was shoved from a second-storey window of the Miners' Union Hall into which he had climbed to attempt to pacify the crowd. It is said the men who pushed the alderman from the windowsill were intoxicated. It is doubtful if those responsible knew whether he was a sympathiser or opponent.

Leafing through the archives and their tales of riots, whorehouses, dog fights, music-halls and opium dens, I'm struck by the rich and extreme history of the place. There should have been a sprawling historical novel by now, or a great juggernaut of a movie, a sprawling tear-jerker going from Castletownbere to Cobh to Boston to Butte, a cross-generational saga of scattered families, political intrigue, mining disasters, drunken violence and plummeting mayors. I particularly like the stories of the Chinese waiter nicknamed 'Spuds' who nearly died after eating nothing but potatoes for six months because an Irishman told him they were better for you than noodles; and of the wild Irish kids of Dublin Gulch who tied cows to front doors and released horses into church, leaped through the theatre skylight on to the heads of the audience, and once tied one end of a rope to a prospector's cabin and the other to a freight train. The prospector had gone four blocks before they dragged him out and took him to hospital.

I drive out of Butte determined to return. I like it here. As Highway 15 swings east then north I can see the whole town, the derelict pitheads standing gaunt but proud against the huge snow-capped peaks on the western horizon. Though the past has gone and they're still waiting for the future to begin, I haven't sensed the sadness I felt in Queenstown, Tasmania. It may not be pretty, but it has a stark beauty of its own. You could never imagine you were anywhere else. In a world where one town is rapidly becoming much like another, Butte is only like itself, and you can't ask much more of a place than that.

And you could always tell them you were allergic to celery.

Having escaped from Van Diemen's Land, Thomas Francis Meagher arrived in New York City on 26 May 1852. He slipped in unnoticed, but within twenty-four hours a crowd of thousands accompanied by the Brooklyn Cornet Band had gathered to greet him, which made it difficult to maintain a low profile. The extraordinary flourishes of his life and career so far were to be eclipsed by the events of the next fifteen years. Within a decade he returned to New York to another rousing welcome, this time as commander of the Irish Brigade which, under a banner of a golden harp on green silk, had fought with great courage and tremendous losses on the side of the union in the American Civil War. When the war ended, he accepted the post of territorial secretary, and subsequently acting governor, in the remote north-western territory of Montana. 'It may be the last time (God only knows) that you shall see me,' he wrote to a friend, 'for I go to a fierce and frightful region of gorillas.' Robert G. Athearn, in his 1949 biography of Meagher, writes: 'A rough and ready Irishman had found a community as tough as he – and a little bit more raw.' He was soon expressing fears for his life at the hands of local political opponents. The heavy drinking for which he had become notorious may have fuelled his suspicions.

In June 1867 Meagher made an exhausting six-day ride in sweltering heat to Fort Benton on the Missouri River in central Montana. On arrival he went to the back room of Baker's Store for a few stiff drinks, as would anyone with any sense after riding for six days, before adjourning for the night to a boat called the *G. A. Thompson* that was moored on the river. People who were there said he drank heavily and went to bed rowdy, ranting that some of those present were plotting to kill him. In the night there were cries of 'Man overboard', and Meagher was discovered to be missing. No body was ever recovered.

The official story was that he must have fallen overboard, a drunken victim of his 'unfortunate habit', but Montana was rife with rumours. A witness claimed that he cried out, 'They're after me!' as he fell; others alleged that he had been murdered, and his body buried south-west of Fort Benton in an unmarked grave. Nothing was ever proven, and it makes a strangely unsatisfactory – or wonderfully mysterious – demise for one of Ireland's, and the fledgling USA's, great heroes; albeit with a strange postscript.

In 1899 the body of a 'petrified man' with a bullet hole in his forehead was found, supposedly on the banks of the Missouri near Fort Benton. It was carted around the country in a pine box to be viewed at 25 cents a pop. Well-attended gigs included Yellowstone Park and the Spokane Fruit Fair. A report in the *Bozeman Chronicle* said: 'the latest fake story about the petrified man is that the rocky remains . . . were once the mortal part of General Thomas Francis Meagher,' and there's no doubt this story was being used to attract paying customers. There were, however, other claimants. A Montana cowboy called Liver Eating Johnson paid his 25 cents, then asserted that the exhibit was his old partner Antelope Charlie – or No-Liver Charlie, as I like to think of him – who he claimed had been killed by Indians twenty years earlier. Others alleged it was neither Meagher nor Antelope, but George Washington. It was due to be examined by the Smithsonian Institute, but never arrived, and instead was transported to Australia – a neat touch – where it ended up doing the rounds of agricultural shows.

Six years later, in 1906, thousands of people turned out for the unveiling of an equestrian statue of Meagher, in front of the Montana state capital in Helena.

And in a few minutes, I should be standing right next to it.

I was supposed to be heading north-west when I left Butte, but after pursuing the Young Irelanders from Cobh to Tasmania I felt I couldn't come this close without popping in to pay my respects to Meagher. The journey north-east from Butte has taken less than two hours, the drive through ravishing snow-capped mountains marred only by Herman's Hermits singing 'Mrs Brown You've Got a Lovely Daughter' on the radio, and by occasional jarring reminders, even in country as wild as this, of the national obsession with very large quantities of food. ALL YOU CAN EAT DRIVE THRU BUFFET, said a sign outside one remote eaterie. How does that work then? Surely you'd be in danger of mowing down all the folks standing round the trestle tables piling their plates with barbecue ribs and pasta salad and waffles. The signs multiply as I reach the outskirts of Helena. LADIES' NIGHT. FREE SLICE

OF PIE WITH *HER* DINNER, says the one outside the Andrea Dworkin Diner; no, sorry, my mistake, I read the sign wrong, it's the Red Garter Restaurant. ALL YOU CAN EAT SCALLOPS THURSDAY, says another; then it's the WOK AND ROLL SUSHI BAR, and now I'm driving through the forest of non-food- and beverage-related announcements that greets you on the outskirts of every God-fearing American town.

THE MOST PRECIOUS THINGS IN LIFE ARE NOT THINGS

SAVE SEX TILL MARRIAGE – IT'S THE SMART CHOICE

BEST-SELLING BIBLE – LEATHER COVER – ONLY $39.95

As well as being warmer than Butte, Helena looks much more prosperous. According to people in Moloney's last night, the rest of the state is rather enjoying Butte's fall from economic grace after decades of dominating the state. Mind you, I did detect a few chips on shoulders. One woman told me that when she went away to college she wore a sweatshirt that said: I'M FROM BUTTE – I CAN'T READ OR WRITE, BUT I'LL FIGHT ANY FIVE PEOPLE WHO CAN. It's a good joke, because it comes from a dark place. Helena seems somehow lighter. Sun is streaming down from a blue sky as I pull up near the Capitol building and park the tiny hire car that's been foisted on me as some kind of practical joke. It's so small I could park it in that Dublin hotel room and still have room for a couple of bikes and a freezer. I prise myself through the door using escapology skills I picked up at a community arts workshop in the 1980s, and take a few moments to luxuriate in the sweet sensation of my knees no longer touching my chin. A hundred yards away, across the lawns that surround the Capitol, I can see the statue. I'm about to walk across to it when I remember something. I open the door, take a banana from the car, then continue on my way.

The Capitol is a huge domed building set back from the road, built in granite with Ionic – or are they Doric? columns. I never did understand the distinction, but Brother Alexander used to go a bit psycho if you asked him questions, so we tended not to bother. Beyond the lawns are neat rows of American Dream houses. Between the legislature and the voters' homes sits Meagher astride a horse, sword in hand, facing north towards Canada. AMERICAN SOLDIER AND STATESMAN, reads a plaque. Alongside it is a quote from Meagher himself.

The true American knows, feels, and with enthusiasm declares that, of all human emotions, of all human passions, there is not one more pure, more noble, more conducive to good and great and glorious deeds than that which bears us back to the spot that was the cradle of our childhood, the playground of our boyhood, the theatre of our manhood.

The words were spoken in Montana in 1866. He is addressing America, but harking back to Ireland to evoke his deepest emotions. His prose may be more purple than the average immigrant's – he was a precursor of the 'this great nation of ours' tears-to-a-glass-eye oratory for which later generations of American politicians have become renowned – but Meagher, in his grand way, is an archetype of the Irish in the New World. A reluctant exile, he nevertheless threw himself with vigour into building a new society; took on responsibilities and powers denied him in his homeland; yet could never forget the land of his birth. In those last moments, Fort Benton must have seemed a very long way from Waterford and Clonmel.

I'm just thinking how touching it is to stand here and read his words and remember the grave of the child he never saw in that churchyard in Tasmania, when I realise that this could start to get very maudlin. Irish-American sentimentality has a quicksand quality to it, and you wouldn't want to venture in too far. Better to remember Meagher, I think, for the wittiest idea he ever had: the pub meals on that bridge thousands of miles away in Tunbridge. I still owe him a lunch for that, because the pie ruined the moment. That's why I've brought a banana. You can't go wrong with fruit.

I take it out, peel it in his honour, and raise it skywards in salute, in imitation of his sword. 'Cheers, Thomas Francis.'

'Get your butt back over here before I spank it,' says a woman's voice, rather alarmingly. I lower the banana and turn round to see a three-year-old girl staring at me. She can stare all she likes. She's not having the banana. It's a political symbol, and would be wasted on a toddler. Her mother drags her away, and I head straight back to the car. If she calls the cops I'll need a head start, and it could take a while to squeeze back into my seat.

Montana is the third largest state in the Union after Alaska and Texas, 750 miles from side to side, with landscape of lyrical grandeur. This is truly big sky country, the road and the railway following river valleys through the mountains, constantly evoking the imagery of nineteenth-century paintings of the west. For a first-time visitor like me, your best expectation of what you might get is exactly what you do get: horses, log cabins, cattle, and space seemingly into infinity. Its impact can take you by surprise, especially if you're a man of a certain vintage who grew up on westerns. You internalised this stuff at an impressionable age, and its emotional charge is just waiting to be reactivated. And if you ever tire of the scenery, there are always the signs, which just keep coming at you, and have a poetry all of their own.

LAST CHANCE MOTEL GUESTS SAY NICEST, CLEANEST

ARTS AND CRAFTS, GUN SALES

COMMUNITY CHURCH OF CHRIST CENTERED

FLATHEAD INDIAN RESERVATION

GODDESS – PRAISE THE FEMALE

BUFFALO BURGERS, HUCKLEBERRY SHAKES

MONTANA SISSY COWPOKE TEA

CEMENT ART – CONCRETE LAWN CRITTERS!

PARADISE - 15 MILES

For a while I listen to the radio. 'Walk of Life' by Dire Straits comes on, which has never been a favourite, but which carries a new charge since meeting Danny – 'Johnny' in the song – in Montserrat. When the road becomes too remote to pick up a station I put the Yank's CD on, taking care not to feed it into any rogue orifice in the body of the hire car. As it starts to play, I pass a huge Winnebago with a Ford Escort strapped to the back for sightseeing when they get wherever they're going. Inside the boot of the Escort, I expect, will be a Fiat Uno, and inside that a Honda 50 with a skateboard strapped to it. Once they get a removal truck to carry the Winnebago round in, they'll be all set.

It's late afternoon and I've just passed hundreds of identical cows, pure black with a single white band round their middles, as if they're wearing rugby jerseys. I'm following a broad, glistening river through dimpled hills on Route 135, about 150 miles north of Butte, when a large fish flies straight past my windscreen. Strange, I'm thinking, for a split-second, until I realise it's being held in the claws of a huge bird of prey; and then it's gone. The bird was flying left to right across the front of the car, from the mountains to the river, which seems a bit arse-about-face. Perhaps it's just found the fish and is trying to save its life; or maybe it's just restocking the river. Either way, it's always a comfort to find such altruism in nature, which sometimes gets a very bad press.

I arrive in Paradise – you could wait your whole life to say that and never get the chance – which turns out to be a pretty little place straddling the railway line. There's a bar called the Pair-a-Dice, and a mile marker that tells me I've less than ten miles to go. The next town is Plains, an abbreviation of Wild Horse Plains. Town is deserted in the soft early evening light. I pass a warning sign that says WATCH FOR FALLEN ROCK, and then I hit the rock. The impact jolts my knees against my chin and the top of my head against the car roof, but I'm so tightly packed in that the damage is only superficial. I carry on for a few hundred yards until I hear an ominous metallic ker-lunk-a-lunk-a-lunk. I'm next to mile marker 70, and my destination is half a mile past 68. Two and a half miles to go after driving nearly 300, and it sounds like I've got a flat front tyre.

I get out and take a look. Yep, flat all right. Ah, sod it. It's a hire car. It's what they're for, as the Channel 4 cameraman used to say before driving another brand-new family saloon along a stream, through a wood, or across a quarry. I'll just limp along at ten or fifteen until I get there. There's no other traffic. I won't be a hazard. It might knacker the wheel, but serves 'em right for adding the $39 a day insurance they hadn't mentioned on the phone. Mind you, it's a bit noisy. Quite alarming really. Still, there's no one to hear it. Except those four people up ahead, working in that lumber yard. They've stopped what they're doing now so they can watch me approach. Must be quite a sight, I suppose, a tinny little grandma's runabout rattling along on three tyres on a road that was designed for the ballsiest pick-up trucks on the planet. So – what to do now? They obviously think I'm barmy, and the fact that I look like a grown-up sitting in a toy car probably isn't helping. Do I drive blithely past, klunk-a-klunk-a-klunk, and give them a little wave, like Coco the Clown driving into the ring before the wheels and doors fall off? Or do I stop and use my remedial mechanical skills to try and change the wretched wheel at the only point on the entire road where I'll have an audience? The noise is dreadful now. I don't mind wrecking the tyre, but writing the axle off would be a different matter entirely. Better stop, eh? I'll give 'em a big smile, a sort of 'Oh, shucks, I guess this kind of thing happens to pioneering folk like you and me most every day,' to break the ice, and they'll come running right over to help.

Nothing. They're just staring. Standing in a row, giving me the evil eye. Behind them a couple of sabre-toothed devil dogs are bouncing off a fence like balls in a squash court, in a desperate attempt to get out of the compound and rip my liver out. What a great spot to try and change a tyre. 'Howdy,' I shout, and wave. The one on the end says something, and the others laugh. I don't like this. But I can't just get back in and clunk off up the road. They might chase me, or release the dogs. Nothing else for it. I'm going to have to put the spare on. I wonder where it is? How do you get it out? Where's the jack? How does it work? Why won't they help?

They've decided to ignore me and are standing in a line throwing concrete blocks to each other, stacking them in a pile at the end. There are two men and two women, all in their twenties. The one who made the funny remark has a close-cropped skull, as if he's just come from an audition for a teen killing-spree movie, although he could be the real thing. He's throwing blocks to a good-looking blonde woman who is much tougher than I am. A less attractive couple with baseball caps and outsize bottoms complete the line. They're probably just pretending to ignore me, and have noticed that it's taken me fifteen minutes to locate the spare and get it out of the boot. As I lie down and start looking under the car for a jack point I realise how vulnerable I am. *The sign diverted my attention just long enough for me to hit the rock it was supposed to be warning me about.* They probably put it there themselves.

Look at them. They're like vultures, keeping their distance, waiting for the car to collapse on me so they can come across, pick me clean, and toss what's left over the fence to Lucifer and Satan, who are barking even more ferociously now they can smell my fear. I'm working as fast as I can, knocking chunks out of my fingers and elbows in my hurry to get out of here. Cropskull just went across and got some sort of ominous-looking power tool out of a huge battered old car, like the ones in the movies that are always parked outside the hillbilly homestead where three generations of the same family have spent their lives making lampshades and tambourines out of skin they've flayed from the corpses of strangers. Right. Done it. The spare's on. It's not much bigger than a doughnut, but it'll have to do for now. There will be no garages open tonight, because there are no garages. I give them a cheery wave as I drive off, and they just stand there, impassive. Maybe they've already got themselves a stranger who they haven't finished with yet, and they didn't want to give the game away.

Perhaps he's under the concrete blocks.

A couple of minutes, and I've reached mile marker 68. And here's the sign, just less than a half a mile further on, exactly as promised. MCCARTHY'S — BEARA WEST. I can see a low wooden house facing the mountains at the end of an unpaved track. I drive up and park. Dogs are barking inside, but they don't sound like they mean it. I open the boot and take out the overnight bag I packed this morning at the Finlen. Inside are a change of clothes, a washbag, and the dossier on the McCarthy Mór I was given in the Dublin hotel. A man is walking down the steps.

'Hi. I'm Larry McCarthy.'

Whether a clan is a real or a bogus thing remains a topic of heated genealogical debate, but as far as I'm concerned it's extremely heart-warming to turn up in a remote place, covered in dust and with bits missing from your digits, and be treated as kin by people you've never met before. Some people find visiting strangers more relaxing than being with family, because no one can see the gulf between what you're saying and what they know you're really like from years of unpleasant experience.

It's been a long day, and I'm more desperate for a drink than Thomas Francis Meagher after a fortnight's gallop through an Arizona duststorm with a hangover and a canteen full of sand.

Our close genetic bond enables Larry to sense this, and an Alaskan amber ale is slapped into my palm before I've had time to try and straighten up from the question-mark stoop into which my back has fused after so long in the Dinky car. The beer's good, cold but full of dark flavour, a sign of the brewing revolution that's taken place in this country in recent years. At last there's an alternative to the loathsome liquid burp produced by the big brand-name brewers. God how I hated those 'Wassup'!' adverts. 'Your beer's shite, pal, that's wassup!' I would scream, which used to upset some of the other parents waiting at the school gates.

Larry isn't drinking because of his recent illness, but he has no qualms about getting me another when he notices I've finished the first one before he's had a chance to close the fridge door. Moments later I'm sitting facing the biggest steak I've eaten since – well, since this morning at M & M, I suppose. I don't think eating steak twice in one day can be very good for you, especially if you've only had a banana in between. Doesn't it lead to those meat-impacted bowel disorders where you wind up on the wrong end of forced high-pressure colonic irrigation from a butch nurse in a rubber dress on the floor of a white-tiled room? Mind you, it's a very good steak. Local, according to Larry. Reared on all that grass I've been driving past today, I suppose, rather than ground-up processed bits of its relatives, as is traditional elsewhere. I've eaten half of it now, and soon I should be able to see the plate.

I first became aware of Larry when I stumbled on to the scandal of the McCarthy Mór and discovered the existence of the North American Clan McCarthy Association, which had distributed Terence's writings and other Celtic-based literature throughout the world, as well as playing a key role in his fund-raising and ceremonial operations. John McCarthy – the banker who once drove from New York to Montana to buy a dog – told me that night in the pub opposite Madison Square Garden that Larry was the man I should see if I wanted to know more about the Mór. I know that he's a paid-up member of the Niadh Nask, the Gaelic chivalric order that Terence either revived or made up, depending on whom you believe; and that he's taken part with Terence in various ceremonial McCarthy bashes, in both Ireland and America. He hasn't, as far as I know, visited him in Tangier; nor is it likely that he's seen the dossier, which I've left down in the basement guest bedroom covered with a tapestry of President Kennedy I found there. Does Larry think Terence is a fraud; or is he still a loyal subject? And how am I going to find out? I don't want to come on like some private eye, with my ridiculous secret dossier. There's Celtic harp music on the stereo, a model of the Rock of Cashel on the bookcase, the snow-capped mountains of the North American Rockies are outside the window, and the casbah of Tangier seems like a distant dream. Suddenly I realise what I have to do, and it doesn't involve interrogating Larry so that I can pin down the truth, which will always be a movable feast. I'll just stick to what I've been doing all year: keep following the connections, and see where they lead me.

For some reason I'd imagined Larry lived up here on his own, but there are four of us at the table. To my left is his wife, and across from me his mother, who is ninety-three years old. She's been telling me about growing up in Butte, how her father came out from Beara and married an Irish girl he met in America, part of the generation who settled the west when it was wild. Wilder. We're laughing and talking about Father Sarsfield's Indian-Irish dancing story, and I'm not prepared for what she tells me when I ask about her childhood.

'I had an older sister who I never met. She was eighteen months old. My mother was somewhere out on the edge of Butte, talking to a neighbour, my sister standing clinging to her skirts, when the ground opened up in front of her, and the little child disappeared into a hole in the ground, 150 feet down a disused mineshaft.'

I'm stunned, overwhelmed by sadness for something that

happened nearly a hundred years ago. How do you recover from something like that?

'I don't think Mother ever did.'

It's almost dark when I finish the steak and Larry brings up the subject of Terence. 'A lot of people over here,' he says, 'are very angry with him.'

Including you, I imagine, as head of the American clan?

'Well, I'll tell you something. I had a wonderful time with Terence. Everything he said he'd do, he did, and he did it all with wonderful grace and generosity. He brought people together – like we are tonight – McCarthys from all over who otherwise had no connection. That was a good thing to do.'

I agree that it was, and decline the ice cream.

'I've never met Conor, but I don't see how he can carry this forward now. It's been discredited. Who's gonna want to put energy, or money, into it? No one. People's questions remain unanswered, and as long as they do, they'll stay mad. This was Terence's thing, and my guess is it'll end with him. He had charisma.'

But are you angry?

'I could never get mad with Terence. Is he happy in Morocco? I hope he's happy. He's a great historian and scholar, he writes real well, and he brought a knowledge of Irish and Gaelic history to people who otherwise would have had none. Part of a clan chief's job is making people aware of the history they share, bring them together, make things happen. If you judge it like that, Terence was a big success. And if he wasn't who he said he was? Well, I'll be honest with you. I'd be disappointed, but I'd still like the guy. All the contact I had with him, I had a wonderful time. Whatever it cost me, I'd happily spend again, but I know other people don't feel that way. But I had my money's worth.'

I'm just wondering how to bring up the subject of the dossier, when Larry seems to read my mind, and answers my question for me.

'Some people say they've seen evidence, but I never have. And you know something? I don't think I want to either. Just more things to argue about and divide us. Terence brought us together. You could say that whether he was who he says he was is irrelevant. I mean, who knows what really went on in Irish history?'

I decide to leave the dossier downstairs with President Kennedy for the rest of the evening.

Next morning I manage the eighty miles to Missoula airport on three wheels and a doughnut without any further mishap. Two soldiers in camouflage fatigues are on duty at the hand-luggage X-ray machine. I don't understand the logic in wearing camouflage if you're not in the jungle or forest. It just makes you easier to spot. There's no doubt that flying in the USA is a more unsettling business these days. If we admit it, we're all nervous. A gangling twenty-five-year-old who looks as if he might still be growing rummages through my bag and takes out the least suspicious item he can find. He stares belligerently at the colourless liquid.

'This water?'

I confirm that it is. He assumes a look of triumph, as if he just got the prime suspect to betray his guilt on tape.

'Okay,' he says, resisting the temptation to add 'wise guy'. 'Then drink some for me.'

This is an intriguing security tactic I haven't previously encountered, and naturally I comply with his request. When I fail to explode or spontaneously combust, he reluctantly lets me through. In the departures lounge an anaesthetist in tennis clothing is on the payphone talking loudly to a patient about upping her dose of steroids and injecting morphine directly into her spine, which isn't what I want to hear before going up to 30,000 feet with a bunch of strangers whose water may not have been checked properly.

The in-flight meal is peanut and caramel-coated popcorn,

served with a fizzy drink. It comes with a little slip of paper that says 'I will praise God's name in song and glorify Him with thanksgiving' by way of explanation.

At Seattle airport the clampdown on drinks continues unabated. I'm stopped going through security by a middle-aged Chinese man in a blazer. He ignores the potentially lethal water, and instead removes the bottle of duty-free Jameson's I bought at Heathrow.

'What's this?'

'Whiskey.'

'Scotch whisky?'

'Irish.'

'No Irish whisky. Whisky Scotch, eh? From Scotland!'

'No. It's from Ireland. Look. It says so on the bottle.'

He removes the bottle from its bag, unscrews the top, gives it a sniff, and looks to me for an opinion.

'Cheaper than Scotch?'

'About the same.'

An Indian guy in a different blazer has come over now. He smiles and says, 'You share that? We have party now?'

'Ireland, eh?' asks the Chinese guy.

'Yes.'

'My mother, all my family, in Toulouse.'

'Toulouse? I see.'

'Yes. Every year, I go to Toulouse. Next time, I remember.'

There's a long pause, but eventually I can't bear it any more.

'Remember what?'

'Jameson's. Irish Scotch. Very good. Have a nice flight.'

He screws the top back on and I go through the X-ray machine, secure in the knowledge that the war on terrorism is doing whatever it takes to make the skies a safer place, particularly in the area of hazardous beverages.

In five hours' time I will be in Alaska; and tomorrow morning I will be on the road to McCarthy.

12

WHERE THE
ROAD ENDS AND THE
WILDERNESS BEGINS

A geeky youth with a too-thin head and disturbing grin is staring at me across the desk. He appears to be looking at someone behind me and slightly to one side, but I just turned round and checked and there's nobody there, so I'll have to add cross-eyed to his list of attributes.

'So, whaddya got ta show me, Peete?'

I like American informality, but this kid's behaving like he's been mixing red wine with his Mogadon, drawling words in a menacing sing-song and stretching out my name like it's some kind of joke. I decide to go terribly British on him, see how he likes that. Usually, they don't.

'I'm sorry. I don't understand what you mean. What do you want? A credit card?'

'Right first time, Peete!'

I give him a green American Express card instead of a slap. He gazes at it as if I've just put the Ark of the Covenant on the counter.

'Wow! Weird design. Far out. Where'd ya get this, Peete? England? No kidding. I guess you got some pretty strange stuff over there?'

Not as strange as Alaska judging by the evidence so far, which is you.

'There you go. Room 3226. You enjoy your stay now, Peete!'

I walk the few yards to the lift and wait for it to arrive. Pinhead stands watching me waiting for it to arrive. It arrives. I'm just about to get in when I decide it might be a good idea to check the obvious.

'Third floor?'

'Nope. Second floor, third building.'

'Third building?'

He nods and grins and points to a depressing parking lot full of dirty half-melted snow.

'Didn't I say that? Out there, second door. Sorry, Peete!'

I pick my way across the slush to the third building. Strangely, there is no sign of the second building. In the lobby a big, tough woman with processed hair is punching a Coca-Cola machine. It may have failed to dispense her beverage of choice, but it seems more likely she's just come down from her room because she needed something to punch. I unpack and head out to look for a bar. It's almost ten and still light, but from what I can see it doesn't look a promising situation. I'm in a mid-budget chain hotel ten minutes from Anchorage airport, on the main road into town. I can see a petrol station, a convenience store, a pizza delivery place, three more chain hotels and some traffic lights, but nothing that resembles a bar. Directly across the four-lane road is a building that looks like the engineering department of a 1970s polytechnic. 'Restaurant', claims the sign, then, more hopefully, 'Cocktails'. I cross the road and find myself in a wood veneer and plastic banquette fast-food joint which is completely empty. If you'd just taken an overdose and needed to wash it down with a drink, you wouldn't have it here because it might depress you.

'Can I get you a table, sir?' asks a dispirited waitress, who seems to be the only other soul on the premises. I mutter some random sounds that don't include any proper words, then look round inquisitively as if I'm checking to see whether my buddies are here, which they're not. For good measure I decide to imply unpunctuality and look at my wrist, where there is still no watch. By now she's looking the other way, so I take the opportunity to slip through the door and escape across the road. Back in the lobby of Building One I ask Pinhead if the hotel has a bar.

'Sure thing, Peete! Through that door, down the stairs, you'll find the bar straight ahead of you. You enjoy now!'

I go down the stairs and find myself in a long, brightly-lit tunnel, a subterranean aluminium tube with an incongruous floral carpet. It's like a set from a Polish science fiction film. At the far end I climb another flight of steps, and emerge inside the restaurant I left two minutes ago.

'Can I get you a table, sir?' asks the waitress, with no apparent awareness that she asked me the same thing moments ago. Yes, I think, you can get me a table, and I'll take it back through the tunnel and hit Pinhead with it. I can't have a drink here. There'd be an awkward, deathly silence, with each of us thinking how sad the other one's life is. My best bet is to have a party in my room, so I walk to the convenience store and buy two bottles of Alaskan amber beer, a bag of nuts and a copy of the *Alaskan Daily News*. GIANT SQUID, says the headline on the front page of the paper, just as I'd hoped it would. In a world where three species become extinct every day, it's comforting to know that Alaska can still lay on weird nature by the bucketload.

Mind you, it would have had to be a big bucket. According to the paper a fisherman was startled to see a deep-sea halibut he'd hooked rise to the surface with a monster on its back. 'I thought it was an octopus,' said the fisherman, 'then thought, this ain't right, it's got a five-foot head.' He realised he was dealing with a rare giant squid, and from somewhere discovered the imagery to deal with the situation. 'It looked like a stained-glass window of a halibut, where the arms and tentacles of the squid were the lead between the panes,' he raved. 'The squid had totally encapsulated the halibut. It was the most fascinating thing.'

Indeed it was. The paper says that 'the mythic giant squids are rarely found and almost never seen alive.' So what did the fisherman do? 'I fried up a little bit just to check it out,' he said, after gaffing and gutting the rarity. 'It was incredibly salty and had a bit of an aftertaste.' Two thousand people turned up to see the remains, and the weight of the crowd started to sink the floating dock on which the unfortunate sea-monster had been carved up. 'It was quite a menagerie,' said the harbour-master. 'I saw the pharmacist, I saw the judge.'

The fisherman had the final word. 'I cut the halibut loose and, my goodness, he was tickled pink to get out of there. This turned out good for everybody involved, except the squid.'

I drain the second beer, turn off the bedside light, and lie there in the dark thinking about my evening: Pinhead, the tunnel and the squid. Ten minutes later I get up again, open my bottle of Irish Scotch, and turn on *Saturday Night Live*. It's showing a sketch about the trend for successful forty-something white men to dump their wives for trophy relationships with elderly black women. When it finishes I station-hop for a while, but I can't find an episode of *Cheers* anywhere. Alaska must be even more remote than I thought.

The road to McCarthy is famous, at least among people who've heard of McCarthy and tried to get there. Known as 'the worst road in Alaska', an accolade that's nailed to a tree near its start, this sixty-mile unpaved track follows the route of an old railway across canyons, past glaciers, and over a wooden-plank bridge that until a few years ago had no sides. Rivets from the old rail still sometimes rise to the surface to puncture tyres. The entire length is populated by bears. To enhance McCarthy's reputation

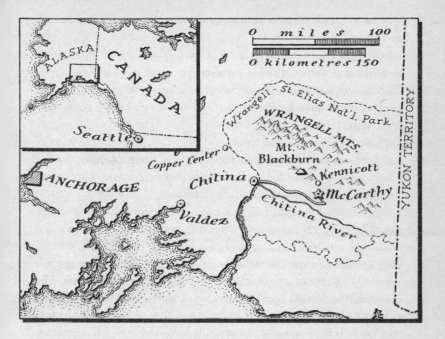

as one of the most remote settlements in North America, the road stops at a river a mile short of town, and you have to walk the rest of the way.

Today the road to McCarthy is closed.

'It's the season after winter and before spring. It's called break-up,' explains Neil from the McCarthy Lodge, which is where I'll be staying if I can get there, which at the moment I can't. 'The snow and the glaciers have started to melt. There's several feet of slush in some places, so even four-wheel drives can't get through, but it's down to the gravel in other places, so neither can snowmachines. Plus, it's snowing hard right now.'

I tell him it's sunny in Anchorage.

'Well, there's a pilot supposed to be flying to Anchorage today, but right now he can't take off. If he makes it, he could bring you back, if he's able to land.'

If he makes it? If he's able to land? What manner of crazy talk is this?

'Or you could try and drive. Get a *big* four by four, with airbags, and plenty of steel between you and the outside world. And if you get stuck, be decisive. You gotta know whether to hike forward, hike backward, or stay in the vehicle till somebody finds you.'

How long would that be?

'Hard to say. Why don't you consider your options, let me know what you plan to do. There's no problem about your room, because there's no other visitors in town.'

I go down for breakfast but can't find it, and have to ask at the desk. There's no sign of Pinhead, but a disarmingly normal woman is on hand to direct me back down the tunnel. When I get to the restaurant, the waitress is missing as well. Maybe she's married to Pinhead and Sunday is their day for halibut fishing. The room that last night had been as cheery as the bar in *The Shining* is now full of happy diners. I take a window seat in the sunshine and consider my options. I think I'll have the reindeer sausages.

McCarthy is a couple of hundred miles east of Anchorage, on the way to the border with the Yukon territory of Canada. It is surrounded by one of the largest areas of wilderness in the world, where four of the great mountain ranges of North America collide. Nine of the highest peaks in the USA are there, surrounded by enormous glaciers, rivers and canyons, and teeming with seriously wild wildlife. McCarthy, old by Alaskan standards, dates from the first decade of the twentieth century, when it developed as a social hub for the copper mines at Kennicott, five miles away. When the mines closed it went into decline, and for a while became a ghost town. The current year-round population, depending on which source you consult, is somewhere between fourteen and twenty. There seems a good chance I'll be able to meet them all, if only I can get there.

Unlike the other places I have been visiting, McCarthy has no known Irish connection. Something about it, though, is calling out. Having adhered for many years to the maxim 'Never pass a bar that has your name on it', it seems only right to add: 'And take pains to seek out any town that does the same'. If you travel in hope rather than certain knowledge, something interesting usually happens; and even if it doesn't, what an absurd affirmation of identity and existence to be able to look at your name on a place sign and say, 'Well. Here I am then.' Hidden at the end of one of the loneliest roads on earth, the town seems the right place to end a journey that has been driven as much by instinct as by design, and which has paid me back with many happy accidents. So I'm going there because we share a name; and because, like most people, I've always fancied going to Alaska, because it's big, scary and far away. Wherever you are, it's far away. But as well as all this, I also have a hunch. I didn't have it when I first set out, but now I want to pursue it all the way to the end of the road.

'Aviation in itself is not inherently dangerous, but like the sea, it is terribly unforgiving of any carelessness, incapacity or neglect,' says a sign on the wall of the hut. Next to it is a handbill. '$15,000 Reward. Find This Aircraft, Lost on a Flight from Anchorage. Pilot and four passengers.' Outside on the airstrip a tiny red and yellow plane sits on its skis among the piles of snow, looking like a toy that has been unwrapped on Christmas morning and abandoned in favour of more impressive gifts. This is how I will get to McCarthy, if the pilot ever comes back. The guy in the hut says he's gone into town to pick up some shopping. I've had a look inside the plane. There are two seats and sixteen cases of beer. Perhaps he's had to go back to pick up the wine and spirits.

I've hopped between tropical islands on these little bush planes, but I've never been in one in the kind of colossal landscape we'll be going through today. It seemed sensible to prepare properly for such a journey, so I went into town for a couple of margaritas. After all, a relaxed coward is a happy coward. I found a comfortable, modern-looking bar called the F St Station, which is according to the menu 'the oldest bar in Anchorage in its original location, originally an Irish pub frequented by aviators . . . to our customers, especially you aviators, thanks very much . . .' I didn't like the sound of that one bit. Aviators don't have any business drinking. That's the passengers' job. My afternoon departure time has already been put back twice while the pilot does his mysterious 'shopping'. What's he really up to? I looked round the bar until my gaze came to rest on the bleary-eyed soak knocking back the bloody marys in the corner. I had a vision of him tottering across the runway with a hand over one eye trying to aim the key at the handle on the cockpit door, and immediately ordered another margarita.

'Hi. I'm Kelly,' says a big, bearded, genial man who's just walked into the hut. He's carrying a brown paper bag containing three bottles of red wine, so he must be the pilot, but at least it isn't the guy from the bar. Is he planning any more errands? No. It's straight out to the plane, squeeze my little bag on top of the beer and wedge the wine down the side, door shut, headphones and seat belt on, taxi what seems like about fifteen yards along the runway, then, whoop, we're up in the air and heading directly towards those enormous snowy mountains. 'This is real flying, eh?' says Kelly, as I nod and smile and try to come to terms with the worrying sensation of being airborne in a Morris Minor. I try to distract myself by reading something, but there is no in-flight movie menu or brochure advertising expensive perfume and alarm clocks shaped like aeroplanes. The only reading matter available is a selection of little dials with warnings about how far it's safe to fall if the engine cuts out. I make a conscious decision, almost certainly margarita-inspired, to stop being such a wuss and enjoy what may well be the flight of my life. I relax the ferocious grip I have taken on the dashboard, so that my fingers are only purple instead of white.

We fly to the left of the mountain range that faces the airstrip, then on through a dreamscape of white peaks we can almost reach out and touch. Far below are frozen rivers and crystalline glaciers glinting turquoise and emerald in the brilliant afternoon sun. Kelly's deft hand on the controls inspires confidence, not least because you sense it's important to him to get those bottles of wine home in one piece. We talk using headsets with microphones attached, looking like singers in a boy band who have fallen victim to a mysterious ageing virus. He's good company, pointing out the different mountain ranges and the snowmachine tracks left by reckless extreme-sporters on mountainsides prone to catastrophic avalanche. As he sees me relax his fund of anecdotes starts to stray from what you want to be hearing when you're hovering above oblivion like a special effect.

'There was a forecast for some turbulence on the way back today, but looks like we might've missed it. My wife and I stopped overnight along the coast one time, were meant to carry on home the next day. The forecast was for extreme turbulence, but we thought we'd try anyway, because sometimes those predictions are way out. Well, it was so wild up there it scared us.'

Well, imagine that, but I wish he'd stop now.

'We decided we'd have to head straight back to the airfield. And then we saw this other little plane, kicking and reeling about right over the ocean – and that is not a place you want to be in turbulent weather. He landed right after us, and he was whiter than the snow on the ground. Said he'd had two gas canisters in there, not tied down, just crashing all round the cockpit. The gusts were so strong they ripped holes in his floorboards . . .'

Floorboards?

'. . . and punctured his roof. Y'know, we think we're in control, and we do our best, but it's only a machine, and if nature decides . . .'

Yeah, okay, Kelly. That's enough now.

'. . . that mountain over there? Well, in the 1960s a freight plane went straight into . . .'

I'm trying to think of something else, but find myself remembering the Australian bush pilot who regaled me with horror stories during our flight into Arnhemland. His favourite was the one about the guy who'd waded across the river at pub closing time for a bet, and had been bitten in half by a crocodile. So he lost the bet.

'. . . down a 12,000-foot crevice. Rumour was, there was a big shipment of gold on board. Nearly forty years now, and no one's ever been able to get near the wreck and find out. Someone tried a couple of years ago, but it was too dangerous, because the snow is so unstable that . . .'

There's a little electronic crystal ball on the dash that says it's only fifty miles to our destination, and now Kelly is pointing out of my wide window and tilting the plane, not to push me out, but to show me the McCarthy road. I can see where it skirts the edge of the glacier and the melting ice has made it impassable. As we're rounding the glacier, hugging the side of the mountain, the winds suddenly hit. It's seriously bumpy for the first time – but, like the man said, this is real flying, and he seems to be in control – and against all my better instincts I find myself wanting it to bump a little bit more as we swoop low over the first buildings we've seen since the hut at the airfield in Anchorage. McCarthy is just a handful of wooden houses, like the cowboy town in *McCabe and Mrs Miller* where Warren Beatty was the business and Julie Christie came to set up the brothel. A little further on we sweep low past the deserted structures of the Kennicott mine. We bank steeply to our left over the glacier, and make a perfect landing on the McCarthy airstrip. Kelly turns off the engine, and I get out and listen to the most silent place I have ever heard.

*

'Beer – It's your Friend', says an ad on the wall of the bar in the McCarthy Lodge. There are two other customers besides me and Kelly, one of whom has green hair. The woman behind the bar has radical eye make-up and facial piercings, but the modern accoutrements of these two young people are offset by the other customer, a long-haired and longer-bearded bib-overall and lumberjack shirt kind of a guy who looks like he's been living in a log cabin without a mirror or running water since 1972. There's an old darkwood bar counter, an impressive mirror marked 'Golden Saloon', and a pool table piled with the cases of beer we've just unloaded from the plane. The Soggy Bottom Boys are singing 'Man of Constant Sorrow' on the stereo, and the Black Butte porter we've airlifted in from Anchorage is full-bodied, rich in flavour, and ideal, as they say in the wine supplements, for drinking now. I mean, what isn't?

First impressions of a bar are crucial. It's like buying a house, only more important. And if you're going to spend a week in a place that's in the middle of nowhere but not so central, you've got high hopes riding on the only bar in town. Right now I'm feeling very relieved. If all else fails – if the weather closes in and the planes don't fly, if the road washes away and I'm trapped for a month; if all the books in town catch fire and there's nothing left to read – then at least I know I'll be able to come and sit in here and be happy. And if they move the beer off the table we might even be able to shoot some pool. All in all, I've been in worse spots.

On the other hand, with a population so small, what happens if I don't like them; or worse still, if they don't like me? If you upset somebody in such a remote place I shouldn't imagine they'd bother with the formality of burying you under a patio. So far the signs are good. Kelly's a diamond, the drinkers in the bar seem friendly enough, and the two guys who own the place have been charming. That's six accounted for. There must only be another dozen or so to meet. 'People here are pretty tolerant, even if they don't agree with you. Places in Alaska can be a lot more redneck than this,' says Doug, one of the owners, over dinner. We're eating pork, sliced into thin fillets, rolled and filled with pistachios and cooked in coconut milk and spices. It's served with home-made poppadoms, lemon rice, oriental pickled vegetables, and salad with honey mustard dressing. The merlot is excellent. My expectations of moose stew and pork'n'beans punctuated by the sound of lumberjacks belching and cowboys farting have turned out to be wide of the mark.

The accommodation is even more of a surprise. Instead of a spartan bunkhouse with too-narrow wire frame beds and a jug of water that freezes in the night so you have to break the ice before you can pour it over your head, I'm in a meticulously designed pioneer-style room with patchwork quilts and one of those knock-me-down hot showers that European plumbers ought to be sent to America to study. I'd had visions of living like a brute for a week, then dumping my clothes in an incinerator back in Anchorage, hosing off the moose shit, and going looking for food that didn't come out of a can. Instead I have been dropped into the Alaskan edition of *Homes and Interiors*. Doug and Neil have done a fine job. There are few more comforting experiences for the traveller than to journey great distances through unfamiliar and threatening landscapes, anticipating an austere and possibly squalid destination, only to discover that catering and interior design are not in the hands of heterosexuals.

As I snuggle down for the night under the crisp linen and embroidered counterpane and cast an eye over the antique lamps and hand-tinted photographs, I realise that if I ever tell anybody how nice it is here they'll all want to come, and it will spoil it; so instead I pull the threadbare bloodstained blanket up to my chin, arch my back against the broken springs, and listen to my teeth chattering above the drunken snoring of Liver Eating Johnson from the rusty toilet bucket on which he collapsed a little while ago. I'm gonna have to be tough to make it through a week in this hell-hole, but if I grit my teeth I've a feeling I just might pull it off. Sissy city folk, though, should stay away.

'You're the first visitor to come through here since that Israeli guy a few weeks ago,' says Jeremy the Dogmusher over breakfast. It's seven o'clock, and I'm dining with the half dozen construction workers who've been working through the winter to fix the town up before the snow melts and the visitors start arriving.

'At least you knew McCarthy was here,' says Neil. How else would you find it? I wonder. It's not as if it's on the way to anywhere.

'Except oblivion.' Jeremy grins. He's about thirty years old with long brown hair and beard, piercing eyes that I think are grey but appear to keep changing colour, and a manic laugh that lights up his whole face, and the rest of the room, like Jack Nicholson on helium. 'This Israeli guy, man, didn't know this place existed. Drove all the way out the McCarthy Road, when it was frozen solid, in a rented Escort. A fuckin' Escort!' He shrieks with laughter, and somewhere in Costa Rica a howler monkey looks round to see what all the noise is about. 'He was trying to get to Valdez, but made a left at Chitina, took a whole day to get here. Didn't even know there was going to be anyplace out here, because the asshole didn't have a map.' He's banging the table with delight now, and the pancakes are bouncing up and down.

'He said he didn't have enough money for a room,' says Neil, 'and could he sleep on the floor in here.' He raises an eyebrow, which I imagine is the same answer the Israeli got.

'So I told him I'd rent him tent space and a sleeping bag,' says Jeremy.

Tent space? Does this lunatic live in a tent, in Alaska, in the winter?

'And he says, "You mean, you sleep outside?"'

'"Yeah," I told him. "Sleep outside, live outside, work outside, run the dogs outside. It's an outside kind of a deal." Gave him a warm suit, two sleeping bags, and a lesson in how to minimize heat loss and stay alive. I woke up next morning, and he was just sitting there, with the warmest bag pulled down over his head, rockin' and kinda makin' a noise.'

There's a mournful-looking man sitting at the far end of the table. He's got another one of those long beards, and a nylon cap printed with a slogan for an electrical supplies shop and a picture of an electric motor. He hasn't uttered a sound since he walked in half an hour ago, but now he looks up and begins to speak in a low-key drawl.

'I usually find . . .'

The others have stopped talking and all eyes are on him.

'I usually find if I can keep both ends warm, the middle part takes care of itself.'

There's a momentary pause, then everyone applauds, bangs on the table and whoops. Then they get up and head out to work. There's just Neil and me left at the table. 'That's Guy the generator guy,' he says. 'Fixes our power supply. The first three months he was here he didn't say a word to anyone. I guess he's really coming out of his shell now.'

'Will some Intelligent person show us why McCarthy is not going to make a Butte . . . we have more Copper in the Immediate vicinity than all Montana holds.'

So said the first issue of a newspaper called the *Copper Bee* in 1916. MCCARTHY BAR, proclaimed an ad in the same edition. FINEST WINES AND LIQUORS. The paper only survived for three issues, but you know what? It was right. They may have called Butte the richest hill on earth, but the one outside McCarthy was even richer, if rather less conveniently situated.

Until the late 1800s few white men had penetrated these remote and forbidding regions. It was not until the Klondike gold rush that prospectors and miners arrived to fulfil the prophecy of local

Native American legend that one day their hunting lands would be lost to a new people with pale skin and yellow hair. In the winter of 1898 many prospectors died in the Wrangell Mountains from hypothermia or falling into crevasses, having arrived unprepared for such extreme conditions. A US government expedition led by Captain William Abercrombie reported of the prospectors that 'over 70 per cent of them were mentally deranged'. I suppose that would explain why they turned up in a place like this wearing thin woolly gloves and threadbare overcoats.

One of Abercrombie's men was sent to explore the Chitina River, but ran into difficulties and out of rations. He was fortunate to stumble upon the camp of a prospector, who lent him horses and supplies. The soldier expressed his gratitude by naming a creek upriver after him. The prospector's name was James McCarthy.

A year later, in 1900, a pair of chancers called Clarence Warner and Tarantula Jack Smith – they never seemed to come up with dull nicknames like 'Smithy', did they? – stopped for lunch by the McCarthy Creek. 'Looks like a good place for sheep,' said Warner, pointing to a green patch high up on the mountain. 'Don't look like grass to me,' said Tarantula Jack, throwing away his bear sandwich and striding excitedly towards the mountain. What they'd spotted turned out to be ore with an astonishing 70 per cent copper content, the richest in the world. They lost out to Butte on quantity, but the quality couldn't be beaten. By 1906 the railroad that now forms the McCarthy road had been laid, and the Bonanza Mine was in full swing.

The mine itself was five miles up the hill at Kennicott, a town owned and run – thanks to a spelling mistake by a clerk – by the Kennecott Mining Company, who maintained an austere regime involving table tennis and hymns. McCarthy flourished as a provider of the service industries essential to the physical and spiritual wellbeing of hundreds of wild-eyed miners stranded in the wilderness on top of a frozen mountain. 'If we got any change out of a ten-dollar bill, it was because they thought we were still sober,' said one ex-miner.

Alcohol was illegal in the early days, but bootleggers thrived and even got free publicity in the local paper. 'There is some beverage on the market in our fair city this week which has a great effect on its consumers,' announced another short-lived organ, the *McCarthy Weekly News*, in 1919. The engineer on the train played a special warning on the whistle if there was a federal agent on board. In 1922 the appositely named US Commissioner Coppernoll wrote to his superiors: 'this place is too tough for me . . . 70 per cent of the population make their living directly or indirectly through the medium of illicit traffic in whiskey.' One popular brand was named Old Slippery. 'Made in the woods,' read the citation on the label. 'Aged three days, bottled thin, tastes like sin.'

Many bootlegging stories have been recorded for posterity – including the time Slim Lancaster was denying everything to the marshal when the still upstairs boiled over and started dripping through the ceiling on to his head – but my favourite concerns the Four-Eyed Kid, and not just because of his name. The Kid was caught bang to rights with a bottle of whiskey in his hand. He was locked up, and the booze was put in the marshal's safe to be produced as evidence; but the locals broke into the safe one night, drank the whiskey and replaced it with water. The case collapsed in court when the Kid's lawyer took a match to the alcohol and tried to ignite it.

Legitimate businesses also flourished, under the stewardship of local shopkeepers like the Crooked Swede and Too Much Johnson. Brothels were a boom industry, and prostitutes were welcomed as respectable members of mainstream society, or at least as respectable as anyone else who'd made it out here. A photograph of the red light district, the Row, shows a huddle of primitive wooden cabins that look so cold the miners would have needed a blowlamp to get their longjohns off. The working girls gloried in such names as the Tramway Queen, the Snake Charmer, the Beef Trust – she weighed in at over 300 pounds – and Tin Can Annie, who 'could play sweet music on anything' if we can believe her publicity, and I think we can.

Copper prices dropped after the First World War, and by the 1930s Kennicott was on the skids. The last train ran in November 1938, at less than a day's notice, and mines and homes were abandoned like the *Marie Celeste*, only colder. The bridge was washed away in 1939 leaving McCarthy isolated, and in 1940 a fire burned down the hotel, the post office and the drug-store. Knowing a good opportunity when they spotted one, the bears then ripped up the railway line. By 1943 only four residents remained.

But who was James McCarthy? And why is so specifically Irish a clan name to be found out here, in a place much handier for Siberia than Skibbereen? The simple answer is that nobody seems to know. I've spent my first day leafing through every book, historical document and antique newspaper I can lay my hands on, and it's turned up next to nothing. Accounts agree the creek and the town were named after him, and that's where the information ends. He was just a prospector. When you come from a part of Europe where name and place origins have been recorded and traced for centuries, it's a shock to discover that recent history can have wiped its tracks so quickly. It's actually possible that there are people still alive who met him; after all, if John the Yank had grown up in Alaska instead of Montana, he would have been a kid when McCarthy was a man.

And then I remember something the Yank said to me when I was sitting in his apartment a few days ago watching the snow drift down.

'Wherever you find copper in North America you'll find the Irish. Especially Cork Irish. Beara Irish.'

At the moment it's still a hunch, but if you follow the connections you never know where they might lead.

*

'The thing with bears is, you gotta know which kind you're dealing with. A grizzly is meaner, more inclined to attack, but if you play dead, there's a chance he'll leave you alone and walk away, although there's also a chance he'll crush your skull with his paw. But with a black bear, you have to fight back. Try and play dead, they'll just start right on eating you. So it helps if you can tell 'em apart.'

It's always stimulating to visit new places, acquire fresh knowledge, and expand your portfolio of nightmares. In a place where there are far more bears than people, it would be foolish not to consider what you would do if you were confronted by one; but try as I may, I can't see myself coming up with much besides the weeping and the incontinence. I understand that my life may depend on being able to identify the bear so I know whether to lie down or start punching it, but I'm afraid the only one I'd recognise is Sooty, and it seems unlikely I'm going to run into him out here. If I did, it's obvious what to do. Shoot Matthew.

'Grizzlies have a kind of a hump between the shoulder blades.'

That's not the kind of thing you'd want to point out, though, is it? They probably get really mean if they start feeling self-conscious.

'Don't worry, Peter. People don't see grizzlies that often. And they're a protected species, remember. That means you can only shoot them if your life is threatened.'

'So you've never had to kill one yourself?' I ask.

'Sure I have. Four in two years.'

I've no reason to disbelieve him. After all, there's one pinned to the wall just above the fireplace.

One of the good things about coming to such a small place when there are no other visitors is that word gets round that you're here, and people start to invite you to their homes. It's hard not to be impressed by the warmth of Alaskan hospitality. Tonight I'm having dinner with Rick and Bonny, who produce the community newspaper. Rick is also a pastor at the non-denominational church. I nearly made a major faux pas by turning up with a bottle of wine, until Neil warned me that alcohol would probably be about as warmly received as a member of the Bin Laden family. Instead of Old Slippery I've brought a loaf of bread, an act that would be seen as a practical joke where I come from. There is already a basket of home-baked rolls on the table, so now I feel guilty for having brought rival bread.

Rick and Bonny live a few miles out of town, in a snug wooden house built on a piece of land that was once a farm supplying fresh fruit and vegetables to the sex- and whiskey-crazed miners. Though winter is long and harsh, there is a prolific summer growing season because of the long daylight hours. At the moment there's a gain of six minutes' light every day. But it can only achieve so much; cabbages do well, pineapples less so.

We're joined for dinner by two neighbours. George is a retired weatherman – a meteorologist, not a sixties' terrorist – and John works as a park ranger during the summer season. The parks service is a controversial body in these parts, where many people have come to live in order to be free of government bodies and regulations. The National Park was only established twenty years ago, and most of the Americans who flock to Yellowstone and Yosemite are unaware of its existence, even though it's the biggest in the country. The parks service has a hundred-year development plan, a curiously Soviet-sounding concept that will significantly expand visitor numbers. But it's wilderness, say the locals; why can't they just leave it alone? In an area with little paid employment people understand that their friends may have to take jobs in the parks, but it doesn't stop them hating the concept. I found this letter pinned to a noticeboard today.

Dear Abby,
I have two brothers, one works for the Parks Service and the other was sent to the electric chair. My mother died of insanity when I was three years old. My father sells narcotics to high school students. My sister is a prostitute.

Recently I met a girl who was released from reform school where she served time for smothering her illegitimate child. I want to marry her. My problem is this: if I marry the girl, should I tell her about my brother who works for the Parks Service?

Sincerely,

Worried

I was about to show it to John, until he asked me, 'Who was the first terrorist?'

I said I didn't know.

'It's in the Bible.'

I still didn't know.

'The serpent, in the Garden of Eden.'

How so?

'Terrorism has two purposes: to spread fear, and to subvert the power of government. That's what Satan did in the garden.'

Only if you think of God as the government, John.

'Exactly.'

I decided not to show him the letter.

Dinner is moose stew – which would have gone nicely with a jammy bottle of that Penfolds Bin 389, but non-alcoholic fruit punch is absolutely fine – served with home-grown-and-pickled beets the size of Maltesers which are sweet and delicious, and would be a perfect match for a peppery Côtes du Rhône, or even a rich Traquair ale. And of course there's masses of home-made bread, always ideal with scrumpy, neat Stolly, or a couple of pints of that fally-down Belgian stuff they serve in a test tube.

So I'm just thinking how refreshing it is to be eating dinner without drinking any alcohol when I notice that John has finished his moose and is following it with bread and home-made plum jam, and now he's been served seconds of moose and he's eating it *with* the bread and jam, which is very interesting. I'm dying to ask about it, but I'm scared he might think I'm weird.

The jam's about the same colour as a Hardy's Cabernet Shiraz.

I'd been hoping to talk to these people about local politics and self-sufficiency and the mental strength you need to live in a place like this, but mostly we've been talking about bears. The notion of sharing living space with wild animals who might kill you is as remote a concept for me as planning permission is to Alaskans, and it holds a grim fascination. I am gripped by an urgent need to talk about bears, possibly as a substitute for ever meeting them. So how many are there out there anyway?

'A lot.'

'You know something?' asks John. 'All this time I've lived out here, been treed by a moose, but never got treed by a bear.'

Treed?

'When you have to climb a tree to get away.'

Rick tells the story of the rogue grizzlies, a mother and two cubs, who terrorised the area a couple of years ago.

'They started with breaking into the trunks of cars looking for food, then got to ripping open four-wheel drives and eating the seats.'

They eat the seats?

'Sure. And the roof upholstery. Seem to love that. One lady was out on a mountain bike, the three bears just jumped out in front of her. She was up a tree nearly two hours till her husband came and found her. Wouldn't come down till she knew he had a gun. After that, they started on people's homes. Didn't they, George?'

'Sure did. It was late at night, I heard this scuffling at my window, looked and saw this black nose and pair of claws trying to get between the screen and the frame. One of the cubs. Looked outside, there was mom standing on her hind legs on the lawn. They don't like it if you get near the cubs, so I went through to the lounge room. There's another nose and set of claws trying to get in there.'

It sounds like the sequel to *The Birds* – 'They're back, and this time they're furry!'

'So I phoned the rangers, but they said they had no one available 'cos it was on a weekend, and I'd have to shoot 'em myself. Thing is, I don't own a gun. Won't have one in the house.'

So what did he do?

'Phoned me, and I shot 'em,' says Rick.

That makes three. What about the fourth?

'Heard a noise from the garage one night, went in and turned on the flashlight, there's a big grizzly on top of the freezer.'

I thought you were only supposed to shoot them in a life-threatening situation, as opposed to on the tops of freezers?

'If I'd asked him to come down, I think we might have had ourselves a situation.'

'Don't worry,' says Bonny as I'm leaving. 'The bears won't bother you. They're still asleep. Have a safe journey back to town.'

'Keep your speed up. They should be waking any day now,' says Rick, roaring with laughter.

A skidoo is another word for a snowmobile, but in Alaska they're known as snowmachines. I rode one a few years ago in Lapland, but the technology seems to have moved on since then. They're bulkier, and the speedo goes all the way up to 120, and that's miles, not kilometres. I'm told the record for the sixty miles from here to Chitina is forty-eight minutes without a crash-helmet. Apparently there's a problem with alcohol-related snowmachine deaths, and you can see why. They bounce around so much you'd be in a serious danger of losing control every time you took a swig. Thirty-five is about my limit, and even then I'm wincing into the wind like old man Steptoe with his nuts trapped in the deep-freeze. I've just reached the footbridge that crosses the river – in the summer this is where the road to McCarthy ends, but in winter you can drive a vehicle or snowmachine right across the frozen river – when I'm confronted by a convoy of antique trucks and buses straggled along the river bank. Several large

St Bernards are tethered to the trucks, straining at their leashes and barking at me. All around the vehicles, standing, sitting, and carrying or pulling things, are people in floppy leather hats, old-fashioned dungarees, floor-length embroidered skirts and buckskin jackets. I appear to have stumbled into a scene from *The Grapes of Wrath*. At the centre of the group a man has stopped to watch me pass. With his folksy clothes, long grey hair and bandana he looks like Willie Nelson on a good day. He waves as I pass, and a couple of children join in. I wave back, and almost lose control of the snowmachine as it goes careering down the riverbank. Thank God I wasn't trying to have a drink at the same time. You can see how those accidents could happen.

'That'll be the Pilgrim family. They said they'd be back. I guess you picked a good time to come.'

Neil and I are sitting up in the bar. There's just the two of us. Midweek can get kind of quiet on the wilderness social calendar. It's late but light, Beth Nielsen Chapman's on the stereo, and it feels like the temperature's dropping. The days have been brilliantly clear and sunny with the snow starting to thaw by lunchtime, then freezing overnight to leave a shiny, glossy crust that crunches underfoot.

Neil has been a perfect host since I got here, digging out books, photos and papers for me, phoning people who might know something about James McCarthy – so far without any luck – and even taking time to give me a masterclass in how to drive a snowmachine.

'This is how you make it go. This is how you make it stop. That's it.'

He and Doug have been partners for fourteen years. They've been running the McCarthy Lodge for eight months. It's one of those crackpot romantic schemes that never work out, only this time it seems that one has. Neil is originally from Boston, but

Doug grew up on a homestead in Alaska. When he was a kid his parents bought the McCarthy Lodge and fixed the place up. Doug hung the moose antlers over the door, and painted ROOMS, COLD BEER, MEALS on the windows. Then, in the 1980s, his parents sold up. Doug promised that one day he'd get it back, just like they do in the kids' story books; and now he has. They closed the deal on the lodge and several other plots and buildings at the end of last summer, and now Doug and Neil own a very large part of a very small place.

As well as the lodge, they have Ma Johnson's hotel, twenty yards away across the street, which is where I'm staying. I'm the only guest, so I can sit behind the desk in reception pretending I'm wearing a waistcoat and a bootlace tie and that Wyatt Earp is about to walk in. Doug has brought his designer's eye to bear on the old building, which was named after the original formidable Finnish owner. There's a burgundy pressed-tin ceiling, green velvet drapes, antique clocks and furniture, and a ceiling fan turning even in winter. Other buildings are being restored in traditional style. There will be a hostel, a deli and another bar. 'There'll still be fewer than sixty beds. McCarthy used to be much bigger than this. We're not aiming to be Las Vegas,' says Neil.

'Pity about the brothels though. If we could have one, we would.'

And now they're facing what might be the biggest redevelopment of all.

'There aren't many towns whose population could be doubled by the arrival of just one family,' says Neil, getting me another Black Butte porter from the old wooden-doored fridge, 'but that's what'll happen when the Pilgrims move in to McCarthy. Were these the guys you saw?' He hands me a large photo album. It's them. 'We all thought we were weird, but these guys just raised the bar.'

*

I wake with a start and look at the bedside clock. Ten past five. So why didn't the alarm go off? I get up, brush my teeth, look at the clock again, and realise it's only ten past three. I ought to be angry, but I'm not. It isn't often you can give yourself a two-hour lie-in when you're getting up at five in the morning.

I get up again two hours later and put on all the clothes I own, together with some I have borrowed. Starting with thermal underwear and ending with a jumper as heavy as an orang-utan, topped by a fleece topped by a woollen jacket topped by a full-length waxed Driza-Bone, I can walk with all the free-flowing grace of a medieval knight in sheet-metal armour who's just been knocked off his carthorse by one of those spiky balls on the end of a chain. I put one foot in front of another, totter out through the lobby and stand on the veranda of Ma Johnson's. No doubt about it, it's cold out here. I pull the sheepskin hat with earflaps hard down on my head. In England people may point and laugh, but out here this piece of comedy headgear is all that stands between me and frostbite of the brain. As I wait I rummage around in the dozens of pockets I have at my disposal for something to provide a little comfort. In the sixth or seventh I strike lucky. It's a grubby packet containing three sweeties of some kind. What does the wrapper say? Lockets! They have melded together and will take some separating once I've scraped the worst of the fluff off. Are they still making them? Surely not. It's possible they've been in my pocket since the miners' strike.

I've just popped the partially upholstered lozenge into my mouth when I hear barking, distant at first, then closer as Jeremy appears at the far end of the frozen street, bang on time at five thirty, standing high on the back of the sled as the eight huskies gallop towards me for all they're worth. Jeremy pulls them to a reluctant halt, throws an anchor into the snow, and I get on board as fast as I can. The sled lurches forward, my head snaps back, and we're off, me sitting down just above ground level,

Jeremy standing behind me holding the reins and mushing the excited little buggers for all he's worth. We hiss past the lodge and now town has gone and we're gliding through woodland wilderness, following the path of the old mining railway up to Kennicott. Thirty miles away to my left the 18,000-foot peak of Mount Blackburn is glowing limpid pink in the first rays of morning. This is a hell of a way to kick-start the day.

The Locket turns out to be a masterstroke. It's like having a coal fire glowing in a cold house in winter, the house in this case being my face, sprayed and spiked with early morning ice and snow, which isn't an altogether unpleasant sensation. The rest of me is warm and comfortable, though I hadn't reckoned on being directly in line with the dogs' bottoms, which have an assertively gaseous, early-morning quality about them.

We're about a mile out of town when I remember what Rick said last night. I hope the bears really are still asleep. After all, I'm not asleep, even though I should be, so what if they've had the same idea? People say the best way to survive a bear attack is to make sure you're with someone who can't run as fast as you; a party of primary-school children, perhaps, or an ageing, infirm relative. Jeremy lives in a tent with a pack of dogs and spends all day climbing around on a roof in sub-zero temperatures hitting things with a hammer. He is intimidatingly fit. In my condition, and dressed the way I am, I doubt if I could outrun the Before woman in the 'I Lost 200 lbs in 10 Days' adverts. My only chance would be that I'm wearing so many layers the bear would tire before it got through to my tasteless battery-produced flesh and would head into town for an organic free-range construction worker instead. And as for getting treed – well, I honestly can't see how you'd manage that. These trees are thin, straight, lacking branches and not very high. I suppose you might be so scared you could leap twelve feet and cling to the top like Velcro, but the bear would just bide his time, grinning and shaking the tree while he worked up an appetite.

We've been going a couple of miles when Jeremy tells me it's my turn to drive. This could be his first big error of the day. We swap places, I whip out the anchor as instructed, and we're off. It's even better standing than sitting. We're on a straight, flat stretch, which is why he's let me have a go, but it seems unlikely I'll ever be able to stop this thing. 'Hit the brake,' screams Jeremy. I drop my full body weight and the huge poundage of clothing on to a saw-toothed metal bar underneath my heel, and we slither to a halt. I fix the anchor into the ice feeling quite pleased with myself. Pete the Dogmusher. This afternoon I'll practise the hill start and reversing round a corner.

We stop at Kennicott and take a look at the old mine buildings. The hundred-year-old timber structures still look solid, though roofs are missing, windows are shattered and paint is peeling. It's recently been declared a national monument or some such, so soon it'll be all done up and looking like it's just been built. I feel a keener link with the past seeing it like this. Everything all came and went so quickly. In 1900 there was nothing here; three decades of intense activity, and it was all gone again. The view has changed as well. Kennicott used to look out on a glacier so big it obscured the mountains behind it. Today the glacier is still there, but so much has melted that now you look down on to it, and across at mountains the miners never saw. On the edge of town someone has nailed a pig's head on top of a post, but you don't like to ask, do you?

Jeremy unleashes the dogs for a rest. They behave like drunken students, rolling round in the snow and eating mouthfuls of it, but show no inclination to run as fast as they can into the far distance as they've been doing all morning. They just frolic round Jeremy, staring up at him, because in their world he is a god. One by one he hitches them back up and they're straining to go. They just can't get enough of this running thing. We stop at the miners' cemetery, its picket fence and wooden crosses peeping out over the top of the snowdrifts, then head back to McCarthy by a route that follows the old wagon trail through the woods. This is how the materials to build the town and the mine were hauled up, and parts of it are very steep. 'You ready for this?' shouts Jeremy, as the dogs start racing hell for leather down a woodland equivalent of the Cresta run. The cold night means conditions this morning are fast. There's a loud scraping sound from behind, because Jeremy has the brake full on to slow us down to an almost-safe speed so we don't career off the trail and disappear down the glacier. It's tremendously exhilarating. We reach the bottom of the hill and I just want to do it again. 'More! Now! Action replay!' But the trail's gone flat and stays like that all the way into McCarthy. Jeremy slows down long enough to roll me out in front of the hotel like a Mafia victim, then off they charge back to his tent, where the dogs will have a huge meal, then spend the rest of the morning smoking cigars and watching daytime TV.

I'm not cold apart from my cheeks and my ears, but the rest of me is tingling in a new and unusual way. I peel back the layers and spend quarter of an hour in the hottest shower I can bear. Awapuhi shampoo with Hawaiian ginger infused with silk and panthenol has been laid on for the wilderness explorer who likes to keep that soft and natural look while he's roughing it. Afterwards I shave, a vivid, sensual experience zinging with imagined shades of deep-frozen aquamarine and crystalline blue. It's time for breakfast, but I don't think I'll bother.

Just joking. I'm so hungry I could bite off Ozzy Osbourne's head and eat it if there was brown sauce to dip it in. I head over to the lodge and join Jeremy and the other site workers in their attempt on the world blueberry pancakes and maple syrup record. Jeremy has to work a nine-hour day in the cold, but I may allow myself a brief sit-down on the generously padded sofa in Ma Johnson's lobby. I feel great. I wish every day started like this.

*

When I wake up, the photo album Neil gave me last night is on the coffee table by the sofa. I pick it up and take another look. It was a lot to absorb in one go. 'To our Neighbours here at McCarthy', says a note in the front. 'Our Pilgrimage has been long and full of hardships and pure joy. We've left a beautiful homeland to follow our Vision which we know is Glory Bound. Examine our Souls – the simplicity and love that years of Mountain Living has brought, and also sent us here. We also have brought a Lot of True Love with us in Jesus.'

The book is their introduction to the people of McCarthy. There are sixteen in the family: Ma, Pa and fourteen kids, with another one on the way. "I am called 'Pilgrim'," writes Pa next to a picture of himself wearing a cowboy hat, playing a guitar and leaning on a tree. "I am a stranger here on this earth, but only for a short season till my Lord comes. I came from Texas and a life of Riches and Pride. Country Rose was young and confused when we met in the deserts of California, having lived her childhood in the glitter of Hollywood's Neon Fame ... together we set out on our Pilgrimage." There is a picture of Country Rose holding an upright double bass. A raven called Shadrak is standing on the end of it.

The album tells their life story. For nearly twenty years they lived in a remote part of New Mexico, adding to their cabin as more children were born, raising goats and horses, and erecting an enormous wooden cross. They tanned their own leather and made their own buckskin. One day they went to a bluegrass music festival and were inspired. They bought a load of second-hand instruments, then drew lots to decide which family member would play which one. When hikers and tourists began to discover their homestead they hit the road, learning their instruments as they travelled and adopting the name Heaven's Hillbillies. For three years they wandered around Alaska in search of a new home, and a few months ago they happened on McCarthy. And yesterday they moved in.

The photographs that accompany the story might have been taken in the sixties, or the Depression, or the nineteenth century. They show settlers heading for a new frontier with their hats, their goats and their Lord. The children, whose ages range from one to twenty-six, have names from a biblical epic relocated to the American west: Elishaba, Job, Psalms, Jerusalem, Hosanna, Lamb. Nobody in McCarthy knows where they plan to live.

I take the album back over to the lodge, where a photograph has arrived by e-mail from Anchorage. 'Copper Nugget – Copyright Miles Bros, 1903', says a caption. Five men are standing by a huge rock, looking like characters from a John Ford western, or the Pilgrim family album. They have hats, whiskers and waistcoats, and need to visit a laundry. The rock is a three-ton copper nugget, one of the biggest ever found. The smallest of the men, fourth from the left with his hand on one hip, hat tilted back, and sporting a bushy walrus moustache, is fixing the camera with a serious, narrow-eyed gaze. This is James McCarthy.

Today is mail day, when the plane that connects McCarthy with the outside world arrives and the townspeople assemble at the airstrip. It's a luminous, glistening morning, cold but dazzlingly bright. A handful of people are gathering packages and letters from the pilot when a pick-up truck arrives carrying sixteen people and three St Bernards, and the Pilgrim family step out to meet the town. I see Pa Pilgrim shake hands with Rick the grizzly-slaying pastor, and wonder how compatible their versions of Christianity will be. I wait till the plane has gone before introducing myself to Pa. The kids gather round, all ages and sizes, men and toddlers and teenagers and young women, listening to everything Pa has to say. 'We've been wandering like Abraham, but the road to McCarthy was the road God intended us to take.' He has a warm smile and extremely bright eyes. To survive the Alaskan winters on the road with fourteen kids takes considerable skill and resources, and is so far removed from most people's experience, and what I could ever achieve, that I'm keen to know more. He squeezes my arm, and says he'll catch up with me later in the week. He picks up one of the smallest children and they all head off to the truck. Before they leave, one of the boys comes back over with one of the St Bernards, which nearly knocks me off my feet. He asks if I'll be in town this evening, and I tell him I have no plans to be anywhere else. We'll come at seven then, he says. Or maybe eight. He smiles, and thanks me – these kids have impeccable manners – then climbs back into the truck and they head off.

Back at the lodge I have one of those defining, line-in-the-sand experiences that teach you an unforgettable lesson about who you really are. It's lunchtime, and the guys come clattering down from the roof to eat. It's the kind of climate that encourages a healthy appetite, and the two large trays of baked lasagne that looked as if they would feed three times as many people are soon empty. There's a happy buzz of conversation, though it doesn't involve Guy the generator guy, who hasn't spoken since breakfast the day before yesterday, though to be fair he made a joke then and it might have worn him out. Bagels were being served, and Guy doesn't like bagels. Someone remarked how good the bagels were in New York. 'Yes,' said Guy, in a Stan Laurel deadpan, 'bagels are very good in New York.' There was a moment's pause while we absorbed his meaning: that the best place for bagels is thousands of miles away from him, in New York. The applause was fulsome and enthusiastic.

So everybody's chatting away, speculating on where the Pilgrims might have bought land and whether the kids have ever taken a boyfriend or girlfriend home to meet the parents, when I look up to pour a glass of water. And there, right across the table from me, Jeremy is eating lasagne and bread and jam at the same time. So it's not just John the part-time park ranger. They're all at it! It's an *Invasion of the Body Snatchers* moment, as I realise that these people share a dark and sinister secret, and

I am not part of it. I'm half expecting the room to go quiet and Neil to pour jam on my pasta. I will look in turn, in big close-up, at each of their stubbled, self-sufficient, weather-hardened faces. 'Go on,' Guy the generator guy will say. 'Eat it.' And now I know that I couldn't do it. This is what it takes to survive in the wilderness – for all I know, a plate of curry and Victoria sponge cake may be next – and I'm just not made of the right stuff.

After lunch I drive the snowmachine out across the frozen river and along the first stretch of the McCarthy road to visit Jim, who I met at the mail delivery this morning. He moved to McCarthy in 1954, and has lived here longer than anyone else. There is a long straight snowy drive up to his house, which turns out to be his runway. In his garage are four planes, three of which he built himself. There's a little local runaround for shopping, a bigger one so he can take friends out, a tiny one on which he's doubled the capacity of the fuel tanks so he can fly to Oregon, and another two-seater he sometimes uses to collect the mail, though usually he prefers the three-mile walk.

Building, maintaining and flying your own plane must be the ultimate vote of confidence in your ability to look after yourself. If something breaks out here, there's nobody else to fix it. He built the house, the outbuildings and the aircraft hangar himself, and installed the solar heating system. He built a water wheel driven by a stream – when it isn't frozen – to power his domestic appliances. We go inside and take off our boots in the tool room he has built onto the house. There are vices, woodplanes, benches, welding goggles and hundreds of tools, each sitting snug in its own special place. You could build a Viking longship, or a space shuttle, in here, and for all I know he already has. For a non-handyman like me, to whom a socket set is as mystifying as the Dead Sea Scrolls, it is an intimidating place.

Inside the house Jim introduces me to his wife. They take out some maps and start showing me the wilderness beyond the wilderness. 'McCarthy is just the beginning. It's really kinda tame. You get into some of these regions' – he points towards coastline and mountain ranges where there are no roads or place names – 'well, it gets real big. And empty.' I think it's empty enough for me right here, thanks all the same. I'm starting to understand my limits. Wherever you go in the world, there will be people to tell you it'll be bigger, stranger, better, more authentic if you take the time to go somewhere else instead; but if you go there, you won't be here. You can only be in one place at a time, and sleep in one bed each night. Sometimes it's good to know where you are when you wake up. But I understand Jim's point, and take his word that McCarthy is where the wilderness really begins, even though to me it feels like the heart of it.

'This area here – now this is real remote. Sometimes we'll fly down there, hop around a bit, stop on beaches, maybe pick wild strawberries. There's one guy lives down there, a recluse called Brad. We call and see him if we're in the area. Last time, I noticed he had a skull on his mantel, so I asked him, "What's that, Brad?"

' "The last tourist," he said.'

You could mistake Jim for a fit, recently retired professional from the suburbs rather than a hermit or a backwoodsman, but this is his place, and he loves it. It's warm in the house – he's just finished building a sunroom with a hot tub – and I've taken off two or three outer layers. When it's time to leave, I put on a green fleece that Neil has lent me to cut back the wind chill on the snowmachine. I try to zip it up, but it catches, so I try again. This time the zip gets wedged on the teeth. I pull and tug it, almost break it, and it comes free. The third time, I can't even get the wretched thing started. I've never been good at zips. I look up, and Jim and his wife are watching me with expressions of quiet pity. I was hoping they hadn't noticed.

'What's the matter? Can't you zip your jacket?'

No, I'm afraid I can't. You can build aeroplanes and water

wheels and pick strawberries where no other man has ever trod, but I can't even zip up a fleece. It's another lasagne and jam moment. I wouldn't last five minutes out here.

The room gets a little darker as the Pilgrims appear at the top of the road. The whole family is walking down towards the lodge in a tight-knit group, like a scene from *Gunfight at the OK Corral*, except they're not carrying any weapons. It's almost eight, but the sun's so bright it feels like late afternoon. They reach the door and come inside in a flurry of 'His' and 'Howdys'. I was wrong about the weapons. Pa's wearing a gun in a holster on his belt. The kids are carrying fiddles, guitars, banjos and mandolins, though sadly there's no sign of Shadrak or the stand-up bass.

Neil and Doug have laid out food and soft drinks on the breakfast table because the family will not set foot in the bar. 'None of the kids has ever drunk alcohol. Pa says they've never smoked dope,' says Neil. 'Never seen TV, watched a movie or listened to a CD either, as far as I know.' The kids have spotted the cheese and fruit and cake and cookies, but make no attempt to eat until someone offers the food around. A couple of them have bare feet. I'm not sure whether they took their boots off at the door or whether they walked down here in the snow like that. They take the instruments out of their cases and sit in a semicircle. There are twenty-six people in the room, and sixteen of them are Pilgrims. Pa makes a little speech of welcome, and then they start playing. It's electrifying, moving and raw. Elishaba, the eldest, alternates lead vocals with nineteen-year-old Joshua as they trade licks on their violins. They have powerful, cutting voices, strengthened by singing outdoors, and sound like themselves rather than imitations of anyone else. Thirteen-year-old Jerusalem is a ferocious mandolin player, standing to take instrumental breaks then taking her seat again as her brothers and sisters, and Ma and Pa, continue the vocals. They've already written two songs about McCarthy, and they play them both tonight. At one point they put all the instruments down and sing a cappella in multi-part harmony. Neil calls out a title, and they start doing requests. By now the three tiniest girls are holding hands and dancing in a circle, and the only ones not involved are two of the boys, about seven and nine years old at a guess – I think it would be hard to keep track even if you were their dad – who are lurking at the back. Suddenly they charge forward and start clog-dancing for all they're worth, legs jiggling and big boots flailing beneath wild grins as the whole room comes alive with them. It's been a special evening. It's hard to believe they've only been playing for four years, and it'll be no surprise if in years to come some of these kids are earning a living playing in brighter lights than McCarthy can offer. By the time they finish, we are indeed in hillbilly heaven.

Afterwards Pa tells me about the land they've bought, in a valley on the McCarthy Creek twenty miles out of town. Some of the locals are saying it's so remote and the trail so inaccessible they won't be able to get the vehicles up there, especially in these freeze-thaw-freeze conditions. 'We're gonna be okay,' says Pa Pilgrim. 'Don't make it in one day, we'll take two. Don't make it in two, then three. Whatever it takes. We got ropes, winches, all kinds of stuff. These kids can do most things.' As if to prove the point a woman has come in looking for help because it's dark now and the headlight on her snowmachine has failed. 'I can do that,' says a small boy, who may possibly be eight-year-old Job, but they're moving round so fast it's difficult to keep track. 'I'll take the light off one of ours, fit it on to hers.' And he goes outside into the snow and the dark, and he does.

Before they leave Pa invites me to come and stay with them up at the Creek next time I'm in town. I have a fleeting vision of lasagne, jam and a big wooden cross, and fear I won't be able to cope, but say yes anyway. Neil takes them across the gleaming sheet-ice to see the work Doug has done on Ma Johnson's, of which he is touchingly proud. Doug and I adjourn to the bar for a drop of the devil's brew. He sees me looking at one of the framed photos on the wall. 'That's my mom outside the lodge hugging John Denver.' I thought it was.

It's almost midnight when I head across to Ma Johnson's to go to bed. Pa Pilgrim and Country Rose and Neil are sitting in the lobby talking, with a selection of children asleep in chairs and sofas all around them. They pick up a couple of the smallest kids, and the big kids pick up some of the medium-sized ones, and they say goodnight and head off into the darkness to their makeshift camp. I wonder how things will turn out for them and the town of McCarthy? Whatever happens, it seems unlikely to be dull. Seventeen people can't fail to make an impact.

Next day there's a fax for me from a National Park historian in a place called Copper Center. He has a little more information about James McCarthy. He staked a major claim, known as the Valdez Lode, above Nugget Creek in 1905; and he drowned while fording the Tonsina River in 1910. And at a time when most prospectors were searching for copper, gold, silver or any damn thing that would make their fortune, McCarthy specialised only in copper.

A copper man, with a West Cork name. Judging from the photograph, he'd have been born around 1870, which would coincide with one of the great waves of Irish emigration. Maybe his father was a mining man who came out from Beara, and James was born out here; or perhaps he even came out from Ireland himself. It's become a puzzle, and now I'm hooked.

Who was James McCarthy?

I call Copper Center, and they tell me they'll check the Alaska records for the census of 1900, and see if anything turns up. In the meantime I decide to take a look in the little museum on the edge of town. It's been closed since September and won't open until summer, but apparently the door at the back is only held shut with a piece of wire, and I can let myself in if I tie it again when I leave.

It's cold outside, but colder in the museum. According to the book I'm the first visitor for seven months. There's a lot of dust and cobwebs, and I feel like a detective shaking the place down for clues as I search for any mention of James McCarthy. There are some fine panorama photographs by J. P. Hubrick, whose studio was converted into the McCarthy Lodge in 1954 by local pilot Mudhole Smith, so called because he once made a mistake and landed in a mudhole. They never let you forget, as I'm sure Moosefondler George will testify.

Another picture shows a bear on its hind legs looking through the window of a fragile-looking wooden building not dissimilar to the one I'm in now. There's an old barber's chair, a cash register and a copper still like the one that dripped on Slim Lancaster's head. Doug told me he has Slim's original, and plans to install it in the new bar when it's built. There's no mention of the man the place was named after, but I do find a newspaper cutting to brighten my day. It's from the *Kennecott Star* of 1938, underneath the headline NEW SHIPMENT OF 30 CASES OF EGGS, BIGGEST EVER:

John Letendre says he has no use for an egg that won't stand up for itself. He says he once had a trained egg that would roll over at the word of command.

He spent a long winter training the egg but while showing it off to some friends one day he made it roll over so many times it became scrambled. As it had been a pet he couldn't eat it himself but, being short of grub, he gave it to his malamute dog. Later in the same evening he was thinking sadly of his lost pal and happened to say the same words he used with the egg. The dog rolled over just the same as the egg had done.

John felt better after that and, he says, he knew the egg had found a good home.

I suppose sometimes the solitude gets to you and there's just nothing you can do about it.

'Hey, dude. Who's that, like, third guy on your shirt, man?'

'I dunno, man. Aerosmith. It's a cheap shirt.'

It's early evening and the bar is packed. There must be about ten or eleven of us. Sun is streaming through the window, people are playing pool, and noisy rock-'n'-roll is on the stereo. There's that feeling of unbounded optimism you sometimes get at the start of a lively drinking session, before it all goes wrong and people start arguing about things they'd never intended talking about in the first place. There's a mood of rapidly escalating euphoria as people order back-to-back rounds of beer and tequila from the bartender.

I am the bartender.

It's a fairly straightforward job. No money actually changes hands. There are just ten or eleven little pads on the bar with ten or eleven names on, and you run a tab until the end of the month. Jeremy's just confused me by ordering what I thought was a soft drink. So what is Long Island Iced Tea, if it isn't something that a non-denominational pastor would drink with his moose stew?

'Shot of tequila, shot of vodka, shot of gin, shot of rum, shot of triple sec, just a splaaaash of Coke. Spirit salad, man!'

He laughs, and somewhere between here and Anchorage there is a small avalanche. Meanwhile someone has managed to worm their way behind me and sneak Queen's *Greatest Hits* onto the stereo. 'Arright! Greatest rock-'n'-roll band in the world,' shrieks Jeremy. 'Pink Floyd,' claims someone else. 'The Who!' shouts someone from the next room.

'They're all English,' I protest. 'Get your own rock bands. You invented it, didn't you? C'mon, who've you got?'

'Led Zeppelin!' comes the reply.

It's a long time since I worked behind a bar, and I'd forgotten what a grandstand seat it gives you for earwigging other people's conversations.

'I see one this year, I'm gonna kill it. I want me a bear rug. Just my luck if I don't have my rifle with me when I see one. Still, I'll always have a pistol. That's the thing with those 45s, that whole Rambo thing. They feel so good to shoot.'

The speaker is the young woman who serves breakfast and lunch.

'Last year I went camping? Wanted to see one so much I left a bowl of beef stew out on a log, still didn't get to see one. Bummer.'

Someone chips in with a story about her friend who came home from school for lunch one day when she was eight and saw a dog sniffing round some groceries on the porch. She smacked its butt and went in and told her mom. Mom went out, then came back and said, 'Honey, it's a bear. That's it. You're having glasses.'

The breakfast lady tells us about the fight she had to break up last night between two of her dogs – 'Had to kick it in the face, split its nose' – and now everyone's joining in with their own hideous dog anecdotes.

'I hate it when you have to force their teeth apart.'

'Like with pit bulls?'

'Right.'

'I've been bit more times with dogs fighting than any other time.'

'Don't be afraid to use a hard object.'

'Baseball bat?'

'No. Might kill 'em. A shovel is perfect. Hit 'em with the handle; that don't work, use the metal end. Still won't kill 'em.'

'And if it does, you can always dig a hole with it.'

A geeky guy in a Ramones T-shirt who could double as a character from *Northern Exposure* has just turned up. He orders a beer, I mark his tab, then he says, 'Bears are awake.' There's a stunned silence – not in the bar, where everyone's still yattering away – but inside my head.

'The little four-year-old kid, plays out on the skis all day? Saw one today behind their house, on the edge of town. Said the bear just ran away. Lucky kid.'

Did I mention that I'm leaving in the morning?

The word is that the road is just about passable. Two women from town, Ali and Chris, are driving to Anchorage in a Toyota pick-up to collect supplies, and they can give me a lift. As we leave after breakfast the Pilgrims are preparing to head up to their mountain valley. I say my goodbyes, and we walk the mile to the truck, which is parked on the other side of the river. As we go I'm weighing up the situation, wondering if I could outrun either of them if it came down to it. This bear anxiety is getting out of control. We reach the truck and I get in, wondering why on earth anything would want to eat seats like these.

It takes three hours to cover the sixty miles to the paved road at Chitina. It's a tough drive through ruts and potholes and glacial debris, but I hope the Alaskan authorities never upgrade it. Easy access would change McCarthy for ever. I can't imagine how the Israeli made it out here in the Escort. Ali says that last year a friend of hers found a rental car in a ditch. The doors were open and there was a bottle of Jack Daniels on the seat. A couple of miles further on he found a Japanese tourist pulling one of those suitcases on wheels with an extendable handle. 'He'd seen some strange things out here, but that was the strangest.' He gave him a lift into town, and the tourist paid Kelly to fly him to Anchorage. 'Just left the car right where it was.'

We stop for a break at the bridge that used to have no sides, just wooden planks, slightly wider than a vehicle, across a 300-foot drop. 'Two guys bought a pig, were bringing it back to town, they bungeed it off here.'

They what?

'They bungeed the pig down the canyon. Pig kinda liked it, and it gave them the idea to bungee some people. To attract business, they offered free jumps to any Alaskans who would jump naked, but there were so many takers they had to stop.'

At the end of the road we pull over to look for the Worst Road in Alaska sign, but the road's so bad we can't find it. Then we hit the highway, and they let me drive through countryside so magnificent it makes Montana look like the Chelmsford ring road. Each time you think the mountains have ended, more appear like a mirage.

As we get close to Anchorage we start to see other cars and people, which feels rather alarming. If you stay in the wilds for years at a time you must get a terrible shock when you come to town, especially if you walk into your hotel dazed and confused after a ten-hour drive, as I have just done, to find thirty women with big hair in the lobby wearing emerald-green velvet evening gowns and singing a barbershop-harmony version of 'Something' by the Beatles. The place is packed with hundreds of other women, many of them with even bigger hair. Three are in powder-blue cowboy shirts, but most have opted for frocks made of upholstery fabric. What in God's name is going on?

'The Sweet Adelines,' says the porter in the lift.

Who?

'A convention of close-harmony singing groups. Two thousand of them in town for the weekend. And the crown princess of Thailand is checking in later, with forty bodyguards.'

Of course she is. She probably comes to Alaska all the time. Will she be singing too?

'I really couldn't say, sir. But the Sweet Adelines are performing a melodrama in the ballroom later tonight.'

And so it is that just before midnight, in a hotel at the end of the world, I find myself watching twenty-five Dustin Hoffman-in-*Tootsie* lookalikes in tassels, polka dots, wigs and rouge sing a barber shop version of 'God Bless America'. Most of them are big women and proud of it, but the one on the end is so thin in comparison with her colleagues that she looks like some kind of optical illusion. The melodrama has just ended, and I am shell-shocked. When I handed in my ticket a woman gave me a bag of popcorn. 'I don't eat popcorn,' I said.

'It's not for eating, silly.'

'What's it for?'

'It's for throwing at the villain.'

The show went by in a blur of colour and unlikely harmonies as I made as many trips to the bar as I could manage without causing an incident. One line from the show has lodged itself forever in my mind: the saying Alaskan women have for the fact that their state has so many more men than women.

'The odds are good, but the goods are odd.'

I'm going up in the elevator when I realise I'm still holding the popcorn. If I bump into the Princess of Thailand, maybe I'll throw it at her.

Back in my room there is a message waiting.

'I checked the Alaskan census records, but couldn't find any mention of our James McCarthy. I suspect he must have been somewhere else when the census was completed, making him very tough to track. Good luck on your journey.'

13

TO TRAVEL IN HOPE

'Have we ever had a bald Taoiseach?'

'I don't believe we have. What's your point?'

'Well, that's my point. Hair matters to the voters.'

'Are you bald yourself?'

'Ah, no. Not completely anyway. I'll admit to follically challenged. If anyone says it's a bald patch, I tell them it's a solar panel for a sex machine.'

I'm listening to one of my favourite talk and phone-in programmes as I head south and west from Dublin airport. It's sunny, but the windscreen-wiper on the rear window is going like fury. As I have never owned a vehicle less than a decade old, the up-to-the-minute technology of hire cars is a source of constant grief. I can't stop the wiper because I don't know how I turned it on in the first place. I've tried pressing and pulling the little stick on the steering column that has a picture of wipers on it, and so far it's sounded the horn, indicated left, and squirted water on a couple who were pushing airport luggage trolleys over a zebra crossing. There were also problems with the radio.

In a desperate attempt to escape the techno music on the pre-sets I hit SEARCH, but the wretched thing just kept racing through the FM numbers without stopping. The combination of wiper squeaking behind and digits flashing in front was too much to bear, and I was reduced to jabbing at the stereo with my left index finger as if I were threatening it with a fight until it finally latched on to a station.

We've already had an item about a guy caught in possession of cannabis who claimed he only used it as resin for rubbing on his guitar strings, and now we've just moved on from the bald Taoiseach debate to a discussion about whether George Lucas is a film-making genius, or the Antichrist. 'I've seen it seventeen times, but I'm not a *Star Wars* anorak. I don't dress up in the costumes or anything mad like that,' says the guy calling in. 'I just collect the little people.'

It's Sunday, and the roads are packed. Most of the cars are as new as the one I'm driving, and the speed, volume and sheer affluence of the traffic is a potent reminder of the relentless pace of social change in Ireland. We did this drive often when I was a kid, and once you left Dublin there were no traffic lights until you arrived in Cork. Today you wouldn't know you were in the same country. The new wealth has provoked a fierce national debate about whether Ireland is on the point of losing the values that once made it distinctive, in a headlong materialist rush to be like everywhere else. The Bed and Breakfast signs tell their own story. Once upon a time they just said 'B&B', then they added 'TV' and 'En-Suite'. I just passed one that said 'Jacuzzi'. Mind you, it didn't mention whether it had gold taps. They really should tell you. You wouldn't be wanting a jacuzzi without gold taps. It smacks of poverty.

'Children are born with their backs to God and their feet towards hell! God wouldn't have given them backsides if he didn't believe they deserved chastisement.'

Well, it's a point of view, I suppose. I turn off the pastor from Antrim, and the ignition, outside the courthouse in Clonmel. I'm expecting the wiper to keep on going, like fingernails growing on a dead man, but it seems to have thrown in the towel. I get out of the car and take a deep breath. What's that peculiar smell?

The building where Meagher, O'Brien and the rest were sentenced looks in fine fettle, its stately columns and arches gleaming much as they might have the day the men were marched down here from the jail. The court's not in session and a caretaker's just closing up, but he lets me nip in for a quick look at the room in which they were tried. The modern fittings can't conceal the fact that it's essentially the same grand Georgian space, and I give an involuntary shiver as I remember Maria Island and Port Arthur. Out in the entrance lobby I spot a lady in an academic cardigan with serious-minded spectacles dangling from a cord around her neck, so I sidle up and ask her if she knows anything about the Young Irelanders.

'Yes'.

Ah, I say, then would you know about the Widow McCormack's Cottage, the one with the cabbage patch?

'I do'.

'Do you know if it's still there?'

There's a pause, as if she's weighing up whether I'm the right kind of person to be in possession of such sensitive information.

'I'd say it's been gone a long time now.'

It's what I've been expecting to hear and my heart sinks a little bit, but I'm determined to get something positive from this encounter.

'How about Hearn's Hotel?'

'Twenty yards away, at the end of the street.'

As I come out into the half-light I notice an underfunded-looking modern building directly across the narrow street. 'Arts Centre', says a sign above the door. I walk across to take a look. It's closed and the place is in darkness, but there's a tiny handwritten note on the front door. TONIGHT 8 p.m. – SHANE MACGOWAN DISCUSSES HIS SONGWRITING. TICKETS ON DOOR. I remember his triumphant performance in the dance-hall in Greenwich Village, and Chris and Rachel and Seanchai and Phil and the actors, and think how strange he should turn up again here, in the wrong part of my story, while I'm trying to find the historic cabbage patch. Perhaps it was meant to happen like this. Maybe Shane knows where the Widow McCormack used to live. I walk up the road to Hearn's, check in, and come back and form a queue behind three young Pogues fans who are sharing a litre bottle of cider.

It might be my imagination, but, now I think of it, the whole town seems to smell of cider.

The show's over, and I'm sitting on a stool at the bar in the hotel. MacGowan is four stools away, staring into a drink. Two musicians are setting up at the far end under the TV, but the people in the room have eyes for only one man. These are not rock'n'roll fans, but the ordinary crowd of unassuming middle-aged drinkers you'll find in any small-town bar in Ireland, yet they seem mesmerised by his presence. Occasionally someone approaches and asks him to sign a beer-mat or cigarette packet, which he does with good grace before reassuming the morose slump and staring back into the bottom of his glass.

It was an intriguing evening. Sixty of us sat in neat rows in a tiny upstairs room, while Shane and a local journalist faced each other on a little podium across a half-pint glass of clear liquid with a slice of lemon in it. At first he seemed unwilling, or unable, to speak, leaving the interviewer with some withering pauses; but then he removed the rock-star shades and seemed to warm to the task, his lived-in eyes shifting in and out of focus as he spoke of songs inspired by bar-stool conversations, and of lyrics forgotten for want of a pencil and paper. Someone in the audience asked what's the most recent song he's written, and he grinned before launching into an a cappella rendition of a ballad about being buggered by a bishop, which had the whole place in stitches. He was most passionate when talking about Irish culture, Irish music and the things he hates about England, despite the fact that a life lived mostly in London has left him with that city's accent. In his black drinking suit – possibly the same one he wore in New York – with drink and fag constantly in hand, he seemed almost consciously to be casting himself as the new Brendan Behan, a rough-and-ready man of the people gifted with poetic brilliance. In an era of boy bands and stadium rockers he makes a convincing keeper of the Irish tradition, despite having been born in Kent and attended Winchester public school. Songwriters are under no obligation to sit in front of people and explain their work, and I admired him for being prepared to do it, especially in his grandparents' county of Tipperary.

I know it's probably a mistake to approach him here in the hotel bar, but I'm intrigued that our paths should cross at such different points in my journey. I'll only regret it if I don't, and I do empathise with his English-Irish dilemma; and anyway haven't I still got that Very Important Paddy laminate from New York, and isn't it the least I could do to thank him? So I edge along the bar and say his name, then say it again, and this time he looks up from the drink and already I feel foolish. Why didn't I just leave the guy alone, but I'm here now and I'll have to go through with it, so I say, 'I'm a friend of Chris and Rachel's.'

Nothing.

'From New York.'

Nothing.

'From Rocky Sullivan's.'

Nothing, though I think I'm sensing contempt.

'I saw the St Patrick's Day show last year. It was really good.'

And he stares at me, eyes half closed yet at the same time full of dislike, and says, 'I already bloody know that.'

As I turn to go a guy standing behind him catches my eye.

Perhaps he's the minder. He shrugs his shoulders and says, 'I think an English accent is the last thing he wants to be hearing in South Tip.' A woman ordering at the bar hears and turns to me and laughs and says, 'Sure doesn't he have one himself.' This is the only occasion in a lifetime visiting Ireland that my accent has ever been an issue, the very first time, and isn't it marvellous that it's come from a guy who sounds like a Brit himself. Funny business, this old identity thing.

Half an hour later the musicians are still playing as Shane gets up from his stool, focuses on the door, then heads slowly towards it. The whole room bursts into a round of applause. Some of them are standing. It's extraordinary. They're clapping him for being him, for existing, for writing those songs, for still being alive. If it's a populist Irish hero he wants to be, then he's got it. Happiness, though, might be another thing entirely.

Though it's seen better days, Hearn's turns out to be a fine place to stay. There's an air of down-at-heel gentility that's reflected in the low price of the rooms, and an all-round mood of atmospheric shabbiness that I find alluring. The place isn't showing off and nobody's trying too hard, and at its heart is an excellent bar with original fittings, and possibly some of the original customers. It is an old coaching inn, and was the hub of Ireland's first public transport system, founded in 1815 by Carlo Bianconi, an Italian who as a boy had walked across the Alps and France on his way to Ireland. Understandably peeved at the discovery that unless you were rich you had to walk everywhere in Ireland as well, he bought a job-lot of horses from the army, who were selling them cheap after Napoleon's defeat at Waterloo, and set up a stage-coach business. By the mid-nineteenth century the whole of Ireland was linked in a network with its epicentre at Hearn's. It can't be long before it's swept up in the tide of affluence washing down from Dublin and is turned into a smart heritage hotel with prices to match, and a plaque saying that Shane MacGowan once drank here, but I have to say I like it fine the way it is.

When I was checking out I solved the mystery of the smell. According to a woman at reception, the all-pervasive fragrance of a carpet after a two-day cider party is a consequence of there being a cider factory in town, and sometimes that's the way the wind blows. I expect it's quite pleasant once you get used to it. It's certainly reassuring to discover it's not just me. When you start smelling cider for no apparent reason, you can be certain the secure sheltered accommodation isn't very far down the line.

The soft rain is falling hard this morning, but even in this dank light the river and the wooded hills rising up beyond it look wonderful. Like the hotel, the town itself has resisted homogenisation. There is a pleasing collection of old buildings and shopfronts, interspersed with the occasional kebab outlet to remind you how things could go if people aren't careful. I walk along O'Connor Street as far as Westgate, the archway through which the Irish were required to leave the walled Anglo-Norman town each day at dusk – the area beyond it is still called Irishtown – and then double back to Jailgate. The prison where the Young Irelanders were held is long gone. All that remains is a gate marked by an inscription.

> *How hard is my fortune*
> *And vain my repining*
> *The strong rope of fate*
> *For this young neck is twining*
> *My strength is departed*
> *My cheek sunk and sallow*
> *While I languish in chains*
> *In the gaol of Cluain Meala*

The prisoners would have walked past Hearn's to get from here to the courthouse, which is what I do now as I head back to the car to go looking for the widow.

*

The weather's closing in from all sides as I drive north from Clonmel towards Ballingarry. There's a lot of water on the road and on a bend near a bridge I'm almost wiped out by a huge Guinness lorry, which would have been a terrible irony, but I suppose a kind of immortality. It would probably be lovely scenery around here if you could see it, but as well as driving through three different kinds of rain simultaneously – soft, hard and wet – an opaque mist has descended, and now the inside of the windscreen has fogged up as well. Perhaps I'm crossing some kind of time barrier, and as I round the next bend a squadron of nineteenth-century troops will loom up out of the mist to trap me in the stories I've been pursuing.

At the precise moment I pass the sign that says BALLINGARRY I'm hit by an overwhelming fragrance of turf-smoke. For me burning peat is one of the most evocative of childhood smells, like potatoes roasting during *Round the Horne*, or the all-enveloping malt and hops of Greenall's Brewery as we used to get off the school bus in St Helens. The prefect for my first year, the big grown-up lad in long trousers keeping an eye out for all us littlies in shorts, was Pete Postlethwaite, who grew up even more and then became a famous actor. Whenever I see him in a film it comes with the sensurround aroma of that brewery in St Helens. It's the same with turf. One of the most memorable things about childhood visits to Ireland was that my uncles could cut lumps out of the ground with a spade, then burn them on the fire. I experimented with bits dug from the lawn in Lancashire, but they barely smouldered. I know these days it's mostly processed briquettes they're burning rather than the real sod, but, like a gust of hops on the air, or a glimpse of Pete Postlethwaite on celluloid, the scent of turf still takes me back to another place and time.

I didn't know whether to expect any memorial or acknowledgement of the Young Irelanders in the village, but in fact there is one, albeit so understated you'd have no sense of its significance unless you already knew: '1848', say two grey marker stones on two grey walls, barely visible through the increasingly monochrome weather in what may be the centre of the village, though it's very hard to tell. It's completely deserted, so there's nobody to ask for directions. I drive on a couple of hundred yards, as far as a ribbon of new houses whose fences are painted in Tipperary sporting colours, and then Ballingarry is no more, so I turn back.

I've brought Thomas Keneally's account of the fateful cabbage patch encounter with me, hoping to use it to pinpoint where the widow's cottage used to be. 'A small two-storeyed two-chimneyed house surrounded by a stone wall, on land named Boulagh Common,' writes Keneally. I drive down the only nearby lanes that might be contenders, because they are the only nearby lanes, but one dwindles to nothing in a farmyard, and the other takes a wrong direction and makes no sense in relation to the events of the fateful day. Back in the centre of the village, at the epicentre of the crepuscular damp, the post office and shop is resolutely closed, and it's possible it's been that way for generations.

I leave the car and walk towards the church, which is barely visible through the radar-defeating weather. As I begin to acclimatise I'm aware of a ghostly chipping sound cutting through the gloom like sonar. Across the hazy jumble of Celtic crosses and headstones I can see a blue plastic sheet draped like a bivouac over a grave, possibly concealing some kind of body-snatcher or amateur pathologist going about his grisly business. From the sound of it he's also talking to himself. They're usually the worst ones. I decide to approach him, because I have already realised there is nothing else to do in Ballingarry today. Hesitantly I creep up, trying both to surprise and not surprise him, as I can't work out which would be more dangerous. I can hear him muttering from beneath his morbid shelter as I approach.

'. . . and it's rumoured that a significant announcement on decommissioning might be forthcoming as early as this afternoon . . .'

So it's not a necrophiliac making pillow talk. It's the one o'clock news on a transistor radio. What peculiar synchronicity. Could the end of my Young Ireland pilgrimage be about to coincide with IRA disarmament? There are rumours of 'significant announcements' every nine months or so, then nothing happens, I'll grant you that, but maybe this time? I suppose you never know.

'Would ye like to come in out of the wet?'

He's peering up at me from under his bender, a Milo O'Shea type with creased laughter lines, snug in a tweed cap and distressed maroon V-neck. He's sitting on a grave, chipping an extra inscription on to a headstone with a hammer and chisel. I try and get a look at the name, just in case it's mine.

'Meanwhile American officials are warning that the Afghan conflict and the wider war against terrorism may not be resolved in our lifetime.'

I stoop under the plastic sheet and hunker down on the grave with him. With the politeness of someone who wants to welcome a stranger into his home but can't give up the company he gets from the airwaves, he turns the radio down, but not off. 'How are ye?' he enquires. I tell him I'm fine. This really is most peculiar.

I know it's an off-chance, I say, but I'm interested in a historical story – he's starting to look embarrassed, like a kid who's been picked out because the teacher knows he hasn't done his homework – a famous battle that was fought near here; well, smaller than a proper battle really. I'm burbling a bit now, because he can hear my accent and we both know the battles were always against the same opponents, and to make matters worse they're wittering on about decommissioning again in the background, but anyway I don't suppose he's heard of, or knows where I can find the site of, the Battle of Widow McCormack's Cabbage Patch?

'D'y'know I'm embarrassed to say it, but I don't know as much about the history of my country as I ought to. I'd say ye might have the advantage on me there.'

He gives a warm smile and I tell him I think the battle was fought barely a mile or two from this very spot, so I wonder if perhaps there's a chance the priest might know?

'Ah, well, maybe he would, but ye know I really couldn't say. I'm not from round here myself. I'm from Callan.'

Callan is just a few miles away. It's where the police who took part in the battle marched from.

'D'y'know what I'd do if I were you now?'

I think I do. I was already thinking that way myself.

'Go for a pint, and while y're in the pub, ask them in there.'

It is an honest working man's panacea, and I'd be a fool to decline it. I emerge from the muggy, plastic-enshrouded necropolis into the real world, where the rain has eased off and the church is now as large as life. There are three pubs in the village; unfortunately all of them are closed, even Meagher's, so depriving me of a unique opportunity to have a pint in a pub named after a famous patriot and governor of Montana, in the very village where it all began to go wrong, or right, for him. As I walk back to the car a hand turns the CLOSED sign in the post office window to OPEN.

'Sure I do,' says the postmistress with an ah-come-on-you-patronising-sod laugh when I ask her if she knows about the battle. 'Is it the house you're looking for? Straight up past the church and the school, turn right at the second crossroads, you'll find it up the hill there.'

What – the house itself? It's still standing?

'I'd say so. The Ministry of Works are doing it up. I think they're hoping it might turn into a tourist attraction.'

I find it where she said it would be, off the lane up a newly laid driveway with creosoted fences and an empty car park. DEPARTMENT OF ARTS, HERITAGE, GAELTACHT AND THE ISLANDS, says a sign. SAFETY GOGGLES MUST BE WORN. HARD HATS MUST BE

WORN AT ALL TIMES. NO ADMITTANCE — AUTHORISED PERSONNEL ONLY. I park up and head on in. It looks just as it appears in the illustrations of the battle – four windows, two chimneys, some outbuildings, a water pump and a fenced-in garden – except there are no cabbages in the garden, and no rifles pointing out the windows, and it looks altogether newer and more pristine than I'd expected. THE WAR HOUSE, claims a rather grandiose inscription. SCENE OF THE 1848 RISING. ACQUIRED BY THE STATE 1998. Then underneath that, TAOISEACH BERTIE AHERN TD. Ain't it always the way: the politician gets his bit of immortality, but poor old Widow McCormack gets nudged out of the picture altogether.

There are none of the sounds you usually associate with a major construction project – work going on, that kind of thing – and I'm just starting to wonder whether perhaps Bertie's got his name on the wall because he's doing it up himself at weekends, when I notice three noses and six eyes watching me from over the top of a wall. They pop down out of sight, as if they're about to reload their muskets, so I walk through the gateway into the courtyard while I still have the advantage of surprise. Three builders are lying in wait looking a bit uneasy and shifty, as if I'm about to ask them why they never turned up to finish that kitchen conversion I paid them cash upfront for last July. There are two young lads and an older chap who looks like the foreman. All are distinguished by a complete lack of safety goggles and hard hats.

'Yes?' says the foreman.

I say that I'm very interested in the story of Smith O'Brien and Meagher and Mitchel and the others, and I've come a long way to be here, and I know it's not open to the public yet, but is there any chance I could take a quick look inside?

'The thing is, it isn't open to the public.'

'I know. I appreciate that. It's just that, like I say, I've come a long way and this story really means a lot to me.'

'It's not open to the public, see, so you can't really come in.'

'I know. I know that. It's just that, having come such a long way, it seems a pity . . .'

'I know. But it's not open to the public, so I can't be letting you in. Do you see my problem?'

'Of course I do. It's just that I've followed the story from Clonmel to Tasmania. Just a quick look would be all I'm after. I appreciate it isn't open to the public.'

'Ye'd better come in so.'

He shows me in while the two lads start hitting a piece of wood with a hammer to feign work in case I'm really some kind of undercover jobsworth from the Department of Arts. He's a most gracious guide, pointing out original floorboards, beams, cupboards and hearths where they remain, though mostly the house has been fixed up, like large parts of the rest of the country, with new materials. Still, I hadn't even expected it to be standing, so I'm just thrilled that it's here at all. I check with him that the small enclosed front garden now laid to lawn was the celebrated cabbage patch, and that O'Brien and the rebels were just twenty or so feet away, out there on the other side of that low garden wall.

'That's right.' He's pleased I know the story. 'They were out there, and the, er . . . in here, looking out, was where, you know . . .' – we make eye contact at this point – '. . . where the British were.' There. He's said it. Wasn't so bad after all, was it? In fact I'm pretty sure that most, if not all, the forces in the cottage were Irish police and soldiers loyal to the crown, but we don't want to go into that now, especially not with all this talk of decommissioning on the wireless.

I thank him for showing me round and he tells me to take a few minutes on my own to get a feel of the house if I want. Despite the just-painted look I feel privileged to be here midway between dereliction and Heritage, the first visitor to a brand-new Attraction. I hope they get it right, and it brings people fresh to the story of O'Brien the globetrotting Protestant fenian, Meagher, Mitchel and their friends. We always need good new stories, and the old ones are often the best.

On the way back to Clonmel the mist evaporates in a ninety-second meteorological epiphany to reveal bright sun pouring down from a cumulus-studded blue sky on to a patchwork landscape of rolling green fields studded with toytown cows. The thicker the mist, the more impressive the special effects that usually follow. You'd have little hope of convincing a new arrival how bleak the weather was looking just twenty minutes ago. The thin film of pure Irish mineral water greasing the tarmac would be the only forensic evidence you could submit in support of your claim, and that's already evaporating beneath my tyres in an incongruous, possibly miraculous, rainbow heat haze. The day still has many hours to run, and I'm not about to rule out the possibility of visions just yet. If the statues are ever going to start moving again, this would be as good an afternoon as any for them to give it a go.

Halfway back I pass through Fethard, a famous horse-racing village packed to the gills, according to its reputation, with those bright-eyed Irish jockeys and urbane matter-of-fact trainers you see forever being interviewed on British TV in the winners' enclosure. If you look closely you can usually see clutches of gleeful Irishmen in the dubious haberdashery of the betting fraternity, brandishing wads of cash on the other side of the railings. Fethard is completely deserted, as if all the people who weren't in Ballingarry an hour ago aren't here either. On my left as I head down the main street I pass a large pub called McCarthy's. I hit the brakes, reverse, park and go in.

There's a bar on the right, a pot-bellied stove on the left, and four lads are chatting at a table just inside the door. A grey-haired man in his sixties who looks as if this isn't the first time he's had a few drinks in the afternoon is sitting at the bar drinking stout, with what appears to be a dead dog on the floor beside him. A solitary barmaid has the look of someone who might do a bit of glass polishing or shelf stocking in a little while, but doesn't feel under any pressure to start just yet. The meteorological special effects were an omen, or possibly an opening sequence. You can't plan these moments. You just have to know them when fate sends them your way, and accept them for what they are.

I sit one stool away from the dead dog owner, order a drink and wait for something to happen. He's sitting sideways reading the paper with his back to me. He doesn't seem to have noticed I'm here, but then he breaks the ice with a classic ploy favoured by solo drinkers all over the world: he starts talking to himself out loud.

'Fockin' nonsense it is! Jaysus, but they must think that we're idiots! If that's what we're expected to believe, then where the fock has the rest of it gone!'

Then he pretends to notice me, as the *Good Drinker's Book of Bar Etiquette* demands. I nod and smile back as required, and he says, 'Is it on holiday y'are? So what part of England would ye be from?' So I tell him and he asks, 'Is that pub still there just across from the dog track in Hove? We did some drinking in that place. Years ago that was now, mind.'

What were you doing in Hove? I wonder.

'Sure I was on tour with the circus.'

This is pub chat of an extremely high calibre. Unhindered by the conventional topics of sport, weather and politics, eager to get off-script as quickly as possible, in seconds he has transported us into a magical-realist world of life as an itinerant circus hand in the Britain of the 1960s and 1970s, and he isn't going to stop while he's ahead, which may be most of the afternoon.

' 'Twas a great life all right, but because I was Irish they thought I knew everything about animals. I soon learned, mind. Shetland ponies? Fockn' vicious bastards they are. People buy 'em for their kids, but they get to six years old and they'll bite fockn' lumps outta ya.'

The dog opens one eye, possibly in rigor mortis, maybe in agreement.

'Chimps? Fockn' bastards! They'd go up the pole in the centre of the ring, then drop down into our arms. Heavy, nasty bastards they were. And the fockn' ostriches! God Almighty! You wouldn't want to go near those fockers!'

He starts to rock forward on his stool with laughter at the memory of it. The beer's already come down my nose twice.

'The fockn' ostriches fockn' escaped once in fockn' Southsea. We had to chase 'em, the nasty bastards' – he can't quite finish the sentence, and has to pinch the centre of his forehead between his thumb and first finger – 'chase the bastards with fockn' nets through the centre of fockn' town. Took seventeen elephants to the sea for a publicity stunt while we were there. Couldn't get the bastards out of the fockn' water. You'll have to excuse my language, but that bull elephant was a right cunt. And we had a fockn' rhinoceros!'

What did a rhinoceros do in a circus?

'I had to feed it fockn' cabbages!'

Dear God, I don't think I can take much more of this.

'I used to go to the fruit and veg shops, get all the rotten stuff for the chimps, fockn' nasty bastards that they were. The PG Tips chimps? Loada fockn' nonsense that was. The owner comes to me one night and says, "the fockn' chimps are drunk. They won't do their fockn' tricks. Fockn' pissed, every last one of 'em." I'd given 'em peaches that were, you know, when they go fizzy up your nose.'

Fermenting?

'That's it. Oh, dear God. We had two giraffes on a bus. Holes cut in the roof to stick their heads through. The fockn' driver skidded and turned the fockn' bus over on a roundabout. Jesus, Mary and Joseph! The fockn' things are concussed. The boss comes along with a fockn' gun this time, because they're licensed to have 'em in case the lions go berserk. He says, "You're a fockn' dead man if anything happens to them giraffes." Ah, Jaysus. And we had five tiger cubs. Little things. Like hats.'

Hats?

'No. Like cats. A guy sold one of them to a publican in Hampshire so he could buy drink. We didn't earn much money, but Christ, the craic. I didn't know anyone there who had money as their god. Lovely men. All very generous people. But those fockn' chimps were bastards.'

It's my round, which provides a welcome hiatus for the wiping away of tears, and a natural change of subject.

'Did ye ever go to Cheltenham?'

I don't think he means the Book Festival.

'I was in Baltimore in County Cork – they've a McCarthy's there as well – delivering a cement mixer for them to take out to Sherkin Island and we're having a few drinks in the evening, and one of the lads accepts a £100 bet that he can't get from Baltimore to Cheltenham on a fockn' Honda 50. Anyway didn't he go there on the fockn' motorway from the ferry? Mother of God! Turns up in the Queen's Hotel with a head on him looking like this! The bike was knackered and he wanted to send it home on the train, but the driver wouldn't let him put it in the fockn' taxi. We stayed at a convent, the five of us.'

What?

'Well, the Mother Superior is from Listowel. She only wanted fifty quid, but we gave her a hundred to kip down in a dormitory. It's more than that for one night at the Queen's, no matter how many you squeeze in the fockn' room. And once you've got your head down it doesn't matter whether you're in the Ritz or a bloody hostel. Got up at seven, went to the shop for a paper, got a bottle of whiskey for Madge and four flagons of cider, you know, the plastic ones.'

The lads by the door have gone now so it's just the two of us, the barmaid and the dog, which appears to have had a relapse. 'Here,' says the barmaid, 'would you like a T-shirt?' MCCARTHY'S

FETHARD COUNTY TIPPERARY, it says. PUBLICAN RESTAURANT
UNDERTAKER.

Undertaker?

'Ah, yeah,' she says. 'Has he told ya about the time he was
barred? Tell him, Jim. The letter's on the wall in case you don't
believe him.'

It seems he was once barred by Mrs McCarthy, Publican,
Restauranteur and Undertaker, for some non-specific misdemean-
our. Distraught at being refused entrance to his home from home,
he attended his local TD's constituency surgery to ask him to
intervene. And where was the surgery held? Here, in the very
pub from which he was excluded. His elected representative duly
wrote to Mrs McCarthy. The officially embossed letter is displayed in a frame on the wall at the far end of the bar.

Dear Annette,

I am writing on behalf of Jim who wishes to apologise for any
alleged disturbance inadvertently created at your premises. He wishes
to be reinstated as an esteemed and valued customer. He promises
to return the glass and continue his custom right to the very end,
including transport to Calvary Cemetery.

Perhaps you might consider this plea under the Mental Health
Act?

Yours sincerely
    Noël Dawson TD

'You know the monsignor who built the airport at Knock?
Well, didn't he die at Lourdes? So a few of us decided to go to
the funeral, you know, to represent South Tip. We set off at
night, in a Transit full of cider with a cooker in the back. Anyway
we got lost, and couldn't find fockn' Knock anywhere. Ended up
getting guided there behind a woman garda with a flashing light
on her car. We went for breakfast in a café full of retired priests
and nuns. One of the lads asked the waiter where was the best
pub in Knock for the craic, so I said, "We're not here for the

craic, we're here for the fockn' monsignor's funeral, so show some fockn' respect." So we went to the pub when it opened, bought some of those disposable razors on the way. One of the lads goes into the toilet and doesn't come out. So in we go, and isn't he only trying to shave without taking the little orange plastic things off the blade, throwing all the razors away and saying "useless fockn' things".'

'Did he tell you about the duck?' asks the barmaid.

'What duck?'

'They reckon he's the only man in Ireland ever had a duck that drowned.'

Drowned, in what sense?

'Well, I took it indoors for the winter, then put it back on the pond when spring came. Its feathers must have dried up, it's natural oils like, in front of the stove, because the poor thing got waterlogged and fockn' keeled over and drowned. Sure it made the newspapers.'

As I head for the door he says, 'I promised Mrs McCarthy she can have my funeral, all paid in advance, just as long as we don't take fockn' Cromwell's route through the town. Good luck now. And remember, you see any Shetland ponies, don't take your kids within a hundred yards of the bastards.'

'Will you visit Cashel?' Terence MacCarthy, the ex-Mór, had asked me. I've taken a short detour so I can approach it from the north and get the full effect of the Rock, towering above and dominating the surrounding landscape. It's the single most impressive sight between Dublin and the south coast, a cluster of ancient ecclesiastical buildings standing high above the town and surrounding lowlands like some medieval fantasy of Ireland. It was here that St Patrick preached when he used the shamrock as a metaphor of the Trinity, and where Cormac MacCarthaigh, King of Desmond, built a spectacular Romanesque chapel in the early twelfth century. The cathedral that adjoins the chapel was sacked by Cromwell, repaired, then abandoned and unroofed in 1748 because the archbishop of the time could not drive his coach and four up to the door, and decided somewhere flatter might be more convenient.

I park outside a branch of Paddy Power, the chain of book-makers that sounds like a revolutionary political movement, and walk up towards the Rock. I go through a small housing estate and past King Cormack's Restaurant, which is offering soups, sandwiches and hot meals. I hadn't realised he'd built a café as well as one of the most beautiful Romanesque chapels of the Celtic Christian world. He picked a good spot as well, right on the approach to the Rock itself, so that those coming to visit this most celebrated of ancient Irish sites would think, 'May as well have one of his pies while we're here.' Vision, you see. That's the key to a top-class tourism product.

There's a fierce wind blowing up on top, and I spend a little time watching clouds scudding against the sky through the ruined cathedral windows. The shadow of a bird of prey hovering high above plays on the grass close to my feet. The view over the town and countryside is breathtaking, and must have served to underline the sovereignty over the people of the kings, and after them the clergy, who held sway up here. In Cormac's Chapel some traces of the original frescoes remain, enough to hint at how magnificently ornate it must once have been. I also can't help thinking how close the blues, reds and yellows are to the paints that have been used to revamp Irish towns and villages. Perhaps I've stumbled on evidence that the colours really are traditional after all.

I walk down through the grounds of the Cashel Palace Hotel and back to the car. I'd been hoping to meet Conor MacCarthy here; the seat of the MacCarthy kings seemed an appropri-ate place to renew my acquaintance with my aspirant clan chief, but letters and messages to Belfast have gone unanswered. It's a pity, for I enjoyed his company and had something to show him; not the Dublin dossier, but a package that arrived recently from Tasmania, containing the prison records of all the McCarthys who were incarcerated in Port Arthur. It's a colourful read.

Whenever I see that ruined abbey standing at the water's edge, I feel like I'm coming home. It's just two minutes up the hill to the Convent, the peerless hilltop guest-house that is really called something else. I stay here whenever I'm passing through West Cork, and also quite often when I'm not. I rang a couple of nights ago to book and the phone was answered by the gardener, who has some idiosyncratic traits. He handed me over to Con, chef, proprietor and raconteur.

'Was the gardener naked?' I asked.

'He was wearing a kind of mini-kilt this time,' said Con.

Fair enough.

It turns out to be a busy night in the tiny restaurant in the former nuns' chapel, and they're a bit stretched for staff, so as well as being a guest I'm also the waiter serving a party of twenty female psychics and mystics from the United States. They arrived on a coach, which seemed a little prosaic. 'We are the Celestials,' said their leader, or possibly their democratically elected spokesperson, as they entered.

Resisting the temptation to say 'I can see that,' and resolving not to go down the no doubt well-worn road of denying them a menu because they must already know what they're having, I showed them through. There was an uneasy hiatus for a while, as the minority of non-teetotallers debated whether eight people would be able to finish a whole bottle of wine, or whether that was just excessive. I pointed out as discreetly as I could that the English couple at the corner table were already on their second bottle between two, but as far as they were concerned this was beyond the realms of the possible, and they refused to believe me. They eventually decided to take a chance on the wine, along with fifty or sixty cups of 'erb tea. In the course of my duties I've been able to glean, among other things, that they are on a three-week tour of the sacred sites of Ireland. 'Sometimes people think we're a regular package tour, which is kinda embarrassing.'

So where are they staying tonight?

'Gee, I dunno,' says the Celestial. 'Some hotel, I guess.'

Upstairs in my room I take out the plastic file that contains the picture of James McCarthy and friends with the giant nugget, and also the prison records from Port Arthur in which the exploits of Patrick, Timothy, Jeremiah, John, Denis, Edward, Florence, Daniel and Francis McCarthy in Van Diemen's Land are recorded. 'Stealing a handkerchief – transported ten years.' 'Making away with his slops – 10 days in cells.' 'Idleness – 4 days solitary confinement.' 'Misconduct in having soap improperly in his possession – 2 months hard labour in chains.' 'Being at the theatre after hours – 4 months hard labour.' I don't recognise the idleness, but the McCarthys have always had a reputation for being fond of soap and the theatre, so I suppose it was inevitable that one day it would get them into trouble. And then of course there's the drink.

John McCarthy was transported in 1844 for stealing gas fittings, though he did have previous for stealing a pane of glass, so you can see what society was up against. His fourteen reoffences in Van Diemen's Land have a relentless quality about them: 'Drunk and insolent.' 'Drunk and out after hours.' 'Drunk and representing himself to be free.' 'Drunk.' 'Misconduct in giving a pot of beer to another prisoner.' 'Misconduct in being in public house on a Sunday.' Given his hobby, the offence that deviates from the pattern comes as no surprise. 'Misconduct in having his clothes on at night in his berth and having a lighted rag in his possession.'

The most shocking record of all is that of Timothy McCarthy, transported in 1835 'for stealing a cap'. Over the course of the next six years, twenty-six separate offences and punishments are recorded. 'Disorderly conduct immediately after being tried – 15 stripes on the breech.' 'Drunk and disorderly – 3 days solitary confinement.' 'Blowing out the lamps – 5 days solitary confinement on bread and water.' On and on it goes, so brutal that it starts to read like a work of dark comic genius, a twisted satire by *Ripping Yarns* out of *The Goon Show*. 'Having a thimble improperly in his possession – 3 days solitary confinement on bread and water.' 'Making away with some thread and some leather – 3 days solitary on bread and water.' A dastardly pattern of needlework-related crime is beginning to emerge. 'Conniving at a fellow boy having thread improperly in possession – 48 hours solitary on bread and water.' I'm about to turn the page to continue this pitiful criminal burlesque when something stops me in my tracks. 'A fellow boy'? I look back over his record, and there it is again. 'Striking a fellow boy – 3 days solitary.' I check the cover page, but although the dates of trial, transportation and arrival in VDL are all present, the date of birth is blank.

In the top corner of the sheet, though, are the initials PP – the abbreviation for Point Puer, the island off Port Arthur where convicted children were sent. I remember its cliffs, 'the traditional place of suicide', and feel a terrible surge of shame at the comfort of my life, sitting here with a glass of wine leafing through these grim pages. For a moment I feel foolish; tens of thousands of people had these experiences, so what's special about a handful of McCarthys to whom I can be connected only in the most remote and tenuous way? Then I realise that if it weren't for the name, I would never have sought out these particular records. A name can connect us to people and places beyond our experience, and take us close to a specific, singular identity through which we can imagine a distant place and time. When I remember Port Arthur I'll always imagine Timmy McCarthy arriving there, wondering how he might cope. Perhaps if he could just get hold of a needle and thread . . .

I finish the wine, go to brush my teeth, and discover I have left my washbag behind in the last place I stayed. Or maybe the one before. I lost my trousers in Montana as well. Perhaps I should stay at home a bit more. Either that, or start travelling with an inventory. As I head for bed, I take a final glance at Timothy's record.

'Concealing a fellow boy's shoes – 48 hours solitary on bread and water.'

Hard but fair, you see. You have to let kids know where they stand.

Seven hours' solitary confinement later, followed by coffee, bread, water, poached eggs, rashers and puddings both black and white, and I'm on the road for the last time. I know this particular stretch well by now, but I'm travelling it this time for reasons I hadn't anticipated. I turn left at Glengarriff, and the Ireland of traffic jams and jacuzzis begins to feel like an elaborate hoax. The Beara Peninsula seems as wild and untamed as ever, though two or three times I spot brown tourist-industry signs proclaiming 'The Ring of Beara', a worrying indication that somebody in an office with a map and a tourism graph on the wall has targeted the coach-choked roads of the Ring of Kerry as a role model. I realise of course that people writing enthusiastic books about unspoiled coastlines and welcoming bars should bear in mind their responsibilities, and am therefore happy to report that sub-standard roads, impenetrable rain, lack of suitable accommodation and marauding packs of carnivorous wolves extinct for centuries in the rest of the country are all endemic here, and you'd do best to stay away. Book with the Celestials instead. They're going to some amazing places. It's just that she couldn't remember what they were called.

'To be honest with you, it's an impossible task. If you had a date of birth, a father's name, or especially a mother's name, I might be able to help you. But as it is – well, I'm afraid you'd be believing what you want to believe. It is a wonderful photograph though.'

I'm sitting in the front room of a bungalow in a tiny, brightly painted village in Beara. The man talking to me is wearing a blue plaid shirt that I suspect he bought in Butte, Montana. John the Yank told me to come and see him next time I was in this part of the world. Riobard is a former teacher who has devoted many years of his life to tracing the genealogy of the peninsula, and has particular expertise in the fragmentation of families in the great exodus to America.

'Twenty thousand people lived here before the famine and the closure of the mines. There are little more than 4,000 now. Most went to America. Many were O'Sullivans and McCarthys. One of these families can have more than forty branches. Parish records are full of errors, wrong dates, names misrecorded, births confused with christenings, funerals that never were. People went away, and were never heard of again. And this fella in Alaska' – he taps the photograph like a lawyer cross-examining a witness – 'you say you don't even know if he was Irish, or if his parents were?'

No, I tell him, but I figured with a name like that he wasn't going to be from Budapest. Anyway, it doesn't matter. It's been kind of him to give me his time. I'm sure he spends half his life besieged by the diasporic descendants of people who probably never existed in the first place, come back to the auld sod to play a little golf and trace their roots while the locals take their euros, and the piss. It's not as if it's going to change anyone's life to know who a little town in Alaska was named after. It was just that – well, the name *and* the copper. It seemed too much of a coincidence.

'But when you phoned, I did a little work. I've come up with some possibilities.'

He passes me a slip of pink paper on which are written seven names. Well, one name actually, seven times. James McCarthy.

At first glance it seems clear that the dates listed are not for the man I'm pursuing. The picture was taken in 1903, so I'm guessing the guy on it must have been born around 1870, give or take two or three years to allow for the hardships of life as a prospector. Riobard agrees. But there is one entry that might fit. 'Born 1868. Eyeries parish. Emigrated. Butte, Montana.' The date is right, and he's the only one with his occupation recorded. 'Copper miner.' Copper. And the time frame is perfect: he could have grown up here, worked in Butte in the late 1880s and early 1890s, had breakfast every day in M&Ms, then gone off to Alaska as it started to open up, to take the opportunity to put his skills to good use. So what does Riobard think?

'I already told you. I think you're believing what you want to believe.'

I drive out to Allihies, through the village, past the signs saying 'Caution – Old Mineshaft', and sit on the hilltop above the last of the stone and brick ruins that are all that remain of the mines, temples to copper on an island of saints. I try and imagine how it must have been when this empty mountainside, swaying today with wild flowers, was teeming with industrial life; but I can't. It hardly seems possible. So instead I turn my gaze on the Atlantic, a glacial shade of turquoise-meets-emerald where it pounds the cliffs, and think of the millions who travelled, or were sent, with nothing but hope. And I know what I must do. I will go across the mountain, to my favourite bar in the world, and raise a glass in their memory.

Or two. Maybe I'll have just the two.

ACKNOWLEDGEMENTS

I owe a particular debt of gratitude to Robert Hughes and Thomas Keneally for their books *The Fatal Shore* (Pan, 1988) and *The Great Shame* (Vintage, 1999).

Other sources that were invaluable on this journey were: *The MacCarthys of Munster* by Samuel Trant MacCarthy (Dundalk, 1922); *An Irish Miscellany* by The MacCarthy Mór, Prince of Desmond, and the Count of Clandermond (Gryfos, Little Rock Arkansas, 1998); *Tangier, City of the Dream* by Iain Finlayson (Flamingo, 1993); *The Orton Diaries* by Joe Orton, ed. John Lahr (Minerva, 1989); *Irish America* by Maureen Dezell (Doubleday, 2000); *Wherever Green is Worn* by Tim Pat Coogan (Random House, 2000); *Port Arthur – A Story of Strength and Courage* by Margaret Scott (Random House, 1997); *English Passengers* by Matthew Kneale (Penguin 2001); *Through Hell's Gates* by Kerry Pink (published by author, 4th edition, Tasmania 1998); *To Hell or Barbados – The Ethnic Cleansing of Ireland* by Sean O'Callaghan (Brandon, 2000); *Volcano Story* by Howard Fergus (Macmillan Education, 2000); *Fire from the Mountain* by Polly Patullo (Constable, 2000); *The Butte Irish* by David M Emmons (University of Illinois Press, 1990); and *Copper Camp – The Lusty Story of Butte* by Montana Writers' Project of Montana (Riverbend Publishing, 2002).

I would like to thank the many people who gave me help, advice and hospitality on my journey, and also told me the stories, far more than I have been able to include here, that were a constant source of inspiration.

In Ireland, Vince Keaney, Michael Martin, Seamus Hosey, Adrienne MacCarthy, Con McLoughlin, Karen Austin, Riobard O'Dwyer and Noel Mannion. In Tangier, Conor, Tommy and Terence MacCarthy. In New York, Chris Byrne, Rachel Fitzgerald, Phil Collis, Jean Tatge and John McCarthy. In Tasmania, Jennifer Waters, Michelle McGinity, Damon Hawker, Peter Mac-Fie, Tourism Tasmania, and Susan Hood and Colin Knight at the Port Arthur Historic Site. In Montserrat, Carol and Cedric Osborne, and almost everybody I met on the island. In Montana, Ellen Crain, Kevin Shannon, Sarsfield O'Sullivan and Larry, Peg and Frances McCarthy. And in Alaska, Neil Darish, Douglas Miller, Jeremy Keller, Geoffrey Bleakley, Dick Anderson and Colleen McCarthy.

Closer to home my thanks also go to Judith Burns, Daphne Daly, Angela Herlihy and Mary Pachnos for being so good at what they do, and to my family, for their patience and understanding during long absences, and for great homecomings.

And if anyone can shed any light on the background of James McCarthy, I'd love to hear from you.

PMᶜC
Brighton
June 2002

Float Copper
Nugget-Nizina.